Introduction to Financial Technology

Complete Technology Guides for Financial Services

Series Editors

Ayesha Kaljuvee
Jurgen Kaljuvee

Series Description

Industry pressures to shorten trading cycles and provide information-on-demand are forcing firms to re-evaluate and re-engineer all operations. Shortened trading cycles will put additional emphasis on improving risk management through front-, middle-, and back-office operations. Both business and IT managers need to effectively translate these requirements into systems using the latest technologies and the best frameworks.

The books in the **Complete Technology Guides for Financial Services Series** outline the way to create and judge technology solutions that meet business requirements through a robust decision-making process. Whether your focus is technical or operational, internal or external, front, middle, or back office, or buy vs. build, these books provide the framework for designing a cutting-edge technology solution to fit your needs.

Readers interested in learning more about the series and Elsevier books in finance, including how to submit proposals for books in the series, can go to:
http://www.books.elsevier.com/finance

Introduction to Financial Technology

Roy S. Freedman

ELSEVIER

AMSTERDAM • BOSTON • HEIDELBERG • LONDON
NEW YORK • OXFORD • PARIS • SAN DIEGO
SAN FRANCISCO • SINGAPORE • SYDNEY • TOKYO
Academic Press is an imprint of Elsevier

Academic Press is an imprint of Elsevier
30 Corporate Drive, Suite 400, Burlington, MA 01803, USA
525 B Street, Suite 1900, San Diego, California 92101-4495, USA
84 Theobald's Road, London WC1X 8RR, UK

This book is printed on acid-free paper. ∞

Library of Congress Cataloging-in-Publication Data
Freedman, Roy S.
    Introduction to financial technology / Roy S. Freedman.
        p. cm.
    Includes bibliographical references and index.
    ISBN-13: 978-0-12-370478-8
    ISBN-10: 0-12-370478-2 (alk. paper)
    1. Financial services industry—Information technology.   I. Title.

HG173.F73 2006
332.101'1—dc22

                                                    2005057181

British Library Cataloguing-in-Publication Data
A catalogue record for this book is available from the British Library.

ISBN 13: 978-0-12-370478-8
ISBN 10: 0-12-370478-2

For information on all Elsevier Academic Press publications
visit our Web site at www.books.elsevier.com

Printed in the United States of America
08 09 10 8 7 6 5 4 3 2

Contents

Preface

This book is for technologists who want to learn about financial systems and for financial professionals who want to learn about the technology that assists them in their work. The goal of *Introduction to Financial Technology* is to explain how financial systems work — how they came to be and how they evolved — from a technological perspective.

The basic approach presents the various topics of financial technology in an interesting and systematic way. This is different from what is frequently done in most financial technology references. This book is not a collection of disjoint articles or vendor comparisons. The topics in *Introduction to Financial Technology* are illustrated with numerous worked out examples, spreadsheet displays and formulas, graphs, diagrams, historical excerpts, biographies, and news stories. Throughout the chapters, text boxes are used for case studies and special topics. The text boxes can also be read independently of the chapters to get a flavor of the material. Each chapter concludes with an annotated list of references, where extensive use of the Web is made to help readers find reference material. Chapters conclude with a set of discussion questions whose purpose is to provoke thought and argument.

The role of mathematics in the book is at an introductory level for technologists and financial professionals. Finance requires mathematical representations. Notation is crucial and could be something as simple as a colon or a decimal point. *Introduction to Financial Technology* surveys price and time notations used for financial computations. In most cases, there are no formal mathematical proofs: this is not a book on finance nor is this a book on engineering. Instead, we use the technology of computer algebra systems to simply and quickly derive financial formulas, valuations, and relationships in order to show the rationale behind financial models. Programs that implement many financial computations and data representations are shown in C, C++, Java, Visual Basic, the MuPAD computer algebra system, and the AMPL model specification language, as well as various XML dialects.

Introduction to Financial Technology is based on several lectures and courses that were given over the years at Polytechnic University in New York and at other places to a mixed audience of finance professionals and technology specialists. Indeed, one purpose was to facilitate communication among technologist, practitioner, regulator, and manager. Consequently, this book is suitable as a reference for full or half-semester introductory courses.

This includes short introductory courses on market vendor systems; financial products (bonds, futures, options, and swaps); financial message standards; clearing and settlement; and financial systems risk. Material in *Introduction to Financial Technology* can be used in selected topics courses for programs in management of information systems, finance, financial engineering, and software engineering. The nonacademic financial community will also find *Introduction to Financial Technology* useful for in-house courses and as a reference for financial notation, terminologies, models, algorithms, message standards, systems, and regulations.

The basic problem in building reliable and interoperable financial systems, actually systems of systems of communication and social networks, has not changed since the opening of the Amsterdam Stock Exchange 400 years ago. How can we develop trading systems, information systems, payment systems, and regulatory systems for financial products (such as stocks, bonds, and contracts) that ensure — on the average — that buyers get delivery, sellers get paid, everyone gets news and market data, everyone (hopefully) makes money, and everyone follows the rules? Events associated with risk (credit, operational, and market) also need a specification. What happens if there is a settlement error, a system shutdown, or a credit default? Can improvements make things worse?

Financial technology has much in common with the technology found in commercial systems, military systems, auction systems, and gambling systems. However, in order to build and maintain financial systems, developers need to be familiar with terms and jargon such as ticker feeds, yields, patent protection, bid, spreads, back-office, credit, quotation, martingales, short squeeze, and clearing house. All of these terms were known by Thomas Edison, whose first successful business was a consultancy for market data vendors. Today, developers also need to be familiar with newer acronyms and identifiers as well, such as ABA, 30/360, 369604, CRD, CUSIP, FIX, FOK, FRED, "the greeks," HOF7, IARD, IBMLU, MMID, TCP/IP, VaR, VWAP, and XML. Some of these identifiers describe systems; some describe products; some are parameters; and some are used as database keys. *Introduction to Financial Technology* reviews and describes them.

The trend to replace physical delivery with virtual delivery (sometimes called straight-through processing) has continued for the past 150 years; current market data and financial message standards evolved from the Chappe and Morse telegraph technologies. In the evolving collaboration between people and computers, it is becoming increasingly difficult to tell who is automated — trader, broker, routing broker, market maker, clearing member, regulator — and who is not. *Introduction to Financial Technology* can help the reader assess these trends and help the reader understand how these financial systems work.

I want to acknowledge the following individuals who provided me with answers and friendly feedback over many years: Roken Ahmed, Levi Baumgarten, Michael Cappi, Louis Calabro, Rinaldo DiGiorgio, Chaim Frenkel, Colin Goldberg, Zvi Halperin, Frank Hilf, Shemaya Katz, Chris Keith, David Kelman, Rafe Konikov, Chuck Lawson, Laura Lawson, Fred Novomestsky, Marvin Preiser, Stan Preiser, Joanne Revson, Andrew Rohman, Bonnie Schnitta, Oran Sharon, William Stahl, Neil Strauss, Robert Tamiso, Misha Vaynshenker, Milton White, and Keni Yip. I also acknowledge my late father, Theodore Louis Freedman, who taught me how to ask questions and who taught me the value of history.

Without the support and encouragement of Stacy Pennebaker and Marie De Luca the writing of this book would not have been possible.

Heinrich Guggenheimer, my teacher, gave me an understanding of the legacy of mathematics and technology. He has been an inspiration to me for many years.

Joseph Mathai, my friend and colleague, worked with me on several innovative financial systems; he was murdered while attending the Financial Technology Conference at Windows on the World on September 11, 2001. May his memory be for a blessing.

Roy S. Freedman
New York City, 2005

CHAPTER • 1

What Is Financial Technology?

Financial technology is concerned with building systems that model, value, and process financial products such as bonds, stocks, contracts, and money. At a minimum, financial products are represented by the dimensions of price, time, and credit. Like commercial systems, financial systems incorporate trading systems and trading technology to enable the buying and selling of products at different times and in different market spaces. This includes arbitrage — the simultaneous buying and selling of the same product in different markets, at the same time.

Financial technology depends on standard secure communication protocols for initiating and synchronizing communication, for authenticating market participants, and for ensuring that the market participants can communicate quickly in a common language. This enables the fast delivery of information, orders, and news on public or private, physical or nonphysical communication networks.

Financial technology integrates mathematical, statistical, computing, and economic models with news and analytical systems; these are further integrated with message, transaction, order processing, and payment systems. Financial systems perform their activities in compliance with rules, procedures, guidelines, and regulations. Like military systems, financial systems are involved with strategy and tactics, logistics, information processing, secrecy, and resource allocation. Like gambling systems, financial systems model risk probabilities such as the risk of loss.

1.1. Financial vs. Commercial Systems

Financial systems share many attributes with commercial systems: both incorporate trading technology.

Trading Technology

Actions associated with trading include auctioning, negotiating, buying, selling, borrowing, leasing, brokering, dealing, clearing, settling, and delivering. It is important to note that these activities require at least two actors (e.g., a borrower and a lender; a buyer and a seller). Places where these actors meet are called markets, trade fairs, exchanges, or auction houses.

.inancial systems and commercial systems is in the products
.d processed. Products that are bought and sold in commercial
.t we eat, drink, plant, wear, burn, or consume. The products
.n financial systems are intangibles that vary over time, such as
.cts, obligations, and shares.

.se a trader wants to buy a contract for the delivery of 15 tons
.usta coffee to a specific New York City warehouse in 6 months
.an be bought or sold through a system called a futures exchange.
.ures exchanges are somewhat different from a retail or wholesale
. from a merchant. In the first case, *contracts* are traded; in the second
. of *coffee* is negotiated between two parties for delivery at the buyer's
locau. .er's ability to pay and the seller's ability to deliver must be evaluated in
a commercu. .ransaction.

On a futures exchange, the same contract can be bought and sold several times before
the delivery date: buyers make money if the value of the contract increases and they sell
the contract to someone else at a higher price than the purchase price. Only the last buyer
(in a potentially long chain of buys and sells) gets the delivery of coffee. The buyer's
ability to pay and the seller's ability to deliver are guaranteed by the exchange through
its associated clearing house.

Systems Support for Buying and Selling — in Any Order

One way to make money is to first buy contracts at a low price and then sell them at a
higher price. Conversely, if a trader has credit, he can first borrow contracts from someone
(and be charged a fee by the lender), immediately sell the contracts and then, at a later
time (when the contract price is lower), buy the contracts back at the lower price (and
return the borrowed contracts back to the lender). Making money by selling high and
afterward buying low is called "selling short."

Financial systems support these two methods of making money. These methods provide
a way for buyers and sellers to bet on price movements and to manage price risk: sellers
lock in prices by selling contracts for products and the buyer essentially purchases the
risks (and rewards) associated with a contract's price fluctuations.

Why would a commercial system evolve to a financial exchange? Primarily for the
following economic benefits:

- **Fair prices**
  Centralized monitoring and compliance technology utilized by the exchange helps
  ensure that prices are fair and that markets are not manipulated illegally.
  Technology can help monitor and audit every trade so that suspicious activities can
  be identified. Enforcing market fairness increases an exchange's appeal as a
  trading place: this brings in more participants, greater liquidity, and ultimately
  more profits to buyers, sellers, and the exchange itself. Exchange communication
  technology also provides an important role in determining and reporting prices:
  local prices communicated by the exchange reflect the local supply and demand
  information better than similar prices reported in other places.

- **Stable prices based on standard clearing arrangements**
  Trading financial products on an exchange implies that buyers and sellers do not
  have to make separate bilateral arrangements with each other to ascertain delivery
  and credit risks: the exchange eliminates these risks through transaction systems

that support order, management, clearing, and settlement technology. The exchange guarantees the quality and quantity of the underlying product; as opposed to bilateral arrangements, traders do not have to view, sample, taste, or inspect them.

- **Different products can be used to reduce risk**
  If producers are given more choices for hedging price fluctuations, then it is easier for them to survive the cyclical ups and downs in the market. Risk from currency fluctuation is reduced if there are local exchanges that price products in the local currency.

The First Financial Exchange

Commercial and financial systems developed in parallel. The major break between the two occurred in 1608 with the organization of the Amsterdam Stock Exchange. Initially, only one financial product was traded at the Amsterdam Stock Exchange: shares (corresponding to a share or percentage of the profits) of the Dutch East India Company.

Box 1-1
The First Exchange-Traded Companies: VOC and WIC

The Dutch East India Company [in Dutch, the *Verenigde Oostindische Compagnie* (VOC) literally the United East-Indies Company] was organized by several wealthy Dutch merchants who raised about 64 tons of gold — enough to build several ships. The VOC was established on March 20, 1602: the date the Dutch government granted the VOC a monopoly on trade with Asia. By 1604, ships were sent to India, where they shipped back cloves, nutmeg, pepper, mace, and other spices used to preserve (and improve the taste of) food.

By 1669, VOC had 150 merchant ships and 40 warships (for protection from pirates) and employed over 20,000 people. VOC became a diversified multinational corporation. VOC ships brought silver from Europe to purchase raw silk in China. The silk was traded in Japan for gold and copper. These were traded for textiles in India, which were further exchanged for spices in Indonesia. The spices were shipped back home.

At the 1604 initial public offering (IPO), an investor could buy one share of VOC for either 500 pounds or 3000 guilders. For the first few years VOC increased working capital in more ships, ports, and employees: the first dividend (distribution of profit) was declared and distributed in 1612. It amounted to 287.50 pounds per share, corresponding to a dividend yield of 57.5% of the original share price. Over the years share prices fluctuated: in 1622, a VOC share cost 1500 pounds; in 1720, the price was 6000 pounds (12 times the IPO price); and in 1781, the price fell to 125 pounds. The average dividend yield was 18% per year, which was payable in cloves, VOC corporate bonds, or other proxies for money. On New Years Eve of 1799, VOC was dissolved after a corporate lifetime of 198 years.

The Dutch West India Company [in Dutch, the *West-Indische Compagnie* (WIC)] was organized (June 3, 1621) in the same way as the VOC: the capitalization was 130 tons of gold. The Dutch government granted the WIC a monopoly on trade with Africa and the Americas.

Initially, shares of WIC and VOC traded at the same value. Because of wars and increased competition with Portugal and England, WIC was not as good an investment as VOC; in the early 1670s, a WIC share was worth 3.5% of a VOC share. WIC went into bankruptcy reorganization in 1674.

Both VOC and WIC were multinational corporations. To solidify their international offices and trading ports, VOC and WIC also engaged in real estate transactions. VOC established its Asian headquarters in Batavia on the island of Java (Indonesia), geographically convenient and the site of large coffee plantations. The most famous WIC real estate purchase — for 60 guilders worth of farming tools — occurred in 1626: WIC bought the New Amsterdam port of Manhattan. (In 1869, 60 guilders were worth 24 U.S. dollars.)

The First Transaction Protocols

The transaction technology used at the Amsterdam Stock Exchange, based on a "handshake protocol," is similar in spirit to the technology used today, with the chief difference being that many of today's actors are computers.

A protocol is a rule, represented by a sequence of actions for two or more actors, which specifies how a particular activity should be performed. The "handshake protocol" for trading was discussed in the 1688 essay by trader Joseph de la Vega:

A member of the Exchange opens his hand and another takes it, and thus sells a number of shares at a fixed price, which is confirmed by a second handshake. With a new handshake a further item is offered, and then there follows a bid. The hands redden from the blows.

After the confirmation handshake (signifying that the trade was *executed*), the protocol commits the seller to deliver VOC shares to the buyer on the 20th of the month (the *closing date*) and the protocol commits the buyer to pay the seller on the 25th of the month (the *settlement date*).

At the Amsterdam Exchange, the buyer could borrow money to pay for the shares: this was called *hypothecation* (today we say that shares are bought *on margin*). Depending on the credit of the buyer, shares could be bought with at least a 20% down payment. The buyer could sell the shares at any time before the 20th, hopefully (for the buyer) at a higher price: the net gain would be payable to him on the 25th. If the buyer defaults and is unable to raise the funds by the 20th, the shares are sold on the exchange and net proceeds are due to the seller on the 25th. All individual gains or losses are adjusted between buyer and seller (today this process is called *netting*).

Some trades required an actual transfer of shares. The protocol was that on the 20th of the month, the seller walks over to the VOC Amsterdam office and tells a clerk to open the record book of VOC shareholders and to transfer shares from the seller's account to the buyer's account. The buyer then pays the seller in "certified bank money" witnessed by officials from the Bank of Amsterdam. Note that neither certificates nor physical securities were exchanged: only database records were updated. Payers would only get a receipt.

Today's stock transfer protocol is similar in that a centralized database of all shareholders is maintained. Database records need to be changed to indicate ownership. The database of shareholders for all U.S. exchange-traded companies is maintained by the Depository Trust Clearing Corporation (DTCC).

According to de la Vega, contracts for shares can be bought and sold for other months, as long as the protocol of settlement on the 20th and payment on the 25th is adhered to. Because of this, the Amsterdam Stock Exchange is similar to a futures exchange (with the financial product being the stock futures of VOC).

In today's terminology, trade execution date is referred to by the capital letter T. Today, on stock exchanges in the United States, all clearing and settlement actions are completed within 3 days ($T+3$). A goal of paperless clearing and settlement [sometimes called *straight through processing* (STP)] is to reduce this time to at most 1 day ($T+1$). On the 17th century Amsterdam Exchange, the earliest clearing and settlement time was $T+5$.

The handshake protocol used at the Amsterdam Exchange was used to initiate and synchronize communication, to authenticate market participants (in order to validate their corresponding identities and roles), and to make sure that the market participants were speaking a common language (i.e., Dutch or French).

Financial communication between market participant "peers" (i.e., actors of the same social rank) and between agents and brokers must be unambiguous. The important characteristics of such unambiguous *peer-to-peer* communication are:

- **Reliability**
  There is an acknowledgment for each message between participants so that if a message is not acknowledged by the listener, the speaker communicates the message again.

- **Error correction**
  Any mistakes made in communication should be detected and corrected wherever possible.

The famous *Transmission Control Protocol* (TCP), part of the *Internet Protocol* (IP), governs reliable communication between "peer" computers on the Internet by requiring computers to acknowledge each message sent to each other.

Handshake terminology is used routinely for other types of computer communication. For example, according to Internet Standard RFC 1334:

> The Password Authentication Protocol (PAP) provides a simple method for the peer to establish its identity using a 2-way handshake. This is done only upon initial link establishment.... The Challenge-Handshake Authentication Protocol (CHAP) is used to periodically verify the identity of the peer using a 3-way handshake. This is done upon initial link establishment, and MAY be repeated anytime after the link has been established.

Another Internet Standard (RFC 3546) describes the *Transport Layer Security Handshake Protocol*, which specifies how computers can authenticate each other and negotiate a method for secure communication before any actual transmission of information.

Note that communication protocols do not have to be reliable or error correcting. For example, news — published in a newspaper, a Web page, or broadcast over television, radio, or the Internet — does not usually require an acknowledgement between sender and receiver.

1.2. Financial vs. Gambling Systems

Other competitive activities that share the characteristics of financial systems are gaming systems. In these systems the element of chance is much more explicit.

Box 1-2

Martingales and Arbitrage

Today a martingale refers to a model of the returns of financial products. Martingale models are used in computational finance to value options, futures, and other securities.

Originally, a martingale referred to a gambling strategy played in *roulette*: a game consisting of a rotating wheel with a notched circumference and a small white ball. The white ball is thrown randomly into one of 38 notches, numbered 1 to 36, 0, and 00. The notches are alternatively colored red and black (except 0 and 00 are colored green). Some believe that roulette was invented by the mathematician Blaise Pascal (1623–1662). The martingale strategy is:

- Bet 1 dollar that the little white ball will fall in a red notch.
- If you win, your next bet is 1 dollar.
- If you lose, you double your previous bet.
- Continue the game until you have won your required profit or lost more than your limit.

For equal dollar bets, the casino always wins when the ball falls on green (notches 0 and 00), which occurs $2/38 = 5.3\%$ of the time.

The martingale strategy is mentioned throughout the Memoirs of Giacomo Casanova (1725–1798), especially in Chapter 21 of Volume 2. In Chapter 4 of Volume 3 (called "The Eternal Quest"), Casanova discusses a few financial strategies used in the 1770s. One was to sell French government bonds "to an association of brokers at Amsterdam, and take in exchange the securities of any other country whose credit was higher than that of France." Today this is called a credit swap. The other was to take advantage of the price discrepancy due to news delays between different markets. (When news reached him, Casanova would buy gold at Amsterdam and then ride a fast stagecoach to Frankfort to sell it at a higher price.) In the English language, the buying and selling of the same product in different markets — at the same time and with little risk of loss — is called *arbitrage* (from the French word for *arbitrate*: to render judgment in order to make a decision); people who make such trade-off decisions are called arbitrageurs. Arbitrage and arbitrageur entered the English language in the late 19th century.

In the 1930s, French mathematician Jean Ville (1910–1988) considered a martingale as a model of "un jeu equitable" (a fair game); this convention was continued by Paul Lévy (1886–1971) and American Joseph Doob (1910–2004), whose student, Paul Halmos (1916–), wrote his 1938 Ph.D. dissertation on the mathematical theory of gambling systems. Doob defined a martingale as a fair coin-flipping game, where a player starts off with some money and wins a dollar for each head and loses a dollar for each tail. In a fair game, the expected value of the gambler's pot on the next flip — given all coin flipping history of the past — is the current value of the pot. In finance, this martingale property is used in *the efficient market hypothesis*: this assumption says that in a fair marker, the best estimate of an asset's future price is essentially its current price (discounted by an interest rate factor specifying the future value of money).

A martingale is also a type of animal collar — a restraint. A collar is also the name of a financial strategy that involves the simultaneous purchase and sale of options.

Risk Management Technology

Gambling is a game where players compete with each other and with fortune, cloaked in the laws of chance and probability. The lure for players is to make money by placing bets, where the "odds" or probabilities of outcomes are known to knowledgeable participants. By a skillful application of asset allocation and knowledge of return and risk, players can win and earn rewards or keep their profits and limit their losses by not playing.

The basic goal of gambling systems is to make money for the casino and its owners. Successful casino operators take great pains to eliminate cheating. Enforcing a game's fairness increases a casino's appeal as a gambling destination: this brings in more players, greater liquidity, and ultimately more profits to the players and the casino.

These characteristics are shared by financial systems — one important difference is that many probabilities in the financial universe are not as well known or as well understood as the probabilities associated with games of chance. However, many of the concepts of and terms of theoretical finance — from martingales to Monte Carlo methods — were developed over 300 years ago as strategies for games of chance. Many terms denoting gaming personnel have a financial connotation (such as dealer, house, bank, and cashier).

Box 1-3
Monte Carlo and the Blanc Brothers

The first real gambling house (*casino* is Italian for little house) was established in Venice in 1626 (just a few years after the 1608 opening of the Amsterdam stock exchange). When gambling was declared illegal in France and Germany, Prince Charles of Monaco saw an opportunity to solve his principality's financial problems. He opened a casino in Monte Carlo in 1863 and hired Francois Blanc to manage the facility with a 50-year contract.

Twin brothers Francois (1806–1877) and Louis Blanc (1806–1850), bankers from Bordeaux and traders on the Paris and Bordeaux Stock Exchanges, were well known in financial circles; Francois was even called the "most brilliant financier of his time" by Lord Brougham, High Chancellor of England. They also studied games of chance. In 1842, they invented a new "single zero" roulette wheel for the Hamburg Casino, which cut the bank's edge in half to 2.7%. The Blanc brothers predicted correctly that reducing the house odds — and making the game fairer — would increase its appeal and bring in more players, more gambling volume, and ultimately more profits.

The Monte Carlo casino was so successful that "Monte Carlo" became synonymous with chance and probability.

"Monte Carlo" returned to its mathematical and financial roots almost a century later. During the development of the atomic bomb, physicists created a mathematical model for neutron diffusion based on *partial differential equations*. Solving these equations was one impetus behind the development of the computer. Mathematicians Mark Kac and Stan Ulam showed that they could solve the equations by simulating the random motion of neutrons under various "what-if" scenarios using computer-generated random numbers. Ulam called this random simulation technique the Monte Carlo Method.

Today, prices of stocks, bonds, and other financial products are modeled by equations that are very similar to the equations of neutron diffusion. These equations can be solved by Monte Carlo Methods. However, instead of simulating the random paths of neutrons, computers simulate the random paths of prices, returns, and interest rates.

Surveillance, Regulation, and Compliance Technology

Financial systems share another important feature with gambling systems: they both operate in a space where participants must follow rules and regulations. Cheating is not allowed. System operators must be officially chartered by governments to comply with laws that are specially designed for these activities.

In the United States, gambling is regulated by state-level gambling control commissions. Financial markets are regulated by federal government agencies such as the Securities Exchange Commission (SEC) and the Commodities Futures Trading Commission (CFTC). By SEC rules, financial exchanges and market participants must make sure that their activities are "fair and orderly."

The relationship between gambling and investing has always been a concern to securities regulators and securities attorneys, both in perception and in actuality.

1.3.   Financial vs. Military Systems and Physical Delivery

From an operational perspective, financial technology shares many characteristics with military technology. Tactical and strategic military systems, such as financial systems, are offensive and defensive. Different types of events and behaviors are monitored, tracked, correlated, predicted, and extrapolated. Moreover, much of this activity is done in secrecy, so messages, orders, reports, are frequently encoded and decrypted so that the public in general (and the enemy in particular) should not be able to eavesdrop.

Military planners frequently speak of the need for *command, control, communications, and intelligence* (C[3]I) technologies. This is similar to the needs in financial technology if command and control refer to the processing of *orders*.

Of course, one key difference is that the focus of these technologies is different: a battlefield is not a marketplace and vice versa, even though sometimes the idiomatic language overlaps (as in "George made a killing in the stock market"). It is also interesting to note that the biggest sponsors of technology research and development traditionally have been the defense and financial establishments.

Delivery and Communication Technologies

Delivery of money, orders, and news is crucial for troops or merchants. Physical delivery requires technology investment in networks — roads, bridges, canals, harbors, ports, hubs, and stations — and in carriers — horses, stagecoaches, railroads, trucks, ships, and airplanes. Before the railroad, the most expensive (and most frequent) method of physical delivery was by road; shipping (the most infrequent method) was the least expensive.

The cost of transportation, which includes the cost of actual physical delivery plus the opportunity costs due to timeliness of delivery, plus the expected cost due to theft, piracy, and terrorism, was, until the 19th century, the most expensive component of a commercial, financial, or military enterprise. The cost of transportation was also crucial for arbitrageurs (such as Casanova) who took advantage of price discrepancies between markets with the fastest transport available.

It is interesting to briefly examine the state of delivery and communication technology before the railroad and the Morse electromagnetic telegraph. Here is what a 200-mile trip from Bremen to Leipzig in the 1820s (a 4-hour trip by commuter train today) was like:

The journey has lasted four days and four nights and the traveler is naturally stiff and bruised. His friends receive him, and he wishes to refresh himself a little.... He goes in search of his inn. This is no easy task, for in the streets an Egyptian darkness reigns, broken only at long distances by the smoky flame of an oil lamp. Here at last he finds his quarters, and wishes for a light. As matches do not yet exist, he is reduced to bruising the tips of his fingers with flint and steel, till he succeeds at last in lighting a tallow candle. He expects a letter, but it has not come, and he cannot now receive it till after some days, for the post only runs twice a week....

In the United States, before the full opening of the Erie Canal System in 1830, it took 4 weeks to travel to Chicago.

Table 1-1 compares some delivery methods used in prerailroad times. Clearly the figures in Table 1-1 demonstrate why centralized financial exchanges and financial markets evolved the way they did. Delivering money, orders, and news via private or public postal networks was very expensive and could take weeks, even in the same country, county, or state. That is why merchants and financiers maintained independent agents (now called brokers) with the power to buy and sell, colocated at centralized markets. Meeting and trading with many brokers at a centralized market (multilateral trading) was much cheaper than making several trips to individual brokers (bilateral trading).

Financial systems became more efficient as the technology for delivering of money, orders, and news became more efficient: for financial systems, there is a direct correlation between transportation networks and modern communication networks.

Public Networks and Toll Roads

Both military and financial communication and transportation networks are based on a grid of interconnected stations, governed by standard protocols. Before the Morse telegraph, stations were specific locations (such as shipping ports or depots) that maintained services for the agents (called carriers or couriers) who physically carried the messages, mail, news, money, and commodities. Today, stations also consist of relays, switching computers, network repeaters, or Internet routers. It is interesting to note that we still use the word "port" to refer to a physical electronic connection point or to a virtual peer-to-peer computer connection point using the TCP Internet standard.

It is still very expensive to build and maintain transportation networks. For the most part, this is a job for governments: the resulting network could be used by anyone for a fee or toll. (In England, toll roads were called turnpikes, named after the turning pike that stopped nonpaying users.)

Public networks were developed in ancient times. For example, the Roman postal service was a public network that integrated all methods of delivery technology: it included the maintenance and supply of horses, ships, vehicles, and messengers. It was used for delivering mail, military intelligence, financial and government documents, news, and commodities.

TABLE 1-1 A Comparison of Delivery Technology

Method:	Relative Cost	Distance (miles/day)	Weather	Frequency
Road:	least expensive	15–25	dependent	most frequent
Barge:	medium	10	least dependent	if rivers/canals available
Ship:	most expensive	60–100	most dependent	least frequent

One of the key military and financial advantages that the Romans possessed was their technology in building and maintaining good all-weather road networks. Vitruvius (70–25 BCE) described the technology: first, the road was outlined by digging two shallow trenches parallel to each and separated by 8 to 15 feet. Earth between the trenches was then excavated; engineers dug until bedrock and if the road was on swampy territory they drove support piles into the ground. Next they filled in the roadbed with four layers of material. According to Vitruvius, the lowest layer consisted of stones "not smaller than the hand could just grasp." The next layer consisted of a mass of broken stones cemented with lime, which was rammed down hard until it was 9 inches thick. Above this came fragments of bricks and pottery, 6 inches thick, also cemented with lime. The top layer, the "pavimentum," consisted of large polygonal blocks of hard stone (usually basaltic lava), irregular in form but fitted together so as to present a perfectly even surface.

The money-making aspect of public toll transport and fee-based communication was not lost on investors. For example, one of the first activities of the Philadelphia Stock Exchange (organized in 1791) was to sell shares in the Philadelphia and Lancaster Turnpike Company whose purpose was to build a modern toll road to New York City (about 100 miles away). One reason for this road was to increase the speed of news delivery from New York. (New York, being east of Philadelphia, was more geographically convenient and was the first port of call for the European mail ships.) The initial public offering was 1000 shares at $300 per share. Dividends would later pay about 6%. Because of demand, the stock price rose to $1000 within days.

Typical turnpike cost (using similar road building technology that the Romans used) in 1800 was about $1500 per mile. Income producing tolls were levied at 4 cents per 10-mile turnpike gate (for single horse) or 25 cents per gate (for fast chariot or stage coach). Based on the index of relative unskilled wage, a messenger on a single horse would pay (in 2003 dollars) $10 per 10-mile turnpike gate, a stage coach would pay the equivalent of $62.50 per 10-mile gate and construction costs would be $375,000 per mile. According to contemporary accounts, 20 express stagecoaches per week, mostly carrying news, financial documents, brokers, and traders, would travel between New York and Philadelphia. Many would take advantage of arbitrage opportunities between the two markets and gladly pay the expensive toll (totaling about $600 in 2003 dollars).

An interesting exploitation of public transportation and communication networks is seen in the arbitrage dealings of financier Jim Fisk in 1865 at the close of the U.S. Civil War. The arbitrage opportunity Fisk took advantage of was the mispricings of Confederate bonds between the New York and London markets. (At the time, there was no real-time trans-Atlantic communication.) After it was known in New York that the South lost, Fisk chartered several ships to England that traveled faster than the mail ships. His ships arrived with orders to his London brokers to sell short Confederate bonds on the London Exchanges. When the mail ships arrived with the news that the South lost, the price of the Confederate bonds went to zero: Fisk made a fortune after selling high and buying low.

From Pony Express to American Express

American Express, Wells, Fargo & Company, and Adams Express are three financial companies that got their start in the transportation technology business. They all started by delivering financial securities, documents, money, and packages between the financial centers of Boston and New York. They grew with the assistance of government contracts. (In British English, an *express* is a messenger or carrier sent out on a special errand.)

Within a few years, people in the delivery business realized that transporting money and financial documents to and from centralized locations was similar to what banks do; consequently, these companies branched into financial services, using their own credit (i.e., the belief that the express companies will pay bills on time) and investments to guarantee the movement of funds. A further demand for delivery services was caused by the end of the Mexican–American War and the subsequent discovery of gold in California. In the western territories of the United States of the 1840s, there was no service for the delivery of military intelligence, financial documents, money, and commodities. Entrepreneurs recognized the opportunity and created competing "Express" companies. By the 1850s, these express companies were government contractors that were part of the *Pony Express*.

The common founder of American Express and Wells, Fargo was John Butterfield (1801–1869). Butterfield was born near Albany, New York, and witnessed the building of the Erie Canal — the great technological enterprise that connected New York to Buffalo and Lake Erie (and thereby to Chicago and the farms in the Midwest) — thus lowering the cost of land transport by an order of magnitude by eliminating the long and expensive trip over the Appalachian Mountains.

Butterfield started his career as a stagecoach technologist. The stagecoach was a special-purpose vehicle, mostly custom built for the roads and the items carried. In the 1820s, Butterfield formed an association of drivers into an express business. The typical charge for document delivery by private company between New York and Buffalo was 6 cents per half ounce; the government service charged 25 cents (in 1830, 6 cents was worth about 1 dollar in 2003).

By 1850, Butterfield convinced his northeast competitors that they could make more money by collaborating (possibly by setting prices like a cartel). On March 18, 1850, Wells & Company, Butterfield, Wasson & Company, and Livingston, Fargo & Company pooled together $150,000 to start American Express. Part of the agreement was that the investing partners were allowed to use their original company names (probably to take advantage of name recognition and product branding) and form other express ventures.

In 1852, Henry Wells (1805–1878) and William Fargo (1818–1881) wanted to extend American Express into California. The American Express board did not want to diversify: they voted down the proposal. American Express would concentrate on business east of the Missouri River and Wells, Fargo & Company would concentrate on business west of the river.

On September 16, 1857, Butterfield won a 6-year $600,000 government contract for a 2800 mile delivery system running twice a week that could carry 600 pounds of mail, starting at Tipton, Missouri, and continuing to Fort Smith (Arkansas), El Paso (Texas), Tucson (Arizona), Los Angeles, and ending in San Francisco. The entire trip was scheduled to take 25 days. The system incorporated 1000 horses, 500 mules, 500 stage coaches, and 800 employees. Based on the unskilled wage rate, the contract would be worth about $90 million today. As was done in ancient Rome, stations were established at set distances (8–25 miles); each station was maintained with teams of horses and supplies of food and water. Some stations had a restaurant, hotel, and garage facilities for repairs. By 1860, more mail was carried by Butterfield than by any other method. The fee was $5.00 per half ounce (about $500 today).

It seems that Butterfield subcontracted most of the work to Wells, Fargo; Butterfield Overland failed to cover expenses, so in March 1860 Butterfield retired and the Butterfield Overland Stage Company was taken over by Wells, Fargo & Company.

The express companies were one of the first adopters of the Morse telegraph and railroad; the better companies quickly integrated these technologies into their stagecoach system. Both network technologies established the legal precedents of "carrier" communication networks used in case law today.

During World War I, movement of troops, government parcels, and war material was given priority over financial and commercial products: all U.S. railroads were nationalized. The government decreed that the railroad operations of the principal express companies (American Express, Wells, Fargo, and Adams Express) would be sold to the new government-operated American Railway Express Company (AREC). The express companies were compensated by receiving a third of the stock of AREC and essentially became passive investors in a corporation run by the U.S. government.

Box 1-4
The Express Companies

American Express
Within 10 years of its founding in 1850, the New York office of American Express (in Tribeca between Hudson and Jay Streets) was the largest privately owned building in New York City. Within 20 years, American Express had 890 offices, employed 1500 people, and operated in more than 10 states. The company had a monopoly on the transport of financial securities and money in New York State. In 1874, American Express set up new headquarters at 65 Broadway; in 1882, they began selling money orders; and in 1891, they created a type of "letter of credit" that could be used for payments around the world that would be guaranteed against loss. This "travelers' check" became a popular way of carrying money; by 1913, $32,000,000 worth of travelers' checks were sold.

American Express grew with the evolution of delivery technology: by 1915, they operated railroads, shipping lines, stagecoach lines, and a banking subsidiary with offices all over the world. After the AREC nationalization, American Express continued operations in financial services and banking.

Wells, Fargo & Company
From its founding in 1852, Wells, Fargo & Company expanded throughout California by merger and acquisition of other express companies. In 1905, its banking component, "Wells Fargo & Co's Bank, San Francisco" formally separated from Wells Fargo & Co Express. This division survived the 1906 San Francisco Earthquake ("Building Destroyed, Vault Intact, Credit Unaffected") and the AREC nationalization.

Adams Express
In 1840, 36-year-old Alvin Adams (1804–1877) began delivering financial securities, documents, and packages between Boston and New York. The total corporate assets consisted of "two men, a boy and one wheelbarrow." Adams Express Company was incorporated in 1854 and consolidated Adams & Company, Harnden & Company, Thompson & Company, and Kinsley & Company. During the Civil War, Adams Express maintained the payroll of both the Union and the Confederate armies. By the 1880s, Adams Express had nearly 8000 employees.

In 1916, Adams Express built their corporate (now landmark) headquarters at 61 Broadway, next door to the American Express. Their shares have been publicly traded on the New York Stock Exchange since 1873. After the AREC nationalization, Adams Express concentrated on its investment portfolio by purchasing additional shares of AREC from American Express and other AREC shareholders. The transformation of Adams Express into an investment company continued with its decision (made in October 1929) to operate the company as a closed-end mutual fund.

Secure Physical Carriers: Avian-Based Networks

One problem with physical delivery systems is that messengers and carriers are vulnerable to activities of hostile adversaries (theft, piracy, terrorism) and nature (accidents, earthquakes, floods, high winds).

One of the more famous financial technology achievements was the secure communication network established by a family business. The Rothschild family set up a multinational banking corporation in the early 1800s; the 5 brothers were located in Frankfurt, London, Paris, Vienna, and Naples. The communication technology was based on coded messages carried by pigeons.

The technology is simple: a written message is folded, rolled, and secured in a small tube that is attached to a trained homing pigeon's leg. Once the pigeon is released, it flies back to its home (for the Rothschild family, a bank in Frankfurt, London, Paris, Vienna, or Naples). When the pigeon arrives, office staff removes the message from the pigeon and then delivers it to the intended recipient.

Pigeon communication technology was used in antiquity in China, Greece, Rome, Persia, and India and continued to be used in the United States until the 1940s. Pliny (23–79 CE) reported that the Romans used hawks to intercept pigeon-based communications. Defensive countermeasures to ensure against interception included diversity techniques (sending more than one pigeon) and coding to ensure authentication and secrecy. Both of these techniques are used in modern military communication systems.

In a recent exhibition, the Museum of London displayed the messages that the Rothschild brothers exchanged via daily pigeon. They were written in coded Yiddish (similar to German, but written in Hebrew characters). Their network enabled their London office to receive news about Wellington's defeat of Napoleon at Waterloo (18 June 1815, near Brussels) 24 hours before the British government.

Reuters, the global financial information provider, started out transmitting financial news and prices using pigeons. As a youth, Israel Baer Josaphat (1816–1899) was familiar with financial services: one of his first jobs was as a clerk in his uncle's bank near Göttingen (Germany). In 1845, he immigrated to London and changed his name to Paul Julius Reuter. He saw an opportunity in setting up carrier pigeon links between end points of the Morse telegraph lines. By 1850, Reuter's carrier pigeon system provided the quickest reports of stock prices from the Paris stock exchange. His fleet of 45 pigeons delivered news and prices between Brussels and Aachen (a distance of 100 miles) faster than stagecoach express or railroad. By 1851, the fleet grew to 200 pigeons.

As Morse telegraph technology became more available, Reuter would open offices close to the main telegraph facilities; his motto was "follow the cable." This motto served the corporation well as the Morse telegraph network evolved into the Internet.

Electronic methods gradually replaced the pigeon in financial systems; however, pigeons continued to be used by the military. Even during World War II, many field commanders had a staff maintaining pigeons. In addition to communication, some pigeons were fitted with cameras to take pictures of enemy positions.

Today there are Internet standards for pigeon communication. RFC 1149 — A Standard for the Transmission of IP Datagrams on Avian Carriers — and RFC 2559 — IP over Avian Carriers with Quality of Service — have been released on April Fool's Day (1 April) in 1990 and 1999, respectively.

Physical Information Security and Privacy

Code techniques were developed for military systems before their adoption in financial systems. Cassius Dio (40–110 CE) reported on the technology used by Julius Caesar:

. . . even if the letter were captured, it should even so be meaningless to the barbarians and afford them no information. In fact, it was his usual practice, whenever he was sending a secret message to any one, to substitute in every case for the proper letter of the alphabet the fourth letter beyond, so that the writing might be unintelligible to most persons.

For example, to send the letter A, transmit E; to send B, transmit F. This is the origin of the Caesar Cipher class of codes used today. In some sense, the Caesar Cipher is another variation of the much older ATBSh method that is alluded to in the Bible (Jeremiah 25:26 and 51:41). Here, A (the first letter of the Hebrew alphabet) is transmitted as T (the last letter), and B is transmitted as Sh (second to the last letter), and so on. Generically, these techniques are called *cryptography* (Greek for *hidden writing*).

A variation of cryptography that addresses the problem of interception is called *steganography* (Greek for *covered writing*). One of the earliest references is noted by Herodotus (485–425 BCE). He reported that Demaratos (who was in Susa, the capital of Persia) wanted to tell his Greek allies about the upcoming military campaign by Persian King Xerxes:

[Demaratos] took a folding wax writing tablet and scraped off the wax which was upon it, and then he wrote the design of the king upon the wood of the tablet, and having done so he melted the wax and poured it over the writing, so that the tablet (being carried without writing upon it) might not cause any trouble to be given by the keepers of the road. Then when it had arrived at Lacedemon. . . Gorgo, the daughter of Cleomenes and wife of Leonidas, suggested a plan of which she had herself thought, bidding them scrape the wax and they would find writing upon the wood; and doing as she said they found the writing and read it, and after that they sent notice to the other Hellenes.

Today, the development of secure and authenticated digital money is based on digital steganography.

1.4. Nonphysical Communication and Delivery

The fastest long-distance communication methods do not require physical carriers: these methods require an encoding of information, which is important for military and financial systems. The information contained in orders and news could easily be abstracted and represented in a simpler form. Delivery risk can be minimized if commodities can be replaced by "information proxies." For example, an information proxy for money (gold, securities, or bills) could be represented by a "letter of credit" — an order to a recipient that provides someone the ability to buy or borrow a certain amount of funds. Such an order can be encoded and transmitted.

In antiquity, short messages were encoded using light or sound; in this century, light and other electromagnetic waves (from voltage pulses to radio) are used. Polybius (c. 200–118 BCE) discussed three signal-based protocols that describe asynchronous, synchronous, and symbol encoding that can be used today for line-of-sight wireless communication.

Semaphore Protocol

This simple protocol specifies how to transmit and receive a predetermined signal. The classic example is the optical *semaphore* (Greek for *symbol carrier*) used for military communication by Paul Revere in his 1775 ride. As described by poet Henry Longfellow (1807–1882):

He said to his friend, "If the British march
By land or sea from the town to-night,
Hang a lantern aloft in the belfry arch
Of the North Church tower as a signal light,
One if by land, and two if by sea;
And I on the opposite shore will be,
Ready to ride and spread the alarm
Through every Middlesex village and farm,
For the country folk to be up and to arm."

Note that with this simple protocol, communication may only be one way; and there may or may not be an acknowledgment of the transmission by the receiver. In any case, information (encoded as a very short message) was sent at the speed of light.

Sound-based (audio) semaphores using drums, bagpipes, or horns were also used in ancient times; information is sent at the speed of sound. (For a biblical example, see Numbers 10:1 to 10:10, where different blasts of special silver trumpets were used to communicate different assembly commands.) The advantage is that sound communication does not have to be line of sight. Because sound waves have a much longer wavelength than light waves, sound can bend around obstacles; the disadvantage of sound is its limited range.

In antiquity it was realized that greater range can be obtained by communicating at night with burning torches. It turns out that the human eye is very sensitive to light in the yellow to yellow–green region of the color spectrum. This sensitivity (about 0.05 lux, equivalent to the detection of a few hundred photons) is heightened at night (via our biological scotopic "night vision") and enables the human eye to see an ordinary wax candle at a distance of 17 miles. Brighter torches can be seen at greater distances, subject to the signal power law (the power intensity decreases inversely with the square of distance. In other words, we need four times the power to transmit twice the distance).

Line-of-Sight Communication

The crucial limitation in optical communication — a limitation seen as well with today's line-of-sight wireless radio communication — is not the sensitivity of the receiver, but the curvature of the earth. Line-of-sight communication is limited by the real distance to the horizon.

Using Euclidean geometry, we can derive the following easy-to-remember formulas: If a transmitter is at height h_t feet above sea level (and this height is small relative to the radius of the earth), then the distance to the horizon in miles is approximately

$$\text{Distance to horizon} = \sqrt{h_t}$$

If the receiver is also at a certain height h_r feet above sea level, then the maximum communication range in miles is

$$\text{Maximum line-of-sight communication range} = \sqrt{h_t} + \sqrt{h_r}$$

So if two communicators are both at elevations of 400 feet, the maximum range that they can communicate with each other is about 40 miles. This is true either for torch technology or for microwave antenna technology. In practice, this means that in order to communicate 100 miles or more, one needs access to very high mountains and a system of relays.

The Talmud (Tractate Rosh Hashanah, Chapter II) describes a relay system that was used in antiquity that covered hundreds of miles. It was used when the officials in Jerusalem needed to broadcast the start of a new fiscal year (before the Jewish calendar was published):

> How were these torches lighted? They used to bring long poles of cedar, and reeds, and olive wood, and flax fluff which they tied to the poles with a string. Someone used to go up to the top of a mountain, and set fire to them, and wave them to and fro, and up and down, until he saw the next one doing the same thing on the top of the second mountain; and so on the top of the third mountain, etc. From where did these torches start? From the Mount of Olives to Sartaba, from Sartaba to Grofina, from Grofina to Hauran. . . the one in Beth Baltin did not stop from there but went on waving to and fro, up and down, until he saw the whole of the Diaspora before him like one bonfire. . . Rabbi Johanan said: between each one and the next there were 8 parasangs. How many were there altogether? Thirty-two. But today there are much more. Abaye said: The roads have been closed.

Relay communication was reliable, as each receiver had to acknowledge the transmitter. The system consisted of 32 relay points, each separated by 8 parasangs, starting from Jerusalem (Mount of Olives, elevation about 2700 feet), traveling north over the mountains, and then to the northern and western communities in Syria, down the Euphrates valley (elevation 900 to 1200 feet), and finally reaching the Academy of Pumbeditha (near what is now Baghdad, elevation about 150 feet).

A Persian parasang is defined as the distance a horse would walk for 1 hour (today assumed to be between 3 and 4 miles). Consequently, if the distance between relays was 8 parasangs (between 24 and 32 miles), the line-of-sight range formula implies that the average torch antenna elevation had to be between 144 and 256 feet. The 32 relays would cover a distance between $(32 - 1) \times 24 = 744$ miles and $(32 - 1) \times 32 = 992$ miles. (Note that the straight-line air distance from Jerusalem to Baghdad is about 550 miles.) It seems that the telecommunications infrastructure expanded by the time of Abaye ("because the roads were closed") and could have been used for other purposes.

Synchronous Communication Protocol

Synchronous communication requires that sender and receiver clocks are set to the same time. More messages can be sent by a single torch, but it requires that sender and receiver clocks be synchronized perfectly. This method also uses the previous semaphore protocol.

In operation, Polybius tells us to first obtain two identical containers, each with a set of calibrated level markings. These containers are our clocks: the key property of the containers is that after they are filled with water, they empty at the same rate after pulling out a stopper on the bottom. The levels denote predetermined messages, such as "Buy 1000," "Sell All," "Sell Short," and so on. Floating corks placed in the containers are used to ascertain the level. Suppose the transmitter wants to transmit the message "Sell 100 Gold," corresponding to a particular level on the container. According to Polybius, the transmitter first raises a torch and waits until the receiver acknowledges by transmitting his torch (this is just the previous semaphore protocol). When both torches are clearly visible, both sender and receiver release their stoppers so that both containers start emptying. When the level is reached at the transmitter's container that corresponds to the message "Sell 100 Gold," the transmitter raises his torch and stops emptying his container. This receiver sees the raised torch and plugs up his container. The receiver then reads the level on the container and notes the corresponding message.

Polybius described a method similar to what today is called "time hopping." A variation of his method is found in a communication scheme called spread spectrum — a noise-resistant digital communications technique.

Symbol Encoding Protocol

This method also uses the semaphore protocol, but with two torch transmitters: one clearly standing to the left and one to the right. Before transmission, Polybius encodes the alphabet into letter groups: A–E (group I), F–J (group II), K–O (group III), P–T (group IV), and U–Z (group V). The protocol is as follows: both the left and the right transmitters raise one torch; they wait for the receiver to acknowledge by raising two torches. After this synchronization, all torches are lowered. Letter transmission requires signaling of the letter group (by the left transmitter) and the order of the letter in the group (by the right transmitter). For example, to send the letter B of BUY, the left transmitter lifts one torch (group I) and the right transmitter lifts two torches (indicating the second letter in the group); to send the letter U, the left transmitter lifts five torches and the right transmitter lifts one torch; to send the letter Y, the left transmitter lifts five torches and the right transmitter lifts five torches. According to Polybius,

> The first letter is kappa. This being in the second division is on tablet number two, and, therefore, he must raise two torches on the left, so that the receiver may know that he had to consult the second tablet. He will now raise five torches on the right, to indicate that it is kappa, this being the fifth letter in the second division and the receiver of the signal will note this down on his writing tablet. The dispatcher will then raise four torches on the left as rho belongs to the fourth division, and then two on the right, rho being the second letter in this division. The receiver writes down rho and so forth. This device enables any news to be definitely conveyed. Many torches, of course, are required, as the signal for each letter is a double one.

This is actually a binary letter encoding system, based on whether a flame is visible or not. It is similar in principle to Morse Code or to the American National Standard Institute (ANSI) codes.

1.5. The First Wireless Network

Almost 2000 years after Polybius, Claude Chappe (1763–1805) developed a sophisticated secure communication system consisting of amplifiers, repeaters, and routers.

Chappe's system consisted of a network of transmitting stations. Each station consisted of a tower hooked up with two wooden arms, with each arm movable to seven distinct positions. Each distinct position encoded a letter, number, or word (the official encodings, written in a codebook, were changed frequently). In 1794, the word *telegraph* (Greek for *writing at a distance*) was first used and referred to this optical communication system; the optical code used in the telegraph towers was called "semaphore."

The telescope (invented in the 1600s) was used as a signal amplifier to increase the daytime sensitivity of the human eye. Operators posted at each station were able to see the semaphore towers — with a telescope — to distances up to 20 miles in clear daytime weather. The Chappe telegraph network technology included the creation of new protocols, the encapsulation of control data, error correction, and routing based on address.

Innovations in the Chappe Telegraph Network

The early optical (semaphore, fires, smoke) and acoustic (drums, horns, shouts) networks relied on broadcasting a signal — either light or sound waves — whose reception depended on the sensitivity of human eyes or ears. Acoustic signals had the shortest range, flares at night had the longest range, and semaphore flags or smoke had an intermediate range, as human eye sensitivity was greatest in the dark. Optical systems depended on the weather, time of day, and height. In general, for all broadcast technologies, the signal power (intensity, loudness, brightness) is proportional to the inverse square of the distance:

$$\text{Power} = \frac{\text{Constant}}{r^2}$$

The constant depends on the network, the weather, and time of day. This is also true in today's wireless systems, which are based on the broadcast of electromagnetic radio waves.

For acoustic waves, ancient technologists also recognized that the range of relatively weak signals can be extended by concentrating the signal in a physical media such as a hollow tube or a hose. Such speaking tubes (essentially acoustic waveguides) were used for communication in palaces or large offices.

Ancient technologists knew that the only way to increase the range of communication was to use repeaters and routers: trusted intermediaries along a communication path. The job of a repeater is to receive a message and relay it to the next repeater (who may be located at the ultimate destination). A router is used when there are more than one possible communication paths: the job of a router is to read part of the address information in the message and to decide which path to use.

Chappe realized that a telescope can amplify daytime signals to match the sensitivity of the human eye at night. The Chappe telegraph network was the first communication system to use amplifiers in a systematic way with repeaters and routers, thereby increasing the range of the system. The telescope amplifiers extended the range between repeaters. This meant fewer repeaters were needed for a given distance; fewer repeaters meant that the *network latency* — the total amount of time it takes a symbol to move across a network from a source to a destination — was also reduced in comparison to other methods. Ultimately, this technology enabled intraday trading and intraday arbitrage for its users.

Data Protocol

The lowest-level Chappe telegraph protocol was concerned with representing an information signal. Each signal was represented physically by a distinct position of the arms, which could be seen clearly with a telescope. Signals were either synchronized (using a system similar to the second method of Polybius, but with synchronized pendulum clocks) or not synchronized (using a system similar to the first method of Polybius). The Chappe telegraph operators did not know the meaning of the encoded message (the code was only known to special individuals called directors). In any case, at station reception, each signal, together with its sequence number, was logged into a book.

Repeater Protocol

The second-level protocol was concerned with station-to-station communication along the network, where a signal that was just received would be repeated or relayed to the next station. Here, the Chappe telegraph operator would, if necessary, encapsulate information signals with control signals. The control codes would precede or follow the information message. Control codes included:

> Start of transmission
> End of transmission
> Suspension of transmissions for 1 or 2 hours
> Conflict (two signals from opposite directions arrived simultaneously at the station)
> Priority (indicates the precedence of one of the conflicting signals)
> Error (cancels the last transmitted signal)
> Idle (indicates the closing of the station or line)
> Minor failure (indicates a small problem or temporary absence of the operator)
> Major failure (indicates a serious problem requiring outside help)
> Rain or fog (indicates restricted visibility)

The repeaters used other signals to control the signal rate (faster or slower) and flow control (retransmission requests based on the logged signal number). This protocol specified transmission error detection and correction and specified conflict resolution between "colliding signals" (signals traveling in opposite directions). These control signals seem to be the origin of our "control keys" found on computer keyboards and ANSI data codes.

Router Protocol

The third-level protocol governed how a message was routed along one tower route or another tower route from source to destination. At special points in the network several tower routes converged. At such a routing point the special network official (a director) had to decode a message in order to extract source and destination addresses. The director would then direct or route the original encoded message to the telegraph tower on the correct path in order to continue transmission.

Transmission Protocol

Finally, the highest-level protocol was concerned with source-to-destination communication and included the following encapsulating control signals:

> Synchronization (tells all stations along the line to synchronize clocks)
> Acknowledgment (indicates the reception of a correctly decoded message at the final
> destination)

This final acknowledgment control signal shows that this high-level protocol enforced reliable communication. With all technology in place, Chappe telegraph operators could reliably and securely transmit about one symbol per minute per 20-mile repeater station. (Note that depending on the codebook used, one symbol can denote a specific message.)

Note that the individual Chappe telegraph signals (from repeater tower to repeater tower) travel at the speed of light, as each signal is optical. However, symbol communication time is much greater because it includes the time that the telegraph operator requires to move the station arms in order to receive and relay (or route) the symbol. This "hidden time" is included in the network latency (latency is from the Latin verb *to lie hidden*). The easiest way to measure network latency is for a sender to measure the round-trip time between the transmission of a short message to a destination and the destination's acknowledgment to the sender. (In modern networks, this process is colloquially called *ping*.)

Napoleon made extensive use of Chappe technology on his campaigns. After Napoleon's defeat, the Chappe telegraph was used exclusively for French government communications: private citizens were forbidden to use the network. By 1852, the network grew to 556 stations (covering about 3000 miles), connected 29 cities to Paris, and employed over 1000 people. After the Morse telegraph appeared, the French were reluctant to use what they initially considered an inferior and insecure technology. The wireless Chappe telegraph system was superior because there were no wires to cut and no batteries to replace.

Chappe telegraph systems were built around the world by government and private enterprises. This technology was used in Europe until the 1880s, especially by the military. In the United States, various hilltop locations were called "Telegraph Hill" in honor of their Chappe telegraph towers.

In the early 1800s, a group of Philadelphia Stock Exchange brokers set up their own private Chappe telegraph system. The repeaters were located on hills traversing New Jersey (including one 400-foot hill on Staten Island). On a good day, a signal could be transmitted 110 miles from New York to Philadelphia in 10 minutes: the fastest alternative was a 100-mile stage coach ride. The Chappe telegraph let the Philadelphia brokers profit on good arbitrage opportunities between the New York and the Philadelphia markets and enabled day trading between markets.

The Need for Repeaters, Routers, Amplifiers, and Multiplexers

The basic Chappe telegraph principles were adapted by the Morse telegraph and all later communication networks using wired and wireless technologies.

The wired Morse electromagnetic telegraph technology was the first competitor to the wireless Chappe network. In the Morse telegraph, a signal was transmitted (in a steel or copper wire) by closing and releasing a switch connected to a battery (a voltage source). A signal corresponded to a voltage or current burst or impulse; these pulses were represented in a patented code due to Samuel Morse (1791–1872).

As the length of the wire increased, signals became difficult to detect (because of the wire's internal resistance). A signal transmitted with a more powerful battery (providing a greater voltage and current impulse) could have a higher range; however, this had to be balanced by the fact that such high power could burn out the equipment and burn off the insulation around the wires. In order to avoid this, the earliest commercial Morse telegraph networks were designed with repeaters: repeaters received weak signals and retransmitted them. Morse telegraph repeaters were faster than the human Chappe telegraph repeaters

---

Box 1-5

Exploiting Technology: Arbitrage in the 1830s

The distance between the Paris Exchange and the financial market in Bordeaux was about 365 miles. News delivered via the regular mail stagecoach took about 5 days. However, the French government's Chappe telegraph to Bordeaux, utilizing the single router at Tours (about 150 miles from Paris), relayed news to Bordeaux in a few hours.

In 1834, before they left banking to concentrate on the casino business, the Blanc brothers figured out how to use the French government's Chappe telegraph as part of their proprietary trading, even though (i) the telegraph was secure and restricted to government use; (ii) the telegraph operators did not know the semaphore encoding for a given message; (iii) any nongovernment message would be detected easily; and (iv) any error codes would be filtered out by the directors at the routing stations.

The Blanc brothers discovered a vulnerable point: the telegraph operator at the repeater tower immediately after the router at Tours. They arranged that on certain days, a trusted Blanc brothers agent would arrive from Paris and tell this operator to please put an extra sequence of control codes (e.g., "Error — cancel the last transmitted symbol") in the next message. The original government message was not modified. In normal operation, operators who made an error would transmit the correction in the next symbol. The control codes and corrections would be propagated by the network repeaters and filtered out by the next router (in this case at Bordeaux). Another agent of the Blanc brothers would be standing near the repeater tower immediately before the Bordeaux router; this agent waited and simply read the control codes transmitted to Bordeaux before they were filtered out by the director. Everyone (agents and naïve telegraph operators) was paid for their trouble.

The pattern of error codes — harmless to the original government message — contained a message coded by the Blanc brothers using the semaphore control codes that indicated the price of securities at Paris. The Blanc brothers figured out how to superimpose this message on a carrier. Their messages, from Paris to Bordeaux, were transmitted in much less time than any other method.

After their discovery, the French courts ruled that the only law that seemed to have been broken was the illegal use of government property. All telegraph operators were acquitted in 1837 and the Blanc brothers were told to leave France. There was no law in France as yet forbidding the use of the telegraph for private messages.

(the Morse operators did not have to climb a tower and swing large wooden arms). Another breakthrough came with the elimination of human repeaters with the Morse patented electromechanical repeaters. The electromagnet used to detect weak signals at the receiving end was hinged to a switch that was used to transmit a strong voltage using a separate battery; consequently, the same signal can be repeated in another wire. These automated repeaters further helped reduce the network latency in the Morse system.

By the 1860s, the electromagnetic Morse telegraph was much less expensive to operate than the wireless Chappe telegraph: fewer (wired) repeaters were needed; at a later time even the routers were automated. The Morse repeaters and routers made real-time trading economical.

By this time, it was becoming apparent that running individual wires for each Morse telegraph line was becoming too expensive. One way to decrease technology costs was to figure out how to transmit and receive multiple messages simultaneously on a single

Morse telegraph line. In 1874, Thomas Edison (1847–1931) developed a special type of repeater that enabled two telegraph operators to simultaneously transmit and receive two messages on the same telegraph line. Edison called his patented invention a quadruplex repeater. Quadruplex helped Western Union save $20 million in wiring costs.

Edison's quadruplex is a special case of what is today called multiplex. A multiplexer (sometimes called a concentrator) is a device that creates a single message from a set of messages for transmission. At the receiving end is a demultiplexer (sometimes called an inverse multiplexer): a device that reconstitutes the original set of messages from a single (multiplexed) message. In the Internet, multiplexing and demultiplexing take place in hubs and switches. The use of multiplex communications further reduces the cost of technology per message as it allows the sharing of more technology resources. This was another major improvement over the Chappe telegraph.

Because a repeater needed its own power supply, it could not be used across distances that traversed the water (it was difficult to configure batteries at the bottom of the ocean). In the 1880s, Oliver Heaviside (1850–1925) proposed techniques that considered a telegraph wire as a kind of speaking tube wave guide: depending on the construction, a voltage pulse can either diffuse through a wire like an explosion or propagate like a sound wave through a speaking tube. Heaviside's model led to the so-called loading coils, which extended the range of the signal in a wire and helped facilitate trans-Atlantic and trans-Continental communication.

The telephone network (that started being built after Alexander Bell demonstrated his invention at the 1876 World Exposition in Philadelphia) was a second application that needed repeaters. Initially, the telephone network used the same wires as the Morse telegraph network. The first telephone repeaters consisted of physically placing the receiving speaker end of one phone on the transmitting microphone end of another phone (mimicking the telegraph repeater): this worked but was not really feasible for long distance. It turned out that the Heaviside loading coil technique for the telegraph was crucial in extending long-distance telephony to several hundred miles.

Wireless electromagnetic telegraphy was a third application that needed repeaters. In 1888, Heinrich Hertz (1857–1894) discovered that some alternating current circuits can be used to produce an electromagnetic wave; the wave could be used to transmit a pulse through space that can be detected at a similar circuit across the room. Consequently, the wireless wave pulses can be used to drive a wireless Morse telegraph. Because these were broadcast signals, the signal power decreased proportionally to the inverse square of the distance. Repeaters were needed here as well to compensate for the sensitive (and expensive) receiving equipment that was needed for long-distance wireless communication.

Early wireless telegraphy was not restricted to line-of-sight operation: it was discovered (by accident) that over-the-horizon communication was possible if the circuit was adjusted ("tuned") to certain frequencies. In 1901, the first (very high power) trans-Atlantic wireless signal was received; regular trans-Atlantic news was broadcast by 1903. Heaviside later explained that there had to be a layer in the upper atmosphere (now called the Heaviside layer in the ionosphere) that acted like a waveguide: the waves propagate up and then propagate down where they can be detected. For example, at "short wave" frequencies, waves reflect off the ionosphere — in several hops — and can enable trans-Continental or trans-Atlantic communication. (On the opposite extreme, very low frequency waves — now used almost exclusively by the military — can pass right through the earth; these waves are used to communicate with submarines. In general, radio waves above microwave frequencies behave just like light beams in Chappe's telegraph.)

What was really needed in these three wired and wireless networks was the analog of Chappe's telescope: an amplifier. The electromagnetic amplifier was actually discovered by Thomas Edison in 1883 (by accident) during his search for the right combination of filaments for light bulbs. Edison observed a current flow between the filaments of a three-pronged light bulb and observed that the strange light bulb could be used as a switch or as an amplifier. After the Edison patent expired, such vacuum tube diodes and triodes (also called thermionic valves) were created and first used in wireless telegraphy and long-distance telephony: weak electromagnetic signals could be received and amplified without the need for expensive equipment. For example, by 1915 these vacuum tube amplifiers enabled a three-way telephone conference call between President Woodrow Wilson in Washington, Alexander Bell in New York, and Bell's assistant Thomas Watson in San Francisco.

Box 1-6
Exploiting Technology: Arbitrage in the 1990s

According to the Securities and Exchange Commission, "Day traders rapidly buy and sell stocks throughout the day in the hope that their stocks will continue climbing or falling in value for the seconds to minutes they own the stock, allowing them to lock in quick profits."

In the 1800s, technology-enabled traders allowed them to discover arbitrage opportunities between New York and Philadelphia and between Paris and Bordeaux. In the 1990s, other technology-enabled traders allowed them to discover arbitrage opportunities between different market makers on the electronic Nasdaq Stock Market System.

Nasdaq is an electronic system that links hundreds of dealers who are allowed to make markets in a particular stock. (In some sense, Nasdaq is a collection of markets, with each market run by a "market maker.") Nasdaq was developed by the National Association of Securities Dealers (NASD) and was deployed in 1971. As opposed to traditional exchanges, Nasdaq market makers can be physically located anywhere: the "floor" is implemented in a fault-tolerant computer system colocated in Trumbull (Connecticut) and Rockville (Maryland). One actively traded stock could have over a hundred markets: each market maker would post their buy and sell prices — their bid and offer quotes — on a device called a Nasdaq II workstation. The idea is that the market makers compete with each other to offer the best price to customers: the actual buyers and sellers of stocks. The best bid and best offers are computed automatically by Nasdaq computers and broadcast in real time to Nasdaq subscribers.

In the early 1990s, a small company called Datek Securities developed a system called "The Watcher." According to the SEC,

> Watcher was designed to run Nasdaq data through Datek Securities computers, which were far faster than a Nasdaq Workstation II. The Watcher system gave Datek Securities traders a significant time advantage because they received last sale and quotation update information before other market participants. The Watcher system also analyzed the data to highlight trading opportunities. These features enabled Datek Securities traders to react more quickly to market activity and to enter and receive execution on their orders more quickly than other market participants.

The basic idea behind "The Watcher" was to identify Nasdaq market makers who did not update their quotes fast enough, and then to buy from one electronic market maker and sell to another. As in Philadelphia 200 years before, Datek used technology to identify arbitrage opportunities in the mispricings between markets.

By the 1930s, research in materials science focused on semiconductor materials with switch-like properties. The advantages of such a "solid-state" (i.e., not filaments in a light bulb) amplifier led to the 1947 invention of the transistor. The first fully commercial product using a transistor as an amplifier was a repeater built for the Bell Telephone System in 1959.

1.6. Notes and References

General References

A good technology encyclopedia available on the Internet is the Wikipedia: an open-content encyclopedia in many languages. It has entries on the Pony Express, Chappe's telegraph, and the most recent Internet standards, as well as entries on classical writers such as Vitruvius, Polybius, Pliny, Cassius Dio, Herodotus, and others.
[0.1] http://en.wikipedia.org/wiki/.

Project Gutenberg maintains the content of several out of print books, memoirs, classics, and other public domain writings, including the Memoirs of Casanova:
[0.2] http://www.gutenberg.net/.

Relative prices and values — at least for the U.S. dollar from 1789 to 2003 — can be computed via a financial calculator that uses five economic series, including the consumer price index (CPI) and the unskilled wage rate. It is hosted at the Economic History site:
[0.3] http://www.eh.net/

A good online source documenting the earliest known uses of some of the words of mathematics is maintained by Jeff Miller at
[0.4] http://members.aol.com/jeff570/mathword.html

The MacTutor History of Mathematics archive, maintained by the School of Mathematics and Statistics of the University of St. Andrews in Scotland, is a good online source for biographies of mathematicians and related fields. It is maintained at
[0.5] http://www-groups.dcs.st-and.ac.uk/~history/

Wall Street & Technology is a monthly news publication covering the financial technologies of compliance, trading, operations, and investment management. Their site is at
[0.6] http://www.wallstreetandtech.com/

CrossTalk, The Journal of Defense Software Engineering is an approved Department of Defense monthly journal (published by the Software Technology Support Center at the Ogden Air Logistics Center) that frequently publishes articles relating to mission-critical financial systems. Their site is at
[0.7] http://www.stsc.hill.af.mil/crosstalk/

Financial vs. Commercial Systems

A picture of the oldest share traded, and a good description of VOC, is at the Web site maintained by Reinhild Tschöpe at
[1] http://www.oldest-share.com/.

Historical surveys on financial innovation were reported at the
[2] Conference on the History of Financial Innovation held at the International Center for Finance (organized by Christos Cabolis, William Goetzmann, and Geert Rouwenhorst), Yale School of Management, March 2003 (see http://icf.som.yale.edu/news/hist_conference.shtml).

Some argue that the tradition of privatizing a corporation into shares goes back to Roman times. For more information, see
[3] Ulrike M. Malmendier, "Shares in Ancient Rome." To appear in *Origins of Value: Innovations in the History of Finance* (edited by K. Geert Rouwenhorst and William Goetzmann). Oxford University Press, ISBN 0195175719. (A preliminary version is in [2].)

The eye-witness descriptions of Joseph de la Vega are found in his short book published in 1680, Confusión de Confusiones, reprinted in
[4] Martin S. Fridon (ed.). *Extraordinary Popular Delusions and the Madness of Crowds and Confusión de Confusiones*. John Wiley & Sons, New York, 1996. ISBN 0 471 13312-4.

Financial vs. Gambling Systems

For a good reference on martingales, the Monte Carlo method, and other topics in probability theory, see
[5] Charles M. Grinstead and J. Laurie Snell. *Introduction to Probability*. American Mathematical Society, Providence 1997. ISBN 0-8218-0749-8. (This book is also freely available under the terms of the GNU General Public License at http://dartmouth.edu/~chance/teaching_aids/books_articles/probability_book/book.html)

Common attributes between gambling and financial systems, especially regarding regulation and compliance, are addressed by the Securities Exchange Commission at http://sec.gov/. The difference between gambling and investing (and a quiz that can help traders decide if they are gamblers) is at the Web site of the Connecticut Council on Problem Gambling:
[6] http://www.ccpg.org/financial.asp

A description of the roulette activities of the Blanc brothers is described at the roulette site
[7] http://www.play-table-roulette.com/

and the site for the Hamburg Casino:
[8] http://spielbank-bad-homburg.de/en/information/information_geschichte.htm

Financial vs. Military Systems and Physical Delivery

The description of the turn-of-the-century (19th) is discussed in
[9] Max Nordau. *Degeneration* (originally published in 1892), University of Nebraska Press; Reprint edition, 1993 (pp. 37–38).

For a review of commercial history in the Middle Ages, see
[10] Meir Kohn. *The Origins of Western Economic Success: Commerce, Finance, and Government in Pre-Industrial Europe*, Working Papers (available at http://www.dartmouth.edu/~mkohn/).

Interesting stories about Fisk and others associated with American finance can be found in
[11] Robert Sobel, *Panic on Wall Street: A History of American Financial Disasters*, Macmillan, New York 1968. ISBN 68 25715.

A history of the Philadelphia Stock Exchange is maintained at their Web site:
[12] http://www.phlx.com/exchange/history.html

Toll roads and turnpikes are discussed in the article by
[13] Daniel Klein and Gordon Fleming. "Private Toll Roads: Learning from the 19th Century." *Transportation Quarterly*, Vol. 46, No. 3, July 1992 (available at http://lsb.scu.edu/~dklein/papers/privateTollRds.html).

Histories of American Express, Wells, Fargo & Company, and Adams Express are maintained at their corresponding Web sites. A history of the Pony Express is maintained by the U.S. National Park Service at
[14] http://www.nps.gov/poex/hrs/hrst.htm

The Rothschild exhibit at the Museum of London is summarized at
[15] http://www.museumoflondon.org.uk/MOLsite/exhibits/roth/index.htm

In 1940, Warner Brothers produced the film *A Dispatch from Reuters* with Edward G. Robinson playing Paul Julius Reuter. The official history of Reuters is maintained at the corporate site:
[16] http://about.reuters.com/aboutus/history/

Nonphysical Communication and Delivery

For a discussion on the sensitivity of the human eye, see
[17] David R. Copenhagen and Tom Reuter, "Phototransduction and Dark Noise in Rod Photoreceptors," in *Night Vision: Current Research and Future Directions*. National Academy of Sciences, Washington, DC, 1987. ISBN 0-309-07796-6 (available at http://www.nap.edu/books/POD259/html/23.html).

Longfellow's works, including the poem "Paul Revere's Ride," are at Project Gutenberg:
[18] http://www.gutenberg.org/dirs/1/3/6/1365/1365.txt

The First Wireless Network

For a description of Chappe's system, described by some today as "Napoleon's Internet," see
[19] Gerard J. Holzmann and Bjorn Pehrson. *The Early History of Data Networks*. IEEE Computer Society Press and John Wiley, November 1994. ISBN 0-8186-6782-6.

The Blanc brothers exploitation of technology for the Paris–Bordeaux arbitrage is discussed by
[20] Gerard J. Holzmann. "Taking Stock." *Inc, Magazine*, September 1999 (available at http://www.inc.com/magazine/19990915/13554.html).

Day trading is described by the SEC at
[21] http://www.sec.gov/answers/daytrading.htm

The arbitrage technology of Datek Securities is described at
[22] http://www.sec.gov/litigation/admin/33-8059.htm

1.7. Discussion Questions

1. Joseph de la Vega stated that "The Exchange business is comparable to a game." Discuss three points where you agree and three points where you disagree.

2. Show how news communication can be neither error correcting nor reliable.

3. How have American Express and Wells, Fargo exploited financial technology?

4. Look up Internet Standard RFC 1149 (IP over Avian Carriers). Discuss how it relates to the standard Internet protocol.

5. Can there be demand for a commodity but no demand for a futures contract on that commodity? Can you give examples?

6. Discuss how improvements in financial technology can increases or decrease the opportunities for arbitrage.

7. The capitalization of the Erie Canal, built between 1817 and 1825, was $7 million. What is the Erie Canal capitalization value in today's dollars?

8. What were the differences among the arbitrage strategies of the Blanc brothers, the brokers at the Philadelphia Stock Exchange, and Datek Securities? Comment on the fairness, legality, and utilization of financial technology.

9. Transportation networks based on physical carriers may be more efficient for transmitting large messages (especially messages with maps, charts, or pictures). Computing the *channel capacity* is one way of comparing two different information transmission methods. For example, suppose we have a financial contract consisting of 5 pages (each page contains 300 words of 5 letters); consequently, together with the "space" used as a word separator, each page contains 1800 characters (letter or number symbols), and the entire document contains 9000 symbols. A 100-mile transmission by Chappe telegraph, at 1 symbol per minute, would require 9000 minutes (150 hours). If we use a messenger traveling 10 miles per hour, the message would be delivered in 10 hours — the channel capacity of the messenger here is 900 symbols per minute. Suppose that we store a large historical set of financial data for thousands of companies containing glossy corporate annual reports, SEC filings, and market data. Data are stored on 1000 DVD disks. Suppose a single DVD holds 10 gigabytes (= 10 billion characters) and our Internet connection is calibrated at 10 megabytes (= 10 million characters) per second. How long would it take to send the 1000 DVD disks from New York to Philadelphia via the Internet? Suppose we have an express courier that is available to drive to New York to Philadelphia: what is the channel capacity of this service?

10. In addition to the telephone, Alexander Bell patented the photophone, which is a device for transmitting voice on a beam of light. Compare Bell's photophone with today's fiber optic networks.

CHAPTER ◆ 2

Prices, Interest, Time

The terms used on the Exchange are not carefully chosen… even the most experienced person needs a new dictionary to understand it… As to the confusion of tongues on the exchange, I am not to be blamed for it. The jargon was coined by the necessities of the business, then became customary, then became practical.

—Joseph de la Vega, Confusión de Confusiones (1688)

A scribe whose hand rivals his mouth, he is indeed a scribe.

—Sumerian proverb (ca. 2000 BCE)

2.1. Financial Terms

Thomas Edison was known as a technologist and inventor. Yet, his recollections were peppered with terms such as premium, bid, corner, quotation, checks, broker, clearing house, and Wall Street. These terms are actors in the financial technology universe. What do these terms mean? This section reviews these terms and other jargon from a financial technology perspective.

Many financial terms are *metonyms*, i.e., words derived from associations. For example, *Wall Street*, a short street in lower Manhattan, is used as an alias or proxy for the entire U.S. financial system because that is where the New York Stock Exchange is located. Similarly, *The City* is used frequently as an alias for the financial district in London and therefore the financial interests of the British economy. Other financial terms are derived from Latin, old English, or slang (American or British). For example, *bread* (short for *bread and honey*) is Cockney rhyming slang for *money*. Other terms are *eponyms* (names that become identified with an object or activity) or *synecdoches* (a kind of metonymy in which a part of something is used for the whole).

What Is Money?

In antiquity, temples were used as banks and depository institutions. Temples were centrally located, well guarded, and had to accommodate the influx and exchange of commodities (agricultural, precious metals, and animals) for religious functions, taxes, and commerce. In pre-Augustan Rome, the Temple of *Juno Moneta* (*Moneta* is a nickname, meaning *she who warns*) was used as the location for financial transactions. All of these fiduciary (Latin *fiduciari*: trust, hold in confidence) activities involved trust. *Moneta* became an eponym for mint, monetary, and money.

Box 2-1
Money in 1704 America

Pay is Grain, Pork, Beef &c. at the prices sett by the General Court that Year; mony is pieces of Eight, Ryalls, or Boston or Bay shillings (as they call them) or Good hard money, as sometimes silver coin is termed by them.; also Wampum, vizt. Indian beads wch serves for change. Pay as mony is provisions, as aforesd one Third cheaper than as the Assembly or Genel Court sets it; and Trust as they and the merchant agree for time.

In general, money is fungible (interchangeable, from Latin *fungi*: to perform); payment can be made in commodities (metal, animals, food) and, more importantly, in "trust" or credit (*credit*: Latin, to have confidence in). As Benjamin Franklin emphasized centuries later, time and credit are also surrogates for money.

Box 2-2
From *Advice to a Young Tradesman, Written by an Old One*
(Benjamin Franklin, 1748)

Remember that TIME is Money. He that can earn Ten Shillings a Day by his Labour, and goes abroad, or sits idle one half of that Day, tho' he spends but Sixpence during his Diversion or Idleness, ought not to reckon That the only Expence; he has really spent or rather thrown away Five Shillings besides.

Remember that CREDIT is Money. If a Man lets his Money lie in my Hands after it is due, he gives me the Interest, or so much as I can make of it during that Time. This amounts to a considerable Sum where a Man has good and large Credit, and makes good Use of it.

Remember that Money is of a prolific generating Nature. Money can beget Money, and its Offspring can beget more, and so on. Five Shillings turn'd, is Six: Turn'd again, 'tis Seven and Three Pence; and so on 'til it becomes an Hundred Pound. The more there is of it, the more it produces every Turning, so that the Profits rise quicker and quicker. He that kills a breeding Sow, destroys all her Offspring to the thousandth Generation. He that murders a Crown, destroys all it might have produc'd, even Scores of Pounds.

Remember that Six Pounds a Year is but a Groat a Day. For this little Sum (which may be daily wasted either in Time or Expence unperceiv'd a Man of Credit may on his own Security have the constant Possession and Use of an Hundred Pounds....

Most relationships between time and money can be measured, as both are quantifiable: for example, time units can be years, months, and days and money units can be in amounts of coin or weight. Note that agricultural money is only useful for a limited amount of time: food and vegetation decay and young animals must be fed and housed (and then they grow old and die). Money based on hard assets such as gold or land would, in some sense, be viewed as more valuable than time-limited assets. This fungibility can be seen today in the different prices stated on futures markets and currency markets.

The measurement of credit is a measurement of a probability to pay. Franklin observed that credit measurements are implicitly factored into the different prices for bonds — binding agreements to repay a loan. For example, someone lending $10,000 to the U.S. government for 3 months will most probably be repaid; would a similar loan to a stranger be repaid? This probability of payment is factored into the compensation to the lender: the *interest* for the loan. A lender might be happy receiving an interest payment of $300 (in addition to the return of the $10,000 lent out) for her 3-month loan to the U.S. government; the same lender might demand an interest payment of $1000 from less credit-worthy characters for taking a higher risk. Note that establishing credit, like other activities measuring an event probability, requires the results of different loan repayment examples over time.

The combination of credit and time led Franklin to the aphorism "money begets money." *Fenus* (Latin: money made by interest) is possibly the origin of the word finance.

What Are Banks?

Temples were the "central banks" of their day. Because temples were centrally located and well guarded, they became the natural places for storing money and other objects for safekeeping (Latin *depositum*: safekeeping). Some deposits earned fungible money from the deposited money (like today's savings accounts), whereas other deposits returned exactly the items that were kept (like a safety deposit box). *Letters of credit*, basically a guarantee from an established and well-known third party that the bearer of the letter will repay (similar to today's credit cards and travelers checks), and checks were mentioned by the Roman writer Cicero. A check (from the old Sanskrit word for dominion, related to the order to *check* in the game of *chess*) is a formal order to a bank to pay someone; money in the checking account is stopped until money from the debit account (Latin *debit*: one who owes, debt, duty) is *paid* (*pay*, from Latin *pax*: peace, pacify) or settled (old English *setl*: to bring to rest in a seat) to the creditor's account. This process is called clearing (clear, from Latin *clarus*: free from debt or charges). Letters of credit and checks indirectly establish a social network of credit and trust. The payment procedures and standards associated with transferring monetary values — clearing and settlement — are a major aspect of financial technology systems today. These activities are performed by intermediaries — called clearing agents — who frequently work for a business called a *clearing house*.

What Are Coins and Currency?

Coin is from the Latin *cuneus*, meaning wedge. (Cuneus is also the origin of *cuneiform* — the wedge-like system of notation used in ancient Sumeria and Babylonia.)

Different societies minted different coins. In antiquity, people would exchange their goods at tables where coins were piled up into little pillars or columns. The tables and benches (*banca* in Latin) are metonyms for banks. The top or capital (*capitellum*, Latin for little head or top of a column) of the column of coins is possibly an origin of the word capital as another metonym for money (others say that the little head of *capitellum* denotes the head of cattle). Note that bench has another metonym used today: because a bench is where a judge sits, a bench denotes a court of law.

At the end of the day, coins were placed in a box (Latin *capsa*: case, chest, or money box; *cassa* in old Italian, *casse* in old French); this money case became slang for cash. The word cashier entered the English language in 1596 to denote the person who had access to the money box.

One problem with using coins for money is that coins can be faked. Before the development of high-quality metal manufacturing processes, coins varied in weight and could be clipped and faked as well. Checking coin quality for large payments could take weeks.

In 1699, an accepted medium (or *standard*, from old French *estendard*: rallying point) for exchange — a *circulation* (something that goes back and forth) — was called a *currency* (like a liquid that flows back and forth). In those days the new financial technology was the development of paper money as a standard; paper money amounted to a kind of standard letter of credit issued by a government. In the United States, the effort to standardize on paper money was led by Benjamin Franklin. (Because Franklin made his living as a printer, he had a financial interest in paper money: one of his company's first government jobs was the printing of Delaware's 1729 paper currency.)

Paper manufacturing technology (based on a chemical process that creates pulp and compressible slurry from soaked organic fibers) was discovered in China about 2000 years ago. By the 8th century, printed paper books and newspapers started appearing in China and Japan. By the 10th century, paper money started being used in China as a medium of exchange. The paper money was backed by precious metal. Paper technology appeared in Europe with the opening of the Fabriano paper mills by the Miliani family in 1268 (the Miliani paper mills still produce 90,000 tons of paper per year). The significant innovation introduced at Fabriano was the invention of the watermark: identification marks produced during paper manufacturing process. The watermark made authentication possible, which led to the increased use of paper for bank notes, certificates, and currency. Sophisticated watermark technology makes the counterfeiter's job more difficult.

One economic problem concerned with paper money is that the public must have confidence in the government's credit: printing more paper money can lead to inflationary crises. This is what happened in China in 1433. After a loss of confidence in its paper currency, the Chinese government converted to money backed by silver in 1450.

The problem of counterfeit money was why most people avoided large payments in cash or coins. Through most of history, most financial transactions were (and are) conducted on the basis of credit: only a few small transactions involved the immediate payment of cash. Coins and currency were used as a standard for value measurement (the underlying credit was denominated in currency units). Moreover, instead of accounting for each individual transaction, merchants typically offset one debt against another. For example, given the following four transactions: party A owes party B $5; B owes A $6; B owes A $5; and A owes B $8. Note that instead of exchanging a lot of cash for all four transactions (totaling $24 in value) they only need to exchange cash for a single transaction and record the details: A owes B $2. The individual transactions are "netted" into a single transaction.

Box 2-3
Clearing (Netting) and Multiplexing, Settling and Demultiplexing

Many financial transactions use intermediaries (also called agents or brokers) who act on behalf of clients (or customers). In financial jargon, client trades are denoted by a buy or sell *position*: an entitlement to receive or obligation to deliver something. Having a *long position* denotes ownership, and having a *short position* denotes an obligation to deliver.

Netting (clearing) refers to the process where an agent creates a single trade (or position) from a set of individual client trades (or positions). The agent matches and cancels positive charges (debits or purchases) with negative charges (credits or sales). Netting leaves a single remaining trade (a purchase or sale, i.e., a long or short position) with the agent that can then be resolved — bilaterally — with another agent. To use a technology analogy: netting multiplexes trades to a single trade. Note that a multiplexer (sometimes called a concentrator) is a device that creates a single message from a set of messages.

The opposite process, called settlement, occurs when an agent needs to fulfill the trading obligations of its clients. Each client with a buy position expects delivery (upon payment), and each client with a sale position expects payment (upon delivery). Settlement demultiplexes a resolved agent-to-agent trade into the original set of individual obligations. Note that a demultiplexer (sometimes called an inverse multiplexer) is a device that reconstitutes the original set of messages from a single (multiplexed) message. The rationale behind netting is that it is easier to process a single trade than to separately process many individual trades. In the Internet, multiplexing and demultiplexing take place in hubs and switches.

This system of clearing or netting was formalized by Luca Pacioli (1445–1517) in his 614 page textbook on business mathematics and accounting, the *Summa de Arithmetica, Geometria Proportioni et Proportionalita* (Latin: Everything about Arithmetic, Geometric Analogies, and Proportions). The Summa was one of the first best sellers printed by Gutenberg (first edition: 1494). It was set in dense print with no punctuation; however, it has a few illustrations by Pacioli's friend and former math student, Leonardo da Vinci. The term "netting" is from the Italian: *netto* clear or final (from Latin: *nitere* bright; related to the English word neat).

Investment and Speculation

The word *interest* is from a 15th century Latin construction derived from the prefix *inter*, meaning "to be between," and refers to a payment made between an initial and final payment. Even in ancient Sumeria it was recognized that investors (from Latin *investire*: someone who clothes or covers) or speculators (from Latin *speculari*: examine, spy) need to be compensated for lending money. Contract terms were stated something like "in one year, 60 shekels of silver produce 8 shekels of silver" — this specifies a *dividend* (Latin *dividendus*: something divided) or interest payment of 8 shekels of silver per year per 60 shekels.

Box 2-4
Babylonian Contracts (568 BCE)

Loan
One manna of money, a sum belonging to Dan-Marduk, son of Apla, son of the Dagger-wearer (is loaned), unto Kudurru, son of Iqisha-apla, son of Egibi. Yearly the amount of the manna shall increase its sum by eight shekels of money. Whatever he has in city or country, as much as it may be, is pledged to Dan-Marduk. (The date is) Babylon, Adar fourth, in Nebuchadnezzar's sixth year.

Financial Partnership
Two mannas of money belonging to Nabu-akhi-iddin, son of Shula, son of Egibi, and one half manna seven shekels of money belonging to Bel-shunu, son of Bel-akhi-iddin, Son of Sin-emuq, they have put into a copartnership with one another. Whatever remains to Bel-shunu in town or country over and above, becomes their common property. Whatever Bel-shunu spends for expenses in excess of four shekels of money shall be considered extravagant. (The contract is witnessed by three men and a scribe, and is dated at) Babylon, first of Ab, in the thirty-sixth year of Nebuchadnezzar.

In Babylonian currency, 1 manna equals 60 shekels. Interest rates per manna ranged from 3 to 20 shekels per year; typical values were 12 shekels per manna for silver (i.e., 1 silver shekel per month). In modern weights, 1 manna is about 500 grams; 60 mannas (a measure known as 1 *talent*) was defined as the weight that an average person can carry easily (approximately 30 kilograms or 66 pounds). The minimum yearly wage for an unskilled worker was 10 shekels; this salary could purchase the equivalent of 300 liters of barley per month. (Because slaves cost between 20 and 90 shekels, it was more cost effective to hire yearly workers.) The Babylonian accounting convention assumed all months had 30 days and all years had 12 months (360 days); there were intermittent religious holidays but no regular weekend breaks.

Compound interest — making money on interest, as opposed to simple interest — was also known in antiquity, despite the fact that computing compound interest tables required substantial skill in financial computing technology. This is possibly why compound interest was frequently outlawed and simple interest was strictly regulated. No one wanted to participate in an activity that they did not understand.

Another way of borrowing money from a lender is to induce the lender to become a business partner: a business can raise money by selling *equity* (from Latin *aequus*: fair, equal) or shares — a proportion of the business risks and rewards to investors.

For example, a business that needs 60,000 shekels can sell shares of itself at 1 manna per share (i.e., 60 shekels) to 1000 investors. With the money, the business makes 40,000 shekels over the year, and the business directors choose to distribute 30,000 shekels back to the 1000 shareholders — each shareholder receives 30 shekels — and the rest of the money is kept as reserve cash for the business. In this case, the investor's annual rate of return on the investment is 30 shekels per manna.

Note that from a *borrower's perspective*, the borrower (i.e., the business) borrowed money and is repaying the money to the lenders (i.e., the shareholders) at the yearly rate of

30 shekels per manna. If this arrangement was truly a loan, such a high interest rate would be culturally classified as *usurious*. However, if this payment is viewed as a dividend yield of 30 shekels per manna, then it would be viewed as a good investment! Note that the key difference between *fixed income* borrowing via a loan and *equity* borrowing via shareholders is that with a loan, the interest payments are specified in advance of the actual performance of the business. Shareholders take more risk: they do not know in advance what the business performance (and payment distributions) will be.

What if the business fails? Typically, in order to manage risk, the lenders have recourse to liquidate some assets of the borrower. For example, in the contract of Dan-Marduk lending 60 shekels to Kudurru (Box 2-4), the assets or *security* (Latin *securitas*: guarantee of safety or surety, related to *securis*: axe, a metonym for power and protection) that can be sold to cover his default is "whatever he has in city or country, as much as it may be."

One of the most difficult ancient problems was in determining the division of profits corresponding to the amount invested. One way of measuring *profit* (Latin: *proficere*: make, effect) is by computing the gain or return on an investment. For *partnerships* (Latin *partition*: part or share) and *corporations* (Latin *corpus*: body), computing a share in the profits was a regulated activity and was an advanced topic in medieval business textbooks.

Box 2-5

Computing Profit per Share (Exercise from a Business Textbook, 1592)

Two merchants made a companie. A put in 300 pound for a monethes and then putteth yet in 100 pound, and 6 monethes aftyer that taketh out 200 pound, and with the rest remaineth until the yeares end. B put in 100 pounds for one moneth and then putteth yet in 700 pound, and 6 monethes after that taketh out a certain summe of money, and with the rest remaineth until the yeares end and then finde to have gained together 400 pounde, wherof B must have 80 pound more than A, the question is how much money B took out of the companie, without reckoning interest upon interest.

From ancient times (until the 18th century), common technology tools used for financial computation included the abacus, clay or wax tablet, and tally stick.

The early abacus was a table covered with fine sand; marks can be drawn and erased as needed (the word abacus is either from the Greek *abax*: table or Hebrew *abk*: dust). Later models used small stones. With skill, the abacus could be used for integer addition, subtraction, multiplication, division, and some computations with fractions. In Roman times, another common name for an abacus was a *calculus* (Latin for pebble, from *calx*: a piece of limestone, probably like today's toy marbles). This metonym gave rise to the activity of *calculare* — calculation. *Calculones* ("pebblers") referred to the slaves who used these devices.

Popular abacus models had grooves for the pebbles; later models had the pebbles sliding on rods (as in the Chinese *suan-pan* models). During the Middle Ages, the English called the little computing pebbles in the abacus *counters* (from old French *compteur*). This eventually became metonymous with the person doing the counting (a *counter* or *accountant*) and with the place at the bench (bank) where the counters worked (a counter is also table top).

As today, gains on investments would be taxed (Latin *taxare*: estimate, touch, assess). The Romans had several systems of taxes, including taxes for import–export (*portorium*), land (*tributum soli*), a census (head or poll) tax per person (*tributum capitis*), income tax tithes (decimae), and a corporate tax on trade and business (*collatio lustralis*).

Financial Market Participants

For traders and dealers, gains on investments are measured as a difference between a *buy price* (price is from the Latin *pretium*) and a *sell price*. *Dealers* (one who portions out, like a card dealer, from Old German *teil*: portion, part), *brokers* (a middleman, agent, or factor, from old French *brocoeur*: negotiator), and market makers (Latin *mercatus*: marketplace, trade) often speak of a *bid price* (the price they will buy something from you, from old German *bitten*: entreat) and an ask or offer price (the price they will offer to sell something to you if you ask them). These two prices always exist, with the bid price less than the ask price (the dealer makes money on the price difference). A *quote* or *quotation* specifies, for a given product, a bid price and bid quantity and an ask price and ask quantity. For example, a silver dealer quote may be bid 200 ducats for 1 ounce and ask 2100 ducats for 10 ounces. Markets that utilize bids and asks are said to be *two-sided markets*.

Dealers make money on the *spread*: the difference between the ask and the bid. Brokers, because they are agents, get paid if they match buyers to sellers. They get a *fee* (from Latin *pecus*: cow, which later became a metonym for *pecunia*: money) or a fixed payment, also called a *commission* (Latin *commissio*: act of bringing together). In American slang, this is also called *vigorish* (Russian for *winnings*) — a term used for the charge taken by a *bookie* (slang for a *bookmaker*: one who determines and publishes the probabilities and payoffs of bets and who also arranges for collections and payments).

Recording Stock Purchases and Sales

One problem with the abacus was that there was no permanent way to record results of computation (today software engineers would say there was no *database* or no *object persistence*). Database records were written on papyrus (an expensive type of flammable paper) or on less flammable but much more expensive animal skin parchment (called *vellum*, related to the word *veal*). One probable impetus for the transition from papyrus to parchment was when the great library at Alexandria burned up in flames, destroying hundreds of thousands of papyrus volumes.

Clay and wax tablets have no problem with persistence. In fact, fired clay is more resistant to fire and water damage than the CDs, disk drives, tape, and floppy disks used today.

The Sumerians, and later, the Babylonians, used fired clay tablets for their database records. They used a standard "high level language" — called cuneiform since the 18th century — that represented numbers in a manner very similar to our representation. Instead of using a decimal (base 10) system, the Babylonians used a sexigesimal (base 60) system for computing. Their cuneiform database records (some over 3000 years old) are completely legible.

The *tally* stick (from French *tailler*, to cut, tailor) was another method that was used to create persistent financial databases. Numbers were represented on a wooden stick by making a mark, notch, or scar. (The word *score* is old English for scar or cut.) Larger scores represented larger numbers, and smaller scores represented smaller numbers. Tally stick methods did not require formal training in literacy or computation. They were first used in preliterate Babylonia almost 4000 years ago.

The procedure to make a financial database entry was as follows. Suppose A lends money to B. The amount recorded (scored) on a tally stick was, according to the 12th century English Dialog of the Exchequer,

> ...the distance between the tip of the forefinger and the thumb when fully extended. The manner of cutting is as follows. At the top of the tally a cut is made, the thickness of the palm of the hand, to represent a thousand pounds; then a hundred pounds by a cut the breadth of a thumb; twenty pounds, the breadth of the little finger; a single pound, the width of a swollen barleycorn; a shilling rather narrower than a penny is marked by a single cut without removing any wood.

After scoring, the wooden stick was split sideways along the length into two unequal pieces (it is difficult to split wood exactly) with both showing the same scores. The bigger side was called the *stock* (old English for *stick*; related to the word *ticket*); it was given to lender A. The shorter side was called the *foil*, probably from the old English term for the Latin *contra*, contrast, or opposite, as in the phrase "foiled again." This shorter piece was kept by borrower B. Lender A was now said to own stock in Company B.

This method for recording financial transactions automatically provided receipts (or stock certificates) that prevented fraud and forgery, as it is impossible to split another piece of wood exactly the same way. The two sides formed a kind of lock and key. Consequently, when accounts or debts were cleared and settled, the two sides were fitted together to see if they would "tally" or align exactly.

Note that today we speak of *sides* of a trade. For example, if you are a buyer, i.e., on the *buy side*, then the *contra side* is your seller; if you are a seller, i.e., on the *sell side*, then the *contra* is your buyer.

Box 2-6
Institutional Jargon: The buy side and the Sell Side

Today there is additional jargon used to describe large institutional traders that probably derives from tally sticks.

The buy side refers to money management firms such as mutual funds, investment advisers, trusts, and pension funds. *The sell side* refers to brokerage firms that make recommendations on what to buy, sell, and hold.

Typically, the buy side is sold financial products by the sell side. Consequently, the sell side can do two types of trading: *agency trading* (where they act as brokerage agent for their buy side customers) or *proprietary trading* (where the sell side trades privately for its own account).

The buy side generates brokerage fees for the sell side. To encourage business, the sell side sometimes delivers to the buy side fungible products and services, like analysis reports on companies, market data from vendors, computers, software, and communication systems. These expenses, called *soft dollar* expenses, are the subject of regulatory attention.

Tally stick technology offered many benefits. Records were long lasting and conveniently stored and transported: delivering tally sticks was easier and less expensive
than delivering other proxies for money, such as gold and agricultural products. Tally
sticks have a very simple user interface: the tallying settlement process was simple and
transparent for the buy side, sell side, tax collectors, and regulators. Moreover, if the
government needed to raise funds, they were able to sell their tally sticks at a discount
to the public (at a tally stick/stock exchange). The purchaser could settle the tally when
the taxes fell due, making this arrangement a kind of *repurchase agreement* (known
colloquially as a *Repo*) for a government bond. (This process is similar to the repurchase
agreements used by the U.S. government when they sell bonds to treasury dealers so that
the dealers can sell them back to the government: the result is a kind of short-term loan
to the government.)

Tally sticks were used in Britain until the mandatory shift to paper records and
watermarked paper certificates in 1826. The sticks were so popular that they were still
used as a backup. This ended in 1834, when the data warehouse of tally sticks somehow
caught fire (and destroyed both Houses of Parliament).

2.2.   Numbers and Prices

Our global standard notation for numerical representation and processing is relatively
recent; most of our notation for prices was standardized within 100 years of the opening
of the Amsterdam Stock Exchange and followed the technology of business printing and
typesetting.

Box 2-7
Punctuation, Prices, and Mathematical Notation

Punctuation marks are symbols that are used to organize or clarify written texts. These
include symbols that separate or group words, sentences, and thoughts; symbols that indicate
pauses, questions, and emphasis; and symbols that signify quotes, omissions, and plurals.
Punctuation symbols evolved into our modern notation for prices and for many symbols
used in finance and mathematics.

Before the invention of printing in the 1450s, there were no standard punctuation symbols
or rules governing their use. (In Latin texts, spaces were not used as standard word separators
until the 9th century; Romans frequently used a dot as a word separator, as E·PLURIBUS·
UNUM.) For the next 200 years after the invention of the printing press, printers experi-
mented with various signs, marks, abbreviations, cases (upper or lower), font, styles (Roman,
bold, italic), typeface (serif, sans-serif, script), size, alphabets (Latin, Greek, Hebrew), special
symbols, and relative positioning (such as superscript text that appears above the normal
line of type, such as N^2, and subscript text that appears below the normal line of type, such
as N_2). All of these were used by various authors to specify — in abbreviated symbolic
notation — mathematical and financial ideas.

Representing Numbers

Today we use a decimal or "base 10" place-value numeral system for representing prices, using the 10 symbols 0–9. Positions of the symbols indicate multiplication by a power of 10, with the *point symbol* (.) used as a separator between the integer part of the number (corresponding to positive powers of 10) and the fractional part (corresponding to negative powers of 10). For example, the number 123.678 is really

$$123.678 = 1 \cdot 100 + 2 \cdot 10 + 3 \cdot 1 + 6 \cdot \frac{1}{10} + 7 \cdot \frac{1}{100} + 8 \cdot \frac{1}{1000}$$

In exponential notation,

$$123.678 = 1 \cdot 10^2 + 2 \cdot 10^1 + 3 \cdot 10^0 + 6 \cdot 10^{-1} + 7 \cdot 10^{-2} + 8 \cdot 10^{-3}$$

and in general, the number PQR.STU is just

$$PQR.STU = P \cdot 10^2 + Q \cdot 10^1 + R \cdot 10^0 + S \cdot 10^{-1} + T \cdot 10^{-2} + U \cdot 10^{-3}$$

Here, P, Q, R, S, T, U can use the 10 numeral symbols 0, 1, 2, 3, ..., 9; PQR represents the integer part and STU represents the fractional part. The *number of places* of the number corresponds to the power of 10; e.g., the fractional part of 123.456, 0.456 has three places; the integer part of 12.3 has two places.

Arithmetic with whole decimal numbers — numbers written with numerals 0–9 (the decimal point was not invented yet) — was popularized in Europe by the merchant Leonardo of Pisa (1175–1250), who was also known as Fibonacci. Over 200 years later, Fibonacci's methods were further popularized by Luca Pacioli (1445–1517) in his 1494 *Summa*.

Real decimal prices were first used in the finance textbook *Künstliche Rechnung mit der Ziffer und mit den Zahlpfennigen* ("The artful skill of calculation with numerals and whole numbers of pennies"), published in 1526 by Christoff Rudolff (1499–1543). Rudolff used a vertical bar as a separator between the integer part and the fractional part of a price instead of today's point.

The decimal point (".") was first used to denote fractions over 400 years after Fibonacci introduced whole decimal numbers. John Napier (1550–1617), a Scottish baron, used the point to illustrate the new computational inventions described in his 1614 book *Mirifici Logarithmorum Canis Descriptio* (Latin: The Description of the Wonderful Canon of Logarithms). Napier was not consistent: he also used the comma as a fraction separator.

The symbols for addition (+) and subtraction (−) first appeared in the finance textbook *Mercantile Arithmetic* by Johannes Widmann (Leipzig, 1489); the symbols originally denoted surpluses and deficits.

The × was first used to denote multiplication in the text *Clavis Mathematicae* (Latin: *Key to Mathematics*), published in London in 1631 by William Oughtred (1574–1660). The middle dot was used for multiplication by the German mathematician Gottfried Leibniz (1646–1716) as early as 1698 because he kept mixing up × with the letter *x*. The convention to use the letter *x* as a symbol for an unknown quantity or variable was first established by Réne Descartes (1596–1650), the French lawyer, soldier, mathematician, and philosopher. Before Descartes, writers used various phrases or abbreviations to denote a variable. In the *Summa*, Pacioli used ".c" for an unknown — an abbreviation for *cosa* — Italian for *thing* or *object*.

Limitations on typesetting technology induced most writers to represent multiplication by simple juxtaposition (placing numbers side by side); this notation for multiplication actually goes back to 10th century India. So $ab = a \times b = a \cdot b$.

The asterisk was used by Swiss mathematician Johann Rahn (1622–1676) in his textbook on algebra (Zurich, 1659), possibly because of typesetting problems with the middle dot. *Fortran* (Formula Translator), one of the first programming languages (born in 1954 and developed by an IBM team led by Jim Backus) established * as the favorite multiplication symbol for most computer implementations. (In this book, we alternately use the middle dot or asterisk as a symbol for multiplication.)

The representation of division and fractions by a numerator on top of a denominator goes back to 10th century India. Fibonacci used the horizontal bar in the 1202 edition of his finance book, the *Liber Abaci* (the Abacus Book); this use of the bar probably originated with Arab merchants. Thus, for example, $\frac{2}{3}$ became $\frac{2}{3}$. Typesetting problems were responsible for the use of the single line slash for division and fractions: forms like 2/3 were found in business documents in 1718. Fortran standardized on this single-line notation for division as well.

Descartes invented a way to represent repeated multiplication. For example, "4 to the third power" is 4 multiplied by itself three times, or $4 \cdot 4 \cdot 4 = 64$. In his 1637 textbook *La Géométrie*, Descartes abbreviated "4 to the third power" with a superscript: $4 \cdot 4 \cdot 4 = 4^3$. Here, superscript 3 is called the *exponent*.

Programming languages are restricted to single-line type. For powers of numbers, Fortran uses the two adjacent asterisks **, and Microsoft Excel and other systems (such as MuPAD and Mathematica) use ^. Thus, $4^3 = 4{**}3 = 4{\wedge}3$. Other programming languages, such as C, C++, and Java, do not have an explicit symbol for powers. The "law of exponents" is the notation

$$b^N \cdot b^M = b^{N+M} \quad \text{and} \quad b^{-N} = \frac{1}{b^N} \quad \text{and} \quad b^0 = 1$$

This rule was established by John Wallis (1616–1703) in 1655 for any N and M. Powers and exponents were connected with the John Napier's concept of logarithms (from Greek: *logos* ratio and *arithmos* number); Napier called logarithms *numerus artificialis* — artful (or artificial) numbers.

Today there are several notations for exponents, powers, and logarithms that are used in financial technology systems. Recall that M is the *logarithm of Y* to a *base b* if

Mathematics superscript/subscript notation:
$Y = b^M$ and the logarithm is denoted as $M = \log_b Y$.

Excel inline notation (not case sensitive):
Y=b^M and the logarithm to any base b is denoted as M=log(Y,b)

MuPAD inline notation (case sensitive):
Y=b^M and the logarithm to any base b is denoted as M=log(b,Y)

Mathematica inline notation (case sensitive):
Y=b^M and the logarithm to any base b is denoted as M=Log[b,Y]

Fortran inline notation:
$Y = b{**}M$; no explicit expression for logarithm to any base b.

C, C++ (and other languages) inline notation:
$Y = pow(b, M)$; no explicit expression for logarithm to any base b.

The notation abbreviating logarithm by log (originally it was "log." but the period was eventually dropped) dates from the mid-1600s; the subscript denoting the base of the logarithm started appearing in the early 1700s.

Napier's idea caught on because logarithms transform multiplication and division into (the much easier to process of) addition and subtraction. In the preface to his 1614 *Mirifici*, Napier wrote that his logarithms should save (human) computers much time and eliminate errors. Logarithm tables were soon implemented in a type of analog computer consisting of two sliding sticks calibrated in logarithmic scale whose relative displacements from each other either added or subtracted logarithms. This first *slide rule*, invented by William Oughtred (1574–1660), was the first computer to execute one multiplication (or division) per unit time. Oughtred's technology is based on the law of exponents that imply the addition properties for logarithms:

$$\text{if} \quad Y = b^M \quad \text{and} \quad X = b^N \quad \text{then}$$

$$\log_b(X^*Y) = \log_b(X) + \log_b(Y) \quad \text{and} \quad \log_b(X^Y) = Y^* \log_b(X)$$

The equality sign was first used by Robert Recorde (1510–1558) in his book on abacus computation called *The Whetstone of Witte* (London, 1557). Professionally, Recorde was a medical doctor (his patients included King Edward VI and Mary Tudor).

In mathematics and finance, = is used for assignment (as in "assert that this expression is that expression") or for comparison (as in "if this expression equals that expression, then the answer is this expression"). Fortran and Excel use = for both assignment and comparison. Other computer languages separate these two meanings. Languages such as Java use a colon before the equal sign := for assignment so that = is reserved for comparison. Other languages (like C) use = for assignment and two adjacent equal signs == for comparison.

The *percent* specification (indicated by the symbol %, originally an abbreviation for *per cento*), used for decimal fractions, was first used in Italy around 1425. With this notation, the percent rate of return (or *interest rate*, or *dividend yield*) on an investment of 60 florins that pay 8 florins per year is

$$yearly\ rate = \frac{yearly\ dividend}{investment} = \frac{8\ florins\ per\ year}{60\ florins} = 13\tfrac{1}{3}\%\ per\ year$$

Another specification used in finance for decimal fractions is the *basis point* (frequently abbreviated by *bp*):

$$0.01 = 1\% = 100\,\text{bp}$$

Note that in modern notation, $0.0333\ldots = \tfrac{1}{3}\%$ is approximately equal to 33.3 basis points. Here we use the *ellipsis* symbol — 3 adjacent dots — "..." to indicate "and so on" or "the pattern repeats." Up until the 19th century, authors used a phrase like *et cetera* (Latin: *and the others*), usually abbreviated as *etc.* or *&/c* or *&c.*, to represent a logical continuation of some pattern.

Box 2-8
The Evolution of Ellipsis

The ellipsis is used to denote an intentional omission. For example, 1,2,...,100 denotes "all numbers from 1 to 100." It is also used to denote that an expression has not terminated and that it will continue to repeat indefinitely, e.g., $\frac{1}{3} = 0.333. \ldots$

The word *ellipsis* is related to the English word for a financial *loan*: both derive from the Greek word *leipein*, meaning *to leave*. An *ellipsis* is a rhetorical figure of speech that involved the intentional omission of words: the words *left out* are implied by the context. A *loan* denotes money that is *left* with someone that earns interest.

One of the earliest explicit marks for ellipsis — used in a printed English book — dates from 1588; several adjacent hyphens are used to indicate the omission of words. Different printers used hyphens, asterisks, points, and also +. (Recall that the dot was used as a word separator in Latin; the dot was also used as a symbol for zero in 8th century India.)

In 17th century books and letters, ellipsis marks in mathematics and finance alternated with "..." and "&c." Both notations are used in the book *Essay D'Analyse sur Les Jeux de Hazard* (Essay Analyzing Games of Chance), published by Pierre Redmond de Montmort (1678–1719) in 1713; Montmort reprints his correspondence with Jean Bernoulli (from 1710) that used both notations. For example, on page 292, Bernoulli shows how many ways you can arrange p objects of which b are of one suit, c are of another suit, d a third suit, e a fourth suit, and so on. The expression he derived is

$$\frac{1 \cdot 2 \cdot 3 \cdot 4 \cdots p}{1 \cdot 2 \cdot 3 \cdot 4 \cdots b \times 1 \cdot 2 \cdot 3 \cdot 4 \cdots c \times 1 \cdot 2 \cdot 3 \cdot 4 \cdots d \times 1 \cdot 2 \cdot 3 \cdot 4 \cdots e \times \&c.}$$

Bernoulli noted that the combinations of suits are related to the coefficients we get when multiplying out the "multinomial" $(b + c + d + e. \ldots)^p$. Today we write Bernoulli's expression as

$$\frac{p!}{b!c!d!e!. \ldots}$$

Here $p! = 1 \cdot 2 \cdot 3 \cdot 4 \cdots p$ denotes what is now called the *factorial function*. The exclamation point notation $p!$ was introduced by Christian Kramp (1760–1826) in *Élémens d'Arithmétique Universelle* (1808) to eliminate typesetting the numbers and the ellipsis. If we have an arbitrary but fixed number n of different suits, we can also eliminate the "&c." and write this expression (with a single ellipsis) as

$$\frac{p!}{b_1! \cdot b_2! \cdot b_3! \ldots b_n!} \quad \text{or even as} \quad \left(\frac{p}{b_1 \; b_2 \; b_3 \; \cdots \; b_n} \right) \quad \text{with} \quad p = b_1 + b_2 + \cdots + b_n$$

The notation with the large parentheses appeared in books published in the mid-1800s and is now standard in mathematics. Newer technology systems have their own notation for Bernoulli's multinomial expression. For example, multinomial expression for three suits having 2, 3, 4 members in each respectively (i.e., $b = 2$, $c = 3$, $d = 4$, so $p = 9$): the expression in Microsoft Excel is =multinomial(2, 3, 4), which evaluates to 1260.

Statistical tests based on the multinomial distribution ascertain the "goodness of fit" between values actually observed and values predicted by a model (e.g., in determining whether a deck of cards is "fair" or whether a trading system makes money). These tests were formalized by Karl Pearson (1857–1936), founder of the science of biometry (and cofounder of the statistics journal *Biometrika*).

Representing Decimal Prices

It is only since April 2001 that a full decimal notation (known in the markets as *decimalization*) has been used in quotes for stock prices. Older price conventions use a combination of decimal notation for a whole dollar amount and an actual fraction for the cents (with the fraction evenly divisible by ($\frac{1}{2}$). For example, a stock price reported in 1990 as $33\frac{1}{8}$ is now reported as 33.125. One reason for standardizing on decimal prices is to reduce the bid–ask spread, thereby making prices more competitive (at the expense of the market maker): a market is more *efficient* with a bid-to-ask spread of 33.125–33.127 than with a bid–ask spread of $33\frac{1}{8}$–$33\frac{1}{4}$.

Note that other symbols, such as the *comma*, have been introduced to "pretty print" numbers and prices, e.g., 1234.567 = 1,234.567. The European convention for numbers and prices frequently reverses the meaning of points and commas. Consequently

U.S. Continental Europe

1234.567 = 1,234.567 = 1234,567 = 1.234,567

Mixing up these conventions can wreak havoc with international financial prices. Countries where the period is used as the fraction separator include Australia, Botswana, English-speaking Canada, China, Costa Rica, Dominican Republic, El Salvador, Guatemala, Honduras, Hong Kong, India, Ireland, Israel, Japan, Korea (both North and South), Malaysia, Mexico, Nicaragua, Panama, Philippines, Puerto Rico, Saudi Arabia, Singapore, Thailand, United Kingdom, and United States.

Countries where the comma is used as the fraction separator include Andorra, Argentina, Austria, Belgium, Bolivia, Brazil, French-speaking Canada, Croatia, Cuba, Chile, Colombia, Czech Republic, Denmark, Ecuador, Estonia, Faroes, Finland, France, Germany, Greece, Greenland, Hungary, Indonesia, Iceland, Italy, Latvia, Lithuania, Luxembourg, Macedonia, Netherlands, Norway, Paraguay, Peru, Poland, Portugal, Romania, Serbia, Slovakia, Slovenia, Spain, South Africa, Sweden, Switzerland, Ukraine, Uruguay, Venezuela, and Zimbabwe.

Representing Prices in Other Bases

In general, a place-value system to any base b represents a number with the following convention:

$$PQR.STU_{(b)} = P \cdot b^2 + Q \cdot b^1 + R \cdot b^0 + S \cdot b^{-1} + T \cdot b^{-2} + U \cdot b^{-3}$$

To avoid ambiguity, we write the base of the number as a subscript in parentheses. Numbers without the base subscript are assumed to be base 10. Note that in general, number systems in base b need b different symbols.

Financial communication systems use binary (*base 2*), octal (*base 8*), hexadecimal (*base 16*), and *base 256* to represent numbers for different quantities and computer codes. For example, the number 257 can be represented as

$$257_{(10)} = 11_{(256)} = 101_{(16)} = 401_{(8)} = 100000001_{(2)}$$

As shown in Chapter 1, binary (using the two symbols 0–1) is convenient for representing on–off signals such as torches. Octal (using the eight symbols 0, 1, 2, 3, 4, 5, 6, 7) is sometimes used as a shorter form for binary: each octal digit (sometimes called an octet or a byte) can represent three binary digits (a binary digit is also called a bit). We could say that if each arm of a Chappe telegraph had eight recognizable positions, then each arm transmits one octal number at a time.

Hexadecimal requires 16 symbols. One convention is to use the symbols 0–9 and the special symbols A, B, C, D, E, F denoting the numbers 10–15. For example,

$$27_{(10)} = 1B_{(16)}$$

Hexadecimal is also used as a shorter form for binary: each hexadecimal digit can be represented as four binary digits.

Another number representation used for bases greater than 10 is the *dotted decimal* notation. Here, the period is used as a digit separator (not as a fraction separator), which helps us avoid making up new symbols:

$$257_{(10)} = 2.5.7_{(10)} = 1.1_{(256)} = 1.0.1_{(16)}$$

Recall that the notation of using a period as a separator goes back to the Romans.

Note that for dotted decimal fractions, we need to introduce a fraction separator different from the point. We use the semicolon. So, for example, $1.10; 2.4_{(16)}$ is the *base 10* fraction 26.140625:

$$1.10; 2.4_{(16)} = 1 \cdot 16^1 + 10 \cdot 16^0 + 2 \cdot 16^{-1} + 4 \cdot 16^{-2}$$
$$= 16 + 10 + 0.125 + 0.015625 = 26.140625$$

Numbers represented by four base 256 ($256 = 2^{\wedge}8$) digits (sometimes called *dotted quad decimal*) are the standard representation for addresses used in the routing tables in the Internet's domain name server system. This representation is called *IPv4*. For example, the base 256 number 192.193.210.24 corresponds to an Internet address of a specific Web server. If all Internet computers are represented by four base 256 digits with each digit having 256 symbols, this implies that the total number of possible Internet addresses is $256^4 = 4,294,967,296$ addresses (actually somewhat less, as many addresses are either reserved or are "invalid" numbers such as 0.0.0.0). The Internet naming standard called *IPv6* expands the number of addresses from 4 base 256 digits to 16 base 256 digits; the standard denotes this as 8 base 65536 ($65536 = 2^{\wedge}16$) numbers, with each base 65536 number specified by 4 base 16 (hexadecimal) digits, with each digit represented by 1 of 16 symbols 0–9, A–E. The IPv6 convention is to use a colon as a separator between two base 65536 numbers. For example, one IPv6 internet address is 1234:5678:9ABC:DE12:A201:0568:75E3:AA83.

In financial systems, colons are also used for prices: the *decimal-colon* notation is used to represent the prices of bonds. In a bond price such as 98:14, the number to the right of the colon (sometimes called a *tick*) is the first place of a *base 32* fraction: it is shorthand for a fraction with denominator 32. In other words,

$$98:14 = 98\tfrac{14}{32} = 98 + 14 \cdot 32^{-1} = 98.4375$$

Investment Evaluation and Bond Pricing Conventions

Suppose someone wants to lend (or invest) a certain amount of money for 10 months with the assurance that he will get back $1,000,000. How much should the investor risk, given that the investor expects a return on the loan and given that the credit is backed by the United States Treasury? One answer for the investor is to purchase a type of bond called a U.S. *Treasury Strip* that "matures" in 10 months. On July 7, 2004, the price of such a bond that matures on May 15, 2005 (in about 10 months) is reported as

MATURITY	TYPE	BID	ASK	CHG	ASK YLD
May 15 05	np	98:14	98:14	-1	1.85

In the aforementioned quote, note that the daily change (CHG) in price, given as -1, is a base 32 fraction: -1 corresponds to

$$-\tfrac{1}{32} = -32^{-1} = -0.03125$$

Newspapers and market data vendors quote the bond price "based on transactions of $1 million or more." What this means is that the market data quote represents a convention for a *set of values* for an investment of any amount (more than $1 million). The procedure is to take the quote — a number usually ranging from 50 to 100 — and normalize it by dividing it by 100 in order to come up with the *discount factor* of 0.984375; the discount factor represents the time value of money (as Ben Franklin would say) that is associated with the bond.

Consequently, the value of a $1 million bond with ask price 98:14 is

$$\frac{98\frac{14}{32}}{100} \cdot \$1,000,000 = \frac{98.4375}{100} \cdot \$1,000,000 = 0.984375 \cdot \$1,000,000 = \$984,375$$

This means that the investor can buy a bond (that matures in 10 months to a value of $1 million) from a bond dealer (exclusive of fees and commissions) at an ask price today of $984,375. This also tells us that for a $1,000,000 bond, the price change from yesterday is down $31,250. If we want to invest $2 million, then this quote indicates that the bond price is

$$0.984375^* \$2,000,000 = \$1,968,750$$

Anther way of looking at this is that our investment of $984,375 will grow to $1,000,000 in 10 months: a profit of $15,625. Let $P(10\ months)$ denote the price at maturity (in 10 months); $P(today)$ represent today's quoted price of our purchase. Here are three methods that can be used to evaluate our investment:

$$\text{10-month profit} = P(10\ months) - P(today)$$
$$= \$1,000,000 - \$984,375 = \$15,625$$

$$\text{10-month return} = \frac{P(10\ months) - P(today)}{P(today)}$$
$$= \frac{\$1,000,000 - \$984,375}{\$984,375} = 1.5873\ldots\%$$

$$\text{rate of change} = \frac{P(10\ months) - P(today)}{10\ months}$$
$$= \frac{\$1,000,000 - \$984,375}{10\ months} = \$1,562.50 \text{ per month}$$

All methods use a different combination of price differences and time differences. Note that the units of profit are dollars and that the units of rate of change are dollars per month. There are no units for return (it is "a dimensionless quantity"): return is a kind of normalized or standardized measure for price change. Also note that the profit and return measures are time period dependent. Box 2-9 further discusses the different notations and conventions used for price differences.

In practice, the method used for evaluation depends on the application. For example, rents and other periodic payments are usually quoted in terms of rate of change. Business ventures need to know about period profit or loss. For applications involving financial products, return is the most popular measure. In our example, our 10-month rate of return for our bond investment is known in advance — it is about 1.6%.

Note that different time units will result in different answers. In order to eliminate the confusion, most investors standardize time differences, typically in units of years. How do we rescale a return over a 10-month period to a 10-month return measured in years? We only need to transform the *timescale* into units of years.

For a 12-month year, the fraction of a year that a 10-month maturity period corresponds to is

$$\frac{10 \text{ months}}{12 \text{ months/year}} = 0.833333\ldots \text{year}$$

Consequently, the 10-month return, rescaled to a timescale measured in years, is

$$\frac{return}{year} = \frac{return}{(^{10}/_{12} \text{ year})} = \frac{1.5873\ldots\%}{0.833\ldots} = 1.90476\ldots\% \text{ per year}$$

This says that the "annualized" 10-month return is 1.90% (rounded off to a basis point — one hundredth of a percent). Note that this is not the same as the return on the investment in 1 year. Annualized returns and yields standardize on the same units of time (years!), not in the investment time period.

Note that the time between July 7, 2004 and May 15, 2005 is exactly 312 days, not 300 days. For a 365-day year, the fraction of a year that a 312-day maturity period corresponds to is

$$\frac{312 \text{ days}}{365 \text{ days/year}} = 0.8547945\ldots \text{year}$$

In this case, the annualized 10-month return is

$$\frac{return}{year} = \frac{return}{(0.8547945\ldots \text{year})} = \frac{1.5873\ldots\%}{0.8547945\ldots} = 1.86\ldots\% \text{ per year}$$

Finally, note that May 15, 2005 is a Sunday — the U.S. markets are closed! According to the U.S. Treasury conventions, we redeem the bond on Monday: 313 days after today. A maturity of 313 days corresponds to a fraction of 0.857534247…year; this corresponds to an annualized 10-month return of 1.851…% per year. This return, rounded to the nearest basis point, is what is reported in the Treasury Strip quote as the Ask Yield (abbreviated as ASK YLD). It is the (standardized) annualized return on the investment over the *actual* maturity time period, assuming a 365-day year.

Box 2-9

Price Differences: Notations and Conventions for Comparing Investments

In order to compare investments, we need a common language for time, price, and profitability. Let

$T1$ denote a particular time
$T2$ denote another, later time: $T2 > T1$ (so $T2 = T1 + h$ for increment h)
$P(T1)$ is an asset price at time $T1$; $P(T2)$ is the price at later time $T2$

These values, depending on time and price differences, help compare investments:

- length of the time period (duration) $= (T2 - T1)$
- profit (or loss if negative, over the time period) $= P(T2) - P(T1)$
- price rate-of-change (over the time period) $= [P(T2) - P(T1)]/(T2 - T1)$
- return (a "normalized" price difference) $= [P(T2) - P(T1)]/P(T1)$
- rate-of-return $=$ return$/(T2 - T1) = [P(T2) - P(T1)]/[(T2 - T1)*P(T1)]$

The return compares price changes that are independent of rice magnitudes. Price differences with respect to any quantity measure the price sensitivity to that quantity. For example, gasoline depends on oil. The price difference of gasoline with respect to oil is

GasPrice (at a larger value of oil) $-$ *GasPrice* (at a smaller value of oil)

Consequently, profit is a price difference or sensitivity *with respect to time.*

Some abbreviations for differences use the letter "D" written in different cases and alphabets. This notation was invented in the 1700's. Some of the popular notations for the difference in price P with respect to an *implicit* quantity include

DP or dP (Latin alphabet, pronounced "D P")
ΔP or δP (Greek upper and lower case letter Delta: pronounced "Delta P")
∂P (Latin cursive or Cyrillic italic, also pronounced "D P")

In MuPAD, a price rate of change at time T with respect to a very small incremental time period is denoted by `diff(P(T),T)`. This notation explicitly represents time. For an example of the implicit notation (using ∂):

- length of the time period (duration): ∂T
- profit (or loss if negative): ∂P
- price rate-of-change: $\partial P/\partial T$ (pronounced "D P D T")
- return: $\partial P/P$ (pronounced "D P over P").
  The P in the denominator denotes the price at the earlier time.

Bond markets are structured in a way so that the final prices (or yields) are always stated; the investor pays for the bond at a "discount" — an amount less than the final $1,000,000 price at maturity. This provides the bond markets with a uniform standard language so that different bonds can be compared. The difference in the buy price and maturity price is known at purchase time and represents the investor's fixed profit, as long as the investor holds the bond until the maturity time. If the investor sells the bond before maturity time, the bond price fluctuates between the purchase price (it could go lower or higher) and the maturity price of $1,000,000.

Decimal-Hyphen Convention

The *decimal-hyphen* convention for pricing bonds is similar to the *decimal-colon* convention: fractions are represented to the right of a hyphen. (Note that this hyphen has nothing to do with subtraction!) The dot-hyphen convention is typically used to price mortgage-backed securities — bonds whose credit is established by the regular payments of different home mortgages.

For example, on July 21, 2004, the following quotes were given for the following mortgage-backed securities:

	RATE	PRICE (AUG) (PTS-32DS)	PRICE CHANGE (32DS)	AVG LIFE (YEARS)	SPRD TO AVG LIFE (YEARS)	SPREAD CHANGE (BPS)	PSA (PREPAY SPEED)	YIELD TO MAT
30-year								
FMAC GOLD	5.50%	100-01	-3	6.9	149	-4	219	5.51
GNMA **	5.50%	100-10	-2	6.6	149	-3	227	5.45

A bond price quoted as 100-10 is just $100\frac{10}{32} = 100.3125$, as in the colon decimal notation. However, a bond price of 100-101 corresponds to a price (in decimal notation) of

$$100 - 101_{decimal-hyphen} = 100 + \frac{1}{32}(10 + \tfrac{1}{8}) = 100.31640625$$

The optional third digit to the right of the hyphen represents eighths of a 32nd. In general, the decimal hyphen notation for a bond price is

$$P - QR_{decimal-hyphen} = P + \frac{Q}{32} + \frac{1}{32} \cdot \frac{R}{8} = P + \frac{Q}{32} + \frac{4 \cdot R}{32 \cdot 32}$$

Here, P represents a decimal whole number for a price. The fractional part actually is a two-place fraction in *base 32*: Q represents a number from 1 to 31; R ranges from 1 to 7, so the second *base 32* digit is either 4, 8, 12, 16, 20, 24, 28. In a dotted decimal notation, this fractional part is

$$QR_{decimal-hyphen} = \frac{Q}{32} + \frac{4R}{32^2} = Q.4R_{(32)}$$

In a dotted decimal notation, this fractional part of the quote corresponds to the following possible prices:

$;1.4_{(32)}$ $;1.8_{(32)}$ $;1.12_{(32)}$ $;1.16_{(32)}$ $;1.20_{(32)}$ $;1.24_{(32)}$ $;1.28_{(32)}$
$;2.4_{(32)}$ $;2.8_{(32)}$ $;2.12_{(32)}$ $;2.16_{(32)}$ $;2.20_{(32)}$ $;2.24_{(32)}$ $;2.28_{(32)}$
. . . .
$;31.4_{(32)}$ $;31.8_{(32)}$ $;31.12_{(32)}$ $;31.16_{(32)}$ $;31.20_{(32)}$ $;31.24_{(32)}$ $;31.28_{(32)}$

So $100 - 101_{decimal-hyphen} = 100;10.4_{(32)}$. Finally, the convention also specifies a new use of the $+$ symbol (here having nothing to do with addition!): a fraction of 4/8 is expressed with a "+" instead of a "4".

For example, the price quote for 100-10+ is

$$100 - 10+_{decimal-hyphen} = 100 + \frac{1}{32}(10 + \frac{4}{8}) = 100;10.16_{(32)} = 100.328125$$

As you can see, one of the interesting aspects of pricing is its reliance on fractions. One reason may be that in many cases fractions are very efficient in conveying information: 98-141 requires only 6 symbols; its decimal equivalent 98.44140625 requires 11 symbols. Other fractions (like $\frac{1}{3} = 0.33333...$) have infinite decimal expansions, which explains why decimal prices are not quoted in thirds, sixths, sevenths, or ninths.

Financial Computation in Antiquity

Babylonian financial technology represented prices in *base 60* (sometimes called *sexigesimal*). Sixty is a nice number because it has a lot of divisors, which simplifies many computations with fractions and avoids infinite expansions for many fractions. For example,

$$\frac{1}{3} = \frac{20}{60} = 0;20_{(60)}$$

The Babylonians did not use 60 different symbols to represent prices; they used a smaller set of symbols in a way similar to the Internet numbering schemes. They used a big circle like an O to represent 10 and a little circle like an o to represent 1. So

O ooooo represents our number 15

They used two basic signs together with a positional notation like we do: a wedge like a V that either had the value 1 or a power of 60 (i.e., $V = 60^n$), and a wedge like a $<$ that had a value of $10*60^n$. Just like in our positional decimal system, the place value n decreases from left to right.

The Babylonians sometimes used a dot (".") or a blank space as a placeholder, like our zero. So the Babylonian numbers

V O ooooo   represents 75

    V. $<$ represents a set of values given by $1*60^{n+2} + 0 + 10*60^n$

          for $n = 0, 1, 2, ...$ or for $n = -1, -2, -3, ...$

  So V. $<$ represents 3610 for $n = 0$ (note that $60*60 + 10 = 3610$), or

          represents 216,600 for $n = 1$ (note that $1*60^3 + 0 + 10*60^1 = 216,600$), or

          represents $60\frac{10}{60}$ for $n = -1$ (note that $60^1 + 10 \cdot 60^{-1} = 60\frac{10}{60}$), or

          represents $1\frac{10}{3600}$ for $n = -2$ (note that $60^0 + 10 \cdot 60^{-2} = 1\frac{10}{3600}$), or...

In general, Babylonian accountants were able to tell the value of a number (represented with the 4 symbols V, O, o, $<$) from the context; they possibly used these forms to represent *a set of values*, similar to our convention for bond prices.

The Babylonians had arithmetic rules similar to our arithmetic that enabled them to compute interest rate tables for loans, bonds, and mortgages, shares for inheritance and profits, commodity calculations (involving areas and volumes), and accurate calendar times for special holidays. Financial databases consist of thousands of tablets detailing contract specifications, shares for inheritance and profits, commodity calculations (involving areas and volumes) and show computations equivalent to 17 decimal place accuracy. The *base 60* notation is still used today in specifications of degrees hours, minutes, and seconds.

Babylonian finance used methods identical and as fast as the methods used today for addition, subtraction, and multiplication. For example, numbers represented in positional notation can be multiplied together by using the distributed law

$$(a+b) \times (d+e) = (b^*e) + (b^*d) + (a^*e) + (a^*d)$$

For example:

$$3.0;2_{(60)} \times 11;45_{(60)}$$

$$= (3^*60^1 + 2^*60^{-1}) \times (11^*60^0 + 45^*60^{-1})$$

$$= 90^*60^{-2} + 22^*60^{-1} + 135^*60^0 + 33^*60^1$$

$$= (1^*60^{-1} + 30^*60^{-2}) + 22^*60^{-1} + (15^*60^0 + 2^*60^1) + 33^*60^1$$

$$= 35^*60^1 + 45^*60^0 + 23^*60^{-1} + 30^*60^{-2} = 35.45;23.30_{(60)}$$

This is similar to our multiplication rules for decimal numbers. (There are no simple rules like this for multiplying two numbers represented as Greek or Roman numerals.)

Their technology for computing a/b was to find the value of $1/b$ (the *reciprocal* of b) and then multiply this number by a. Here is an example of the Babylonian procedure for finding the sexigesimal reciprocal of 7:

To represent 1/7 by the number denoted by 0; abcdef...

Step 1. $\dfrac{1}{7} = \dfrac{a}{60}$ so a $= 60/7 = 8+4/7$

Step 2. $\dfrac{4}{7} = \dfrac{b}{60}$ so b $= 240/7 = 34+2/7$

Step 3. $\dfrac{2}{7} = \dfrac{c}{60}$ so c $= 120/7 = 17+1/7$

Step 4. $\dfrac{1}{7} = \dfrac{d}{60}$ so d $= 60/7 = 8+4/7$

(observe that this is the same result as Step 1)

If we continue, we find that 1/7 has an infinite repeating representation (the pattern 8.34.17 repeats forever) in *base 60*

$$\frac{1}{7} = 0;8.34.17.8.34.17.8.34.17.\ldots\ldots_{(60)}$$

This process is very similar to our "long division."

Note that in practice, there must be rules that tell us when to stop. Babylonian computers typically stopped computing after 17 sexigesimal places. Other stopping rules can be specified in terms of accuracy (e.g., stop when the difference between the results in subsequent steps is less than a predetermined threshold) or time (keep working for a specified time period).

A well-defined problem-solving procedure or recipe that specifies, for some actor or agent, a specific sequence of steps (together with a rule for specifying when to stop) is called an *algorithm*. The method used by the Babylonians for finding reciprocals is now called the *Euclidean algorithm*. For humans, going through the steps of the Euclidean algorithm is tedious and time-consuming; consequently, the Babylonians precomputed thousands of reciprocals (most to 17 sexigesimal places) and stored them in cuneiform databases.

Today, the Euclidean algorithm is used extensively in applications involving encryption with prime numbers.

2.3. Time Is Money: Loans and Interest

The importance of different representations of prices from a financial technology perspective is in the ease of understanding, communicating, and computing.

As Franklin observed, time becomes money when evaluating loans. This is illustrated by showing how loan computations were processed efficiently thousands of years ago. Box 2-10 shows an example from an ancient finance textbook.

Box 2-10

Student Problem in Financial Time Value (2000–1600 BCE)

Suppose I loan a manna of silver to a person at 12 shekels per year. At the end of the loan I receive as payment 1 talent and 4 manna. What was the length of time for the loan?

Babylonian Textbook Solution: 30 years.

Note: 60 shekels = 1 manna; 60 manna = 1 talent.
[Source: Tablet VAT 8528 (Vorderasiatische Abteilung Tontafeln), Museum of Berlin]

Babylonian Interest Computation

The way the Babylonians represented the time value of money and compounding illustrates the basic principles of today's finance and financial technology. The student problem specifies a fixed yearly payment of 12 shekels ($= \frac{1}{5}$ manna $= 0.2$ manna) on a general loan committment of 1 manna. This implies a yearly rate of return — the *interest rate* or *yield* — of 20% per year. This rate commitment is also called the *spot interest rate*. Note that if we only consider the simple yearly payment of $\frac{1}{5}$ manna per year, it would take 320 years to grow to 64 mannas ($320 \ years \times \frac{1}{5} manna/year = 64 \ manna$). Because the given answer is 30 years, the Babylonians have introduced compounding — making money from money.

Babylonian financial technology for bond computation was based on doubling. Their solution is to reduce the problem into two subproblems.

1. How many years does it take to reproduce (i.e., double) the investment at the simple interest rate that is given?

   Solution: Assuming we are only allowed to collect what we are told to collect, after 5 years, at a rate of collection of $\frac{1}{5}$ manna per year, 1 manna yields another $\frac{1}{5} + \frac{1}{5} + \frac{1}{5} + \frac{1}{5} + \frac{1}{5} = 1$ manna: in the Babylonian convention, 1 manna doubles every 5 years. In general, given an initial investment of 1 manna and a simple rate of r mannas per year, Babylonian compounding assumes that 1 manna doubles in $1/r$ years.

2. How many doublings does it take to create 64 mannas from 1 manna?

   Solution: Note that

   > After 1 doubling we have 2 mannas
   >
   > After 2 doublings. . . . .$2*2 = 2^2 = 4$ mannas
   >
   > After 3 doublings. . . . .$2*2*2 = 2^3 = 8$ mannas
   >
   > After 4 doublings. . . . .$2*2*2*2 = 2^4 = 16$ mannas
   >
   > After 5 doublings. . . . .$2*2*2*2*2 = 2^5 = 32$ mannas
   >
   > After 6 doublings. . . . .$2*2*2*2*2*2 = 2^6 = 64$ mannas
   >
   > After 7 doublings. . . . .$2*2*2*2*2*2*2 = 2^7 = 128$ mannas
   >
   > (and so on...)

In modern notation, this amounts to finding the number of doublings D, where

$$2^D = 64$$

According to this table, after 6 doublings, 1 manna yields 64 mannas.

We now combine the answers to the two subproblems. Because 1 manna at 20% reproduces in 5 years, 6 reproductions yields 64 mannas in 6*5 = 30 years — the answer indicated on the cuneiform tablet *VAT 8528*.

Note that to solve other kinds of doubling problems, we can precompute powers of 2 and save them in a cuneiform database. Archeological records show that the Babylonians had extensive tables of powers of 2 so all they had to do was to look up the number of mannas on the right-hand side of the table and the number of doublings was adjacent on the left.

Textbook solutions are usually chosen for their simplicity. Here is a modification of the problem showing some real world complications: Suppose I loan a manna of silver to a person at 12 shekels per year. At the end of the loan I receive 100 mannas as payment. What was the length of time for the loan?

By inspecting the table given earlier, the answer is *between* 6 doublings (30 years) and 7 doublings (35 years). For a more precise answer, the Babylonians invented a technology that approximates unknown values from two known values in a table. Today this procedure is known as linear interpolation.

Linear interpolation is essentially a kind of weighted average of values. Given the table values

After 6 doublings. . . . . .64 mannas

After X doublings. . . . . 100 mannas

After 7 doublings. . . . . .128 mannas

Then X is found by first computing values A and B, where

$$A = \frac{128 - 100}{128 - 64} = \frac{28}{64} = 0.4375$$

$$B = 1 - A = 0.5625$$

Finally, the value for X is approximated by

$$X = A^*6 + B^*7 = 0.4375^*6 + 0.5625^*7 = 6.5625 \text{ doublings.}$$

This corresponds to $5^*6.5625 = 31.8125$ years. Linear interpolation can be generalized given the table values

Known values X1. . . . . .Y1

Unknown X. . . . . known Y

Known values X2. . . . . .Y2

where Y is between Y1 and Y2, then X is found by first computing A and B where

$$A = \frac{Y2 - Y}{Y2 - Y1}; \quad B = 1 - A$$

Finally, the value for X is approximated by

$$X = A^*X1 + B^*X2$$

In modern notation, note that the number of doublings is the *logarithm* of the number of mannas to base 2. According to Babylonian compounding, if mannas grow at the rate of r mannas per year, money doubles every $1/r$ years. So in general after T years, an investment today of $P(0)$ mannas is worth:

Future Value of investment after T years: $P(T) = P(0) \cdot 2^{r \cdot T}$

We can use this expression to derive other relationships. The value of an initial investment $P(0)$, given the final investment $P(T)$ after T years and the fact that the $P(0)$ mannas grow at rate r mannas per year, is

Present Value of investment: $P(0) = \dfrac{P(T)}{2^{r \cdot T}} = P(T) \cdot 2^{-r \cdot T}$

If we use these formulas to solve for r, then we can derive the yearly manna growth rate. In mathematical notation (using logarithms to base 2), this is

$$\text{Manna growth rate: } r = \frac{1}{T} \cdot \log_2\left(\frac{P(T)}{P(0)}\right)$$

Similarly, if we solve for T, we derive the number of years T needed to grow $P(0)$ mannas into $P(T)$ mannas:

$$\text{Number of years: } T = \frac{1}{r} \cdot \log_2\left(\frac{P(T)}{P(0)}\right)$$

These formulas can be used for computations of Babylonian treasury strips.

Box 2-11

Babylonian Compounding

A Babylonian treasury strip matures in 10 months with a value of 1 million mannas. Today the purchase price (exclusive of fees and commissions) is 984,375 mannas. What is the interest rate under Babylonian compounding?

Solution: Note that according to the Babylonian time convention of 30 day months and 360 day years, 10 months is $300/360 = 10/12$ year.

So $r = \dfrac{1}{(^{10}/_{12} \, year)} \cdot \log_2(1{,}000{,}000/984{,}375) = 2.7264\%/\text{year}.$

With Babylonian compounding, at this rate money doubles in about $1/r = 1/0.02764 = 36.68$ years (i.e., at Babylonian compounding of 2.73%, money doubles in about 36 years, 7 months, and 2 weeks).

Note that if we can compute base 2 logarithm tables then we can dispense with the Babylonian interpolation approximation procedure. Recall the following problem. Suppose I loan a manna of silver to a person at 12 shekels per year. At the end of the loan I receive 100 mannas as payment. What was the length of time for the loan?

The Babylonian solution by interpolation was computed as 6.5625 doublings, corresponding to 31.8125 years. Assuming we have a complete base 2 logarithm table, a more accurate answer is

$$T = \frac{1}{0.2} \cdot \log_2\left(\frac{100}{1}\right) = \frac{1}{0.2} \cdot 6.64385619 = 33.2192809 \text{ years.}$$

Compounding Conventions of Return-Based Compounding

The compounding convention we use today is based on returns over time. Let us look at an investment over a set number of years, and let us assume we know the actual future prices at the end of every year.

Box 2-12

Modified Student Problem in Financial Time Value

Suppose I loan \$1 at 20% per year. We assume that this interest rate is fixed over several years. At the end of the loan I receive \$64 as payment. What was the length of time for the loan?

Solution: Note that money from year to year increases at a constant rate of 20%. In other words, if at the start of year 13 we have P dollars, then at the start of year 14 we have $P + 20\% \, P = (1 + 20\%)^* P = 1.2^* P$ dollars. So (rounding off to the nearest cent):

After 1 year we have $1^*(1 + 20\%) = 1.20$ dollars
After 2 years ....$1.20^*(1 + 20\%) = (1.20)^2 = 1.44$ dollars.
After 3 years..........$1.44^*(1 + 20\%) = (1 + 20\%)^3 = 1.73$ dollars
After 4 years..........$1.73^*(1 + 20\%) = (1 + 20\%)^4 = 2.07$ dollars
After 5 years...........$2.07^*(1 + 20\%) = (1 + 20\%)^5 = 2.49$ dollars
(and so on...)
After 22 years.........$46.00^*(1 + 20\%) = (1 + 20\%)^{22} = 55.21$ dollars
After 23 years.........$55.21^*(1 + 20\%) = (1 + 20\%)^{23} = 66.25$ dollars

In general, return-based compounding is recursive: if the interest rate is R, then at the start of year K we have $P(K)$ dollars, then at the start of year $K + 1$ we have $P(K + 1)$ dollars, where

$$P(K + 1) = (1 + R)^* P(K)$$

According to the aforementioned computation, \$64 is reached somewhere between years 22 and 23 (closer to year 23). Using (Babylonian) linear interpolation, the solution is

$$X = A^* X1 + B^* X2 = 0.125^* 22 + 0.875^* 23 = 22.875 \text{ years.}$$

Again, a more exact answer requires logarithm tables: to find the number of years N, where

$$(1 + 20\%)^N = 64$$

The properties of logarithms imply that, to any base,

$$N \log_b(1 + 20\%) = \log_{10} 64 \quad \text{so} \quad N = \frac{\log_b 64}{\log_b(1.20)}$$

Within 75 years of the opening of the Amsterdam Stock Exchange, tables of base 10 logarithms were compiled to 13 decimal places and were readily available. Consequently,

$$N = \frac{\log_{10} 64}{\log_{10}(1.20)} = \frac{1.806179974}{0.079181246} = 22.8107041 \text{ years.}$$

Compounding Periods

Returns can be compounded for any timescale. For example, suppose the 1-year spot rate is 20% and $P(0) = \$1$. Then in 1 year, the value of $1 becomes

$$P(1) = (1 + 20\%) \cdot P(0) = \$1.20 \ (20\% \text{ annual compounding per year})$$

Let us shrink the timescale to 1 month (1/12 year). If we compound at the same yearly rate by the month, the investment grows $20\%/12 = 1.666667\%$ for each month of 12 months. So compounding over 12 monthly periods yields

$$P(1) = (1 + 20\%/12)^{12} = \$1.21939\ldots (20\% \text{ annual compounding per month})$$

Let us shrink the timescale again to 1 week (1/52 year). If we compound at the same yearly rate per week, the investment grows $20\%/52 = 0.3846154\%$ for each of 52 weeks, so compounding over 52 weekly periods yields

$$P(1) = (1 + 20\%/52)^{52} = \$1.22093\ldots (20\% \text{ annual compounding per week})$$

If we compound at the same rate per minute, the investment grows $20\%/525600 = 0.0000381\%$ for each of 525,600 minutes in a 365 24-hour-day year, so compounding over 525,600 periods yields

$$P(1) = (1 + 20\%/525{,}600)^{525{,}600} = \$1.22140\ldots (20\% \text{ annual compounding per minute})$$

In general, if we divide the year into N time units and we compound at the same yearly rate, the investment grows $20\%/N$ for each of N time units in a 365 24-hour-day year, so compounding over N periods yields

$$P(1) = (1 + 20\%/N)^N (20\% \text{ annual compounding per } 1/N \text{ time unit})$$

Continuous Compounding

What happens when we compound over "infinitely many" periods of "infinitesimally small" time duration? In other words, what happens as N grows arbitrarily large? Jacob Bernoulli (1654–1705) solved the general problem of infinitesimal compounding in 1683. Bernoulli was very familiar with interest rate problems: he came from a family of merchant bankers and spice traders. (The family emigrated from Amsterdam to Basel in the 1570s.)

Using techniques that are now standard in calculus, Bernoulli showed that as the number of time periods N grows without bound, the value of $P(1)$ becomes

$$P(1) = 1 + 20\% + \frac{(20\%)^2}{2} + \frac{(20\%)^3}{2*3} + \frac{(20\%)^4}{2*3*4} + \frac{(20\%)^5}{2*3*4*5} + \cdots$$

$$= 1 + 20\% + \frac{4\%}{2} + \frac{0.8\%}{6} + \frac{0.16\%}{24} + \frac{0.032\%}{120} + \cdots = 1.22140276\ldots$$

(Note that this is an *infinite* sum: to make the equation exact we would have had to add the individual terms forever. The good news is that the partial sums converge quickly, so that in practice we only have to add as many terms as needed to achieve enough accuracy as we need, usually 10 terms or so.)

In general, for any rate R, as the number of compounding periods N increases without bound, the value of $P(1)$ converges to a number that can be approximated according to the formula

$$P(1) = 1 + R + \frac{R^2}{2} + \frac{R^3}{6} + \cdot\frac{R^4}{24} + \frac{R^5}{120} + \frac{R^6}{720} \cdots$$

Bernoulli also showed that as the number of time periods T increases without bound, the value $(1 + 1/N)^N$ converges to a constant number called e, where

$$e = 1 + 1 + \frac{1}{2} + \frac{1}{6} + \frac{1}{24} + \cdots = 2.71828\ldots$$

Using this number e simplifies the notation. Recall that in 1 year, 1 dollar grows at R percent interest compounded over N periods to

$$P(1) = (1 + R/N)^N \text{ dollars.}$$

Let us define the value M so that $N = M \cdot R$ so $\frac{1}{M} = \frac{R}{N}$. Substituting M for N gives

$$(1 + R/N)^N = (1 + 1/M)^{M \cdot R} = \left[(1 + 1/M)^M\right]^R$$

which approaches e^R as M increases without bound. Consequently, in 1 year, the future value $P(1)$ of an amount $P(0)$ that grows at a yearly rate R *continuously compounded* (over infinitely many periods of infinitesimally small time duration) is just

$$P(1) = P(0) \cdot \left[1 + R + \frac{R^2}{2} + \frac{R^3}{6} + \cdot\frac{R^4}{24} + \frac{R^5}{120} + \frac{R^6}{720}\cdot\right] = P(0) \cdot e^R$$

In T years, the future value $P(T)$ of an amount $P(0)$ that grows at a yearly rate R *continuously compounded* is

$$P(T) = P(0) \cdot e^{R \cdot T}$$
$$= P(0) \cdot \left[1 + (R \cdot T) + \frac{(R \cdot T)^2}{2} + \frac{(R \cdot T)^3}{6} + \frac{(R \cdot T)^4}{24} + \frac{(R \cdot T)^5}{120} + \frac{(R \cdot T)^7}{720} \cdots\right]$$

This shows that if we have exponential (and logarithm) tables for powers of e, then we can solve any problem of continuous compounding.

Note that e^R is written as =exp(R) or =EXP(R) in Microsoft Excel and other systems (i.e., Fortran, C, C++, Java, MuPAD).

A few years before Bernoulli's general solution, James Gregory (1638–1675) wrote a letter to a friend in 1670 detailing a solution to a specific problem concerned with daily compounding: given an annual interest rate of 6% a year compounded daily (i.e., $R = 0.06$), what is the value of an investment of $1 in 1 year? The correct answer is

$$(1 + 0.06/365)^{365}$$

There was no way that anyone could compute this expression in 1670. Gregory approximated the daily compounded solution by the series for continuous compounding

$$\left[1+0.06+\frac{(0.06)^2}{2}+\frac{(0.06)^3}{6}+\frac{(0.06)^4}{24}+\frac{(0.06)^5}{120}+\cdots\right]$$

For daily compounding, the real answer (using Excel) is

=(1+0.06/365)^365   or $1.061831311.

For continuous compounding, the exact answer (using Excel) is

=EXP(0.06)   or $1.061836547

Gregory's answer, using five terms in the series, is accurate to the real answer to five decimal places:

$$1+0.06+0.0018+0.000036+0.00000054=\$1.06183654$$

Gregory, the first chairman of the mathematics department at the University of Edinburgh, was one of the inventors of the reflecting telescope. He wrote the letter to John Collins (1625–1675), a math teacher and accountant who wrote books on computational finance, including *An Introduction to Merchant's Accounts* (1652) and *Doctrine of Decimal Arithmetick* (1664).

In some sense, by using continuous compounding, we have recovered an exponential base that was seen in the Babylonian interest rate convention. In fact, the only difference is that the Babylonians used base 2 as their exponent; continuously compounded rates use base e. Because e is bigger than 2, continuously compounded returns are greater than Babylonian doubling returns.

For example (to the nearest cent), the value of $1 at 20% interest that is continuously compounding is $e^{0.2}=\exp(0.2)=2.71828^{\wedge}(0.2)=\$1.22$; the value of $1 at 20% interest using Babylonian (doubling) compounding is $2^{0.2}=(2^{\wedge}0.2)=\$1.15$.

Formulas for present value, future value, interest rate, and time are similar to those derived for Babylonian compounding: the difference is that we replace powers (and logarithms) to base 2 by powers (and logarithms) to base e. The value of an investment after T years of an amount $P(0)$ that grows at a yearly rate R continuously compounded is

$$P(T)=P(0)\cdot e^{R\cdot T}=P(0)^*\exp(R^*T)$$

The value of an initial investment $P(0)$, given the final investment $P(T)$ after T years and given the fact that $P(0)$ grows at continuously compounded rate R per year, is

$$\text{Present Value of investment: } P(0)=\frac{P(T)}{e^{R\cdot T}}=P(T)\cdot e^{-R\cdot T}=P(T)^*\exp(-R^*T)$$

If we use either formula to solve for R, then we can derive the yearly interest rate. In modern notation (using logarithms to base e), this is

$$\text{Continuously compounded interest rate: } R=\frac{1}{T}\cdot\log_e\left(\frac{P(T)}{P(0)}\right)$$

Similarly, if we solve for T, the number of years T needed to grow $P(0)$ into $P(T)$ is

$$\text{Number of years: } T = \frac{1}{R} \cdot \log_e \left(\frac{P(T)}{P(0)} \right)$$

Efficient technologies exist for computing logarithms to *base e*. One formula used for its computation is

$$\log_e(x) = 2 \cdot \left[\left(\frac{x-1}{x+1} \right) + \frac{1}{3} \cdot \left(\frac{x-1}{x+1} \right)^3 + \frac{1}{5} \cdot \left(\frac{x-1}{x+1} \right)^5 + \frac{1}{7} \cdot \left(\frac{x-1}{x+1} \right)^7 \cdots \right]$$

Other formulas were also derived and used in the 17th century. Note that the *base e* logarithm, sometimes called the *natural logarithm*, has another notation:

$$\log_e(x) = \ln(x)$$

The "ln" notation was first used in 1893 by Irving Stringham (1847–1909) in his book *Uniplanar Algebra* (possibly to help his typesetter avoid subscripts).

There are different conventions for log used today when the base is not specified: $\log(x)$ means $\log_{10}(x)$ in Excel. For base e logarithms, Excel also uses $\ln(x)$; means $\log_e(x) = \ln(x)$ in most mathematics and finance writings and in Fortran, C, C++, and Java languages. Note that C, C++, and Java define log10(x) to refer to base 10 logarithms. Some Fortran dialects use ALOG and ALOG10.

In the 17th century, natural base e logarithms were also used to build logarithm tables to any base, especially base 10. For example, because

$$N = e^A = 10^B \quad \text{then} \quad \log_{10} N = B \quad \text{and} \quad \ln N = B \ln 10$$

Consequently, when we equate expressions for B:

$$\log_{10} N = \frac{\ln N}{\ln 10} = B$$

We can transform rates within compounding conventions. For example, what is the relationship between the T-year Babylonian doubling rate R_B, the T-year continuously compounding rate R_C, and the T-year yearly compounding rate over N periods R_N? Note that the future values — the end result — must be the same whatever compounding method we use

$$P(T) = P(0) \cdot e^{R_C \cdot T} = P(0) \cdot 2^{R_B \cdot T} = P(0) \cdot \left(1 + \frac{R_N}{N} \right)^{T \cdot N}$$

After simplifying and taking natural logarithms, we find

$$R_c = R_B \cdot \ln 2 = N \cdot \ln(1 + R_N)$$

So a Babylonian rate $R_B = 20\%$ is equivalent to a continuously compounding rate $R_c = 13.86\%$ and is equivalent to a twice-a-year compounding rate ($N = 2$) rate $R_N = 14.35\%$.

These relationships are summarized in Box 2-13.

Box 2-13
Rates and Prices: Summary of Conventions for a T-Year Investment

Given today's price $P(0)$, a price $P(T)$ at time T, and rate R.

Note: You can replace year and period time units by any consistent time units.

Babylonian compounding: Money doubles in $1/R$ years. For a T-year investment:

Present Value: $P(0) = P(T) \cdot 2^{-R \cdot T}$

Future Value: $P(T) = P(0) \cdot 2^{R \cdot T}$

Rate: $R = \dfrac{1}{T} \cdot \log_2 \left(\dfrac{P(T)}{P(0)} \right)$

Time: $T = \dfrac{1}{R} \cdot \log_2 \left(\dfrac{P(T)}{P(0)} \right)$

Continuous compounding: In 1 year, 1 dollar becomes e^R dollars. In T years:

Present Value: $P(0) = P(T) \cdot e^{-R \cdot T}$

Future Value: $P(T) = P(0) \cdot e^{R \cdot T}$

Rate: $R = \dfrac{1}{T} \cdot \log_e \left(\dfrac{P(T)}{P(0)} \right)$

Time: $T = \dfrac{1}{R} \cdot \log_e \left(\dfrac{P(T)}{P(0)} \right)$

N-period yearly compounding: 1 year consists of N periods (i.e., 12 months).

Given annual interest rate R, in one period, 1 dollar becomes $(1 + R/N)$ dollars. In T years:

Present Value: $P(0) = P(T) \cdot (1 + R/N)^{-N \cdot T}$

Future Value: $P(T) = P(0) \cdot (1 + R/N)^{N \cdot T}$

Rate: $R = N \cdot \left[\left(\dfrac{P(T)}{P(0)} \right)^{1/(N \cdot T)} - 1 \right]$

Time: $T = \dfrac{1}{N} \cdot \dfrac{\log \left(\dfrac{P(T)}{P(0)} \right)}{\log(1 + R/N)}$, log to any base

Transformations of Babylonian R_B, simple N period R_N, and continuous compounding R_C:

Babylonian to continuous: $R_C = R_B \cdot \ln 2 = 69.31\% \cdot R_B$

Continuous to Babylonian: $R_B = R_C / \ln 2 = 1.44 \cdot R_C$

Babylonian to simple: $R_N = N \cdot (2^{R_B/N} - 1)$

Continuous to simple: $R_N = N \cdot (e^{R_C/N} - 1)$

Simple to Babylonian: $R_B = N \cdot \log_2(1 + R_N/N)$

Simple to continuous: $R_C = N \cdot \ln(1 + R_N/N)$

2.4. Days, Months, and Years

So far, our standard unit of time is a year, which we said has 12 months, 52 weeks, and 525,600 minutes. But does a real year have 52 weeks? Does a real year have 365 days? How do we count holidays and weekends? This is an important question. For financial computations involving loans, rents, and bonds, counterparties need to determine the number of days or months between payment dates and the time periods needed to charge interest.

Time must also be synchronized among market participants. For audit applications, how can we assure that a trade was executed at a particular time? Without adequate synchronization, traders and brokers (on different sides) and exchanges might record different times for the same trade; in case of a dispute, reconstructing time events associated with trading, clearing, and settlement would be difficult.

Calendar Conventions

Most units of time used in our calendars are not constant. A lunar month (corresponding to a complete rotation of the moon around the earth) is not an integer number of days: it is about 29 and a half days. A solar year (corresponding to a complete rotation of the earth around the sun) is not an integral number of days: it is about 365 and a quarter days. Twelve lunar months do not add up to a year either: they add up to about 354 days. This implies that the financial technology of interest rate, return, and loan computations must involve calendar conventions to determine the exact length of time durations.

These problems were known to the Babylonians. Using water clock records over several centuries, the Babylonians established that the average duration of the lunar month was 29 days and $12 \frac{793}{1080}$ hours. Consequently, to make an integral number of lunar months correspond to the solar year, they periodically added an extra month to a year: normal years were 12 lunar months and special years were 13 lunar months. Special years are variously called intercalated, interpolated, or leap years.

In the Babylonian system, the interpolated year pattern would repeat every 19 years (the Greeks later called this the Metonic cycle). Their interpolation algorithm made sure that fixed solar dates would not drift too much into the wrong season (e.g., it ensured that July 4 was always celebrated in the summer and not in the spring). This basic Babylonian algorithm was adapted for the Jewish calendar, which required spring holidays to be celebrated in the spring. (The algorithm was published in 359 CE when the signal flare method that announced the new month proved unworkable. A variation of the calendar is also used in the computation of the date of Easter.)

For purely financial computations, the Babylonians used a year of 360 days with twelve 30-day months. Yearly payments were made at the end of the year. The 360-day year simplified fractional parts of years (360 has many divisors; also note that $\frac{1}{1080}$ hour $= \frac{1}{1080} \cdot 60$ minute $= \frac{1}{18}$ minute).

The financial world now uses a variation of the Gregorian calendar based on a purely solar Roman model published during the time of Emperor Julian (46 BCE). In the Julian system, normal years were fixed at 365 days and "leap years" were 366 days; every 4 years, a day is added to February (which is normally set to 28 days). A year has 12 "months," each non-February month is arbitrarily given a set number of either 30 or 31 days. Months in the Julian system have no correspondence with lunar months. (For example, a "blue moon" refers to a month having two full moons; the second full moon is the "blue moon.")

Box 2-14
Time, Financial Technology, and NASD (and SEC) Regulations

In the last chapter we saw how Polybius used a water clock for secure military communication. Centuries before Polybius, the Babylonians used accurate water clocks to measure time for religious and financial affairs. The Babylonians called their water clocks *dibdibbu* (possibly sounding like drip drop). Their water clock involved filling a vessel with water to a marked line and then letting a quantity of water escape. Unlike the Greeks, the Babylonians did not measure time by the difference of water levels — instead, they more accurately measured the volume of water that was collected into a container. Since they saved the water, they maintained a permanent time stamp. For example, water flowing at a certain standard rate would fill up a given standard volume in 1 hour; a 60th of that volume would be filled in 1 minute, a 60th of that would be filled in 1 second.

Modern synchronized clocks make digital communication, computation, and finance possible. The National Association of Securities Dealers (NASD), in NASD Rule 6957, mandates that all computer clocks and mechanical clocks (including manual devices) used to record the time associated with electronic order handling or execution must be synchronized "to any source that is accurate to within three seconds of the National Institute of Standards and Technology." According to NASD Rule 6953, member firms must document and maintain their clock synchronization procedures, and members should keep a log of the times when they synchronize their clocks and the results of the synchronization process, including notice of any time the clock drifts more than 3 seconds. According to the Securities Exchange Commission rule SEC Rule 17a-4(b), clock synchronization logs must be maintained and must be accessible for at least 3 years.

The NASD requires the use of the standard clock kept at the Technology Administration of the U.S. Department of Commerce — the National Institute of Standards and Technology (NIST) formerly known as the National Bureau of Standards (NBS). NIST maintains an atomic clock that tracks (since 1955) Temps Atomique International (TAI), also known as International Atomic Time. TAI is an average of the atomic clocks maintained by several countries; each clock is calibrated on the radioactive decay of cesium. The International Bureau of Weights and Measures oversees the averaging.

The international legal standard for time is called Coordinated Universal Time (UTC), broadcast through radio, satellite navigation systems, telephone, and special portable clocks. The TAI atomic clocks show that the rotation of the earth is slowing: the day is gradually becoming longer. The solution (adapted from the Babylonian method) is to periodically insert a leap second into UTC: one special minute thus has 61 seconds in some years. The insertion is coordinated by the International Earth Rotation and Reference Systems Service (IERRSS). So far, 32 leap seconds have been inserted on an ad hoc basis by the IERRSS. Occasionally having a 61-second minute may cause problems in some systems.

The problem with the Julian system was that spring holidays started drifting toward the winter. During the time of Pope Gregory XIII (1502–1585), modifications to the Julian system were introduced and standardized. The Standard Gregorian Algorithm is add a day if the year is evenly divisible by 100 and evenly divisible by 400 (e.g., add a day to 1600 or 2000, but not to 1800 or 1900) or add a day if the year is evenly divisible by 4 (e.g., add a day to 1604 or 2004, but not to 1601 or 2003). As in the Julian system, months are arbitrarily given a set number of days that have no relationship to the true lunar month.

Box 2-15

When Was the Gregorian Algorithm Adopted?

1582:   Rome and most Catholic countries

1700:   Denmark, Norway, and the Protestant parts of Germany

1752:   British Empire (including the United States). At adoption time, it was necessary to correct by 11 days: September 2, 1752 was followed by September 14, 1752.

1753:   Sweden. At adoption time, it was necessary to correct by 11 days: February 17 was followed by March 1. Before 1753, Sweden alternated between Julian and Gregorian calendars; because of this, Sweden had a February 30 in 1712.

1873:   Japan

1918:   Russia. At adoption time, it was necessary to correct by 14 days: January 31 was followed by February 14.

1924:   Greece

The last day of the Julian calendar was October 4, 1582; the next day was declared to be October 15, 1582. This created major problems: 10 days vanished from financial computations. Some people were paid for days worked; others were required to pay a full month's rent. As part of the reform, the first day of the year was standardized as January 1. (Other countries had different first days: England started the year on March 25.)

A standard is only successful if it is used and recognized universally: the Gregorian calendar was not an immediate success. It took almost 400 years for the Gregorian calendar to become a common time standard.

Financial technology systems have additional standards (called a *day count basis* or *basis* for short) for specifying the number of days per month and the number of days per year that may be different from the Gregorian standard. By convention, a day count basis is specified with the form N/M, with N denoting the number of days per month and M denoting the number of days per year.

For example, suppose we specify dates by the triple of numbers (Year, Month, Day). Suppose we want to know the number of days between two dates (Year1, Month1, Day1) and (Year2, Month2, Day2). A different day count basis will yield a different answer.

Here are the most commonly used day counts:

- **30/360**

  This is the Babylonian standard that is still used today. All months have 30 days; all years have 360 days. The number of days between the two dates is given by the following algorithm:

  If Day1 = 31 then set Day1 to 30;

  If Day2 is 31 and either Day1 = 30 or Day1 = 31 then change Day2 to 30; otherwise, leave Day2 at 31;

  Number of Days = 360*(Year2-Year1) + 30*(Month2-Month1) + (Day2-Day1)

Note that if Day1 = 31, set Day1 = 30. If Day2 is 31 and Day1 is 30 or 31, change Day2 to 30; otherwise, leave Day2 at 31. According to 30/360, there are 29 days between May 1 and May 30, 30 days between May 1 and May 31, and 30 days between February 1 and March 1.

Microsoft Excel has a built-in function, DAYS360, that computes dates with 30/360; for example, the Excel formula

`=DAYS360(''2/1/2004'',''3/1/2004'')` evaluates to 30.

The 30/360 day count basis is used in the United States for many bonds, especially money borrowed by corporations, agencies, and municipalities; mortgage-backed securities such as those issued by Freddie Mac; floating rate bonds; and certificate of deposits (CDs).

- **30E/360**

  This is the European version of 30/360. Again, all months have 30 days; all years have 360 days. The number of days between the two dates is given by the following algorithm:

  If D1 = 31 then set D1 to 30;

  If D2 = 31, then set D2 to 30;

  Number of Days = 360*(Y2-Y1)+30*(M2-M1)+(D2-D1)

According to 30/360E, there are 29 days between May 1 and May 30, and 29 days between May 1 and May 31, as D2 was reset to 30.

Microsoft Excel has a built-in function, DAYS360, that computes dates with 30E/360; for example, the Excel formula

`=DAYS360("5/1/2004","5/31/2004", TRUE)` evaluates to 29.

The 30E/360 day count basis is used for many European bonds.

- **Actual/360**

  The actual calendar days for months are counted; all years have 360 days. For multiyear periods, the whole number of years has 360 days; we then count the actual number of days for the fractional part. For example, there are actually 30 days between May 1 2004 and May 31 2004; with Actual/360, there are 360 days between May 1 2004 and May 1 2005; consequently there are 390 days between May 1 2004 and May 30 2005.

The Actual/360 day count basis is used for many money market securities (CDs and floating rate notes), mortgage-backed securities (such as those issued by Freddie Mac); and U.S. Treasury bills.

- **Actual/365**

  The actual calendar days for months are counted; all years have 365 days. For multiyear periods, the whole number of years has 365 days; we then count the actual number of days for the fractional part. For example, there are actually 30 days between May 1 2004 and May 31 2004; with Actual/365, there are 365 days between May 1 2004 and May 1 2005; consequently there are 395 days between May 1 2004 and May 30 2005.

The Actual/365 day count basis is used with many U.S. Treasury bonds, foreign government bonds, and floating rate bonds.

- **Actual/Actual or Actual/365 (366)**

  Actual calendar days for months and years are counted; all years have either 365 or 366 days, if the year includes a leap year. This basis is used with many U.S. Treasury bonds.

Box 2-16
Actual/360, Treasury Bills, and Discount Rates

U.S. Treasury bills ("T bills") are short-term loans to the U.S. government for a minimum of $10,000 with terms of 91 days (13 weeks), 182 days (26 weeks), and 364 days (52 weeks). They are auctioned throughout the year on Thursdays and are priced with the Actual/360 day count basis. Consequently, a T bill is a bond with maturity price $P(T)$ (at least $10,000), with T being 91, 182, or 364 days. Quotes for Treasury bills are not given in present value $P(0)$; rather, quotes are given in terms of a *discount rate r*, where by definition.

$$P(0) = P(T) \cdot (1 - r \cdot T)$$

For example, on July 21, 2004, the following quote is given for a T bill that matures on September 16:

MATURITY	DAYS TO MAT	BID	ASK	CHG	ASK YLD
Sep 16 04	56	1.19	1.18	-0.01	1.2

Note that for rate quotes, *the bid rate is greater than the ask rate*. Using the discount rate definition and the Actual/360-day count:

$$\text{Bid price} = \$10,000 \cdot \left(1 - \left[1.19\% \cdot \frac{56}{360}\right]\right) = \$9981.49$$

$$\text{Ask price} = \$10,000 \cdot \left(1 - \left[1.18\% \cdot \frac{56}{360}\right]\right) = \$9981.64$$

Note that *the bid price is less than the ask price*. Also note that the prices would be different for a different day count basis.

Computer Time Conventions

Other problems that need to be addressed in financial systems regard the treatment of days where the markets are closed (such as holidays and special closing days). These days depend on the product traded, the exchange, the state, and the country. For example, which markets are open on July 4? July 14? August 15? Which markets are open on the Friday after Thanksgiving? If products are not traded on certain days, certain conventions may have to be established to fill in "blank" quotes and prices for financial computations. Different implementations of dates and times can lead to compatibility problems for financial applications.

For example, Microsoft Excel represents dates as integers called "serial values." In the Windows Excel representation, January 1, 1900 is serial number 1, and January 1, 2008 is serial number 39448 because it is actually 39,448 days after January 1, 1900. (Excel stores time as decimal fractions because they consider time as a fraction of a day.) The Macintosh Excel date representation is not compatible with the Windows representation: on the Macintosh, January 1, 1904 is serial number 1. By examination, the latest version of Excel can represent dates up to the year 9999.

Unix represents date and time as a 32-bit integer (32 base 2 digits, corresponding to 4 octal digits, or 4 bytes) representing the number of seconds since January 1, 1970. Because the maximum value of a 32-bit integer is $2^{31} - 1$, dates recycle approximately every 68 years; the next Unix date recycle will be reached in year 2038, so that, after 2038, dates will roll over to 1970. In C, the value of this 32-bit integer is returned by C's local time function.

Newer Unix implementations represent time as a 64-bit integer; this allows a time representation for 292 billion years after January 1, 1970. To implement this fix across all implementations, all older Unix systems would have to be recompiled. In Java, the getTime() function returns the number of milliseconds since January 1, 1970, represented as a 64-bit number. In practice, Unix time is generally synchronized with UTC, although there are some questions on how to handle leap seconds.

Box 2-17
Time Synchronization and the Network Time Protocol

Most computers have their own clocks, typically based on a quartz oscillator and a hardware counter, that are accurate on the order of 10^{-7} second. How can such clocks be synchronized with a common clock standard? At the speed of light, it takes a signal about 10 milliseconds (10^{-2} second) to travel across the United States without considering the network latency effects introduced by routers, repeaters, and other factors.

One cost-effective solution to the problem of time synchronization is to organize a set of time servers whose purpose would be to synchronize a larger number of clients and other servers in a common network.

One protocol that does this is the Network Time Protocol (NTP), one of the oldest continuously operating Internet protocols. NTP enables clock synchronization for distributed networks. The protocol specifies how time can be read from a server clock, how time stamps are communicated, and how client clocks can be adjusted for network latency and other factors.

On the Internet, NTP (version 4) can maintain time to within 10^{-2} second; over local area networks, NTP can synchronize clocks to accuracy on the order of 10^{-4} second.

The NTP time is defined by a 128-bit signed (base 2) integer. The first 64 bits measure a whole number of seconds and the second 64 bits represent a fraction of a second. This representation yields a timescale that cycles approximately every 10^{16} years with precision of about 10^{-20} second.

The prime epoch (epoch 0) is January 1, 1900, with positive values representing times after and negative values representing times before. Conversion between different time formats and the NTP format is done by computing the difference in seconds and fractional seconds between starting points of the other format and the NTP base epoch.

Sometimes we do not need the full NTP precision. An *NTP time stamp* is an NTP time represented as an unsigned 64-bit integer, formed by concatenating the first (most precise) 32 bits of the NTP seconds part with the second (least precise) 32 bits of the fraction-of-a-second part. The NTP time stamp can represent 136 years from 1900 to 2036 to a precision of about 10^{-12} second.

The latest versions of Microsoft Windows supports the synchronization of computer clocks with NTP "Internet Time" by connecting via NTP with a time server at either time.windows.com or time.nist.gov (this is enabled via the Windows *Date and Time Properties*).

Standards organizations are actively defining date and time specifications. One standard is ISO 8601 (Data elements and interchange formats – Information interchange – Representation of dates and times). One particular problem this standard focuses on is the international representations of dates: it turns out that a representation like 08/04/02 has at least six different interpretations around the world (i.e., 8 April 2002, 4 April 2008,...). Representations that are standardized by ISO 8601 include calendar dates, ordinal dates, week dates, time of day, time zone and time zone offsets, time intervals, durations between dates and times, and repeating intervals.

2.5. Notes and References

Quotes from Joseph de la Vega are found in his 1680 Confusión de Confusiones, reprinted in
[0.1] Martin S. Fridon (ed.), *Extraordinary Popular Delusions and the Madness of Crowds and Confusión de Confusiones*. John Wiley & Sons, New York, 1996. ISBN 0 471 13312-4.

Quotes from Sumerian and Babylonian financial texts are from
[0.2] Karen Rhea Nemet-Nejat. *Cuneiform Mathematical Texts As a Reflection of Everyday Life in Mesopotamia*. American Oriental Society, 1993. ISBN 0940490757.

General References

In addition to the general technology references in Chapter 1, another reference for material in this chapter is the 1911 edition of the Encyclopedia Britannica, now in the public domain, at
[0.3] http://1911encyclopedia.org/

Financial Terms

A good historical survey of the technology of money, financial computing, and the origin of many financial terms (including the quotes in Box 2-1 and Box 2-5) is found at
[1] David E. Smith. *History of Mathematics* (published in 1925). Reprinted by Dover Publications, Mineola, 1958. Vol. 1 ISBN 0486204294 and Vol. 2 ISBN 0486204308.

Franklin's essay (Box 2-2) can be found at
[2] The Writings of Benjamin Franklin: Philadelphia, 1726–1757 (available at http://www.historycarper.com/).

During some excavations in the 1700s, Pietro della Valle found tablets of script that he called cuneiform (Latin *cuneus*: wedge). Many early translations were done by George Smith (1840–1876), a bank note engraver. Translations of many Babylonian financial texts are in
[3] George Aaron Barton, "Contracts," in *Assyrian and Babylonian Literature: Selected Transactions* (with an introduction by Robert Harper), New York, D. Appleton & Company, 1904 (available at http://www.fordham.edu/halsall/ancient/mesopotamia-contracts.html).

[4] Karen Rhea Nemet-Nejat. *Daily Life in Ancient Mesopotamia*. Hendrickson Publishers, Inc., Peabody (MA) 2002. ISBN 1-56563-712-7.

Pictures and descriptions of 13th century tally sticks (with a translation of the Dialog of the Exchequer) are maintained by the National Archives of England, Wales and the United Kingdom (from Domesday Book of 1086 to recently released government papers). [5] http://www.nationalarchives.gov.uk/

Numbers and Prices

The original work of Fibonnaci and others is reprinted in
[6] D.J. Struik (ed.), *A Source Book In Mathematics, 1200–1800*. Harvard University Press, Cambridge, 1969.

The Archimedes project is a research digital library for the history of mechanics and engineering from antiquity to the Renaissance. It has the complete text of Luca Pacioli's 1494 *Summa de Arithmetica et Geometria, Proportioni et Proportionalita* (also see Box 2-3) at
[7] http://archimedes.mpiwg-berlin.mpg.de/cgi-bin/toc/toc.cgi

A history of mathematics notation is maintained by Jeff Miller at
[8] http://members.aol.com/jeff570/mathsym.html

The 1713 second edition of the de Montmort's book analyzing gambling systems is still in print:
[9] Pierre Remond de Montmort, *Essay d'Analyse sur les Jeux de Hazard*. Photographic reprint by the American Mathematical Society. ISBN 0-8284-0307-4.

Strips is an acronym for Separate Trading of Registered Interest and Principal of Securities. U.S. Treasury Strips started trading in January 1985. They are described at
[10] http://www.publicdebt.treas.gov/of/ofstrips.htm

Formulas used by the U.S. Treasury are described in the Appendices of
[11] Treasury Security Tender Submission Guide. U.S. Federal Reserve (available at http://www.publicdebt.treas.gov/of/ofguide.htm).

[12] "Estimating Yields on Treasury Securities." Fedpoints (a reference series explaining the structure and functions of the Federal Reserve System, available at http://app.ny.frb.org/aboutthefed/fedpoint/fed28.html).

Time Is Money: Loans and Interest

A history of interpolation technology is by
[13] Erik Meijering. "A Chronology of Interpolation: From Ancient Astronomy to Modern Signal and Image Processing." *Proceedings of the IEEE*, Vol. 90, No. 3, March 2002 (available at http://bigwww.epfl.ch/publications/meijering0201.html).

Gregory's letter to Collins concerning the daily interest rate compounding problem is in [6].

Days, Months, and Years

NASD and SEC rules are listed in the
[14] NASD Manual Online (http://nasd.complinet.com/)

Some recent problems dealing with coordinating NIST, UTC, and IERRSS are discussed by
[15] Keith Winstein. "Why the U.S. Wants To End the Link between Time and Sun: Astronomers Say Wait a Sec, Sundials Would Be Passé; Mean Blow to Greenwich." *Wall Street Journal*, July 29, 2005.

2.6. Discussion Questions

1. Comment on the relative persistence of databases implemented in clay tablets, tally sticks, paper, skins, magnetic tape, magnetic disks, CDs, and DVDs. Compare their performance with respect to the amount of data stored, ease of use, and their vulnerability to flood, fire, and theft.

2. Many hardware and software vendors that helped create "legacy databases" have gone out of business. Consequently, corporate archived financial data (such as email) might be rendered useless in a legal case if there are no programs that know how to access and read the emails. Compare this software archeology to conventional archeology. Has this happened in the financial community? Is this situation avoidable?

3. What is the difference between a bookie and a market maker?

4. What was more important for the development of financial computation: the 10 symbols for decimal numbers or the invention of the decimal point?

5. Theoretical mathematical notation evolved from handwritten manuscripts using superscripts, subscripts, different fonts, and different font styles. However, notation for financial computation developed with the technology of in-line typesetting. Which notation is easier for people? Which notation is more practical? Are there any programming languages that can parse expressions written with superscripts, subscripts, different fonts, and different font styles?

6. How complicated is it to write a program that would translate U.S. decimal prices (with commas and points) to Continental decimal prices (with commas and points)?

7. Why are bonds quoted in base 32 fractions?

8. Instead of asking about daily compounding, suppose Collins asked Gregory about hourly compounding. How would Gregory solve this problem?

9. Is the 3-second Rule 6957 sufficient for fast markets? At your favorite Internet source for real time prices, can you determine how many trades per second occur for very active securities? Using the current version of NTP, can you propose another rule?

10. What are the advantages and disadvantages of keeping more than one day count basis?

11. Comment on the cost to the financial industry regarding the so-called Y2K problem. What about the Unix Epoch problem?

12. After a leap second was added on January 1, 1996, the computer systems at the Associated Press and other organizations crashed. Comment on the quality of a financial order trail if leap seconds are added — not according to any fixed schedule — every year or so.

13. Mathematical notation evolved from typesetting technology. Notations for programming languages evolved from single-line typesetting technology. Comment on the use of fixed-width non-proportional fonts in programming languages.

CHAPTER ◆ 3

Algorithms and Financial Technology

A mind which does not know accounting, is it a mind that has intelligence?
— Sumerian proverb (ca. 2000 BCE)

3.1. Financial Algorithms

Financial technology is concerned with the representation and processing of financial algorithms. Financial algorithms are systematic procedures. They are used to specify financial communication protocols; compliance rules for regulatory authorities; clearing and settlement operations; coded representations of financial information (prices and orders); and authentication schemes. Financial algorithms also describe decision rules for buying and selling. Financial algorithm developers are typically finance professionals — mathematicians, economists, statisticians, quantitative analysts, risk managers, and traders. Operational properties of representation and processing include correctness, reliability, speed, accuracy, availability, maintainability, flexibility, and scalability. Implementation of financial algorithms involves programmers, software and systems engineers, communication network specialists, database designers, project managers, technical writers, and quality assurance staff.

The word *algorithm* was coined to refer to the systematic procedures associated with arithmetic and computing. The word may be derived from the Greek *algos* (*white sand* — used with the abacus) or *arithmos* (*number*); another possibility is that it is an eponym, derived from the last name of Persian textbook author Mohammed Bin Musa al-Khowarizmi (780–840) — Khwarizm being a city in present-day Uzbekistan. The second word in the title of al-Khowarizmi's book (written in 830), *Kitab Al-jabr w'al-Muqabala* (Arabic: *Rules of Restoration and Reduction*), is a metonym for *algebra*, a word that entered the English language in 1551. (Al-Khowarizmi did most of his work at the great academy near Baghdad; his writings on arithmetic, trigonometry, sundials, geography, and the Jewish calendar are still available.)

Christoff Rudolff (1499–1543), the merchant who showed how to use decimal numbers for prices, published one of the first books dealing systematically with known but arbitrary quantities in 1525. He titled his book *Cosa*, Italian for thing: cosa — "thing" — what Renaissance Italian authors (like Pacioli) called "a variable" or "an unknown." However,

71

unlike Pacioli, Rudolff used special symbols (not abbreviations) to denote variables. (Rudolff used a symbol that looks like a script K for a variable; he also used different symbols to denote different powers of an unknown.) People who were trained to work with abstract quantities were called algebraists or cossists; algebra was also called the "cossic art" (see Webster's 1913 English dictionary, available on the Web). Today we would call this cossic art a *technology*, consisting of notational rules, formal procedures (for manipulating expressions denoting unknown quantities), and computing tools (such as logarithm tables and slide rules). Note that *technology*, a word first used in English in 1859, is from the Greek *techne*: art.

Notational Rules and Language

To avoid mistakes, algorithms must be specified in formal unambiguous language. We have seen how symbolic mathematical language has evolved with the development of the typesetting conventions used for the printing press.

From another perspective, algorithms are always written in a language suitable for the current computing technology. Before the electronic computer, algorithm processing technology included the abacus, writing tablet, table lookups, pencil and paper, and devices such as "Napier's Bones" and the slide rule. In order to do business, merchants had to be familiar with the evolving set of tools and algorithm notations.

Today, programmers translate algorithm specifications into another representation that computers can process (this representation of an algorithm is called a program; note that one meaning of *programming* is *scheduling*, as in radio or television programming). Since the 1950s, these representations are called *programming languages.*

Many programming languages are developed by corporations; some have been developed in academia or under government sponsorship. The technology marketplace determines which languages become popular and which do not. Some reasons for popularity include ease of learning, ease of writing algorithms, low license cost, speed of the program when executed, and availability on different computer platforms. Most popular languages eventually are regulated by different standards organizations in order to ensure common implementations across platforms.

There are three different ways we can classify programming languages.

Syntax

The syntax of a language refers to the rules used that specify how well-formed expressions, functions, commands, and other language constructs appear in text. For example, C and Java have a similar syntax in that all commands end with a semicolon. Excel has a totally different syntax; e.g., all worksheet functions must begin with an equal sign.

A low-level *lexical* syntax specifies what "words" look like; in programming languages, words are made up of letters, numbers, and symbols belonging to *character sets*. For example, the letter e is part of the ASCII character set (used in C); the letter é is part of the Unicode character set (used in Java). Different "words" are "spelled" differently; e.g., the comparison operator for Not Equal in C is written as != and in Excel it is written as <>. "White space," namely blank (single space) or tabs (used for indentation), also needs a specification, as does the length of lines. *Comments* are text that is ignored by the computer; they are used to improve human readability. In ANSI C, comments begin with a /* and terminate with a */, all text within and including these markers are ignored by the compiler. In C++ and other languages, comments begin with // and continue to the end of the line.

Another lexical construct is concerned with how names are formed. (This is similar to the problems that early algebraists and cossists faced when deciding how to name unknown quantities.) Because most languages are case sensitive, x and X stand for different objects and log and Log stand for different names of functions (note that Excel is not case sensitive). In most languages, names begin with a letter; many special symbols (such as mathematical operators $+, -, ^*, /$) are usually not allowed to be used in names.

Semantics

The semantics refers to the meanings of syntactical constructs. For example, most languages provide ways of encapsulating the operations of algorithms into *functions* and *procedures* (in Fortran, these are called *subroutines*). Functions, such as $\log(x)$ or $\exp(x)$, return values; they correspond to mathematical abbreviations. Procedures are useful for representing a sequence of steps, such as the Euclidean algorithm or procedure specifying multiplication derived from the distributive law. Most programming languages provide programmers with the ability to specify arbitrary functions and procedures.

Many languages have constructs specifically for mathematical and financial applications. The advantage of having such built-in functions is that extra programming steps can be minimized or eliminated. Languages that are more oriented toward financial and mathematical applications include spreadsheet systems such as Microsoft Excel and numerical systems such as MuPAD. For example, a C programmer would have to write a procedure to compute the logarithm to an arbitrary base; in Excel, the logarithm to an arbitrary base is already part of the system.

Other languages represent and process symbols in order to simplify expressions in algebra and calculus and to do arithmetic to precision of any number of digits (this is sometimes called *bignum arithmetic*). Most languages have separate facilities for acquiring, manipulating, and displaying different data types and data structures, such as character strings; whole numbers (integers); decimal numbers (usually called *floating point numbers*); and tables of these objects.

Data structures that have varying degrees of built-in language support include arrays (an *array* is a multidimensional generalization of a two-dimensional row and column table), lists (a *list* is an *ordered* collection of objects), and trees (used to represent hierarchies). For example, the programming language Lisp was designed explicitly to model lists (Lisp is an acronym for *List Processing*). Most programming languages provide programmers with the ability to specify arbitrary data structures built on more elementary component data structures.

Languages such as AMPL and GAMS demonstrate yet another type of semantics: in this case, a problem *specification* (not a procedure outlining a step-by-step solution) is submitted to a computer system; part of the specification indicates which algorithm to use to obtain a solution. Because the problem specification is separate from implementation, a potential solution can be directed to different *solvers*. A solver can be any computer platform and can be hosted anywhere. This technology paradigm is called an *algebraic modeling language*.

Financial technology languages for control and communication applications have their own set of semantic constructs. *Threads* (called *processes* or *tasks* in pre-1970s languages) enable programmers to create modules (threads) that execute concurrently. On a single computer, each thread is given a small amount of time to execute; on a multiple (networked) system, threads can be allocated to a different processor. In either case, these languages support the semantics of thread creation: scheduling, prioritization, and termination.

Other semantic constructs are used to package software systems into independent but interoperating components. The most popular constructs, developed in the 1970s, are *objects* and *classes* (in older languages these constructs were called flavors, mixins, actors, and agents). Objects encapsulate functions, procedures, and threads together with a collection of underlying data structures.

Pragmatics

The pragmatics of a language refers to how the language is used by a community of application developers and other users.

Some languages are *interpreted*: after a command is typed, it is processed (or *executed*) immediately. The program that executes these languages are called *interpreters*. Other languages are *compiled*. Compiled languages utilize special software tools (called *compilers*) that translate complete program texts into an optimized representation; once translated, these optimized representations can be saved in a file (one convention is to name the file with the last three letters being *exe*) for execution at arbitrary times.

Many operating system languages, such as DOS, Unix, and Linux, are interpreted; sometimes the interpreters are called *the shell*; programs written in these languages are called *macros* or *shell scripts*. Other system languages used for shell scripts include Perl and Python. Interpreted languages utilize a command box (i.e., a DOS *command prompt* in Windows) or a command line.

Mathematical and financial oriented languages such as MuPAD, Excel, Mathematica, and SciLab are also interpreted. In Excel, the *Formula Bar* acts as the command line; worksheet functions typed in the Formula Bar are interpreted. Other commands are interpreted through a menu or dialog system [commonly called a Graphical User Interface (a GUI), pronounced "gooey"].

Compiled languages have complex tool sets called Software Development Environments (SDE) that are used to manage several configurations of programs and projects; some, like Microsoft's Visual Studio, use a GUI; others, like the public domain GNU Compiler Collection (GCC), are based on shell commands. Sometimes interpreted languages have a compiled version, and vice versa.

3.2. Spreadsheets

A spreadsheet is a table that represents information organized in ordered rows and columns. Usually, on the top of each column and on the side of each row, information labels (called *headers*) are present. Also, rows and columns are separated by thin lines (called *grid lines*). Headers and grid lines are display utilities that help the reader understand the information in the table.

Spreadsheets have been used since ancient times. Why? In antiquity it was discovered that most people find spatial and tabular processing easier than sequential list processing. It is easier to visualize the relationships between objects in space than it is to mentally represent relationships in sequential order. Since 1993, Microsoft Excel has been the most popular spreadsheet system; consequently, Excel's syntax and semantics today represents a kind of *de facto* spreadsheet standard.

Spreadsheet Syntax

One of the most famous Babylonian spreadsheets is a 4000-year-old tablet known as Plimpton 322 (after the G. A. Plimpton Collection at Columbia University; photographs of Plimpton 322 are available at dozens of sites on the Web). In Microsoft Excel, the Plimpton 322 has the representation shown in Box 3-1.

Box 3-1
Plimpton 322 (Excel Representation)

	A	B	C	D
1		width	diagonal	
2	1.59.0.15	1.59	2.49	1
3	1.56.56.58.14.50.6.15	56.7	1.20.25	2
4	1.55.07.41.15.33.45	1.16.41	1.50.49	3
5	1.53.10.29.32.52.16	3.31.49	5.9.1	4
6	1.48.54.1.40	1.5	1.37	5
7	1.47.6.41.40	5.19	8.1	6
8	1.43.11.56.28.26.40	38.11	59.1	7
9	1.41.33.45.14.3.45	13.19	20.49	8
10	1.38.33.36.36	8.1	12.49	9
11	1.35.10.2.28.27.24.26	1.22.41	2.16.1	10
12	1.33.45	45	1.15	11
13	1.29.21.54.2.15	27.59	48.49	12
14	1.27.0.3.45	2.41	4.49	13
15	1.25.48.51.35.6.40	29.31	53.49	14
16	1.23.13.46.40	56	1.46	15
17				

The 2003 version of Excel has "built-in" column headers: the letters A,B,C,.... continue through AA, AB, AC,...BA, BB, BC,...,...to IT, IU, IV (denoting a maximum of $65,536 = 2^{16}$ columns). Rows labeled with "built-in" headers also range from 1...65,536. The letter–number row–column convention is similar to that seen in many geographical maps; it is a convenient address convention.

Plimpton 322 has four columns: the last column displays the row number and the second and third column headers are labeled width and diagonal. The other 15 rows and four columns are aligned left with base 60 cuneiform numbers. The Excel representation translated the original cuneiform numerals into our dotted decimal notation. Thus, cell C16 contains either the value $1\frac{46}{60}$ or, according to Babylonian convention, numbers such as $106(= 60 + 46)$ or 646 and so forth (it is not clear from the tablet context which power of 60 is meant). Some people think Plimpton 322 is a table of square roots.

Spreadsheet Evolution

The modern computer-based spreadsheet owes its design to Dan Bricklin and his 1979 release of VisiCalc for the Apple II personal computer.

VisiCalc pioneered the technology of spreadsheet formulas: cells have formula properties as well as display properties. For example, suppose you want to add the contents in cell D12 and D15 and place the result in cell E15. To do this, first select the cell E15.

Then type the formula text =D15+D12 (your typed text will be visible in the spreadsheet command box, called the *Formula Bar*). Typing an equal sign tells the spreadsheet interpreter that the following text must be evaluated as a formula or other expression. After you correctly type in the formula (and terminate it with the Enter or Return key), it is "entered" in cell E15. So if cell D15 displays the value 13 and cell D12 displays 10, then cell E15 will display 23(13+10).

Note that if we change the value in D12 to 20, then the value displayed in cell E15 is immediately updated to 33(13+20). This feature of automatic updating and propagation to all spreadsheet cells was so unique for a programming system that it was discussed in many books on artificial intelligence in the early 1980s. According to Bricklin,

> The idea for the electronic spreadsheet came to me while I was a student at the Harvard Business School, working on my MBA degree, in the spring of 1978. Sitting in Aldrich Hall, room 108, I would daydream. "Imagine if my calculator had a ball in its back, like a mouse . . . imagine if I had a heads-up display, like in a fighter plane, where I could see the virtual image hanging in the air in front of me. I could just move my mouse/keyboard calculator around, punch in a few numbers, circle them to get a sum, do some calculations, and answer "10% will be fine!"

In 1983, Lotus Software (now part of IBM) released Lotus 1-2-3. Lotus outsold VisiCalc and became the spreadsheet standard for DOS platforms. Microsoft Excel was first released in 1985 for the Macintosh platform; in 1987 it was released for Windows. Within 1 year Excel outsold all competitors (see Figure 3-1).

The "Sheet" in Spreadsheet

Within 10 years from its first appearance in 1979, the electronic spreadsheet (now in the alias of Microsoft Excel) became a financial technology standard for the syntax (display) and semantics (computation) of financial information. However, financial algorithms, bookkeeping reports, and spreadsheet formats were standardized much earlier.

One of the first financial uses of computers was in the "data processing" of financial records. Some of the first programming languages, such as Cobol (developed in 1959; Cobol is an acronym for COmmon Business Oriented Language), were designed to generate reports in standard "spreadsheet" format that bookkeepers and accountants were familiar with; any system that generated spreadsheet reports was always in demand.

The spreadsheet-based accounting and financial report standards we use today were formalized by Luca Pacioli in his 1494 *Summa* (see Box 2-3). Today's accountants call Pacioli the "Father of Accounting" because of his chapters on business systems and information management.

Pacioli's spreadsheets were based on the "modern" system used by the 15th-century Venetian merchants that he was familiar with. In the *Summa*, Pacioli reviewed how financial data should be laid out, processed, and presented in journals, books, and ledgers; his famous dictum is that accountants should not go to sleep until the debits account matched the credit account. His ledger recording system specified accounts for assets, receivables, inventories, liabilities, expenses, capital, and income. Pacioli specified the procedures for closing accounts at the end of a fiscal year and showed how to prove that a ledger was balanced. Pacioli specified financial algorithms in terms of positive numbers only became mainstream by the time of Descartes.

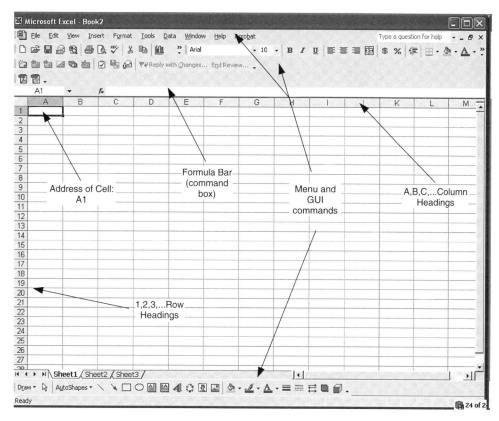

FIGURE 3-1   Excel spreadsheet system.

Box 3-2
Accounting, Spreadsheets, and Pacioli

Management Information Systems (MIS) technology has always been a major expense for financial and commercial applications. The technology of paper drove the technology of accounting and bookkeeping. As paper manufacturing technology developed and improved (from the 13th century onward), so did the algorithms used for MIS. However, paper remained expensive: in the 16th century, 24 sheets of paper cost the equivalent of a day's pay for a laborer. One could probably say that the goal of "straight through processing" and the "paperless office" probably dates from the 13th century.

In 13th century Italy, business schools (called *Liber Abbaci* or abacus schools) were open to students 12 years old and up. In Florence there were 6 abacus schools in the 1200s; by 1613, Nuremberg had 48 *Liber Abbaci*. The course curriculum (teachers were typically paid directly by the student) included arithmetic, abacus, decimal numbers, exchange rate algorithms, weights and measures, and accounting. The only textbooks in use at the time were too theoretical for most financial applications: these were either Fibonacci's book *Liber Abaci* or a Latin translation of al-Khwarizmi's *Al-jabr*. Consequently, Pacioli's *Summa* became an instant Gutenberg best seller.

In 1494, Pacioli showed students the concise and efficient Venetian report layouts for financial information on *fogli* (Italian: sheets) of paper; the sheets were eventually bound in books. In his book, Pacioli also helped students on the business ethics of accounting.

According to Pacioli, a typical layout (e.g., for a *foglio bilancio* or *balance sheet*) would have header columns for categories horizontally across the top and header rows denoting invoices listed vertically; the amount of each invoice–category payment would be in the area (cell) where row and column intersect. In practice, this layout would involve spreading a sheet of paper (with grid lines) across a desk (from Italian *desco*: table or work area). In 1555 the English coined the word *bookkeeper* to denote the person who records business accounts and transactions in a book of bound sheets. In 1588 England, the sheet layout was called a *ledger* (from an old English word *leggen*: to lay).

Accountants trained in Pacioli's Venetian method would visit their clients carrying collections of their sheets — a *portafoglio* (*porta*: to carry). In Italian, a portafoglio denotes a billfold, wallet, or "pocket book"; it has become a metonym for a set of commercial papers, financial papers, or a collection of securities. (The word *portfolio* entered the English language in 1722.)

In modern Italian, a spreadsheet (such as Excel) is called *fogli di calcolo* (calculating sheets) or *foglio elettronico* (electronic sheet); the "spread" does not appear.

Using Spreadsheet Technology

Chapter 2 showed that in T years, the future value $P(T)$ of an amount $P(0)$ that grows at a yearly rate R *continuously compounded* is

$$P(T) = P(0) \cdot e^{R \cdot T}$$

$$= P(0) \cdot \left[1 + (R \cdot T) + \frac{(R \cdot T)^2}{2} + \frac{(R \cdot T)^3}{6} + \cdot \frac{(R \cdot T)^4}{24} + \frac{(R \cdot T)^5}{120} + \frac{(R \cdot T)^7}{720} \cdots \right]$$

Figure 3-2 shows a spreadsheet that computes the six-term series approximation with Excel and compares this result with the Excel built-in function for exp.

Note that the Excel display commands (also called *graphical user interface* or GUI commands) help us define different font styles (i.e., **bold**) and numerical formats

	A	B	C	D	E	F
2						
3		R=	20%			
4		T=	1			
5		R*T =	0.2			
6						
7		k	fact	(R*T)^k	num/denom	
8		0	1	1	1.0000000000000000000	
9		1	1	0.2	0.2000000000000000000	
10		2	2	0.04	0.0200000000000000000	
11		3	6	0.008	0.0013333333333333300	
12		4	24	0.0016	0.0000666666666666667	
13		5	120	0.00032	0.0000026666666666667	
14		6	720	0.000064	0.0000000888888888889	
15						
16				**sum**	1.2214027555555600000	
17				**built-in**	1.2214027581601700000	
18						

FIGURE 3-2   Spreadsheet computations for continuous compounding.

(i.e., display 19 decimal places of precision). The interest rate input R is in cell C3, time T in years is in cell C4, and cell C5 computes the intermediate value $R^*T(=0.2)$. The numerator and denominator terms in the series are in columns C and D. For example, the term $\dfrac{(R \cdot T)^3}{6}$ corresponds to the row where k=3: 3!=6 is in cell C11 (the denominator) and $(R \cdot T)^3$ (the numerator) is in cell D11; the final result (numerator/denominator) for this term is cell E11.

When all these terms are entered, the results are all added: the final sum is shown in cell E16 and the value of Excel's built-in function $\exp(R^*T)$ is shown in cell E17. Note that these two expressions agree to nine decimal places. [The Excel built-in function computes $\exp(R^*T)$ to more than six terms.]

Note that this sheet only displays the results. We specified the actual computation via the = worksheet commands. We can display the worksheet computation by pressing CTRL + ` (grave accent); Figure 3-3 shows the actual formulas in each cell. (Note that typing CTRL + ` again toggles back to displaying values.)

Each cell starting with the equal sign specifies a computation that was entered manually. For example, cell C5 specifies that its content corresponds to the value in C4 multiplied by the value in C3. Cell C11 shows that its value is specified by the Excel's built-in factorial function FACT using the value B11 as input (because B11 displays 3, this is just 3!). The value in C11 is computed by raising the value in C5 to the power corresponding to the value displayed in B11; this is 0.2^3. Finally, the formula in E11 shows the value of the numerator (cell D11) divided by the denominator (cell C11). Results are summed in cell E16 using the Excel built-in function SUM, which as input works on the content displayed in the cell range from E8 to E14. The exp function formula is shown in E17.

Note that cell C5 is addressed as $C$5 in column D. This is Excel spreadsheet syntax for an *absolute reference*. An ordinary reference (i.e., C5 is called a *relative reference*). What is the difference? The answer is in how formulas can be copied and pasted on a sheet.

When formulas are copied and pasted, relative spatial positions are preserved according to Excel's spreadsheet programming rules; if, however, we want to always reference a *particular cell*, we need to make its reference absolute.

	A	B	C	D	E	F
2						
3		R=	0.2			
4		T=	1			
5		R*T =	=C4*C3			
6						
7		k	fact	(R*T)^k	num/denom	
8		0	=FACT(B8)	=$C$5^B8	=D8/C8	
9		1	=FACT(B9)	=$C$5^B9	=D9/C9	
10		2	=FACT(B10)	=$C$5^B10	=D10/C10	
11		3	=FACT(B11)	=$C$5^B11	=D11/C11	
12		4	=FACT(B12)	=$C$5^B12	=D12/C12	
13		5	=FACT(B13)	=$C$5^B13	=D13/C13	
14		6	=FACT(B14)	=$C$5^B14	=D14/C14	
15						
16				sum	=SUM(E8:E14)	
17				built-in	=EXP(C5)	
18						

FIGURE 3-3 Spreadsheet computations for continuous compounding (formulas).

A relative cell reference in a formula, such as the formula in cell C8 (that references cell B8), is based on the relative position of the cell that contains the formula and the cell the reference refers to. When you copy the formula across rows or down columns, the reference adjusts automatically. For example, when you copy the formula in cell C8 to cell C9, it changes the reference from B8 to B9 automatically. By default, all new Excel formulas use relative references.

An absolute cell reference in a formula, such as the reference to cell $C$5 in the formula in cell D8, always refers to a cell in a specific location. When you copy the formula across rows or down columns, the absolute reference does not adjust. For example, when you copy the formula in cell D8 to cell D9, the reference to $C$5 is not changed in cell D9.

The ability to handle both relative and absolute references reduces the development time for spreadsheet applications. For example, first type in the three formulas in cells C8, D8, E8 explicitly. For step 2, select the region C8:E8 by dragging with the mouse. Next, for Step 3, invoke the Excel Copy command (in the Edit menu); after that, in step 4, select the range C8:E14 by dragging with the mouse. Finally, for step 5, invoke the Excel Paste command (in the Edit menu): all formulas are then inserted correctly. In five simple steps formulas are inserted in 18 spreadsheet cells.

3.3. Interpreters and Compilers for Procedural Languages

Let us see some examples showing how traditional procedural languages are used for financial applications. As an example, we will specify the future value algorithm (that we computed with Excel in the previous section) in a few different procedural languages. Recall that the future value $P(T)$ of an amount $P(0)$ that grows at a yearly rate R *continuously compounded* is

$$P(T) = P(0) \cdot e^{R \cdot T}$$

$$= P(0) \cdot \left[1 + (R \cdot T) + \frac{(R \cdot T)^2}{2} + \frac{(R \cdot T)^3}{6} + \cdot \frac{(R \cdot T)^4}{24} + \frac{(R \cdot T)^5}{120} + \frac{(R \cdot T)^7}{720} \cdots \right]$$

The C Programming Language

C is one of the most popular languages; one reason is that it has a simple procedural semantics that translates very well into machine instructions: compiled C programs are fast and efficient. The popularity of C and Unix was enhanced further by nonrestrictive licensing terms to academic and research organizations.

C was developed between 1969 and 1973 at the AT&T Bell Telephone Laboratories by Ken Thompson and Dennis Ritchie. One of the primary applications for C was in the control and operation of telephone switches (in the 1970s, the telephone system evolved from mechanical to digital switching). The new Bell Labs computer operating system (called Unix) was also written in C in 1973.

In the 1980s, C became the language of choice for engineering and scientific programming on Unix platforms (these computers were called "engineering workstations");

C became the language of choice for DOS and Windows personal computer platforms as well. In 1983, the American National Standards Institute (ANSI) formed a committee to establish a C standard; in 1989 ANSI X3.159-1989 was adopted and C was also standardized by the International Organization for Standardization (ISO) as ISO/IEC 9899 in 1990.

Today, most Unix platforms provide a C compiler, called gcc, that is distributed by the GNU Project (part of the Free Software Foundation). The stated goal of the GNU project, which started in 1984, was to develop a free "Unix style operating system." Linux is one example of a GNU Unix system. (GNU is an acronym for *GNU's Not Unix*; it is traditionally pronounced *guh-noo*.)

C on Unix or Linux

To program in C, we first create one or more files containing text (the files are said to contain *source code*) that correspond to our ANSI C program. Then we use the C compiler and other translation tools: the compiler translates the text files into a computer readable representation and creates files with the last letters named .o (these files are said to contain *object code*).

The last step is to package the object code files with precompiled utilities and libraries (some specific to the computer that the resultant application will run on) to create an executable file (with the last letters usually named .exe). Sometimes these translation steps can be performed by a single command.

For example, suppose we have the algorithm represented in C that computes the future value of $1 that grows for 1 year at a continuously compounded annual rate of 20%. We save the program text in file PriceAppxC.c. Suppose we are in a Unix or Linux command box (sometimes called *the shell*); the prompt looks something like this

```
-bash-2.05b$
```

The Unix or Linux shell interpreter is waiting for commands; here, all commands are typed after the $. The gcc *compiler* is invoked with the following shell command:

```
-bash-2.05b$ gcc PriceAppxC.c - c
```

This tells gcc to compile source code file PriceAppxC.c into object code and save the result in file PriceAppxC.o (gcc creates this file and saves it to the current directory).

We next need to package the object code file with precompiled utilities and libraries to create the executable file PriceAppxC.exe (note that we can call this file any name we like). This step (called *linking*) is also accomplished with gcc. At the prompt, the gcc *linker* is invoked with the following command:

```
-bash-2.05b$ gcc - o PriceAppxC.exe *.o -lm
```

This command tells gcc to link all files ending in *.o with all precompiled library utilities (-lm) and then create file PriceAppxC.exe (which is an executable file). Note that the Unix or Linux commands are rather terse, which is good for experts and confusing for novices. The dashed letters are sometimes called compiler *switches*; different switches can also be used to affect different configurations and optimizations.

At this point, we can get the answer to our future value problem: we just need to execute PriceAppxC.exe and view the output. At a Unix or Linux shell prompt, execution is enabled by typing the name of the executable program, prefixed by a "./" (denoting the current directory). Box 3-3 shows the display.

Box 3-3
Executing a Program at the Unix Prompt

```
-bash-2.05b$ ./PriceAppxC.exe

1.2214027555555556000 : 6 Term Price
1.2214027581601699000 : Built-In Price
-bash-2.05b$
```

Figure 3-4 shows the entire process displayed in a Linux shell. The actual C program contained in file PriceAppxC.c is shown in Box 3-4.

In C, commands are terminated by a semicolon. A *main* program invokes component procedures or functions, which, in general, process their own data structures. One important innovation is *separate compilation* — separately compiled C components may be used by including their headers in the program specification (the instructions to the compiler are indicated by the "include macros"). Note that the executable program has no GUI or graphics; the C source file was compiled and linked as a simple *Console Application* — an application that runs in a command box. Embedding a GUI in the program would involve several hundred extra lines of C program text that would be necessary for specifying and controlling the GUI.

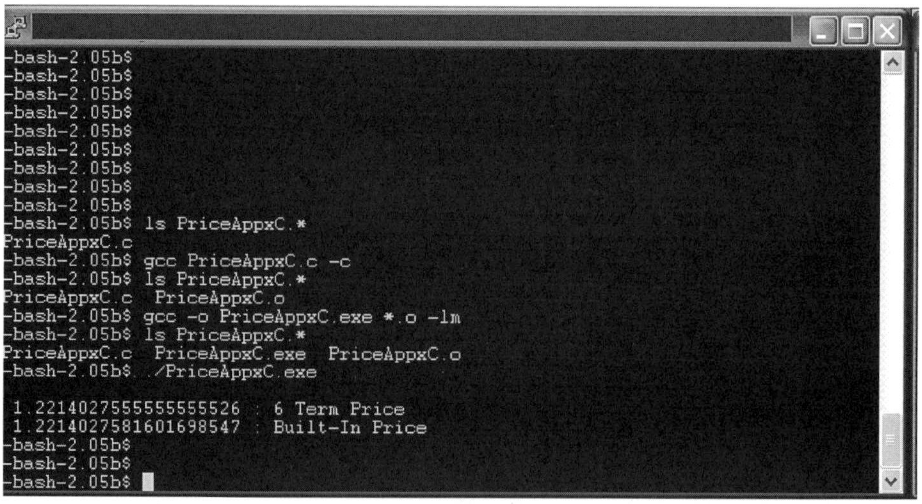

FIGURE 3-4   Compiling and executing a C program in a Linux shell.

Box 3-4
C Program for Continuous Compounding

```c
/* ANSI C Source: PriceAppxC.c; Target: PriceAppxC.exe
- Compute value of $1.00 at 20% continuous compounding.
- Compare built-in exp with a 6 term series  approximation.
*/
#include <math.h>
#include <stdio.h>

double PriceAppx(double T, double R){
     double sum=1.0, num=1.0, denom=1.0, RT;
     int i;
     RT = (R*T);
     for (i=1; i<=6; i++) {
          num = RT * num;
          denom = denom * i;
          sum = sum + num/denom;
     }
     return(sum);
}
int main() {
     double myPrice, builtinPrice;
     myPrice = PriceAppx(1.0, 0.20);
     builtinPrice = exp(1.0 * 0.20);
     printf("\n %20.19lf : 6 Term Price", myPrice);
     printf("\n %20.19lf : Built-In Price \n", builtinPrice );
     return 0;
}
```

C++ on Windows

Object-oriented (OO) constructs are designed to create and manage objects (packages of data structures, functions, and procedures) via a hierarchy of classes. As the OO paradigm became popular in the 1980s, OO constructs were wrapped around C (in an effort led by Bjarne Stroustrup at Bell Labs). The result was C++ (in 1998, becoming international standard ISO/IEC 14882).

We use the menu commands in Microsoft's Visual Studio to create a C++ console application that computes the future value of $1. Visual Studio is a development environment with its own set of menus, commands, and file configuration utilities for building applications.

We first need to create a project workspace for a console application. A workspace contains all the source code, object code, and executable files for our application (plus any other intermediate results). A workspace can be any name; if we name the workspace hello, then Visual Studio creates a directory called hello, saves all files in the directory, and saves all workspace information in files called hello.wpp and hello.dsw. Visual Studio also creates two subdirectories — Debug and Release — for different development configurations.

Next, we create our text file, PriceAppxCpp.cpp, containing our C++ program that computes the future value. Visual Studio has a Build menu that contains the command

```
Compile PriceAppxCpp.cpp
```

that translates and links the C++ text file into the executable representation. (Intermediate files are saved in a directory created by Visual Studio; the default directory is the Debug directory, but this can be changed with the Set Active Configuration... command on the Build menu). Linking is done with the Build hello.exe command on the Build menu. Note that these commands are combined with the single command Rebuild All. Figure 3-5 shows the Visual Studio display.

After the executable application hello.exe is created, it can be invoked directly within the Visual Studio environment with the Execute hello.exe command on the Build menu. In order to execute the application outside of the Visual Studio environment, the file hello.exe must be moved from the configuration directory (Debug or Release) and moved to a directory of choice. Then, at a Windows command box (sometimes called the *Command Prompt*), execution is enabled by typing hello.exe at the command prompt (see Box 3-5).

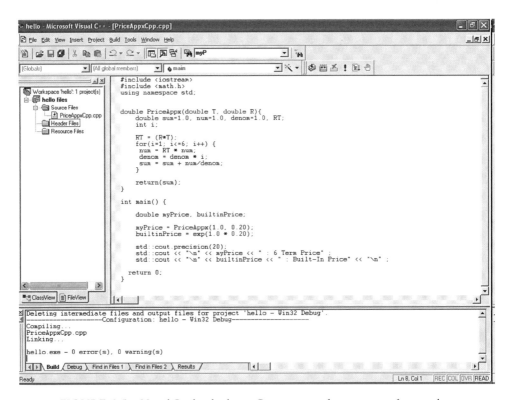

FIGURE 3-5   Visual Studio display: a C++ program that computes future value.

Box 3-5
Execution of C++ Program from Windows Command Prompt

```
C:\>hello.exe

1.2214027555555556 : 6 Term Price
1.2214027581601699 : Built-In Price

C:\>
```

The Windows Command Prompt looks just like a Unix or Linux shell (see Figure 3-6).

The C++ program is shown in Box 3-6. The syntax of C++ is almost identical to the syntax of C as far as commands are concerned. The only OO features used in this example involve the display of the output. The command

```
std::cout.precision(20);
```

is a syntactical construct termed a "method call" for the cout object in class std; it is used here to change the output precision for the numerical display. The symbol << is an "overloaded operator" for the output stream defined in class std.

Even though C++ is a descendant of C, there are incompatibilities and conflicting constructs that can confuse developers who program in both languages: programs and component libraries must be modified for compilation or execution as one or the other.

FIGURE 3-6   Windows Command Prompt.

Box 3-6
C++ Program to Compute Future Value

```cpp
// C++ Source: PriceAppxCpp.cpp; Target: PriceAppxCpp.exe
// Value of $1.00 in 1 year at 20%; continuous compounding.
// Compare C++'s built-in function for exp with a 6 term series.

#include <iostream>
#include <math.h>
using namespace std;

double PriceAppx(double T, double R){
      double sum=1.0, num=1.0, denom=1.0, RT;
      int i;
      RT = (R*T);
      for(i=1; i<=6; i++) {
            num = RT * num;
            denom = denom * i;
            sum = sum + num/denom;
      }
      return(sum);
}
int main() {
      double myPrice, builtinPrice;
      myPrice = PriceAppx(1.0, 0.20);
      builtinPrice = exp(1.0 * 0.20);
      std::cout.precision(20);
      std::cout << "\n" << myPrice << "  : 6 Term Price";
      std::cout << "\n" << builtinPrice << " : Built-In Price" << "\n";
return 0;
}
```

Visual Basic for Applications (VBA)

Another popular language used for financial applications is an implementation of Microsoft's Visual Basic that comes with all of the component tool kits of Microsoft Office.

VBA works very nicely with Microsoft Excel, as it can be used to specify financial algorithms based on procedural semantics in a way that utilizes Excel's GUI and graphics; unlike C and C++, VBA is integrated with Excel. Programmers do not have to spend time building customized user interfaces.

Here is the output of a VBA program, compiled as a *worksheet function*, called PriceAppx, that computes the future value of $1 that grows for 1 year at a continuously compounded annual rate of 20% (see Figure 3-7).

The VBA program specification is in cell C6; cell C7 shows the value of exp(0.20). Figure 3-8 shows the formula display.

	A	B	C	D
3				
4		**R**	20%	
5		**T**	1	
6		**6 term price:**	1.22140275555556000000	
7		**Built-In price:**	1.22140275816017000000	
8				

FIGURE 3-7

	A	B	C	D
3				
4		**R**	0.2	
5		**T**	1	
6		**6 term price:**	=PriceAppx(C4,C4)	
7		**Built-In price:**	=EXP(C4*C5)	
8				

FIGURE 3-8

We create the *VBA* program from the Visual Basic Editor, which is part of the Tools/Macro menu on a normal *Excel* spreadsheet. (When the Visual Basic Editor is launched, the Excel menubar changes to a VBA menu.) The VBA program is typed into a VBA *module* that is attached to the spreadsheet. The actual VBA program is shown in Box 3-7.

Box 3-7
VBA Program for Future Value Computation

```
'Visual Basic for Applications (VBA)
'Value of $1.00 in 1 year at 20%; continuous compounding.

Function PriceAppx(T As Double, R As Double)
    Dim sum As Double, num As Double, denom As Double
    Dim RT As Double

    RT = R * T
    sum = 1#
    num = 1#
    denom = 1#

    For i = 1 To 6
        num = RT * num
        denom = denom * i
        sum = sum + num / denom
    Next i
    PriceAppx = sum
End Function
```

The structure looks similar to the C and C++ function PriceAppx. One obvious syntax difference is that commands do not terminate with a semicolon: commands terminate with a "carriage return" or new line indicator. Note that spreadsheet cell input data are specified as a "Double," which is VBA for a decimal number.

Computer Algebra Systems

Computer algebra systems (CAS), typically based on interactive command interpreters, do symbolic mathematics. For example, typing in the text $2^*x + 2^*x$ in a command box would display 4^*x. These systems started appearing in the 1970s.

A CAS generally implement arbitrary precision arithmetic (colloquially called *bignum arithmetic*), which permits the evaluation of fractions to as many decimal places as desired (instead of being limited to approximately 16 places of "double precision" seen in C, C++, and VBA).

Powerful matching utilities implement algebra rules so that complicated algebraic expressions can be simplified. These systems embed rules of algebra, trigonometry, calculus, differential equations, and other subjects. They also have powerful tools for charts and graphs. Because of these facilities, CAS are starting to be used in many financial technology environments.

Box 3-8 shows a session with the MuPAD computer algebra system. Again, the goal is to compute the future value of $1 that grows for 1 year at a continuously compounded annual rate of 20%.

The MuPAD interpreter reads a line and displays a result. Like most interpreters, if it is unable to evaluate a command, it either returns the expression or it returns an error message. Note that both C and C++ style comments are supported.

The MuPAD text

```
PriceAppx:=(T,R)->sum((R*T)^k/fact(k),k=0..6)
```

uses the built-in factorial function and sum function (that adds an arbitrary number of terms). Note also that this expression

```
sum((0.2)^k/fact(k),k=0..infinity)
```

evaluates to

```
1.22140275816016908339
```

which is the MuPAD value of exp(1.0*0.2). Note that if you typed this expression into MuPAD

```
sum((R*T)^k/fact(k),k=0..infinity)
```

it evaluates to

```
exp(R T)
```

because the symbolic rules associated with series expansions of different functions are implemented in the system.

Box 3-8
MuPAD Session for Future Value Computation

- // MuPAD Session: note the dot is the MuPAD command prompt.
- // The interpreter ignores all text to the right of // (comments)
- // Value of $1.00 in 1 year at 20%; continuous compounding.
- // Compare MuPAD's built-in function exp with a 6 term series.
- // First: define function PriceAppx (a one line definition)
- PriceAppx := (T,R)->sum((R*T) ^k/fact(k), k=0..6)

  (T,R) -> sum((R*T) ^k/fact(k), k = 0..6)

- // Next: evaluate it for T=1 and R=20%
- PriceAppx(1,0.2)

  1.221402756

- // Change precision to 20 places and evaluate again
- DIGITS:=20

  20

- PriceAppx(1,0.2)

  1.2214027555555555556

- // Compare the result with the Built-In exp function
- exp(1.0*0.2)

  1.2214027581601698339

Most computer algebra systems also support conventional programming language control semantics: procedures can be written separately in an editor and either pasted or read in by the system. For example, the following procedure prints out all approximating terms of the continuously compounded problem

```
Pnew:=proc(T,R)
begin
    xsum:=0;
    for k from 0 to 6 do
    xsum:=xsum+(R*T)^k/fact(k);
    print(xsum)
    end_for
end_proc
```

The procedure can be saved in a file or typed directly in MuPAD (typing CTRL-ENTER or SHIFT-ENTER tells the interpreter to continue onto the next line).

Declarative vs. Procedural Semantics

As we have seen, most popular programming languages emphasize procedure and sequence. This is understandable because the original application communities were concerned with control of communication equipment. A *procedural semantics* corresponds to the following specification:

To accomplish a task:

1. Do this first.
2. Do this second.
3. If some condition is true
   3a. Do this
   3b. Otherwise, do this
4. Then do this while another condition is true
5. Finally, do this.

This specification (which looks like a cooking recipe) illustrates the "structured" way of describing the steps in an algorithm. The paradigm of *structured programming* — the set of semantic structures that recommend using a small set of syntactic control structures — originated with Edsger Dijkstra (1930–2002) in 1968. This structured approach is different from a purely procedural approach where each command is numbered or labeled and control can jump to any other labeled region of the text, as in "Go to step 13."

A spreadsheet specification is totally different. Its geometrical layout corresponds more to a map than to a recipe. Nevertheless, many financial algorithms are specified in terms of spreadsheets. The type of semantics that does not explicitly describe sequence is called *declarative semantics*.

In some sense, spreadsheet cells are equivalent to functions or variables in the procedural semantics paradigm. Cells may contain values and a formula that can use the contents of other cells. Spreadsheet formulas can also be linked to external data sources, such as real-time price feeds or a quote server.

Cells can also be considered as separate processes or as separate computer systems, each individually computing an answer in its cell and propagating that answer to other dependent computer system cells. Depending on the spreadsheet cell topology (and dependency network), formula operations can be executed in parallel. This implies that the spreadsheet model can be used to specify algorithms for distributed computing systems characterized by parallel and asynchronous execution. (Today, this parallel computing paradigm is called *grid computing*.)

3.4.   Spreadsheet Algorithms for Interpolating Prices and Rates

Banks (and other lenders) compete among themselves for investors. One way they compete is by offering different rates of return on money that an investor can earn over time, with the understanding that rational investors are attracted by higher return rates. For example, on November 1, 2005, Acme Trust Company publishes the following spreadsheet that lists the rates investors will receive if they purchase their *certificates of deposit* (see Figure 3-9).

	A	B
3	**Time**	**Interest**
4	**(Years)**	**Rate**
5	1	2.25%
6	2	2.50%
7	3	3.00%
8	5	4.00%
9	10	5.00%

FIGURE 3-9

	A	B	C
12	**Time**	**Interest**	**$100 is**
13	**(Years)**	**Rate (Spot)**	**worth**
14	1	2.25%	$102.25
15	2	2.50%	$105.06
16	3	3.00%	$109.27
17	5	4.00%	$121.67
18	10	5.00%	$162.89

FIGURE 3-10

These rates are *spot rates*; recall from Chapter 2 that a spot rate is a rate-of-return commitment over time on an investment starting today. In other words, an investor who commits money for 5 years (i.e., who lends Acme money for 5 years) by purchasing an Acme Trust 5-year CD will earn 5% per year. An alternate way of specifying this is by indicating how much a given amount of money would be worth at the end of the time period (see Figure 3-10).

This spreadsheet specifies what $100 would be worth at the end of 1, 2,…10 years. Note that rate and time are not the only parameters the bank uses; the bank must also specify the algorithm it uses for compounding. The aforementioned spreadsheet specifies annual compounding; this method is made clear when we look at the formulas (in Excel, made visible by toggling with CTRL-`) shown in Figure 3-11.

Each year money earns the quoted rate per maturity time; e.g., with the 5-year CD, money earns 4% each year. Note that for each maturity time, Acme knows in advance how much it has to return to the investor. If Stacy purchases a 5-year $100 CD on November 1, 2005, then Stacy will receive $121.67 on November 1, 2010. Note that these rates change: for example, on December 1, 2005, Acme's 5-year rate may jump down to 3.25% or may jump up to 5.25%. This does not affect Stacy's contractual commitment to 4% a year for the next 5 years.

	A	B	C
12	**Time**	**Interest**	**$100 is**
13	**(Years)**	**Rate (Spot)**	**worth**
14	1	0.0225	=100*(1+2.25%)
15	2	0.025	=100*(1+B15)^2
16	3	0.03	=100*(1+B16)^3
17	5	0.04	=100*(1+B17)^5
18	10	0.05	=100*(1+B18)^10

FIGURE 3-11

However, suppose that Stacy has an Aunt Daisy who is scheduled to pass away in exactly 3 years. Aunt Daisy plans to leave Stacy $100. Suppose Stacy plans to purchase a 2-year CD at that time. Stacy does not like uncertainty and she thinks that the CD rates will go down in a few years so her potential earnings will be less than the CD rates today. She asks Acme Trust if they can enter into a contract with her today, on November 1, 2005, for a 2-year CD that would start 3 years from now. What rate should Acme quote?

Here is another problem: suppose Stacy wants to commit money for 9 years. In this case, what rate should the bank quote? Should it be 4%, 5%, or something intermediate? These problems involve the jargon and algorithms of spot and forward rates and how prices and rates should be computed and interpolated.

Spot Rates and Interpolation

The rates specified earlier by the Acme Trust spreadsheets for their certificates of deposits are *spot rates*: a rate-of-return commitment over time on an investment starting today. For example, a T-year annually compounded spot rate R represents the constant yearly return on an investment. If P is initially invested, in T years, the investment grows to

$P \cdot (1+R)$ at the end of year 1

$P \cdot (1+R) \cdot (1+R)$ at the end of year 2

$P \cdot (1+R) \cdot (1+R) \cdot (1+R)$ at the end of year 3

. . .

$P \cdot (1+R) \cdot (1+R) \cdot (1+R) \ldots \cdot (1+R) = P \cdot (1+R)^T$ at the end of year T.

Spot rates can be compounded over different periods. Suppose the published Acme rates are compounded quarterly or compounded continuously. In these cases, the investor receives (for 1- and 2-year maturities) (see Figure 3-12). Note that as the compounding period increases, the returns on the investment increases. The spreadsheet formulas for this computation are shown in Figure 3-13.

Spot rates are really a surrogate for how prices evolve today to another time in the future. Suppose we are given today's price $P(0)$ and a price $P(T)$ at time T. The T year *spot rate* compounded over N periods is defined as the number R such that

$$P(T) = P(0) \cdot (1 + R/N)^\wedge (T^*N)$$

The T year *spot rate* compounded continuously is defined as the number R such that

$$P(T) = P(0)^* \exp(R^*T)$$

	A	B	C
21	**Time**	Compounded	**$100 is**
22	**(Years)**	Quarterly	**worth**
23	1	2.25%	$102.27
24	2	2.50%	$105.11
25		Compounded	
26		Continuously	
27	1	2.25%	$102.28
28	2	2.50%	$105.13

FIGURE 3-12

	A	B	C
21	**Time**	Compounded	**$100 is**
22	**(Years)**	Quarterly	**worth**
23	1	0.0225	=100*(1+2.25%/4)^4
24	2	0.025	=100*(1+B24/4)^(A24*4)
25		Compounded	
26		Continuously	
27	1	0.0225	=100*EXP(2.25%*1)
28	2	0.025	=100*EXP(B28*A28)

FIGURE 3-13

For example, today's 5-year spot rate compounded quarterly is the value R that satisfies

$$P(5) = P(0) \cdot (1 + R/4)^{\wedge}(5*4)$$

The formulas in Box 2-13 summarize the relationships among R, T, $P(0)$, and $P(T)$.

Interpolation Technology

How much interest should the Acme give Stacy for a 9-year investment? (Note that Acme can also refuse Stacy's business, claiming that they do not do execute "nonstandard" contracts.)

Suppose Acme gives Stacy the 5-year rate for a 9-year CD. This rate (the *lower constant threshold*) may be good for Acme but bad for the customer (and noncompetitive). Conversely, suppose Acme gives Stacy the 10-year rate for a 9-year CD. This rate (the *upper constant threshold*) may cause Acme to lose money.

Figure 3-14 shows a MuPAD-generated chart that shows CD rates with the upper constant threshold convention. To generate this chart, we need to first define the CD interest rate function $R(t)$ via

- R:=t->piecewise([t>0 and t<=1,0.0225],[t>1 and t<=2,0.0250], [t>2 and t<=3,0.03],[t>3 and t<=5,0.04], [t>5 and t<=10,0.05])

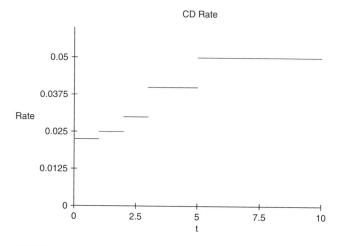

FIGURE 3-14   CD rates: upper constant threshold convention.

This specifies the same CD rates that are in the Excel spreadsheet: the difference is that it also provides an unambiguous upper constant threshold rule as to when to apply the rates. For example, in this specification, Acme gives the 10-year rate for a 9-year CD (note that the 10-year rate of 5.00% is given for all years greater than 5).

The MuPAD command that graphs the rate function $R(t)$ is

- `plotfunc2d(R(t),t=0.0..10.0, rate=0..0.06, Title="CD Rate")`

Here, the horizontal axis (labeled "t") ranges from 0 to 10, and the vertical axis (labeled "rate") ranges from 0 to 0.06.

Using either the lower or the upper constant threshold may cause problems for Acme; because of this, Acme may decide to use an interpolation algorithm.

Suppose Acme's policy is to use linear interpolation. Given (time, rate) pairs $(T1, R1)$ and $(T2, R2)$, the interpolated value for time value t between $T1$ and $T2$ is given by the weighted sum

$$X = A^* R1 + B^* R2$$

with

$$A = \frac{T2 - t}{T2 - T1}; \ B = 1 - A$$

In the Excel spreadsheet specification, A, B, and the interpolated 9-year CD rate are shown in Figure 3-15. The formula specification is shown in Figure 3-16.

Linear interpolation is intuitively appealing because it can be proved graphically with a little knowledge about similar triangles, as Figure 3-17 shows.

There are other interpolation technologies. The Babylonians had interpolation algorithms that required three or more values where they would fit "higher order curves" such as parabolas and circles to data. These as well as other techniques were formalized in the 18th century by Isaac Newton (1642–1727) and Joseph Louis Lagrange (1736–1813).

Today, the most popular interpolation algorithms used in financial technology applications are linear interpolation and cubic spline interpolation. Cubic spline interpolation

	I	J	K
43	A	B	Rate
44	0.2	0.8	4.80%

FIGURE 3-15

	I	J	K
43	A	B	Rate
44	=(10-9)/(10-5)	=1-I44	=0.2*4%+0.8*5%

FIGURE 3-16

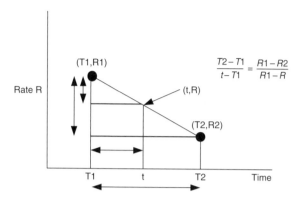

FIGURE 3-17   Linear interpolation: geometric rationale.

is used in most graphing and charting tools when requesting smooth looking plots. For scatter plots, Excel uses linear interpolation for charts showing "data points connected by lines" and cubic spline interpolation for charts showing "data points connected by smoothed lines." (Interpolation formulas are built into the charting tools; they are not generally available as Excel formulas.)

Yield Curves and Spline Interpolation

The U.S. Treasury uses cubic spline interpolation when creating a yield curve — a smooth graph showing interest rates over maturity times. According to the U.S. Treasury,

> The Treasury's yield curve is derived using a quasi-cubic hermite spline function. Our inputs are the...bid yields for the on-the-run securities....Treasury does not provide the computer formulation of our quasi-cubic hermite spline yield curve derivation program. However, we have found that most researchers have been able to reasonably match our results using alternative cubic spline formulas.

Figure 3-18 shows the yield curve for the Acme Trust CD rates using linear interpolation. The yield curve using cubic spline interpolation is shown in Figure 3-19. Which yield

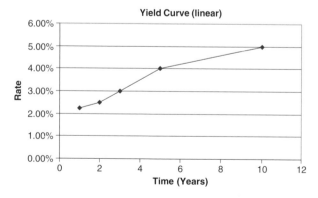

FIGURE 3-18   Yield curve for Acme Trust CD rates (linear interpolation).

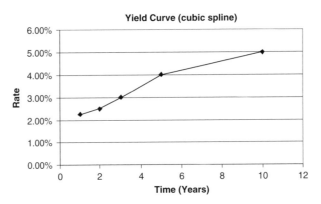

FIGURE 3-19   Yield curve for Acme Trust CD rates (cubic spline interpolation).

curve is correct? The answer depends on the contract agreement, not on the technology. (Note that the U.S. Treasury uses linear interpolation for computing values of its Treasury Inflation Protection Securities.)

Many finance professionals use the shape of a yield curve to induce the state of an economy. Some yield curve heuristics are summarized in Box 3-9.

Box 3-9
Yield Curve Heuristics

A *heuristic* (from Greek *heuriskein*: to find or discover; related to the word *eureka*) is a problem-solving method going back to ancient times that is characterized by experimental or trial-and-error procedures. Today, heuristics denote simple and easy-to-implement rules used for solving complex problems with uncertain or incomplete information. They cannot be rigorously proved. The idea is that heuristics "probably" will be successful in most (unexceptional) situations.

IF   the yield curve Slopes Upward
THEN   this implies a healthy economy.
A yield curve that slopes gently upward is frequently called a *normal* yield curve.
The yield curve in Figure 3-19 is normal

IF   the yield curve Slopes Downward
THEN   this implies a near term economic slowdown.
This is frequently called an *inverted* yield curve.

IF   the yield curve is Flat
THEN   this implies a transitional economy.
Pessimists induce a potential near term economic slowdown.

IF   the yield curve has a Steep Upward Slope
THEN   this implies an improving economy.
Optimists induce a potential quick near term economic expansion.

	D	E	F	G
40	**Time**	**Spot Rates**		
41	**(Years)**	**Spline0**	**Spline1**	**Spline3**
42	0	2.25%	2.00%	2.00%
43	**1**	2.25%	2.25%	2.25%
44	**2**	2.50%	2.50%	2.50%
45	**3**	3.00%	3.00%	3.00%
46	4	3.00%	3.80%	3.54%
47	**5**	4.00%	4.00%	4.00%
48	6	4.00%	4.20%	4.35%
49	7	4.00%	4.40%	4.60%
50	8	4.00%	4.60%	4.78%
51	9	4.00%	4.80%	4.90%
52	**10**	5.00%	5.00%	5.00%
53	11	5.00%	5.20%	5.10%
54	14	5.00%	5.80%	5.65%
55	16	5.00%	6.20%	6.48%

FIGURE 3-20

The spreadsheet shown in Figure 3-20 compares different interpolation algorithms. The known maturity times (1, 2, 3, 5, and 10 years) are in bold. The first interpolation method, called Spline0, is the upper constant threshold; Spline1 is linear interpolation and Spline3 is cubic spline interpolation. All algorithms were programmed in VBA. The spreadsheet shown in Figure 3-21 displays the formulas for Spline3 (the formulas for Spline0 and Spline1 have similar ranges).

Box 3-10 shows VBA implementation of the first two interpolation algorithms: upper constant threshold (Spline0) and linear interpolation (Spline1). Note that most of the work is concerned in determining the correct interval of the given known values (known values are sometimes called *knots*).

	A	B	D	G
40	**Time**	**Interest**	**Time**	
41	**(Years)**	**Rate**	**(Years)**	**Spline3**
42	1	0.0225	0	=spline3($A$42:$A$46,$B$42:$B$46,D42)
43	2	0.025	1	=spline3($A$42:$A$46,$B$42:$B$46,D43)
44	3	0.03	2	=spline3($A$42:$A$46,$B$42:$B$46,D44)
45	5	0.04	3	=spline3($A$42:$A$46,$B$42:$B$46,D45)
46	10	0.05	4	=spline3($A$42:$A$46,$B$42:$B$46,D46)
47			5	=spline3($A$42:$A$46,$B$42:$B$46,D47)
48			6	=spline3($A$42:$A$46,$B$42:$B$46,D48)
49			7	=spline3($A$42:$A$46,$B$42:$B$46,D49)
50			8	=spline3($A$42:$A$46,$B$42:$B$46,D50)
51			9	=spline3($A$42:$A$46,$B$42:$B$46,D51)
52			**10**	=spline3($A$42:$A$46,$B$42:$B$46,D52)
53			11	=spline3($A$42:$A$46,$B$42:$B$46,D53)
54			14	=spline3($A$42:$A$46,$B$42:$B$46,D54)
55			16	=spline3($A$42:$A$46,$B$42:$B$46,D55)

FIGURE 3-21

Box 3-10
VBA Implentation of Spline0 and Spline1

```
Function spline0(Ts, Ys, x)
    n = Ts.Rows.Count
    For j = 1 To n
        If x < Ts(j) Then Exit For
    Next j
    If x >= Ts(n) Then j = n + 1
    If j <= 1 Then j = 2
    spline0 = Ys(j - 1)
End Function

Function spline1(Ts, Ys, x)
    Dim A1 As Double, B1 As Double
    n = Ts.Rows.Count

    For j = 1 To n
        If x <= Ts(j) Then Exit For
    Next j
    If j <= 1 Then j = 1
    If j >= n Then j = n - 1
    A1 = (Ts(j + 1) - x) / (Ts(j + 1) - Ts(j))
    B1 = 1 - A1
    spline1 = A1 * Ys(j) + B1 * Ys(j + 1)
End Function
```

MuPAD and other systems have built-in cubic spline interpolation functions. For example, in MuPAD, the following defines spline function S3 and uses it to evaluate the interest rate for a 9-year investment given Acme data

- S3:=numeric::cubicSpline([1,2,3,5,10],
      [0.0225,0.0250,0.0300,0.0400,0.0500], Natural)
      proc S3(z)...end

- S3(9)
      0.04900392157

Forward Rates

Aunt Daisy plans to leave Stacy $100. Suppose Stacy plans to purchase a 2-year CD at that time. Stacy does not like uncertainty and she thinks that the CD rates will go down in a few years so her potential earnings will be less than the CD rates today. She asks Acme Trust if they can enter into a contract with her today, on November 1, 2005, for a 2-year CD that would start 3 years from now. What rate should Acme quote?

Box 3-11

The Technology of Spline Interpolation

Spline interpolation was one of the most significant and useful innovations for financial technology applications involving prices, rates, and graphs that appeared in the last 200 years. It was invented by Isaac Schoenberg (1903–1990) during the years 1943–1945. Schoenberg worked as a mathematician at the U.S. Army Ballistic Research Laboratory in Aberdeen, Maryland (the Aberdeen Proving Ground). In a biographical note, Schoenberg recalls the problem:

> The morning in August 1943 of my reporting for duty, Major A. A. Bennett, of Brown University, then Chief of the Computing Branch of the BRL [Ballistics Research Laboratory], told me what my particular problem was to be: Trajectories of projectiles were until then computed with desk calculators by hand…. In performing these computations on the ENIAC, which was very fast, a much simpler integration method of very small step could be used. In these methods, the accumulation of the round-off errors was unacceptable due to the rough drag-function tables; they needed to be smoothed by being approximated by analytic functions. To do this was my problem. I solved this problem by what later I called Cardinal Spline Interpolation and Cardinal Spline Smoothing. To insure the smoothness, to 8 decimal places, of the second derivative of the approximant of the drag-function, I used the heat-flow equation on the real axis to produce approximations regular on the entire real axis. Only the fine resources of the BRL made this work possible. We had advanced (but not electronic) punched-card machines which were well suited for this work.

Schoenberg's essential idea was to create special curves that maintained certain smoothness constraints: corners were to be eliminated as much as possible. He called his algorithm after a ship builder's *spline* tool — a flexible piece of wood that could be nailed in place and warped to fit a desired smooth shape without any breakage or sharp corners. As computing power got less expensive and more reliable, Schoenberg's splines became the method of choice for interpolation, graphing, and computer-aided design.

Schoenberg's computer, the ENIAC (Electronic Numerical Integrator And Computer), was the first programmable electronic computer. It weighed 30 tons and could execute about 400 multiplications per second (it could also do almost 40 divisions per second). It was installed at the Aberdeen Proving Ground in May 1943; a computer program involved rewiring thousands of switches and cables (with a team of eight programmers). ENIAC was used for over 12 years. In operation, one of its 17,468 vacuum tubes would burn out every other day (it once ran 5 days without crashing).

Contracts that specify future interest rates are called forward rate agreements. Figure 3-22 shows how Acme can specify these agreements today. The spot rates given by the different CDs specify how much $100 will earn 1, 2, 3, 5, and 10 years from today. We use these results to compute the returns on investment from years 1 to 2, 2 to 3, 3 to 5, and 5 to 10.

	A	B	C	D	E	F	G
12	Time	Interest	$100 is				
13	(Years)	Rate (Spot)	worth			Return	Annualized Rate
14	1	2.25%	$102.25	From year	...to year	on Investment	(Forward Rate)
15	2	2.50%	$105.06	1	2	2.75%	2.75%
16	3	3.00%	$109.27	2	3	4.01%	4.01%
17	5	4.00%	$121.67	3	5	11.35%	5.52%
18	10	5.00%	$162.89	5	10	33.88%	6.01%

FIGURE 3-22

We use the formulas in Box 2-13 for R in terms of T, $P(0)$, and $P(T)$ to compute the annual rates under yearly compounding from years 1 to 2, 2 to 3, 3 to 5, and 5 to 10. The formulas are displayed in Figure 3-23.

These rates showing price evolution (given today's spot rates) from years 1 to 2, 2 to 3, 3 to 5, and 5 to 10 are called *forward rates*. These are the rates that Acme should quote Stacy today for a *forward rate agreement*.

For quarterly compounding, the forward rates are shown in Figure 3-24. The quarterly compounded formulas are displayed in Figure 3-25. For continuous compounding, the

	D	E	F	G
13			Return	Annualized Rate
14	From year	...to year	on Investment	(Forward Rate)
15	1	2	=(105.06-102.25)/102.25	=(C15/C14)^(1/(A15-A14))-1
16	2	3	=(C16-C15)/C15	=(C16/C15)^(1/(A16-A15))-1
17	3	5	=(121.67-109.27)/109.27	=(121.67/109.27)^(1/(5-3))-1
18	5	10	=(C18-C17)/C17	=(C18/C17)^(1/(A18-A17))-1

FIGURE 3-23

	A	B	C	D	E	F	G
21	Time	Compound	$100 is				
22	Years	Quarterly	worth	From	..to	Return on	Ann. QC Rate
23	1	2.25%	$102.27	year	year	Investment	(Forward Rate)
24	2	2.50%	$105.11	1	2	2.78%	2.75%
25	3	3.00%	$109.38	2	3	4.06%	4.00%
26	5	4.00%	$122.02	3	5	11.56%	5.51%
27	10	5.00%	$164.36	5	10	34.70%	6.00%

FIGURE 3-24

	D	E	F	G
22	From	..to	Return on	Ann. QC Rate
23	year	year	Investment	(Forward Rate)
24	1	2	=(105.11-102.27)/102.27	=((C24/C23)^(1/(4*(A24-A23)))-1)*4
25	2	3	=(C25-C24)/C24	=((C25/C24)^(1/(4*(A25-A24)))-1)*4
26	3	5	=(122.02-109.38)/109.38	=((122.02/109.38)^(1/(4*(5-3)))-1)*4
27	5	10	=(C27-C26)/C26	=((C27/C26)^(1/(4*(A27-A26)))-1)*4

FIGURE 3-25

Box 3-12

Spot Rates, Forward Rates, and Prices: Summary of Relationships

Suppose that we know the spot rate $R(0, T)$ at time T, the spot rate $R(0, TA)$ at time TA, and the forward rate $R(T, TA)$ from T to TA. Note that the price at time T is $P(T)$ and the price at time TA is $P(TA)$, with $P(T)$ evolving to $P(TA)$ at forward rate $R(T, TA)$. Also, $P(0)$ evolves to $P(T)$ at spot rate $R(0, T)$ and also $P(0)$ evolves to $P(TA)$ at spot rate $R(0, TA)$. Pictorially, this is represented as

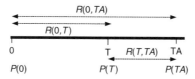

Under N-period compounding, the evolution of $P(T)$ to $P(TA)$ is given as

$$P(TA) = P(T) \cdot (1 + R(T, TA)/N)^{(TA-T) \cdot N} \text{ or}$$

$$P(TA) = P(0) \cdot (1 + R(T)/N)^{T \cdot N} \cdot (1 + R(T, TA)/N)^{(TA-T) \cdot N} = P(0) \cdot (1 + R(TA)/N)^{TA \cdot N}$$

This simplifies to

$$(1 + R(T)/N)^T \cdot (1 + R(T, TA)/N)^{(TA-T)} = (1 + R(TA)/N)^{TA}, \text{ so}$$

$$R(T, TA) = N \cdot \left(\left[\frac{(1 + R(TA)/N)^{TA}}{(1 + R(T)/N)^T} \right]^{1/(TA-T)} - 1 \right) = N \cdot \left(\left[\frac{P(TA)}{P(T)} \right]^{1/(TA-T)} - 1 \right)$$

Under continuous compounding, evolution of $P(T)$ to $P(TA)$ is given as

$$P(TA) = P(T) \cdot e^{R(T,TA) \cdot (TA-T)}, \text{ so}$$

$$P(TA) = P(0) \cdot e^{R(T) \cdot T} \cdot e^{R(T,TA) \cdot (TA-T)} = P(0) \cdot e^{R(TA) \cdot TA}$$

This simplifies to

$$R(T, TA) = \frac{R(TA) \cdot TA - R(T) \cdot T}{(TA - T)} = \frac{1}{(TA - T)} \ln \left(\frac{P(TA)}{P(T)} \right)$$

Under continuous compounding, the formula for the forward rate in terms of the two spot rates resembles the formula for linear interpolation.

	A	B	C	D	E	F	G
29	Time	Compounded	$100 is				
30	Years	Continuously	worth	From	..to	Return on	Ann. CC Rate
31	1	2.25%	$102.28	year	year	Investment	(Forward Rate)
32	2	2.50%	$105.13	1	2	2.79%	2.75%
33	3	3.00%	$109.42	2	3	4.08%	4.00%
34	5	4.00%	$122.14	3	5	11.62%	5.50%
35	10	5.00%	$164.87	5	10	34.99%	6.00%

FIGURE 3-26

	D	E	F	G
30	From	..to	Return on	Ann. CC Rate
31	year	year	Investment	(Forward Rate)
32	1	2	=(C32-C31)/C31	=(1/(E32-D32))*LN(C32/C31)
33	2	3	=(C33-C32)/C32	=(1/(E33-D33))*LN(C33/C32)
34	3	5	=(122.14-109.42)/109.42	=(1/(5-3))*LN(122.14/109.42)
35	5	10	=(C35-C34)/C34	=(1/(E35-D35))*LN(C35/C34)

FIGURE 3-27

forward rates are given in Figure 3-26. The continuously compounded formulas are shown in Figure 3-27. Note that the forward rates are not the future rates. Because CD spot rates can change from day to day, forward rates can also change from day to day: future spot and forward rates today are, in general, different from today's spot and forward rates. Box 3-12 summarizes the relationships between forward and spot rates.

3.5. Notes and References

Quotes from Sumerian and Babylonian financial texts are from
[0.1] Karen Rhea Nemet-Nejat. *Cuneiform Mathematical Texts as a Reflection of Everyday Life in Mesopotamia.* American Oriental Society, 1993. ISBN 0940490757.

Financial Algorithms

See the general technology and history references of Chapter 1.

Spreadsheets

A picture of Plimpton 322, together with a commentary, is available at the
[1] MacTutor History of Mathematics archive, maintained by the School of Mathematics and Statistics of the University of St. Andrews in Scotland
http://www-groups.dcs.st-and.ac.uk/~history/HistTopics/Babylonian_Pythagoras.html

The idea of VisiCalc, together with some spreadsheet history, is at inventor Dan Bricklin's Web page at
[2] http://www.danbricklin.com/history/saiidea.htm

The VisiCalc electronic spreadsheet was considered an artificial intelligence application (a "numeric constraint propagation for adder-multiplier networks") in Chapter 3 of
[3] Patrick Winston. *Artificial Intelligence* (2nd edition). Addison-Wesley Publishing Company, Reading, MA, 1984. ISBN 0-201-08259-4.

Interpreters and Compilers for Procedural Languages

The history and development of the C language is described by inventor
[4] Dennis Ritchie. "The Development of the C Language." In *History of Programming Languages-II* (ed. by Thomas J. Bergin, Jr. and Richard G. Gibson, Jr.), ACM Press (New York) and Addison-Wesley, Reading, MA, 1996. ISBN 0-201-89502-1 (available on the Web).

Structured programming owes its start to the Letter to the Editor written by
[5] Edsger Dijkstra. "Go To Statement Considered Harmful." *Communications of the ACM*, Vol. 11, No. 3, March 1968 (available at http://www.acm.org/classics/oct95/).

The spline methods used by the U.S. Treasury are described at
[6] http://www.treas.gov/offices/domestic-finance/debt-management/interest-rate/

The development of splines is described by their inventor in
[7] Isaac Schoenberg. "A brief account of my life and work." In I. J. Schoenberg, *Selected Papers* (ed. by C. de Boor), Birkhäuser, Boston, 1988. ISBN: 0-8176-3378-2 (available at http://www.cs.wisc.edu/~deboor/HAT/sch.html).

The MuPAD computer algebra system is available at
[8] http://www.mupad.de

3.6. Discussion Questions

1. What was the impact of VisiCalc and Lotus 1-2-3 on Wall Street in the 1980s?

2. Compare the development speed among the spreadsheet version of the future value problem, the C version, the C++ version, the VBA version, and the MuPAD version. Which language requires the most training? Which requires the most computer resources? Which executes faster? Which language is better for interactive applications? Which is better for automated applications that run on a Web server? Using these factors, which is less expensive to use? Does the market agree with your answers?

3. What are the advantages and disadvantages of the different spline methods used to interpolate a yield curve?

4. Why won't the U.S. Treasury make the spline algorithm that they use public?

5. Find an implementation of a cubic spline algorithm in C, C++, and VBA.

6. Are forward rates the actual future spot interest rates?

7. Why do you think the Babylonian accountants were held in such high esteem?

8. In later editions of [3], spreadsheets were no longer being used as examples of artificial intelligence. Why?

9. Pacioli 1494 accounting standards did not rely on negative numbers: they were not yet invented. Explain how modern accounting avoids negative numbers.

10. Show an example of a spreadsheet in Pacioli's 1494 *Summa* (see [7] in Chapter 2).

CHAPTER ◆ 4

Financial Products

> At the place where man goes to study the scribal art,
> In the place of learning the secret arts,
> Subtracting, Adding, Counting, and Accounting, he completes
> The regulations of the nation,
> Their given wisdom I have also mastered…
>
> — Sumerian poem attributed to King Shulgi (ca. 2094–2047 BCE)

4.1. Technology of Cash Flows

Suppose it is known that Stacy's farm crop always produces $300 a year in agricultural produce. Marie enters into a contract with Stacy today to purchase the crops for the next 3 years. How much is Marie's contract worth?

Cash Flow Valuations and Interest Rates

To solve the problem, we need to sum the value of the three cash flows — discounted to today's present value. If we use rates given in Figure 3-9 for the Acme Trust Company CDs as a surrogate for spot rates, we find (rounded off to the nearest cent):

$$\text{the value today of \$300 at the end of year 1 is } \frac{300}{(1+2.25\%)} = \$293.40$$

$$\text{the value today of \$300 at the end of year 2 is } \frac{300}{(1+2.50\%)^2} = \$285.54$$

$$\text{the value today of \$300 at the end of year 3 is } \frac{300}{(1+3.00\%)^3} = \$274.54$$

The sum of these three cash flows, discounted to the present assuming the Acme CD rates, is $853.49.

In financial mathematics, discounted cash flow sums are denoted with the Greek letter sigma (Σ). Sigma is the Greek capital "S" (or "Sh"). The sigma notation corresponding to the solution of the aforementioned problem is

$$CF = \sum_{t=1}^{3} \frac{300}{(1+R(t))^t} = \frac{300}{(1+2.25\%)} + \frac{300}{(1+2.50\%)^2} + \frac{300}{(1+3.00\%)^3}.$$

In the sigma notation, CF represents the present value of future cash flows. The value $R(t)$ is a function that represents the spot rate for maturity at time t, measured in years. Note that t is used as an index in the summation, corresponding to the years 1 to 3.

The sigma notation is similar to those found in algebraic systems such as MuPAD:

- ```// Create the interest rate function R(t)```
- ```R:=t->piecewise([t>0 and t<=1,0.0225],[t>1 and t<=2,0.0250],```
- ```[t>2 and t<=3,0.03],[t>3 and t<=5,0.04],[t>5 and t<=10,0.05])```
- ```//```
- ```sum(300/(1+R(t))^t,t=1..3)```

```
853.4853497
```

In Excel, the cash flow summation problem is represented by the spreadsheet shown in Figure 4-1, with formulas shown in Figure 4-2. Note that all spot rate data and intermediate computations are represented in cells; the Excel Sum function in cell F8 adds the values displayed in its input cell range.

	C	D	E	F
2	Cash Flow	Spot		Present
3	Year	Rate	Discount	Value
4	1	2.25%	0.97799511	$293.40
5	2	2.50%	0.951814396	$285.54
6	3	3%	0.915141659	$274.54
7				
8			Sum:	$853.49

FIGURE 4-1

	C	D	E	F
2	Cash Flow	Spot		Present
3	Year	Rate	Discount	Value
4	1	0.0225	=1/(1+D4)^C4	=300*E4
5	2	0.025	=1/(1+D5)^C5	=300*E5
6	3	0.03	=1/(1+D6)^C6	=300*E6
7				
8			Sum:	=SUM(F4:F6)

FIGURE 4-2

Box 4-1

Technology of Discounted Cash Flow Sums and Sigmas

The sigma notation for sums was invented in 1755 by Leonhard Euler (1707–1783). Some programming languages and computer algebra systems have a Σ-style sum defined as a built-in function. Keyboard conventions require that all symbols be located on one line. For example, the summation

$$CF = 300^* \sum_{t=1}^{3} \frac{1}{(1+20\%)^t}$$

is written in MuPAD as

```
CF := 300 * ( sum( 1/ (1+0.20)^t, t=1..3 )
```

or in AMPL as

```
CF := 300 * ( sum{t in 1..3} 1/ (1+0.20)^t );
```

Each cash flow in the summation is discounted to the present via multiplication by

$$\frac{1}{(1+R(t))^t} \quad \text{or} \quad \frac{1}{(1+r)^t}$$

These values are sometimes called *discount functions*.

Note that Both AMPL and MuPAD allow expressions like this

```
CF := 300 * ( sum {t in 1..3} c(t) * B(t) );
```

as long as c(t) and B(t) are defined somewhere in the program. In some sense, the result of multiplying c(t)*B(t) is passed to the sum function. (In lower level languages like C, this is implemented using a construct called function pointers.)

Microsoft Excel's has a built-in sum function, but it is not a Σ-style sum. Excel's SUM adds a set of numbers that are given explicitly in a list or in a reference to spreadsheet cells. For example,

=SUM(3,4,5) evaluates to 12
=SUM(B2:B4) sums up the numbers in cells B2, B3, and B4.

However, Excel implements built-in functions for specific financial applications that can be used to evaluate sums if the spot interest rates are all equal (such as the PV function for present value and the FV function for future value).

General Specifications of Discounted Cash Flows

Suppose we know the annual spot rate function $R(t)$ and the cash flow function $c(t)$; these provide us with the yearly spot interest rates and the yearly future amounts that the crops are worth. The sum of the yearly discounted cash flows is denoted by

$$CF = \sum_{t=1}^{T} \frac{c(t)}{(1+R(t))^t} = \left(\frac{c(1)}{(1+R(1))} + \frac{c(2)}{(1+R(2))^2} + \cdots + \frac{c(T)}{(1+R(T))^T} \right)$$

In MuPAD notation this is just

```
CF:=sum( c(t)/(1+R(t))^t, t=1..T )
```

Note that for yearly continuously compounded rates, the summation is

$$CF = \sum_{t=1}^{T} c(t) \cdot e^{-R(t)} = c(1) \cdot e^{-R(1)} + \cdots + c(T) \cdot e^{-R(T)}$$

and in MuPAD notation this is just

```
CF:=(sum( c(t)*exp(-R(t), t=1..T )
```

Suppose we divide the cash flow for each year evenly into a set of partial cash flows across the year. For example, instead of paying one payment of $300 for the crop at the end of the year, we can make one payment for $150 on July 1 and another payment for $150 on December 31, with each payment 6 months apart.

In general, suppose we have N cash flows per year; each payment is $c(t)/N$ dollars, payable at regular intervals $1/N$ years apart, where we have a total of $N \cdot T$ payments, with each payment compounded over each period: the interest rate for each fractional yearly time period is $R(t/N)/N$, with t ranging from 1 to $N \cdot T$. The cash flow sum is

$$CF = \sum_{t=1}^{N \cdot T} \frac{c(t/N)/N}{(1+R(t/N)/N)^t}$$

and in MuPAD notation this is just

```
CF :=(sum( (c(t/N)/N)/(1+(R(t/N)/N))^t, t=1..N*T )
```

For example, for monthly cash flows and monthly compounding ($N = 12$), the crops generate $300/12 = \$25$ per month. The total cash flow amount is then

- ```sum((300/12)/(1+(R(t/12)/12))^t,t=1..3*12)```

    863.0641633

As the number of cash flows increases without limit, we are adding an infinite number of infinitesimal cash flows — a sum of a continuous cash flow. For example, for daily cash flows with daily compounding (for a 365-day year), we have

- ```sum((300/365)/(1+(R(t/365)/365))^t,t=1..3*365)```

    863.9203579

Note that according to the results on continuous compounding shown in Box 2-13, via a change of timescale, we get

$$(1 + R(t/N)/N)^t = (1 + R(s)/N)^{N \cdot s} \quad \text{for} \quad s = t/N \quad \text{and} \quad t = 1..N \cdot T$$

As N increases,

$$(1 + R(s)/N)^{N \cdot s} \quad \text{converges to} \quad e^{s \cdot R(s)}$$

In 1822, Jean Baptiste Joseph Fourier (1768–1830) established the notation convention used today to denote this limiting sum, so as N increases,

$$CF = \sum_{t=1}^{N \cdot T} \frac{c(t/N)/N}{(1 + R(t/N)/N)^t} \quad \text{is represented by} \quad \int_0^T e^{-t \cdot R(t)} \cdot c(t) \cdot dt$$

Infinite sums of infinitesimal quantities are called *integrals*. They were first used by Archimedes (287–212 BCE); he approximated the areas under arbitrary curves by summing the areas of rectangles of smaller and smaller widths. So in some sense, the present value of the cash flows from 0 to T is related to the area under the curve $y(t) = e^{-R(t) \cdot t} \cdot c(t)$ formed by the spot rate $R(t)$ and the cash flow function $c(t)$.

The elongated S was first used by Gottfried Wilhelm Leibniz (1646–1716) in 1675 in his development of integral calculus. Tables of integrals and methods for their evaluation are embedded in most computer algebra systems. In MuPAD, the (numerical – not symbolic) evaluation of the integral for continuous cash flow is

- `numeric::int(300*exp(-t*R(t)), t=0..3)`

  863.9495042

Suppose the yearly spot rates and cash flows are constant (and are both positive): $c(t) = A(>0)$ and $R(t) = r(>0)$. In this case, closed form formulas can be derived for fixed and continuous cash flows over T years.

In MuPAD notation, the formulas are

- `//Interest rates, cash flow, periods must be positive`
  `assume(r>0),assume(A>0), assume(N>0):`

- `//Formula for Yearly compounding`
- `sum(A/(1+r)^t,t=1..T)`

```
        /   1   \ T
   A - A |  ----- |
        \ r + 1 /
   ------------------
           r
```

- `//Formula for N-period compounding: 1 year = N periods`
- `sum((A/N)/(1+(r/N))^t,t=1..N*T)`

```
        /   N   \ N T
   A - A |  ----- |
        \ N + r /
   ------------------
           r
```

- `//Formula for Continuous Cash Flow:`
- `int(A*exp(-t*r), t=0..T)`

$$\frac{A}{r} - \frac{A}{r\,\exp(T\ r)}$$

So, for example, for $A = \$300$, $T = 3$ years and $r = 3\%$, we have

$$\text{CF} = \$848.5834065 \text{ for yearly compounding}$$

$$\text{CF} = \$859.6616275 \text{ for monthly compounding}$$

$$\text{CF} = \$860.6881473 \text{ for continuous cash flow}$$

The language of cash flows is used most often when evaluating bonds and mortgages.

A bond is a loan for a set amount of money P (called the *principal* or *face value*) for a length of time T (called the maturity); periodically, the borrower may provide the lender a predetermined cash flow. At time T, the value P is repaid. In bond terminology, each cash flow $c(t)$ is called a coupon (entering English in 1822, from French: *couper* to cut, as the interest payment is cut out of the bond).

Sometimes the coupons are expressed as a fixed percentage (called a *coupon rate*) of the principal. For example, if the bond's principal is $10,000 and its coupon rate is 4%, then the coupons are all $4\%*\$10,000 = \$400$.

If there is no credit risk (i.e., the borrower will not default and everything will be repaid), the present value of a bond (today at time $t = 0$) that pays principal P at maturity time T and that also pays a yearly cash flow $c(t)$ is

`Bond:=sum(c(t)/(1+R(t))^t, t=1..T)+P/(1+R(t))^T`

In other words, the present value of a *coupon bond* today is the present values of its cash flows and the present value of the principal returned at time T:

`Bond:=CF+P/(1+R(t))^T`

For period compounding

`Bond:=sum(c(t/N)/(1+R(t/N))^t, t=1..N*T)+P/(1+R(N*T))^(N*T)`

Another type of bond is a mortgage. The cash flows in a mortgage are used to sum up to an agreed upon value (called the principal). In other words, given a principal P and a spot rate function $R(t)$, the problem is to find the period cash flows $c(t)$ such that

`sum(c(t/N)/(1+R(t/N))^t, t=1..N*T)=P`

If the yearly spot rates and cash flows are constant (and are both positive): $c(t) = A(>0)$ and $R(t) = r(>0)$. In this case, closed form formulas for the bonds and for the coupon can be derived for fixed and continuous cash flows.

For bonds (N period compounding): Present value of principal $P =$

- `sum((A/N)/(1+r/N)^t, t=1..N*T)+P/(1+r/N)^(N*T)`

$$\frac{P}{\left(\dfrac{r}{n}+1\right)^{N\,T}} + \frac{A - A\left(\dfrac{N}{N+r}\right)^{N\,T}}{r}$$

Box 4-2

Mortgages, Vivgages, and Bonds

Ancient Rome provided two different types of loans or bonds. A *pignus* (Latin: *pawn*, to deposit in pledge) required that the security for the loan (e.g., property) be given to the lender; the security will be returned on repayment of the loan. In a *hypothec*, the security remained with the borrower, but could be seized by the lender if the borrower defaulted. (The use of *hypothecated* loans on the Amsterdam Stock Exchange was discussed by Joseph de la Vega; see Section 1.1.) Differences concerned the cost of litigation in the event of default. For pignus, the borrower paid the cost for litigation; for hypothec, the lender bore the cost. As in many real estate trials today, Roman courts usually ruled in favor of the borrower; they rarely took the side of the lender who is suing to seize a security from a borrower. Consequently, most bonds were pignus rather than hypothec. In the United States, most rental agreements are pignus since the landlord holds the security.

What if the security earns money? The practice in a pignus was that all extra income from the security went to the lender (who held the security). Could this income be used to reduce the loan? There are two answers. The *vivgage* (live pledge) specified that the extra income to the lender be used to reduce the current principal; as soon as the loan was repaid the lender returned the security. The *mortgage* (dead pledge) specified that the extra income to the lender should be used to compensate the lender for making the loan in the first place; repayment of principal was due after a predetermined number of years; the extra payments did not reduce the principal (in the case of default, the security became the property of the lender). Consequently, the vivgage was more popular with borrowers and the mortgage was more popular with lenders. Note that today's mortgage is actually a vivgage.

For bonds (continuous cash flow): Present value of *Bond* =

- `int(A*exp(-t*r), t=0..T)+P*exp(-r*T)`

$$\frac{A}{r} + P\,\exp(-T\ r) - \frac{A}{r\,\exp(T\ r)}$$

So for $P = \$1000$, $r = 6\%$, $N = 12$, $T = 15$ years, *Bond* = \$917.82; for continuous cash flows, *Bond* = \$917.64.

For mortgages (N period compounding): Constant cash flow (each period) A =

- `P/sum(1/(1+r/N)^t, t=1..N*T)`

$$\frac{P\ r}{N - N\left(\frac{N}{N+r}\right)^{N\ T}}$$

For mortgages (continuous cash flow): Constant cash flow A =

- `P/int(exp(-t*r), t=0..T)`

$$\frac{P}{\dfrac{1}{r} - \dfrac{1}{r\,\exp(T\ r)}}$$

So for $P = \$200{,}000$, $r = 6\%$, $N = 12$, $T = 15$ years, $A = \$1687.71$ per month, or $\$20252.56$ per year (monthly compounding). For continuous cash flows, $A = \$20221.41$ per year (or $\$1685.12$ per month).

4.2.   Technology of Yields

How do investors and traders compare different types of bonds and mortgages? The prices depend on cash flows and maturity, as well as on credit, so a pure price comparison between bonds and mortgages can be misleading.

Yields Are Surrogates for Price

The most popular terms are the investment yield, annualized yield to maturity, bond equivalent yield, coupon equivalent rate, the effective yield, and the interest yield. Yield can loosely be interpreted as the constant rate of return that an investor expects over time.

The U.S. Federal Reserve Bank defines *the investment yield* of a with no cash flows (like a Strip or a Treasury Bill) having price $P(0)$ today and price $P(T)$ at time T as

$$r = \left(\frac{P(T)}{P(0)} - 1 \right) \cdot \frac{1}{T}$$

Suppose we know the present value of a set of cash flows:

$$CF = \sum_{t=1}^{N \cdot T} \frac{c(t/N)/N}{(1 + R(t/N)/N)^t}$$

The *investment yield* of a sum of cash flows is defined as the fixed value r that satisfies

$$CF = \sum_{t=1}^{N \cdot T} \frac{c(t/N)/N}{(1 + r/N)^t} = \sum_{t=1}^{N \cdot T} \frac{c(t/N)/N}{(1 + R(t/N)/N)^t}$$

For example, consider Marie's crop contract using the Acme CD rates Q and the three cash flows of $300 per year:

- `R(t):=t->piecewise([t>0 and t<=1,0.0225],[t>1 and t<=2,0.0250],`
  `[t>2 and t<=3,0.03],[t>3 and t<=5,0.04],[t>5 and t<=10,0.05])`

The present value of the cash flow CF is $853.59. The yield is the rate r such that

`sum(300/(1+r)^t, t=1..3)=853.59`

In general, no closed form formulas exist for yields; however, efficient numerical methods exist, based on the mathematical methods refined in the 18th and 19th centuries for finding roots of equations.

In the MuPAD computer algebra system, the solve command finds the required solution:

- `solve(sum(300/(1+r)^t,t=1..3)=853.49, r)`

      `{0.02700707689}`

The solution is $r = 2.701..\%$. The price can be reconstructed from the yield by using the definition

- `sum(300/(1+0.02701)^t,t=1..3)`

853.4851847

Note that we rounded off the yield to one basis point. Also note that in general, we can also compute the yield r by the following yield equivalent specification:

- `solve(sum(300/(1+r)^t,t=1..3)=sum(300/(1+R(t))^t,t=1..3), r)`

{0.02700989985}

For bonds, the expression for yield, given the current bond price B, is

`solve(sum(c(t/N)/(1+r/N)^t, t=1..N*T)+P/(1+r/N)^(N*T)=B,r)`

Yield Examples

Given a yield, we can always compute the price. For example, suppose a bond matures in 10 years; it has a yearly fixed coupon of $300 and a principal at maturity of $10,000. Let us assume that the spot rates are given by the Acme CD rates (see Figure 3-9).

The present value is

`sum(300/(1+R(t))^t, t=1..10)+10000/(1+R(10))^(10)`

8513.314752

and the yield is $4.917...\%$:

`solve(sum(300/(1+r)^t, t=1..10)+10000/(1+r)^10=8513.314752, r)`

{0.04917631604}

If the bond is evaluated with monthly compounding, the present value is

`sum((300/12)/(1+R(t/12)/12)^t, t=1..12*10)+10000/(1+R(10))^(10)`

8545.170361

and the yield is $4.9295...\%$:

`solve(sum((300/12)/(1+r/12)^t, t=1..12*10)+10000/(1+r)^10=8545.17, r)`

{0.04929563197}

For continuous cash flow, the present value is

`numeric::int(300*exp(-t*R(t)),t=0..10)+10000*exp(-R(10)*10)`

8474.299475

and the yield is $4.9328...\%$:

`numeric::solve(int(300*exp(-r*t),t=0..10)+10000*exp(r*10)=8474.299,r)`

{0.04932813104}

Excel has a built-in function for the yield of a bond for the special case where all cash flow coupons are identical and for three different compounding conventions:

= YIELD(buyDate, maturityDate, couponRate, CurrentPrice, MaturityPrice, frequency, basis)

where

buyDate	the date when the bond is traded or bought
maturityDate	the maturity date of the bond
couponRate	the annual coupon rate
CurrentPrice	the price of the bond at buyDate, normalized to $100
MaturityPrice	the price of the bond at maturityDate, usually $100
frequency	denotes the payments per year (1: annual; 2: semiannual; 4: quarterly)
basis	day count basis (0: 30/360; 1: Actual/Actual; 2: Actual/360; 3: Actual/365; 4: 30E/360)

The Federal Reserve (in Fedpoint 28, "Estimating Yields on Treasury Securities") states that

Formulas used by Treasury to calculate the investment yield on notes and bonds are complicated and vary, depending on the maturity of the issue. However, the investment yield on a bond or note held to maturity can be approximated with the following formula. . .

In our notation, the Treasury yield formula for bonds paying a coupon rate A (in units of percent) twice a year (i.e., $N = 2$) is

$$r = \frac{A + (P(T) - P(0)/T}{(P(T) + P(0))/2}$$

Note that the Treasury does not specify a day count basis for the time to maturity T.

Technology of Yield Algorithms

The YIELD function of Excel and the solve command of MuPAD are implementations of "root-finding algorithms." Root-finding algorithms are used extensively in finance. They have their origins in antiquity: one basic method, a variant of linear interpolation, is called the *secant method*. The principles are shown in Figure 4-3.

The goal is to find a point z on the curve $y = f(x)$ such that $f(z) = 0$. We first look at the line that interpolates the curve $y = f(x)$ at two points, b and a. We extend the line until it crosses the horizontal axis at point r. We solve for r as shown in Figure 4-3:

$$r = b - f(b) \cdot \frac{b - a}{f(b) - f(a)}$$

Box 4-3

Using Yields

On July 21 2004, this quote is given for a Treasury bill that matures on September 16:

MATURITY	DAYS TO MAT	BID	ASK	CHG	ASK YLD
Sep 16 04	56	1.19	1.18	-0.01	1.2

A US Treasury Bill matures in one year or less (it does not issue coupons). The discount rate formula (Box 2-16) uses this *investment yield* to find the Ask price: $9,981.64.

On July 21 2004, these quotes are given for Treasury notes (bond with maturities between 1 and 10 years) and Treasury Bonds (maturities greater than 10 years). Both issue coupons payable twice a year:

RATE	MATURITY MO/YR	BID	ASKED	CHG	ASK YLD
13.875	May 11	120:02	120:03	-5	2.48
5	Aug 11n	105:04	105:05	-8	4.15
4.75	May 14n	102:03	102:04	-8	4.48

The RATE column indicates the coupon rate as a percent: bid, ask, and price changes use the base 32 colon convention. Maturity dates are typically on the 15th of the month. The "n" next to the year indicates that the bond is a Note. For the last Bond (maturing on May 15, 2014):

	R	S	T	U
32	Settlement:	7/21/2004	Basis:	1
33	Maturity:	5/15/2014	Principal:	100
34	Coupon (%):	4.75%	Frequency:	2
35	Price:	102.125	**YIELD:**	**4.4793%**

Microsoft Excel's YIELD computes the yield as 4.4793%; the formula spreadsheet is:

	R	S	T	U
32	Settlement:	38189	Basis:	1
33	Maturity:	41774	Principal:	100
34	Coupon (%):	0.0475	Frequency:	2
35	Price:	=102+(4/32)	YIELD:	=YIELD(S32,S33,S34,S35,U33,U34,U32)

The published Ask Yield rounds this to the nearest basis point. The Federal Reserve Approximation Formula requires years to maturity: this is 3585 days (Actual/365) or 3585/365 = 9.8219 years. Here the yield is

$$r = [c + (P(T) - P(0))/T]/[(P(T) + P(0))/2]$$

$$= [4.75 + (100 - 102\tfrac{4}{32})/9.8219]/(100 + 102\tfrac{4}{32})/2 = 4.486\%$$

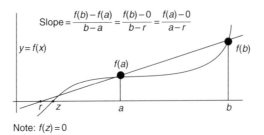

FIGURE 4-3   The secant method for root finding.

We repeat the process with the two points a and r and continue repeating using the last two points until sufficient accuracy is reached or until a maximum number of repetitions.

Root finding is another way of finding the "inverse function." For example, if $y = f(x)$, then we can also say that $x = f^{-1}(y)$, where f^{-1} is called "f inverse" or "the inverse function of f." The secant method finds $f^{-1}(0)$ — the value z where $f(z) = 0$. Note that in general, in order to find a point u such that $f(u) = A$, then all we need to do is construct the function $g(x) = f(x) - A$ and apply the secant method to $g(x)$. Note that the point u found in the secant method has the property that $g(u) = 0$: this implies $g(u) = f(u) - A = 0$ or $f(u) = A$.

A variation of the secant method is in Pacioli's 1494 *Summa*. Because this method requires two arbitrary points, it has been called a "rule of false position" (Latin: *regula falsi*). Pacioli references it as the "regola ditta El cataym," which indirectly references al-Khowarizmi's 840 text: the Arabic *hisab al-khata'ayn* is literally the "rule of two falses." The algorithm has been seen in earlier Indian manuscripts and it is assumed that it can be traced back to the Babylonians.

One of the earliest applications of this algorithm may have been to compute yields. As an example, consider a bond that matures in 3 years with principal of $10,000 and a coupon of $30 per year. If we assume the Acme CD spot rates, the bond price today is $9236.765.

The MuPAD built-in solver solution for the yield is $r = 2.998..\%$:

- assume(r>=0):
- solve(30*sum(1/(1+r)^t,t=1..3)+10000/(1+r)^3=9236.765,r)

        {0.02998172672}

There is no built-in Excel function for the secant method. Hoewever, we can implement it easily using the copy-and-paste conventions for spreadsheet cells. Figure 4-4 shows one implementation. Note that the values converge to eight places after five repetitions. The formula spreadsheet is shown in Figure 4-5.

The bond value is computed in cell J36 using the Acme CD rates. The first two guesses are $a = 0$ and $b = 5\%$ (in cells I38 and I39); their corresponding yield function valuations are in cells J38 and J39.

The secant method itself is first implemented in cell I40. Note that the formulas in J39 and I40 were copied and pasted throughout the two column range to row 44; each row represents an iteration of the algorithm (e.g., I43:J43 corresponds to the fourth repetition).

Box 4-4 shows the yield computation using the secant method implemented in C. Note that the algorithm is written for an arbitrary function f.

	I	J
36	Today's Price	9236.765
37	r	f(r)
38	0.0000%	853.2349
39	5.0000%	-516.6917
40	3.1142%	-31.03843
41	2.9936%	1.216251
42	2.9982%	-0.002737
43	2.9982%	-2.41E-07
44	2.9982%	0

FIGURE 4-4

	I	J
36	Today's Price	=30*(1/(1+2.25%)+1/(1+2.5%)^2+1/(1+3%)^3)+10000/(1+3%)^3
37	r	f(r)
38	0	=30*(1/(1+I38)+1/(1+I38)^2+1/(1+I38)^3)+10000/(1+I38)^3-$J$36
39	0.05	=30*(1/(1+I39)+1/(1+I39)^2+1/(1+I39)^3)+10000/(1+I39)^3-$J$36
40	=I39-J39*(I39-I38)/(J39-J38)	=30*(1/(1+I40)+1/(1+I40)^2+1/(1+I40)^3)+10000/(1+I40)^3-$J$36
41	=I40-J40*(I40-I39)/(J40-J39)	=30*(1/(1+I41)+1/(1+I41)^2+1/(1+I41)^3)+10000/(1+I41)^3-$J$36
42	=I41-J41*(I41-I40)/(J41-J40)	=30*(1/(1+I42)+1/(1+I42)^2+1/(1+I42)^3)+10000/(1+I42)^3-$J$36
43	=I42-J42*(I42-I41)/(J42-J41)	=30*(1/(1+I43)+1/(1+I43)^2+1/(1+I43)^3)+10000/(1+I43)^3-$J$36
44	=I43-J43*(I43-I42)/(J43-J42)	=30*(1/(1+I44)+1/(1+I44)^2+1/(1+I44)^3)+10000/(1+I44)^3-$J$36

FIGURE 4-5

Prices, Yields, and Defaults

What happens to the price of a bond if the issuer does not make a payment? If there is a risk of default, the lender needs to be compensated for taking more credit risk. In this case, lenders would demand a higher return on the investment, which translates into a lower present value for the bond and a higher yield.

For example, suppose an oracle who sees the future knows that Stacy's second crop will fail. From the oracle's perspective, the value of the cash flows is reduced to from $853.49 to $567.94 (=293.40 + 274.54) and the yield increases from 2.7%

- assume(r>0):
- solve(sum(300/(1+r)^t,t=1..3)=853.49,r)

$$\{0.02700707689\}$$

to 2.8%:

- solve(300/(1+r)+300/(1+r)^3=567.94,r)

$$\{0.02803377012\}$$

Let us see how the oracle performs with bonds. Recall the bond that matures in 10 years has a yearly fixed coupon of $300 and a principal at maturity of $10,000, with rates given by the Acme CDs. The present value was computed to be $8513.31 and the yield 4.91%. Suppose that the oracle knows that the issuer will miss three coupon payments — the third through fifth coupons. From the oracle's perspective, the bond value is

- sum(300/(1+R(t))^t,t=1..10)-sum(300/(1+R(t))^t,t=3..5)
- + 10000/(1+R(10))^(10)

$$7735.752865$$

Box 4-4

Computing Yields and Inverse Functions: The Secant Method in C

```c
#include <stdio.h>
#include <math.h>

double PresentBondValue;

double computeBond() {
    double CF, bond;
    CF = 30*(1/(1+.0225)+1/pow(1+.025,2)+1/pow(1+.03, 3) );
    bond = CF + 10000/pow(1+.03,3);
    return(bond);
}

// This is the function y = f(r)
double f(double r) {
    double CF, bond;
    CF = 30*(1/(1+r)+1/pow(1+r,2)+1/pow(1+r, 3));
    bond = CF+10000/pow(1+r, 3);
    return (bond - PresentBondValue);
}

// returns approximation to z where f(z) = 0
double SecantMeth(double a, double b, double error, int repeats) {
    int n;
    double d;
    for (n = 1; n <= repeats; n++)
    {
        d = (b-a)/(f(b) - f(a)) * f(b);
        if (fabs(d)< error)
            return b;
        a = b;
        b = b - d;
    }
    return b;
}

int main(void){
    PresentBondValue = computeBond();
    printf("\n a = 0; b = 0.05; error = 10^(-8); MaxIteration = 100 \n");
    printf("\n Yield = %10.8f \n", SecantMeth (0, 0.05, 1.0E-8, 100) );
    return 0;
}
```

and the yield increases to 6.09%:

- `solve(sum(300/(1+r)^t,t=1..10)+10000/(1+r)^10=7735.75,r)`

  `{0.06089439393}`

If we have no oracles, we can still determine an *expected value* of the cash flows. To do this we need the probability of default — a value that is best assessed today by credit reporting and credit rating agencies.

The principles behind expected value were determined in the gambling casinos. In the simplest case, suppose Acme Corporation owes us $100. If p is the probability that Acme will pay, then $1-p$ represents the probability that Acme will not pay (Acme's *default probability*). Further, suppose that if Acme does not pay, we may be able to sue Acme and recover a percentage of the money due to us. Let us denote this *recovery rate* by d.

The expected value for Acme paying back $100 is

$$\text{Expected value of Acme's payment} = p^*100 + (1-p)^*100^*d$$

For example, suppose we are 95% certain that Acme will pay us back, and that if Acme does not pay us back, we can recover 10 cents on the dollar (10%) then

$$\text{Expected value of Acme's payment} = 95\%^*100 + (5\%)^*100^*10\% = \$95.50.$$

Expected value is usually denoted by a boldface capital **E** surrounding an event in brackets, with the probabilities and other parameters being assumed (this notation dates back to 1901). So

$$\mathbf{E}[\text{Acme's payment}] = 100^*p + 100(1-p)^*d$$

In the special case that we cannot recover anything from the occasion of a default ($d = 0$), the expectation is simply

$$\mathbf{E}[\text{Acme's payment}] = 100^*p + 100(1-p)$$

We can generalize this to cash flow payments. Let us first look at Marie's crop deal with Stacy. Let us assume that the probability of payment is the same for every year and that the recovery rate is 0%. Then the expected value of Marie's cash flow is

- `sum(300*p/(1+R(t))^t, t=1..3)`

  `853.4853497 p`

If Marie is 90% sure that the crops will all succeed, then the expected value of the cash flow is reduced from a value of $853.49 to an expected value of $853.48*90% = $768.14; the yield increases from 2.7% to an expected yield of 8.36%:

- `solve(sum(300/(1+r)^t, t=1..3)=768.14,r)`

  `{0.08359593896}`

Box 4-5

Social Networks, Credit Reporting and Credit Ratings

In 1826, Arthur (1786–1865) and Lewis (1788–1873) Tappan opened a textile importing firm in New York. Their family had an extensive social network. Within a few years, annual sales grossed over $1 million. In 1827, Arthur invested $30,000 to start a financial newspaper with religious overtones (no work on Sundays). The first issue of *The Journal of Commerce* appeared on September 1, 1827. During 1828–1832 Arthur sold these businesses to Lewis and others and concentrated on anti-slavery politics and education.

On December 16, 1835, the Pearl Street Fire damaged the company. However, the business ultimately failed because of the 1837 financial crash. Their clients could not pay their bills: the social network established by letters of credit (the traditional way of establishing payment probabilities) broke down. Unless someone personally knew the contra side there was no way of knowing whether the letters of credit were fakes. Other businesses suffered from the same problem. There was a need for someone to issue credit reports.

On August 1, 1841 Lewis Tappan created the Mercantile Agency: a subscription-based *credit reporting* service. Essentially Tappan outsourced his own social network – traders, lawyers, bankers, brokers – for establishing credit. His newspaper publishing experience enabled the Agency to deliver credit reports to subscribers several times a year, detailing data such as business longevity, net worth, liabilities, and "character." Subscription fees depended on client sales: in 1841, a small company ($100,000 in sales) paid $150 per year. (Tappan also required subscribers to have the Agency process their collection claims.) By 1900 there were 7,000 subscribers and reports on a million businesses. Credit agents (including US presidents Lincoln, Grant, Cleveland and McKinley) were experts in communication technology and used stagecoaches, railroads, and the Morse telegraph.

In 1849, Tappan retired and Agency control was given to Benjamin Douglass. That year, John Bradstreet formed a competing agency in Cincinnati. Bradstreet proposed a new product: a *credit rating* (released in 1851). In 1859, Graham Dun, Douglass' brother-in-law took over the Mercantile Agency; it became R. G. Dun & Company. The competing Dun and Bradstreet companies merged in 1933 to form Dun & Bradstreet.

Also in 1849, Henry Varnum Poor (1812–1905), started publishing credit statistics for railroad companies. In 1868, Poor and his son Henry William (1844–1915) formed Poor's Publishing Co. and released *Poor's Manual of the Railroads of the United States*. In 1916, they publishing credit ratings for financial products. Poor's Publishing merged with Standard Statistics in 1941 to form Standard & Poor's (S&P). S&P merged into McGraw Hill in 1966.

In 1900, John Moody (1868–1958) published *Moody's Manual of Industrial and Miscellaneous Securities*. In 1909, subscriptions included company analysis and *rating symbols* to summarize relative ruality. By 1924, Moody's Investors Service rated nearly every US bond. Moody's was acquired by Dun & Bradstreet in 1962.

Let us assume that the payment probability is 90% for the 10-year bond (with a yearly fixed coupon of $300 and a principal at maturity of $10,000, with rates given by the Acme CDs). Let us also assume that the probability of payment is the same for every year.

Given this credit risk, then the expected values of the bond is reduced from $8513.31 to $7661.98:

- `sum(300*0.90/(1+R(t))^t,t=1..10)+0.90*10000/(1+R(10))^(10)`

    `7661.983277`

and the expected yield increases from 4.91% to 6.21%:

- `solve(sum(300/(1+r)^t,t=1..10)+10000/(1+r)^(10)=7661.98,r)`

    `{0.06207997469}`

The credit assessments are very important. For example, if the default probability is not 90% but is really 85%, then the bond price is reduced further to $7543.27 and the yield increases to 6.40% — a difference of 20 basis points for the yield.

If we have two identical cash flows — one with a 100% payment probability and the other from a source with riskier credit risk — then we can determine the payment probability for the risky cash flow from the market prices of the securities (if the payment probability is the same for every time period). For example, given

$$\text{Risk-free cash flow: } CF = \sum_{t=1}^{T} \frac{c(t)}{(1+R(t))^t}$$

$$\text{Credit risky cash flow: } CRCF = \sum_{t=1}^{T} \frac{p \cdot c(t)}{(1+R(t))^t}$$

Then by factoring out the p

$$CRCF = p \cdot \sum_{t=1}^{T} \frac{c(t)}{(1+R(t))^t} = p \cdot CF \quad \text{so} \quad p = CRCF/CF.$$

For example, suppose the price of a risk free bond is $10,212.50 and the price of a credit risky bond is $9,907.10 and the bonds have the same coupons and payment dates. Then the payment probability for the credit risky bond is 97% and the default probability is 3%.

This formulation of expected value was made explicit in the theological gaming models of Blaise Pascal (1623–1662). In his 1660 book *Penseés* (French: *Thoughts*), Pascal sets up the following situation in Chapter 233:

> *God is or is not.* But which side do you incline? Reason can resolve nothing: there is an infinite chaos that separates us. Let's play a game at the extremes of this infinite distance, and set it up as heads or tails. What do you wager?

The bet is now called *Pascal's wager*. The payoff for belief is very large (Heaven) and is zero for nonbelief; even if the probability for existence is small, the expected payment for belief is greater than for nonbelief.

Box 4-6
Price, Yield, and Credit

On July 21 2004, the following quotes are given for the most active coupon bearing bonds issued by corporations.

COMPANY (TICKER)	COUPON	MATURITY	LAST PRICE	LAST YIELD	EST SPREAD	UST	VOL 000's
General Motors (GM)	8.375	Jul 15 2033	104.853	7.944	274	30	450,007
Ford Motor Credit (F)	7.000	Oct 1 2013	101.807	6.731	226	10	412,634
Liberty Media (L)	5.700	May15 2013	99.071	5.835	137	10	207,708

The cost for credit is given by the estimated yield spread in basis points over the closest Treasury. For example, for Ford and Liberty Media bonds, the corresponding Treasury bond is the 10 year 4.750 coupon Treasury that matures in May 2014; recall that its yield is 4.48%, about 2.26% below the Ford bond and 1.37% below the Liberty Media bond.

On July 21 2004, the following quotes are given for the following Mortgage-Backed Securities (MBS):

	RATE	PRICE (AUG) (PTS-32DS)	PRICE CHANGE (32DS)	AVG LIFE (YEARS)	SPRD TO AVG LIFE (YEARS)	SPREAD CHANGE (BPS)	PSA (PREPAY SPEED)	YIELD TO MAT
30-year								
FMAC GOLD	5.50%	100-01	-3	6.9	149	-4	219	5.51
GNMA **	5.50%	100-10	-2	6.6	149	-3	227	5.45

Bonds that are backed by mortgages are more complicated to analyze because homeowners have the option to pre-pay their mortgages early: consequently, the maturity time for the corresponding bonds depends on the probability of payment at a particular time. The above quotes publish the average life of the bond (computed by the Bear Stearns prepayment model), together with other statistics. For these two MBS, the spread above the closest Treasury (the 7 year Aug 2011 bond with yield of 4.15%) is about 1.49%. Note that the GNMA bond is a little more expensive (and has lower yield to maturity): this is because GNMA bonds are backed by the credit of the US Government.

4.3. Zero Credit Risk/Zero Coupon Bonds

What if a bond has no risk of default and no coupons? Financial analysts define the following special zero coupon bond $B(T)$:

A normalized zero risk/zero coupon bond $B(T)$ is the value today (at time 0) of a bond that returns $1 at time T, with no risk of default.

Sometimes the value of $B(T)$ is called a *discount factor*. (Note that when there is no chance of ambiguity, normalized zero risk/zero coupon bonds are referred to as *zero coupon bonds*.)

Zeros and Interest Rates

Zero coupon bonds simplify most of the present and future value relationships because they do not explicitly represent the type of compounding used. For example, given a price $P(0)$ of something today and a price $P(T)$ of something at time T, the discount relationship is

$$P(0) = P(T) \cdot B(T)$$

This is valid whether we use N-period compounding, where

$$B(T) = (1 + R(T)/N)^{-N \cdot T}$$

or continuous compounding, where

$$B(T) = e^{-R(T) \cdot T}$$

In analogy with the forward rate $R(T, TA)$ from time T to TA (see Box 3-12), we define a forward price $P(T, TA)$ from time T to TA. The forward price is

$$B(T, TA) = \frac{1}{(1 + R(T, TA)/N)^{N \cdot (TA - T)}} \text{ for } N\text{-period compounding;}$$

$$B(T, TA) = e^{-R(T, TA) \cdot (TA - T)} \text{ for continuous compounding.}$$

Consequently, the relationship between today's spot prices and forward price is just

$$B(T, TA) = B(TA)/B(T))$$

Note that the specific type of compounding is not explicit in this price relationship.

Cash flows are conveniently expressed with zero coupon bonds. For example, the present value of a bond of principal P and maturity T for a set of periodic cash flows is just

$$P \cdot \sum_{t=1}^{T} c(t) \cdot B(t) + P \cdot B(T)$$

The actual type of compounding is not explicit.

By convention, the forward price from time 0 to time T is just the spot price: $B(T) = B(0, T)$. Also note that as the time t increases to the maturity time T, $B(0, T)$ approaches maturity value \$1.

For example, Figure 4-6 shows how the prices of both $B(1) = B(0, 1)$ and $B(2) = B(0, 2)$ evolve through $B(ta, 1)$ and $B(tb, 2)$ and approach the maturity value \$1 in 1 year (since $0 \leq ta \leq 1$) and 2 years (since $0 \leq tb \leq 1$), respectively. The forward price $B(1, 2)$ also evolves to $B(tc, 2)$, where $1 \leq tb \leq 2$; $B(tc, 2)$, approaches \$1 as time tc increases from 1 to 2 years.

In the U.S. Treasury market, a set of zero coupon Treasury bonds are the Treasury Strips: because they are backed by the credit of the U.S. government, the risk of default is generally assumed to be zero.

Box 4-7 shows the relationships between spot and forward rates and spot and forward zero coupon bond prices.

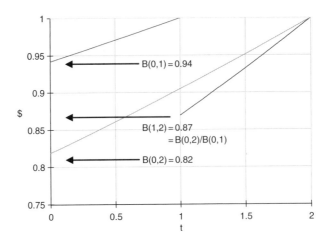

FIGURE 4-6   Price evolution of forward prices to maturity.

Term Structure

Figure 4-7 shows July 21, 2004 quotes for U.S. Treasury Strips. How do we translate these quotes into a set of zero coupon bonds $B(T)$, spot rates, and forward rates? The result of this translation is usually called the interest rate *term structure*.

To create the normalized zero coupon bonds $B(T)$, we first need to standardize on time. Let us assume that our day count basis is Actual/365. Then we compute the difference between today (July 21 2004) and the maturity date for the Strips. The Strips usually mature on the 15th of the month. So, for example, the duration of time between the Aug 04 Strip and today (July 21 2004) is 25 days, which corresponds to 25/365 year $= 0.068493151$ year. (We assume the reported quotes are current quotes: newspaper quotes are usually yesterday's quotes: they are lagged one day.)

Next, we translate the ask prices from the base 32 fractional representation; e.g., $99:30 = 99\ 30/32 = 99.9375$. Because the Strips are normalized to a principal of \$100, we need to divide 99.9375 by 100 to get the value of $B(0, T)$.

We then use the $B(T)$ to generate the spot rates. Let us assume we want continuously compounded spot rates. Let us use the relationship

$$R(T) = -\frac{1}{T}\ln B(T)$$

Note that if we want monthly $(N = 12)$ or semiannual compounding $(N = 2)$, then we can use the formula that transforms continuous rates into N-period compounding rates:

$$R_N = N \cdot (e^{R_c/N} - 1)$$

The spreadsheet in Figure 4-8 summarizes the spot zero coupon bond prices and spot interest rates (continuous compounding). Figure 4-9 shows computations that are in the formula spreadsheet. These prices for $B(T)$ are charted in Excel (with Excel's smooth cubic spline interpolation) in Figure 4-10.

Figure 4-11 shows the zero coupon interest rate term structure: the (continuous) spot rate yield curve (with Excel's smooth cubic spline interpolation). This yield curve is sloping upward (which indicates a good economy, according to the yield curve heuristics in Box 3-9).

Box 4-7

Summary of Conventions for a *T*-Year Investment between Spot Rates *R(T)* and Forward Rates *R(T,TA)* and Spot Prices *B(T)* and Forward Prices *B(T,TA)* of Zero Risk/Zero Coupon Bonds

Continuous compounding: In 1 year, 1 dollar becomes $e^R = 1/B(1)$ dollars. In T years,

$$\text{Present Value:} \quad P(0) = P(T) \cdot B(T) \quad \text{with} \quad B(T) = e^{-R(T) \cdot T} \quad \text{and} \quad B(0) = 1$$

$$\text{Future Value:} \quad P(T) = P(0)/B(T)$$

$$\text{Rate:} \quad R(T) = \frac{1}{T} \cdot \ln[B(T)]$$

$$\text{Time:} \quad T = \frac{1}{R} \cdot \ln[B(T)]$$

N-period yearly compounding: 1 dollar becomes $(1 + R/N)^N$ dollars in 1 year. In T years,

$$\text{Present Value:} \quad P(0) = P(T) \cdot B(T) \quad \text{with} \quad B(T) = (1 + R(T)/N)^{-N \cdot T}$$

$$\text{Future Value:} \quad P(T) = P(0)/B(T)$$

$$\text{Rate:} \quad R(T) = N \cdot ([B(T)]^{1/(N \cdot T)} - 1)$$

$$\text{Time:} \quad T = \frac{1}{N} \cdot \frac{\log[B(T)]}{\log(1 + R(T)/N)}, \text{ log to any base}$$

Today's forward rate from T to TA for period or continuous compounding:

$$R(T, TA) = -\frac{1}{(TA - T)} \ln\left(\frac{B(TA)}{B(T)}\right) \quad \text{or} \quad R(T, TA) = N \cdot \left(\left[\frac{B(TA)}{B(T)}\right]^{1/(TA-T)} - 1\right)$$

Today's forward price from T to TA: $B(T, TA) = B(TA)/B(T) = B(0, TA)/B(0, T)$ with

$$B(T, TA) = e^{-R(T,TA) \cdot (TA-T)} \quad \text{or} \quad B(T, TA) = \frac{1}{(1 + R(T, TA)/N)^{N \cdot (TA-T)}}$$

Present Value of sum of cash flows for period or continuous cash flows:

$$CF = \sum_{t=1}^{T} c(t) \cdot B(t) \quad \text{or} \quad CF = \int_0^T c(t) \cdot B(t) \cdot dt = \int_0^T c(t) \cdot e^{-t \cdot R(t)} \cdot dt$$

Present Value of a bond of principal P and maturity T for period or continuous cash flows:

$$bond = P \cdot [CF + B(T)] = P \cdot \sum_{t=1}^{T} c(t) \cdot B(t) + P \cdot B(T) \quad \text{or} \quad P \cdot \int_0^T c(t) \cdot B(t) \cdot dt + P \cdot B(T)$$

	C	D	E	F	G	H
3						ASK
4	MATURITY	TYPE	BID	ASK	CHG	YLD
5	Aug 04	np	99:30	99:30	...	1.11
6	Nov 04	bp	99:17	99:17	...	1.47
7	Feb 05	ci	99:01	99:01	-1	1.81
8	May 05	np	98:13	98:13	-1	1.99
9	Aug 05	np	97:23	97:23	-3	2.17
10	Aug 06	np	94:18	94:18	-3	2.74
11	Aug 07	ci	90:20	90:20	-5	3.24
12	Aug 08	np	86:29	86:29	-5	3.48
13	Aug 09	np	82:18	82:18	-6	3.82
14	Aug 10	np	78:12	78:12	-8	4.06
15	Aug 11	np	74:07	74:07	-7	4.26
16	Aug 12	np	70:09	70:09	-8	4.42
17	Aug 13	np	66:18	66:18	-8	4.54
18	Aug 14	ci	61:25	61:25	-6	4.84

FIGURE 4-7   July 21, 2004 quotes for U.S. Treasury Strips.

	A	B	C	D	E
19	7/21/2004	Today			Continuous
20	Date	Time (years)	Strip ($)	B(T) ($)	Spot Rate
21	8/15/2004	0.068493151	99.9375	0.999375	0.9128%
22	11/15/2004	0.320547945	99.53125	0.9953125	1.4658%
23	2/15/2005	0.57260274	99.03125	0.9903125	1.7001%
24	5/15/2005	0.816438356	98.40625	0.9840625	1.9678%
25	8/15/2005	1.068493151	97.71875	0.9771875	2.1597%
26	8/15/2006	2.068493151	94.5625	0.945625	2.7029%
27	8/15/2007	3.068493151	90.625	0.90625	3.2081%
28	8/15/2008	4.071232877	86.90625	0.8690625	3.4471%
29	8/15/2009	5.071232877	82.5625	0.825625	3.7785%
30	8/15/2010	6.071232877	78.375	0.78375	4.0134%
31	8/15/2011	7.071232877	74.21875	0.7421875	4.2164%
32	8/15/2012	8.073972603	70.28125	0.7028125	4.3679%
33	8/15/2013	9.073972603	66.5625	0.665625	4.4857%
34	8/15/2014	10.0739726	61.78125	0.6178125	4.7803%

FIGURE 4-8   July 21, 2004 continuous spot rates.

	A	B	C	D	E
19	38189	Today			Continuous
20	Date	Time (years)	Strip ($)	B(T) ($)	Spot Rate
21	38214	=(A21-$A$19)/365	=99+30/32	=C21/100	=-(1/B21)*LN(D21)
22	38306	=(A22-$A$19)/365	=99+17/32	=C22/100	=-(1/B22)*LN(D22)
23	38398	=(A23-$A$19)/365	=99+1/32	=C23/100	=-(1/B23)*LN(D23)
24	38487	=(A24-$A$19)/365	=98+13/32	=C24/100	=-(1/B24)*LN(D24)
25	38579	=(A25-$A$19)/365	=97+23/32	=C25/100	=-(1/B25)*LN(D25)
26	38944	=(A26-$A$19)/365	=94+18/32	=C26/100	=-(1/B26)*LN(D26)
27	39309	=(A27-$A$19)/365	=90+20/32	=C27/100	=-(1/B27)*LN(D27)
28	39675	=(A28-$A$19)/365	=86+29/32	=C28/100	=-(1/B28)*LN(D28)
29	40040	=(A29-$A$19)/365	=82+18/32	=C29/100	=-(1/B29)*LN(D29)
30	40405	=(A30-$A$19)/365	=78+12/32	=C30/100	=-(1/B30)*LN(D30)
31	40770	=(A31-$A$19)/365	=74+7/32	=C31/100	=-(1/B31)*LN(D31)
32	41136	=(A32-$A$19)/365	=70+9/32	=C32/100	=-(1/B32)*LN(D32)
33	41501	=(A33-$A$19)/365	=66+18/32	=C33/100	=-(1/B33)*LN(D33)
34	41866	=(A34-$A$19)/365	=61+25/32	=C34/100	=-(1/B34)*LN(D34)

FIGURE 4-9   July 21, 2004 continuous spot rates (formulas).

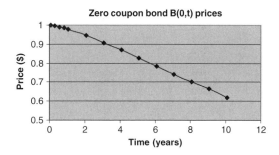

FIGURE 4-10   July 21, 2004 zero coupon prices.

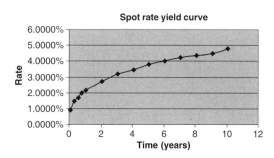

FIGURE 4-11   July 21, 2004 zero coupon yield curve (term structure).

Let us compute the 1-year continuously compounded forward rates from

$$R(T, TA) = \frac{1}{(TA - T)} \ln\left(\frac{B(T)}{B(TA)}\right)$$

For 1-year forward rates, $(TA - T) = 1$. Note that we can only provide 1-year forward rates for the years (2004–2005) to (2013–2014). Figure 4-12 shows the results. Computations are in the formula spreadsheet shown in Figure 4-13.

Figure 4-14 shows the chart of 1-year forward rates (with smooth cubic spline interpolation).

4.4. Equities, Dividend Discounts, and Laplace Transforms

Suppose it is known that Stacy's farm crop always produces $300 a year in agricultural produce. Marie enters into a contract with Stacy today to purchase the crops — forever! How much is Marie's contract worth?

A variation of this problem is the following: Acme Corporation always pays a dividend of $2.26 per share. What is 1 share of Acme Corporation worth? Using the MuPAD notation discussed earlier, the total present value of Stacy's crop is just

```
sum(300/(1+R(t))^t, t=1..infinity)
```

	A	B	C	D
37	**Date**	**Time (years)**	**B(0,T)**	**R(T,T+1)**
38	8/15/2004	0.068493151	0.9994	2.2452%
39	8/15/2005	1.068493151	0.9772	3.2832%
40	8/15/2006	2.068493151	0.9456	4.2531%
41	8/15/2007	3.068493151	0.9063	4.1900%
42	8/15/2008	4.071232877	0.8691	5.1274%
43	8/15/2009	5.071232877	0.8256	5.2051%
44	8/15/2010	6.071232877	0.7838	5.4488%
45	8/15/2011	7.071232877	0.7422	5.4512%
46	8/15/2012	8.073972603	0.7028	5.4364%
47	8/15/2013	9.073972603	0.6656	7.4541%
48	8/15/2014	10.0739726	0.6178	

FIGURE 4-12

	A	B	C	D
37	**Date**	**Time (years)**	**B(0,T)**	**R(T,T+1)**
38	38214	0.0684931506849315	0.999375	=LN(C38/C39)
39	38579	1.06849315068493	0.9771875	=LN(C39/C40)
40	38944	2.06849315068493	0.945625	=LN(C40/C41)
41	39309	3.06849315068493	0.90625	=LN(C41/C42)
42	39675	4.07123287671233	0.8690625	=LN(C42/C43)
43	40040	5.07123287671233	0.825625	=LN(C43/C44)
44	40405	6.07123287671233	0.78375	=LN(C44/C45)
45	40770	7.07123287671233	0.7421875	=LN(C45/C46)
46	41136	8.07397260273973	0.7028125	=LN(C46/C47)
47	41501	9.07397260273973	0.665625	=LN(C47/C48)
48	41866	10.0739726027397	0.6178125	

FIGURE 4-13

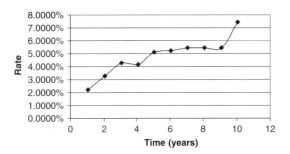

FIGURE 4-14   One-year forward rates.

In practice we will never know the infinite set of current spot rates. However, since Marie will offer Stacy a price for the (infinite) set of crops, we can assume that the price is associated with a particular yield r. In this case, MuPAD computes the total present value of Stacy's crop as

- assume(r>0):
- sum(300/(1+ r)^t, t=1..infinity)

```
 300
 ---
  r
```

For example, if Marie offers Stacy $2000, then the yield on the set of infinite cash flows is

$$r = \frac{\$300}{\$2000} = 15\%$$

Conversely, suppose Stacy looks at a collection of similar agricultural deals and suppose she finds out that the average yield r of these deals is 3%. Then Stacy can value her crops at

$$\frac{\$300}{r} = \frac{\$300}{\$0.03} = \$10,000$$

Annuities and Perpetuities

This use of using a set of infinite cash flows (sometimes called a *perpetual annuity* or *perpetuity*) to value a farm or estate has been used since ancient times. MuPAD can evaluate the infinite sum because it recognizes that it can be written in the form of what is now called a *geometric series*. Formulas for the sum of geometric series were given by Euclid over 2300 years ago (see Box 4-8).

For example, in the 11th century, landlords would sell a set of infinite cash flows — in the form of rents — in order to raise money. Social laws at that time treated a sale of rents differently from a loan or a sale of a coupon bond. This was important: usury laws might be triggered on a loan with 15% interest or a bond with a 20% coupon rate but might not be triggered for a sale of rents. In addition, lawsuit costs in the event of default were treated differently. Cash flows were viewed as part of a total payment — not as interest: it was considered an actual sale and not a pignus, hypothecated loan, or bond. Consequently, creditors had less difficulty in seizing the security in case of default.

In sigma-style notation, the expression for the present value of a periodic cash flow $c(t)$ is

$$CF = \sum_{t=1}^{\infty} \frac{c(t)}{(1+R(t))^t} = \frac{c(1)}{(1+R(1))} + \frac{c(2)}{(1+R(2))^2} + \cdots$$

The symbol ∞ denoting "infinity" was first used by John Wallis (1616–1703) in 1655, possibly from the old Roman symbol for 1000, which the Romans later wrote as M. As in the case of fixed sum cash flows, the yield can be found by solving for r, where

$$\sum_{t=1}^{\infty} \frac{c(t)}{(1+r)^t} = \sum_{t=1}^{\infty} \frac{c(t)}{(1+R(t))^t}$$

Using the formula for geometric series, closed form formulas can be found for simple cash flows. For example, the formula for a constant positive yield and constant cash flow function where $c(t) = A$ is

$$CF = \sum_{t=1}^{\infty} \frac{A}{(1+r)^t} = \frac{A}{r}$$

For continuous cash flows with cash flow function $c(t)$ the present value expression is

$$CF = \int_{0}^{\infty} e^{-t \cdot R(t)} \cdot c(t) dt$$

Box 4-8

Euclid's Geometric Series

The technology for summing a set of periodic cash flows is quite ancient. Euclid (ca. 365–275 BCE), a teacher and mathematician at the academy in Alexandria, derived the results in *The Elements*, one of the most popular mathematics textbooks in history. (Many of his results came from Babylonian sources; Euclid did not give references). Proposition 35 of Book 9 states

> If as many numbers as we please are in continued proportion, and there is subtracted from the second and the last numbers equal to the first, then the excess of the second is to the first as the excess of the last is to the sum of all those before it.

In modern notation, $c_1, c_2, \ldots, c_T, c_{T+1}$ is in continued proportion if $c_2/c_1 = c_3/c_2 = \ldots = c_{T+1}/c_T$. For example, $z, z^2, z^3, \ldots, z^T, z^{T+1}$ is in continued proportion: $z^2/z = z^3/z^2 = \ldots = z^{T+1}/z^T = z$. Proposition 35 says that for a set of numbers $c_1, c_2, c_3, \ldots, c_T, c_{T+1}$ in continued proportion:

$$\frac{c_2 - c_1}{c_1} = \frac{c_{T+1} - c_1}{\sum\limits_{t=1}^{T} c_t} \quad \text{or} \quad \frac{z^2 - z}{z} = \frac{z^{T+1} - z}{\sum\limits_{t=1}^{T} z^t} \quad \text{so} \quad \sum_{t=1}^{T} z^t = z \cdot \frac{z^{T+1} - z}{z^2 - z} = \frac{z^{T+1} - z}{z - 1} = \frac{z - z^{T+1}}{1 - z}$$

Cash flow expressions in the yield formulas are in continued proportion. (Today, a sum of numbers in continued proportion is called a *geometric series*.) Note that for $z^t = 1/(1+r)^t$.

$$\sum_{t=1}^{T} \frac{1}{(1+r)^t} = \frac{1}{(1+r)} + \ldots + \frac{1}{(1+r)^T} = \frac{\left(\frac{1}{1+r}\right) - \left(\frac{1}{1+r}\right)^{T+1}}{\left(\frac{r}{1+r}\right)} = \frac{1 - \left(\frac{1}{1+r}\right)^T}{r}$$

Euclid proved Proposition 35 geometrically. Here is a picture showing a four-term sum with $z = 1/4$:

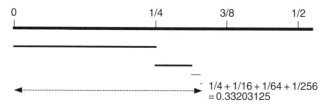

Here, Proposition 35 says that

$$\frac{1}{4} + \frac{1}{16} + \frac{1}{64} + \frac{1}{256} = \frac{1}{4} \cdot \frac{(1/1024) - (1/4)}{(1/16) - (1/4)} = 0.33203125$$

As T increases, z^T in the series gets smaller and the sum approaches $\dfrac{z}{1-z} = \dfrac{(1/4)}{(3/4)} = \dfrac{1}{3}$.

As in the case of fixed sum cash flows, the yield can be found by solving for r, where

$$\int_0^\infty e^{-rt}c(t)dt = \int_0^\infty e^{-t \cdot R(t)} \cdot c(t)dt$$

For an arbitrary but fixed positive yield r, this infinite sum over all time (from the present at time $t = 0$) of infinitesimal cash flows is denoted by

$$CF = \int_0^\infty e^{-rt}c(t)dt$$

Laplace Transforms of Cash Flows

The expression for an infinite sum over all time (from the present at time $t = 0$) of infinitesimal cash flows is well known among technologists — it is called the *Laplace transform* of the cash flow $c(t)$. Note that the Laplace transform of a cash flow does not depend on time t; it only depends on the yield r.

More formally, the Laplace transform of a cash flow $c(t)$, denoted by $L[c(t)]$, is

$$L[c(t)] = C(r) = \int_0^\infty e^{-rt}c(t)dt$$

The Laplace transform has been analyzed for over 200 years; its original formulation dates back to Euler, in his 1737 paper *De Constructione Aequationum* (Equation Construction). Pierre-Simon Laplace (1749–1827) acknowledged Euler's invention in his 1812 *Théorie Analytique des Probabilités* (Analytic Theory of Probabilities). In the 20th century, its "operational calculus" methodology was popularized by Oliver Heaviside (1850–1925) and Norbert Wiener (1894–1964) for solving technology problems arising in electric circuits and other systems.

MuPAD and other computer algebra systems have built-in tables of Laplace transform pairs. For example, suppose a continuous cash flow of a crop grows quadratically with time and is given by

$$c(t) = 300 {}^* t^2$$

The present value of the set of infinite cash flows is found by

- transform::laplace(300*t^2, t, r)

```
      600
      ---
       r^3
```

So if the yield is 10%, then the present value of all the crops is $600/10\%^3 = \$600,000$.

An inverse Laplace transform answers questions such as given a present value $C(r)$, what is the value in time of each cash flow? For example, suppose a company is valued according to the following yield relationship:

$$C(r) = \frac{\$0.25}{r - 0.02}$$

The value in time of each cash flow is given by

- `transform::invlaplace(0.25/(r-0.02),r,t)`

$$0.25 \exp(0.02\,t)$$

This cash flow increases exponentially in time. Figure 4-15 shows a small table of Laplace transform pairs for several cash flow functions.

Valuation of Equities

The same cash flow formulas can be used to value business entities. We just replace the discounted value of the crops by the discounted values of dividends or earnings. This is why the modeling, forecasting, and timely communication of corporate earnings are so important: unexpected changes can have major valuation consequences.

Company cash flows are difficult to ascertain. Cash flows can be positive or negative. As seen in the case of the Dutch East India Company (Box 1-1), dividends do not necessarily follow a fixed mathematical formula. A company might have large earnings and may prefer to keep the profits in the company instead of distributing profits to the shareholders in the form of dividends. Tax liabilities also factor into this decision: it is all up to the corporate board of directors. In any case, any quality estimate of corporate earnings that differs from the expected value may, when broadcasted to the investment community, affect the business evaluation and ultimately the share price.

One popular accounting ratio is *earnings per share*: the net income (obtained from an audited corporate balance sheet) divided by the total number of shares. There are accounting and financial models that enable analysts to forecast and transform earnings per share into cash flows. Unfortunately, some companies may use fraudulent accounting methods, inducing investors to believe that the expected value of the company (and share price) is worth more than it actually is.

What should the yield r be? Recall that a yield is a surrogate for price. Some analysts say we should look at a collection of similar stocks and compute an average yield. Depending on the time period of the collection sample, an average yield for U.S. stocks ranges from 4 to 14%.

For example, suppose that a company produces a constant dividend of $A per share of stock. A set of infinite discounted dividends sums to

$$\frac{A}{r}$$

This model for equities is the simplest version of the very popular *dividend discount model*. Let us look at the consequences of this formula for a real company.

On August 11, 2004, Consolidated Edison reported its last dividend as $2.26. If this dividend remains constant, the price per share should be

$$\frac{\$2.26}{0.06} = \$45.20 \text{ assuming a 5\% yield for stocks}$$

$$\frac{\$2.26}{0.09} = \$25.11 \text{ assuming a 9\% yield for stocks}$$

$$\frac{\$2.26}{0.14} = \$16.14 \text{ assuming a 14\% yield for stocks}$$

Continuous Dividend Cash Flow c(t)		Present Value of Discounted Dividends (Laplace Transform)
Constant A		$\dfrac{A}{r}$
Constant Exponential Growth $A \cdot e^{a \cdot t}$		$\dfrac{A}{r - a}$
Linear Growth $A \cdot t$		$\dfrac{A}{r^2}$
Oscillating $A \cdot (1 - \cos w \cdot t)$		$\dfrac{A \cdot w^2}{r(r^2 + w^2)}$
Asymptotic Constant Growth $A \cdot (1 - e^{-d \cdot t})$		$\dfrac{A \cdot d}{r \cdot (r + d)}$
Growth and Maturity $A \cdot t \cdot e^{-d \cdot t}$		$\dfrac{A}{(r + d)^2}$
Piecewise Growth Continuous $\begin{cases} A \cdot e^{a \cdot t}, 0 \leq t < TA \\ B \cdot e^{b \cdot t}, TA \leq t < TB \\ C \cdot e^{c \cdot t}; t \geq TB \end{cases}$ $B = A \cdot e^{TA \cdot (a-b)};$ $C = B.e^{TB \cdot (b-c)} = A \cdot e^{TA \cdot (a-b) + TB(b-c)}$		$\dfrac{A}{r-a} \cdot (1 - e^{-(r-a) \cdot TA}) +$ $\dfrac{B}{r-b} \cdot (e^{-(r-b) \cdot TA} - e^{-(r-b) \cdot TB}) +$ $\dfrac{C}{r-c} \cdot (e^{-(r-c) \cdot TB})$

FIGURE 4-15   Table of Laplace transforms for different cash flows.

The value of Consolidated Edison on August 11, 2004 is $40.69, corresponding to a yield (in this model) of 2.26/40.69 = 5.55%. If stocks actually yield 9%, then Consolidated Edison is overvalued.

The seven cash flow models in Figure 4-15 are based on the following assumptions:

1. Constant earnings
   This model assumes a constant dividend A. It is the simplest "discounted cash flow" model.

2. Constant exponential growth
   This model assumes a constant dividend A that grows at an exponential rate a in time. This version of the discounted cash flow model requires the growth rate of dividends or earnings. It is sometimes called the Gordon (or Williams) model.

3. Linear growth
   This model assumes a constant dividend A that grows linearly in time. In other words, in N years, earnings increase N times.

4. Oscillating earnings
   This model assumes a constant dividend A that cycles between 0 and A. The cycles repeat approximately every 6.283/w years.

5. Asymptotic constant growth
   This model assumes a dividend that grows from 0 to a maximum value of A. In $1/d$ years, the dividend reaches 63% of its value.

6. Growth and maturity
   This model assumes a dividend that grows from 0 to a maximum value in $1/d$ years; thereafter, the dividend declines gradually. The maximum value of the dividend is about $0.37 \cdot A/d$.

7. Piecewise growth continuous
   This model assumes that a dividend grows at different exponential rates (a, b, c) in three periods: from 0 to TA, from TA to TB, and from TB on. No jumps are allowed; the dividend flows are continuous.

Let us see how these models perform in practice. We use the following parameters to estimate the value of Consolidated Edison stock:

A	$2.26	the current dividend
r	9%	growth rate for stocks
a	5%	dividend growth rate for constant growth model and first period of piecewise growth continuous model
w	1	so cycle repeats about every 6.283 years
d	15%	for asymptotic constant growth model Growth and maturity model (peaks at $5.54 in 6.67 years)
TA	5	from 0 to 5 years, dividend growth rate is 5%
TB	10	second period from 5 to 10 years, third period after 10 years
b	4%	from 5 to 10 years, dividend growth rate is 4%
c	2%	after 10 years, dividend growth rate is 2%

Here are the equity valuations:

Model	Present Value
Constant earnings	$25.11
Constant exponential growth	$56.50
Linear growth	$279.01
Oscillating	$24.91
Asymptotic constant growth	$15.69
Growth and maturity	$39.24
Piecewise growth continuous	$39.01
Con Ed today (August 11 2004)	$40.69

The financial professionals who compute and publish earnings estimates, dividend estimates, and price forecasts and who use these estimates to recommend purchases or sales of stock are called *equity research analysts*.

Equity research analysts work at sell-side, buy-side, or consulting firms. Brokers or dealers employ sell-side analysts to make recommendations as to which securities to buy, hold, or sell for their clients or for their proprietary accounts. Institutional money managers employ buy-side analysts to make recommendations on which securities to buy, hold, or sell for their funds. Independent analysts typically sell their research reports to any investor as a subscription service.

4.5.   Databases for Past, Present, and Future Prices

A *financial database* is a collection of information that is used by a financial system. For example, price information (such as the current collection of bids, asks, quotes, and executions) are reported, like the news, by *market data vendors*. Associated with a market data vendor is a data format and encoding scheme for representing and saving information permanently. Historical prices saved in price databases can be used for research (analyzing the past in order to predict future prices) and for compliance (assessing whether reported prices corresponded with those of reported transactions, orders, quotes, or other messages).

Tick Data vs. Time Series

Prices can be recorded for every transaction, which is colloquially called *tick data*. (In equities and futures, a tick is a measure of the smallest allowable price change; in currency transactions, a *tick* is sometimes called a *pip*.) At a minimum, tick data consist of a price and a time stamp for every transaction (which reports a price increase, a price decrease, or a "no price change").

For many types of statistical analyses, it is convenient to record prices at the end of a predetermined time interval; this is colloquially called a *time series*. A price time series database records a price at the end of every day, week, month, hour, minute, second, or any other specified time period. Even though many products trade every day around the clock, it is convenient to consider a trading day for a particular market. Different markets specify different trading days (which can overlap across different time zones). This makes it possible to report official prices for the market open and market close, as well as the price high and low during the trading day.

Box 4-9
Estimating and Reporting Corporate Earnings

Analyst estimates and reports provide a type of marketing for sell side firms: a common practice among sell side firms is not to charge clients for sell side research reports. An optimistic earnings report can help the sell side make money by generating more purchases of stock: stock purchases through the sell side results in buy side commissions.

"Wall Street estimates" or "analyst earnings expectations" usually refers to the equity earnings estimates collected and distributed by First Call, a division of Thomson Financial. First Call was founded in 1984 by Thomson Financial (52%); the other 48% partners were 8 sell side institutions. In 2001, Thomson Financial bought out the other partners. Multex, First Call's first competitor, was founded in 1993; in 2003, Multex became part of Reuters.

First Call distributes financial research (mostly done by sell side analysts) on thousands of companies in over 100 countries. In operation, hundreds of analyst teams submit estimates (e.g., buy, hold, sell recommendations; corporate growth rates; earnings for quarterly, fiscal-year, calendar-year; other accounting items) in real-time. The service tabulates and statistically processes the estimates to create a median consensus. The estimates are instantly disributed to tens of thousands of users through different networks using a variety of protocols. Some earnings reports eventually become available through third-party distributors and media outlets. During busy periods, First Call receives and distributes over 10,000 estimate revisions per day. (Another service, First Call Notes, distributes analyst meeting notes, intraday research broadcasts and other commentary.)

Investors also rely on public or private social networks. Such "unofficial" earning estimates discussed in the financial community (in clubs, in Internet chat rooms, or emails) are called "whisper numbers." Some whisper numbers are derived by multiplying formal estimates by a certainty factor that depends on the source.

Note that some sell side analysts may work for brokerages that sell the equities being analyzed. These relationships may lead to some conflicts of interest between the investment and brokerage departments and the analysis departments. For example, an unfavorable earnings report might cause a company to look elsewhere for future investment banking services for its stock. Analyst compensation arrangements can also skew earnings estimates, especially if sell side firms link compensation to the profitability of the investment banking or brokerage division. This conflict also appears if the analyst (firm or even a friend) owns stock in the companies that the analyst covers. Because of this, the NYSE and NASD have rules that bar investment banking firms from issuing an optimistic earnings report on a company within an *embargo* or *quiet period* (e.g., subject to a *release time* of 40 days after an initial public offering). There are also rules that prohibit research analysts from being supervised by the investment banking department and disclosure rules on analyst compensation and trading.

Historical Price Databases

On July 21, 2004, the published value of the Treasury Strip that matures in 390 days on $T =$ August 15, 2005 is $97\frac{23}{32} = 97.71875$. What was the price of the Strip 15 days ago?

	A	B	C	D	E	F	G	H
2		Maturities T:						
3	**Dated**	**May-04**	**Aug-04**	**Nov-04**	**Feb-05**	**May-05**	**Aug-05**	**Aug-06**
4	7/21/2004		99:30	99:17	99:01	98:13	97:23	94:18
5	7/20/2004		99:30					
6	7/19/2004		99:31					
7	7/18/2004		99:30					
8	7/17/2004		99:31					
9	....		99:32					
10	5/17/2004		98:23					
11	5/16/2004		98:13					
12	5/15/2004							
13	5/14/2004	99:31						

FIGURE 4-16 Time series indexed by date and maturity date (absolute maturity representation).

To answer this question, we simply look up the price of the Strip $B(T)$, where $T =$ August 15, 2005, in a time series database indexed by maturity. The database can be either published by a data vendor or can be an archived financial news source (e.g., a newspaper published 15 days ago). Figure 4-16 shows the structure of such a database in spreadsheet format.

The values shown in Figure 4-16 can be denoted by table entries $b(d, T)$, where d refers to the price date (in column A) and T refers to the maturity (in row 3). We use a lowercase b so there is no ambiguity between the spot price entries in this table and the forward prices $B(d, T)$ of a zero coupon bond. For example, cell F6 holds the July 19, 2004 price of the Strip that matures on May 15, 2005.

Note that for each date, the price of the specific Strip $B(T)$, with T being a specific maturity, is provided. Note that the prices of the Strip maturing on May 15, 2004 only appear below the May 14 date; there is no price for the May 15 Strip after its maturity date of May 15. Similarly, there might not be a price for the Strip maturing on August 15, 2004 if that Strip is derived from a 3-month Treasury Bill. Because of this, financial time series databases of specific products with specific maturities have "gaps" for time periods after the products matured and before the products were offered on the market. We call this time series database an absolute maturity representation.

One way of eliminating the gaps is by organizing the maturities according to relative time duration instead of by absolute maturity date. Figure 4-17 shows the structure of such a database in spreadsheet format.

Again, the values in this time series table can be denoted by $b(d, T)$, where d refers to the price date and T refers to the maturity — measured from today's date. [Again, we

	A	B	C	D	E	F	G	H
21		Maturities T:						
22	**Dated**	**1 Month**	**3 Month**	**6 Month**	**1 Year**	**18 Month**	**2 Year**	**3 Year**
23	7/21/2004	99:30	99:18	99:01	98:13	97:23	94:18	93:18
24	7/20/2004	99:31	99:18					
25	7/19/2004	99:30	99:16					
26	7/18/2004	99:30	99:14					
27	7/17/2004	99:30	99:13					
28	....	99:30	99:13					
29	5/17/2004	99:30	99:11					
30	5/16/2004	99:30	99:12					
31	5/15/2004	99:30	99:11					
32	5/14/2004	99:31	99:11					

FIGURE 4-17 Time series indexed by date and maturity date (relative maturity representation).

use a lowercase b so there can be no ambiguity between the spot price entries in this table and the forward prices $B(d, T)$ of a zero coupon bond.] For example, cell F26 holds the July 18, 2004 price of the Strip that matures 18 months from now on January 14, 2005 (assuming a 30/360-day count basis). We call this time series database a relative maturity representation.

The problem with both representations is that not every maturity is represented. The first time series represents all traded Strips of a given maturity at a given date. For example, the July 20 price of a Strip maturing on July 15, 2005 would have to be interpolated. The second time series represents prices of Strips that mature at a date that is offset from today's date. This table also does not represent the prices of all securities: the July 20 price of a Strip maturing on July 15, 2005 would also have to be interpolated. Both of these types of time series are used in practice to generate continuous prices of products.

Forward Prices vs. Prices in the Future

On July 21, 2004, the published price of the Treasury Strip that matures in 390 days on $T =$ August 15, 2005 is $97\frac{23}{32} = 97.71875$. What is the price of the August 15, 2005 Strip 15 days in the future?

Only an Oracle knows what the value of the Strip is in 15 days. However, there are several competing predictive models derived by research teams in industry and academia. Many of them use forward prices as a parameter for prediction.

Recall that the forward price in d days is just the price induced by today's zero-risk interest rate term structure. For example, for a zero coupon zero-risk bond $B(T)$, the d day forward price is

$$P_d = \frac{P_0}{B(d)} = \frac{B(T)}{B(d)} = B(d, T)$$

Using the actual/365 day count basis, $d = 15$ days corresponds to 0.04109589 years. To find $B(d)$ we can use an interpolation formula in the interval with $B(0)$ (which is always assumed to have the price of $0) and $B(TA)$, where TA is the shortest maturity time in the table (August 2004). The result for $B(d)$ for linear interpolation is

$$B(d) = M \cdot B(0) + N \cdot B(TA) = 0.4*1 + 0.6*99.9375 = 99.9625$$

$$\text{So the forward price is } B(d, T) = \frac{B(T)}{B(d)} = \frac{97.71875}{B(d)} = \frac{97.71875}{99.9625} = 97.7554083$$

Note that for either absolute or relative maturity times, forward prices can be computed for any date d, given spot prices $B(T)$.

However, 15-day forward prices are not the prices of 15 days in the future. One predictive model for future prices sets the future value of the Strip in d to the following:

$$B(d, T) = \frac{B(0, T)}{B(0, d)} \cdot e^{-G(d,T)}$$

with

$$G(d, T) = \frac{s^2}{4L} \cdot \left[\frac{\left(1 - e^{-L(T-d)}\right)}{L} \right]^2 \left(1 - e^{-2L \cdot d}\right)$$

The parameters s and L are derived from a statistical model; let us suppose $s = 0.4$ and $L = 0.1$. The value with this model is slightly less than the forward value:

$$B(d, T) = \frac{B(0, T)}{B(0, d)} \cdot e^{-G(d,T)} = 97.75541 * 0.99999755 = 97.75517$$

Predictive models come in all flavors. For example, the following spot rate model is an example of a simple *autoregressive* model:

$$R(d) = A \cdot R(d - 1) + B$$

This model essentially says that tomorrow's spot rate is the sum of today's rate (multiplied by constant A) and another constant B, where A and B are *model parameters*.

How close are the forward prices or the model prices to the real price? Figure 4-18 shows the August 5, 2004 quotes for the U.S. Treasury Strips (15 days after July 21; compare with Figure 4-7). The value of the August 2005 Strip is $97\frac{30}{32} = 97.9375$, an increase of $\frac{7}{32}$ over the July 21 price.

Figure 4-19 compares zero coupon bond computations for the continuously compounded spot rates. The yield curve (computed 15 days apart) shown in Figure 4-20 shows a shift between the spot rates.

Forward prices are not the prices in the future: if today is July 21, we do not know exactly what the market will pay on August 5 for a Strip that matures on August 15, 2005.

4.6. Notes and References

Quotes from Sumerian and Babylonian financial texts are from
[0.1] Karen Rhea Nemet-Nejat. *Cuneiform Mathematical Texts as a Reflection of Everyday Life in Mesopotamia*. American Oriental Society, 1993. ISBN 0940490757.

	C	D	E	F	G	H
3						ASK
4	**MATURITY**	**TYPE**	**BID**	**ASKED**	**CHG**	**YLD**
5	Aug 04	np	99:31	99:31	...	1.35
6	Nov 04	bp	99:19	99:19	...	1.53
7	Feb 05	ci	99:05	99:05	1	1.62
8	May 05	np	98:17	98:17	1	1.94
9	Aug 05	np	97:30	97:30	1	2.05
10	Aug 06	np	94:27	94:27	1	2.65
11	Aug 07	ci	91:00	91:00	2	3.15
12	Aug 08	np	87:09	87:09	3	3.41
13	Aug 09	np	83:03	83:03	4	3.73
14	Aug 10	np	78:31	78:31	5	3.97
15	Aug 11	np	74:29	74:29	6	4.16
16	Aug 12	np	70:30	70:30	5	4.33
17	Aug 13	np	67:07	67:07	5	4.45
18	Aug 14	ci	62:16	62:16	6	4.75

FIGURE 4-18   August 5, 2004 quotes for U.S. Treasury Strips.

	J	K	L	M
18		21-Jul	5-Aug	
19		Forward Aug 5 Price	Actual Aug 5 Price	Difference
20	Maturity Date T	B(d,T)	B(0,T)	July-August
21	8/15/2004	0.999749906	0.9996875	0.00624%
22	11/15/2004	0.995685882	0.9959375	-0.02516%
23	2/15/2005	0.990684007	0.9915625	-0.08785%
24	5/15/2005	0.984431662	0.9853125	-0.08808%
25	8/15/2005	0.977554083	0.979375	-0.18209%
26	8/15/2006	0.945979742	0.9484375	-0.24578%
27	8/15/2007	0.906589971	0.91	-0.34100%
28	8/15/2008	0.869388521	0.8728125	-0.34240%
29	8/15/2009	0.825934726	0.8309375	-0.50028%
30	8/15/2010	0.784044017	0.7896875	-0.56435%
31	8/15/2011	0.742465925	0.7490625	-0.65966%
32	8/15/2012	0.703076154	0.709375	-0.62988%
33	8/15/2013	0.665874703	0.6721875	-0.63128%
34	8/15/2014	0.618044267	0.625	-0.69557%

FIGURE 4-19   Comparison of zero coupon bonds: 21 July and 5 August.

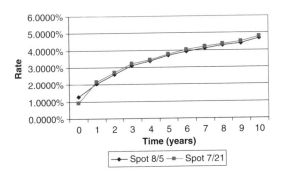

FIGURE 4-20   Comparison of yield curves: 21 July and 5 August.

Technology of Cash Flows

Cash flows are described in many books on accounting, finance, and on different sites on the Web. A good reference is by

[1] Aswath Damodaran. *Investment Valuation: Tools and Techniques for Determining the Value of Any Asset* (second edition). John Wiley & Sons, 2001. ISBN 0471414905.

Technology of Yields

Formulas used by the U.S. Treasury are described in the Appendices of

[2] Treasury Security Tender Submission Guide. U.S. Federal Reserve (available at http://www.publicdebt.treas.gov/of/ofguide.htm).

Fedpoints (a reference series explaining the structure and functions of the Federal Reserve System, available at

[3] http://app.ny.frb.org/aboutthefed/fedpoint/fed28.html

A history of regula falsi and other root finding methods is in

[4] David E. Smith. *History of Mathematics* (published in 1925). Reprinted by Dover Publications, Mineola, 1958. Vol. 1 ISBN 0486204294 and Vol. 2 ISBN 0486204308.

A history of credit rating and credit reporting is by
[5] Richard Sylla. "A Historical Primer on the Business of Credit Ratings." *Proceedings of the Conference on the Role of Credit Reporting Systems in the International Economy*. The World Bank, Washington, DC, March 1–2, 2001 (available at http://www1.worldbank.org/finance/html/credit_report_references.html).

Information about the Tappan family (and other prominent American families) is from
[6] James Grant Wilson, John Fiske, and Stanley L. Klos (eds.). *Appleton's Cyclopedia of American Biography* (6 volumes). D. Appleton and Company, New York 1887–1889 and 1999 (available on the Web at http://famousamericans.net/).

John Moody's 1919 book on railroad companies is available at Project Gutenberg
[7] John Moody. *The Railroad Builders; a Chronicle of the Welding of the States* (available at http://www.gutenberg.org/etext/3036).

Pascal's Penseés are available on the Web. See, for example,
[8] http://eserver.org/philosophy/pascal-pensees.txt

The Bond Market Association is the trade association that represents the fixed income securities markets (in total value of transactions, estimated at $48 trillion; this market is the world's largest). A survey of fixed income technology (from yield tables and slide rules to Monroe calculators and Bloomberg) was presented at the Panel on the Evolution of Technology in the Bond Market at the Bond Market Association Annual Meeting (April 2003) by
[9] Andrew Kalotay. Evolution of Technology in the Bond Markets (available at http://www.kalotay.com/articles/).

Zero Credit Risk/Zero Coupon Bonds

An example of the use of zero coupon bonds for yield curve computations is in
[10] Robert Jarrow, Stuart Turnbull. *Derivative Securities*. South-Western College Publishing. Cincinnati, 1996. ISBN 0-538-84255-5.

Equities, Dividend Discounts, and Laplace Transforms

Different cash flow evaluation models are described in [1]. They trace their origins to
[11] John Burr Williams. *The Theory of Investment Value* (first published in 1938). Reprinted by Fraser Publishing, 1997. ISBN 087034126X.

[12] Myron J. Gordon. *The Investment, Financing, and Valuation of the Corporation*. R. D. Irwin, 1962. Reprinted by Greenwood Press, Westport CT, 1982. ISBN 0-313-23542-2.

The Laplace transform and its relationships to Heaviside's methods is discussed by
[13] N. Wiener. "The Operational Calculus." *Mathematische Annalen*, Vol. 95, 1926 (archived at the Center for Retrospective Digitalization at the University of Göttingen, at http://gdz.sub.uni-goettingen.de/en/).

Databases for Past, Present, and Future Prices

A collection of a financial time series databases, containing over 3000 different components, is the Federal Reserve Economic Data (also known as FRED). FRED data are accessible in Microsoft Excel and various text formats. FRED is available at
[14] http://research.stlouisfed.org/fred2/

Since 1992, the TORQ (Transactions, Orders, Quotes) database was used by researchers to establish and verify many models for equities. TORQ is an audit trail sample of 144 NYSE stocks from November 1990 through January 1991. TORQ is described by Joel Hasbrouck in
[15] http://pages.stern.nyu.edu/~jhasbrou/Research/WorkingPaperIndex.htm

Exchanges now charge license fees order and transaction data. For example, the NYSE Daily Trades and Quotes (TAQ) and other databases are available at
[16] http://www.nysedata.com/

4.7. Discussion Questions

1. In the example in Section 4.1 relating to the value of Stacy's farm crop, what is the value today of the crop in year 30? In year 50? In year 100? In how many years will the value today of the crop be less than 1 cent?

2. In the example in Section 4.1 relating to the value of Stacy's farm crop, what is the total value today of the crop in 30 years? In 50 years? In 300 years? What is the average lifetime for a business? For a shareholder?

3. What would happen today if our mortgages were turned into real (dead pledge) mortgages (Box 4-2)?

4. Use the secant method to compute the yield of a zero coupon zero risk bond.

5. Was Samuel Morse in the social network of Lewis Tappan?

6. Use the expected value methods in Section 4.3 to compute a default probability of a high-yield bond.

7. Suppose a company's cash flow oscillates for 5 years and then it starts to grow and mature after that. What is the company worth? Use some real parameters to estimate the value per share.

8. Are there any recent SEC cases where analysts have violated the quiet period?

9. Compliance and regulatory analysts frequently talk about the Chinese wall. What is it?

10. Build a term structure model and yield curve using data from FRED.

11. Use the Laplace transform methods to value a company of your choosing. Which method is closest to the share current price?

12. Use FRED to compute a yield curve.

CHAPTER • 5

Identifying Financial Objects

> The scribal art, receiving a handsome fee, is a bright-eyed guardian, the need of the Palace.
> — Sumerian proverb (ca 2094–2047 BCE)

5.1.   Symbology: Identifying Issuers and Owners

Three hundred years ago, when the Amsterdam Stock Exchange traded stock in only one company, financial messages consisted of verbal or written instructions to representatives on the exchange. Transaction processing was completed with an authenticating handshake and a visit to the VOC offices across the street: the VOC shareholder ownership record would be updated (and witnessed by a Bank of Amsterdam employee). Before the 20th century, issuers of financial products, buyers, sellers, brokers, and the products themselves were all described by verbal descriptions either orally or textually in a message, letter, or contract.

Today there are thousands of companies traded on the U.S. equity markets. Different companies may issue different classes of equity stock. Thousands of companies, government agencies, and municipalities issue different types of bonds as well. For example, there are over a dozen different equity products for General Motors traded on the New York Stock Exchange; several dozen General Motors bonds also trade in the U.S. fixed income market. To make matters more complicated, this market structure replicated internationally. How can thousands of stocks and bonds be unambiguously identified for price reporting, trading, and settlement? What current technology is equivalent to the authenticating handshake and record book update? How are millions of buyers and sellers identified?

In order to process the products in financial databases, transaction systems, and messaging systems, we need to name them. *Product symbology* denotes the set of financial naming standards and technologies used to unambiguously identify what the buy side and sell side are buying and selling.

Symbology includes product abbreviations and encoding schemes, both a function of communication. For example, the financial messages based on the Rothschild pigeon protocols and the Chappe telegraph protocols used abbreviations, frequently encrypted, to identify financial products and their prices: long messages waste *information bandwidth* — precious message-carrying space (on the pigeon) or broadcasting time (on the telegraph). Financial message abbreviations are part of the financial jargon of the day.

Financial databases and messaging systems need to provide information on products identified by some unique name; these unique names must be consistent across trading platforms (through the buy side, exchanges, and sell side) as well as clearing and settlement systems. It also goes without saying that unique product names must also be consistent within a firm's internal operations, consisting of client account management systems, portfolio valuation systems, risk management systems, and compliance systems.

Names and Financial Database

If financial data is organized systematically, then information can be found and processed quickly. For example, suppose we have a financial database consisting of a small table of 64 different bonds; the columns indicate the security name, maturity date, coupon rate, coupon delivery date, and current bond ask price; each row corresponds to a specific bond. The spreadsheet in Figure 5-1 shows the first few rows.

A *database query* corresponds to the activity of finding information contained in a database. Suppose we want to find a particular bond issued by Acme corporation whose price is $88.75. If the table entries are arranged randomly, then in a worst-case scenario, we may have to search every entry in the price column to find a bond whose price matches $88.75: this amounts to at most 63 comparisons per query. This is how the Excel *Find* command works.

If the prices are sorted from low price to high price, we can use the following *bisection algorithm* to return the closest match: Call the bond with the lowest price F and the bond with the highest price L. (If there are 64 bonds, $F = 1$ and $L = 64$.)

1. Look at the price in bond F.
   If this price is greater or equal to $88.75, then return this bond and stop.
2. Look at the price in bond L.
   If this price is less or equal to $88.75, then return this bond and stop.
3. Otherwise, pick the middle bond M (for a table of 64 bonds, $M = 32$).
   If the price of bond M is greater than $88.75, then set $F = M$. If the price of bond M is less than $88.75, then set $L = M$. Go to step 1.

In a sorted table of 64 prices we need only perform at most six price comparisons per query (since at each step, the number of bonds that have to be compared is halved: from 32 bonds to 16 to 8 to 4 to 2 to 1 bond). In general, for a sorted table of N bonds, we need to perform at most:

$$\log_2 N \text{ price comparisons per database query for a sorted table}$$

$$N - 1 \text{ price comparisons per database query for an unsorted table}$$

	H	I	J	K	L	M	N	O	P
9	Name	Price	Coupon (%)	Maturity	Yield	Rating	Frequency	Coupon Date	Type
10	GM AC	104.39	6.125	15-Nov-07	4.501	BBB	Quarterly	15-Feb-03	Corporate
11	GM AC	105.34	6.75	15-Oct-07	4.725	BBB	Monthly	15-Feb-02	Corporate
12	GM AC	102.31	5	15-Dec-05	2.621	BBB	Monthly	15-Jan-03	Corporate
13	...								

FIGURE 5-1   Financial database of bonds.

For a table of 1 million bonds, we would need to perform at most (in Excel notation)

$$= \text{LOG}(1000000,2) \text{ or about 20 price comparisons per query}$$

At the rate of 1 second per comparison, this would take about 20 seconds per query. The unsorted table would require about a million comparisons; at a second per comparison, this would take over 11 days working around the clock. (Note that today's PC implementations are calibrated to perform approximately 1 million numerical comparisons per second.)

Current versions of Excel are limited to 1,048,576 rows ($=2^{\wedge}20$). Financial databases requiring more rows are based on a different technology, generally called Database Management Systems (abbreviated DBMS).

As long as a table has at least one column (sometimes called a *database field*) that is sorted or *indexed* in ascending (or descending) order, algorithms similar to bisection search can be applied to find information associated with one or more rows (sometimes called *database records*). Of course someone would have to spend time sorting (or indexing) the tables. This needs to be done once. Note that it is also relatively easy to insert new bonds into a sorted table that preserves the order.

Data in the bond table can be sorted by date (i.e., maturity date, coupon date, or earnings announcement date), times (i.e., trade time, settlement time), name (i.e., in alphabetical order by issuer name), and geography (i.e., zip code, city, and state of the issuer's address). We can also develop more sophisticated queries that depend on comparing values in different fields or on field values in other tables. For example, a bond database can be developed consisting of several tables, with each table cross listed by a bond name. In general, information can be found quickly as long as there is an unambiguous way of naming, organizing, and comparing data values. Note that queries can be simplified if there is a database field name that uniquely identifies each bond. *Keys* are (one or more) database fields that uniquely identify entire database records.

Identifying Banks: ABA Routing Numbers

One of the earliest and most important keys developed for financial databases was set up in 1911 by the *American Bankers Association* (ABA). The ABA "routing number" (also referred to as the ABA number or ABA routing transit number) is an unambiguous identifier of a bank (or other financial institution that can process payments); today ABA numbers are used for electronic funds transfer and online banking.

By the early 1900s, there were thousands of banks in the United States, with each bank potentially having thousands of accounts. The primary communication network was physical delivery (although many banks were starting to be linked by telegraph). There was ambiguity in account holder names (many account holders had similar names, e.g., John Smith) and bank names (many banks had similar names, e.g., First National Bank). The ABA routing number was designed to eliminate the ambiguity in identifying banks; its use speeded up the routing, delivery, and processing of money, securities, and checks.

It took several years of research for the ABA to come up with the standard nine-digit identifier. The ABA chose not to go into the key assignment and distribution business; the ABA outsourced these tasks to Rand McNally & Co., a well-known publisher. They were given an exclusive contract to publish the "Key to the Universal Numerical System" in

1911. [In 1990, Rand McNally was purchased by Thomson Financial Publishing (TFP), which in 2005 renamed itself SourceMedia.]

The nine-digit ABA routing number has not essentially changed in almost 100 years. Originally, the first two digits specified 12 geographical territories of the growing United States: (01 Boston; 02 New York; 03 Philadelphia; 04 Cleveland; 05 Richmond; 06 Atlanta; 07 Chicago; 08 St. Louis; 09 Minneapolis; 10 Kansas City; 11 Dallas; 12 San Francisco). If the first two digits are 00 then the check or payment is issued by the U.S. government. The first two digits for traveler's checks are assigned 80. Before 1985, the first two digits for savings banks, savings and loan associations, and credit unions (called *thrift institutions*) were assigned numbers ranging from 21 to 32 (the geographical territory is obtained from a thrift number by subtracting 20).

These two digits were used as the primary routing key for railroad and stagecoach delivery across the United States. After the creation of the Federal Reserve System in 1913, these 12 ABA territories became the 12 *Federal Reserve Districts*, and the main territory banks became the Federal Reserve District banks.

The third digit denotes a specific office at the territory's bank, indicating which branch office of the territory the payment should be routed through. Main offices are denoted by 1; branch offices (typically in other cities) are denoted by numbers ranging from 2 to 5.

The fourth digit indicates the availability of funds and payment speed. A 0 indicates immediate availability; the availability indicated by other numbers is dependent on a funds availability schedule (now enforced as *Regulation CC* by the Board of Governors of the Federal Reserve System). The second set of four digits (originally assigned by Rand McNally) uniquely identify the bank or other financial institution.

The last (ninth) digit is used to reduce to probability of transcription error (either recording wrong digits or recording the correct digits in the wrong order) or fraud (recording a payment to a nonexistent or nonvalid bank). The ninth digit is computed from the previous eight digits by an algorithm.

For example, the algorithm that computes the last digit for 0210 0002 1 (JPMorgan Chase Bank) is shown in Figure 5-2. The first 8 digits are multiplied by the weights given successively as 3-7-1-3-7-1-3-7 (i.e., $0*3, 2*7, 1*1, \ldots$). All products are then added; the result here is 29. We then divide 29 by 10 to get the remainder (not the quotient): the remainder resulting from dividing 29 by 10 is 9. The final step is to subtract this from 10, so the ninth ABA digit (also known as the *checksum digit*) for JPMorgan Chase

	S	T	U
42	**8 Digit**		
43	**Number**	**Weight**	**Product**
44	0	3	0
45	2	7	14
46	1	1	1
47	0	3	0
48	0	7	0
49	0	1	0
50	0	3	0
51	2	7	14
52	Sum Products		29
53	10-mod(S,10)		1
54			
55	**9-Digit**		
56	**ABA:**	0210 0002 1	

FIGURE 5-2

	S	T	U
42	**8 Digit**		
43	**Number**	**Weight**	**Product**
44	0	3	=T44*S44
45	2	7	=T45*S45
46	1	1	=T46*S46
47	0	3	=T47*S47
48	0	7	=T48*S48
49	0	1	=T49*S49
50	0	3	=T50*S50
51	2	7	=T51*S51
52		Sum Products	=SUM(U44:U51)
53		10-mod(S,10)	=10-MOD(U52,10)
54			
55	**9-Digit**		
56	**ABA:**	0210 0002 1	

FIGURE 5-3

is 1. In today's computer systems, we find remainders by using the modulo function: the remainder resulting from dividing 29 by 10 is denoted by

mod(29,10) in Excel
29 Mod 10 in VBA
29 mod 10 or modp(29,10) in MuPAD
29 % 10 in C

Figure 5-3 shows the spreadsheet formulas.

The checksum digit helps implement valid authenticated financial communication that is reliable and error correcting. For example, suppose a courier delivers a check to a receiving bank. If the computed checksum digit is different from the observed checksum digit recorded on the received check, then the receiving institution can request the courier to return to the originating bank and request a retransmission of the check.

In July 1956, almost 50 years after the initial ABA specification, the ABA Bank Management Commission approved guidelines incorporating Magnetic Ink Character Recognition (MICR) for processing checks. The ABA number and customer account numbers would be printed with magnetized ink: this magnetized symbols could be read by a scanner similar to that embedded in a reel-to-reel tape recorder. The technology, developed by Kenneth Eldredge (then at Stanford Research Institute), was awarded U.S. Patent Number 3,000,000. Check sorting, routing, and processing — initially done by hand — could now be automated by integrating MICR readers with computer database management systems.

Today, most checks are printed showing the ABA number (and the bank's customer account number) in the distinctive 14 character MICR font called E-13B. E-13B was accepted as the MICR standard by the ABA in 1959 and by the American National Standards Institute (ANSI) in 1963. Other countries (Canada, Japan, Australia, the United Kingdom) have also standardized on E-13B (CMC-7, another MICR font, is the standard in Brazil, France, and other European countries). Figure 5-4 shows the 14 (0123456789ABCD) E-13B symbols. The symbols for A, B, C, and D are similar to those used in bar codes.

FIGURE 5-4

Box 5-1

Identifying Owners: The Social Security Administration and the Internal Revenue Service

The IRS was originally called the Commissioner of Internal Revenue in 1862: the original purpose was to enact an income tax to pay for the Civil War (the income tax was repealed in 1872, revived in 1894, and declared unconstitutional by the U.S. Supreme Court in 1895). In 1913, the same year that the Federal Reserve system was established, the 16th Amendment to the U.S. Constitution was ratified to give Congress the authority to enact an income tax on individuals and corporations.

The 9 digit US Social Security Number (SSN) was first issued by the newly formed Social Security Administration in November 1936. The SSN was, like the ABA Number, originally geographically based: the first three SSN digits were determined from the applicant's post office. Over 415 million Social Security numbers have been issued to individuals since 1936. An SSN is a unique database key: SSNs are not assigned to two different people and are not recycled or reused.

According to current IRS documents, "a taxpayer identification number must be furnished on all returns, statements, and other tax–related documents and must be given upon request to any other person who must include it on a return or statement." For most individuals this is a Social Security Number. However, some taxpayers do not have (and are not eligible for) an SSN (e.g., foriegn workers). In this case, the IRS issues an Individual Taxpayer Identification Number (ITIN), a nine-digit number that always begins with the number 9 and has a 7 or 8 in the fourth digit. According to the IRS, "ITINs are not valid identification outside the tax system."

The IRS also issues a 9 digit taxpayer identifier to business entities such as employers, sole proprietors, corporations, partnerships, nonprofit associations, trusts, estates, and government agencies. This number is called an Employer Identification Number (EIN); it is also called the Federal Tax Identification Number (or Federal Tax Id). Note that an individual can control several corporations who in turn control other corporations: each corporation would have their own EIN. Consequently, the IRS issues the following warning: "Please be advised that it is against the law to use an EIN for anything other than business use. An EIN cannot be used as a Social Security Number."

Another reason why the EINs, ITINs, and SSNs are not the best database keys is that there is no authenticating checksum digit to help prevent fraud (by inventing new SSNs or EINs or to prevent mistakes when the numbers are manually recorded). True identities can also be stolen, masked, or concealed by fraudulent practices. In any case, using codes based on social security and tax identification may be in violation of personal disclosures and privacy laws.

Identifying Accounts: Credit Cards

ERMA (Box 5-2) demonstrated that computer technology — based on encoding schemes that identified banks and internal customer accounts numbers — helped banks reduce paper-processing costs. This possibly led the Bank of America to issue letters of credit to thousands of applying customers — in the form of credit cards. Checking account identification numbers evolved to letters of credit account identification numbers — credit card numbers.

Box 5-2
Project ERMA and Check-21

ERMA

Stanford Research Institute (SRI) developed (MICR) under contract with the Electronic Recording Machine-Accounting (ERMA) Project, sponsored by the Bank of America (BoA). BoA was the largest bank in California in 1950 and was a major check processor. In those days, checking accounts were identified by name, and clerks needed to manually alphabetize the checks in order to identify the accounts to be cleared. Branches needed to close several hours early for manual check processing.

In July 1950, SRI proposed an idea that would immediately speed up BoA's check processing: the assignment of unique identification numbers for checking accounts. The account numbers (as well as account names) would be printed on each check. This simplified check sorting and the creation and maintenance of new accounts. In November, SRI started designing one of the first financial applications of computer systems: a database integrated with a machine that read checks imprinted with magnetic ink. The ABA routing number and the new BoA account number were imprinted in a special readable font on each check (bar codes were rejected because they are not easily readable). The resulting system read 10 checks a second with very few errors, which was much faster than manual processing. In January 1952, SRI started building a working prototype.

The 1955 version of ERMA weighed about 25 tons (it contained more than a million feet of wire) and required 80,000 watts of power. The hardware consisted of MICR input consoles, magnetic memory drums, a check sorter, a printer, 12 magnetic tape drives (each holding two reels), and several power supplies. General Electric won the contract to take the prototype out of the research lab; their task was to build and install 32 systems deployed at several BoA locations. (GE proposed to replace the prototype's 8000 vacuum tubes with a new technology based on transistors.) The first system was installed in 1959; by 1966 the ERMA systems handled more than 750 million checks a year. The original ERMA computers were replaced over the next 10 years as technology evolved.

Check 21

The 2004 Check Clearing for the 21st Century Act, known as Check 21, lets complying financial institutions exchange digital images of checks instead of routing and physically delivering paper checks across the country via railroad trains, trucks, and airplanes. Faster exchange implies faster clearing: there is less time between the instant a check is written and the time when funds are debited from an account. (The time lag between receipt and clearing is called *the float*.) Cross continental checks clear in minutes instead of days. Because of this, Check 21 was viewed as the first major financial technology check processing innovation since the 1956 MICR standardization.

Check 21 also lets merchants eliminate manual check processing. Merchants can pass customer checks through an MICR reader and convert the check into an electronic transaction at the point of sale. The merchant's MICR processor prevents mistakes or fraud that can occur when transactions are recorded manually. It lets the merchant know, at the time of sales, if the customer has sufficient funds to cover the amount. After a few seconds of processing, the customer account is debited, the merchant's account is credited, and the check is returned to the customer. The merchant does not need the paper check.

The BankAmericard was released in 1958 (it was renamed VISA in 1975). Diners Club (released in 1950 and acquired by Citicorp in 1981), originally designed to let restaurants extend credit to their dining customers, was the only credit card available before that time. American Express also released their first credit card in 1958 and substituted actual plastic cards for paper in 1959. Seven years later, the Interbank Card Association (a group of banks led by the United California Bank, now part of Wells Fargo) released MasterCard International.

Credit card numbers follow separate conventions for the first few digits and the number of digits. The first two digits for American Express numbers are either 34 or 37; for MasterCard they range from 51 to 55; for Diners Club they range from 300 to 305 and also include 36 and 38; and for VISA, the first digit is 4. For American Express the number of digits in the credit card number is 15; for MasterCard the number of digits is 16; for Diners Club the number of digits is 14; and for VISA the number of digits is either 13 or 16.

For all credit cards, the last digit is the checksum digit. For example, the following 16-digit VISA credit card number 4495 7654 3210 9991 has checksum 1, computed according to the algorithm shown in Figure 5-5.

Since the late 1960s the checksum algorithm used is due to Hans Luhn (1896–1964). Some people call Luhn the "father of information retrieval" — at IBM, he developed indexing schemes such as *Key Word in Context* (abbreviated as the KWIC method). Luhn's algorithm is now international standard ISO/IEC 7812.

The difference between Luhn's algorithm (known as the "mod 10" algorithm, or the "mod 10 double-add-double" formula) and the 1911 ABA algorithm is that there is a step in which the digits of the products are added before taking the mod 10.

Formulas for the Luhn algorithm are shown in Figure 5-6. In Luhn's algorithm, the weights are 2-1-2-1-...2 if the total number of credit card digits is an even number or 1-2-1-2-...2 if the total number of credit card digits is an odd number. (When applying Luhn's algorithm, the rightmost digit — the check digit — must always be multiplied by 1 and not by 2.)

	L	M	N	O
52	**15 Digit**			**Sum**
53	**Number**	**Weight**	**Product**	**Digits**
54	4	2	8	8
55	4	1	4	4
56	9	2	18	9
57	5	1	5	5
58	7	2	14	5
59	6	1	6	6
60	5	2	10	1
61	4	1	4	4
62	3	2	6	6
63	2	1	2	2
64	1	2	2	2
65	0	1	0	0
66	9	2	18	9
67	9	1	9	9
68	9	2	18	9
69		Sum Single Digits S:		79
70		10-mod(S,10) :		1
71	**16 Digit Credit**			
72	**Card:**	4495 7654 3210 999 1		

FIGURE 5-5

	L	M	N	O
52	**15 Digit**			**Sum**
53	**Number**	**Weight**	**Product**	**Digits**
54	4	2	=M54*L54	8
55	4	1	=M55*L55	4
56	9	2	=M56*L56	=1+8
57	5	1	=M57*L57	5
58	7	2	=M58*L58	=1+4
59	6	1	=M59*L59	6
60	5	2	=M60*L60	=1+0
61	4	1	=M61*L61	4
62	3	2	=M62*L62	6
63	2	1	=M63*L63	2
64	1	2	=M64*L64	2
65	0	1	=M65*L65	0
66	9	2	=M66*L66	=1+8
67	9	1	=M67*L67	9
68	9	2	=M68*L68	=1+8
69			Sum Single Digits S:	=SUM(O54:O68)
70			10-mod(S,10) :	=10-MOD(O69,10)
71	**16 Digit Credit**			
72	**Card:**	4495 7654 3210 99		

FIGURE 5-6

Identifying Financial Products

In the 1950s, trade processing at the New York Stock Exchange was similar to the processing done 100 years earlier: after each trade, stock brokers would exchange physical certificates for checks; these were physically delivered throughout the day by hundreds of couriers who ran through the streets of downtown Manhattan with bags of checks and securities.

By 1961, the average daily volume on the NYSE exceeded 4 million shares, nearly triple the volume just 15 years earlier. The buy-side and sell-side institutions were also experiencing a paperwork crisis that was similar to the one faced by the Bank of America in the early 1950s. What was needed was a system that identified the issuer of securities (such as publicly traded corporations, government agencies, municipalities, states, and the Federal government) issuers and financial products that they issued (different classes of stocks and bonds). A unique identifier assigned to each issuer (with a suffix identifying a specific product) would reduce the confusion and delays in securities processing. Brokers, banks, exchanges, and institutions would have a common database key that could be used for reporting, trading, messaging, transaction reports, transfers, shareholder proxy voting, and dividend processing.

Partly to address this growing problem, the New York Clearing House Association (Box 5-3) formed a Securities Procedures Committee in 1962 that would uniquely identify stocks, bonds, and other securities, possibly along the same methods as the nine-digit ABA number that was developed in 1911.

The Clearing House soon contacted the American Bankers Association, and in July 1964, the ABA formed the Committee on Uniform Security Identification Procedures (CUSIP). The committee developed a standard numbering system of nine symbols (symbols include numbers 0–9 or letters A–Z) for identifying securities and announced the specification in January 1967. Meanwhile, by August 1967, the NYSE needed to close every Wednesday (and to shorten trading hours on other days) because of the "paperwork crisis."

Box 5-3
The New York Clearing House

In 1841, bank cashier George D. Lyman proposed the then novel idea that New York banks send and receive checks to a central processing office and to organize an association that would "maintain conservative banking through wise and intelligent cooperation." Twelve years later, on October 4, 1853, The New York Clearing House Association was organized to implement Lyman's idea. The first central processing office for checks was organized 1 week later across the street from the New York Stock Exchange, in the basement of 14 Wall Street. At the New York Clearing House (NYCH), 52 banks exchanged checks, bonds, coupons, and other securities; all net changes were recorded to each bank's clearing house account. Accounts among banks were settled each business day. As a service, nonmember NYCH institutions were also allowed to clear their checks and securities through NYCH member banks.

After the Federal Reserve System was created in 1913, net changes were also recorded at the banks' accounts maintained at the New York Federal Reserve Bank.

The manual task of exchanging paper checks, bonds, coupons and other securities was replaced in 1970 by the Clearing House Interbank Payments System (CHIPS), and the Automated Clearing House (ACH) in 1975; this became the Electronics Payment Network (EPN) in 2000.

By November 2003, the Chicago Clearing House Association (established in 1865) and the Western Payments Alliance (known as WesPay, established in 1876) merged with the New York Clearing House: the merged organization became known as The Clearing House. In July 2004, The Clearing House further consolidated their payment operations — consisting of Small Value Payments Company (SVPCo), Clearing House Interbank Payments System (CHIPS), Electronic Payments Network (EPN), Electronic Clearing Services (ECS), and National Check Exchange (NCE) — into the Clearing House Payments Company.

On its first operating day in 1853, the NYCH exchanged checks worth $22.6 million. In 2005, The Clearing House Payments Company consists of a global payment systems infrastructure that clears and settles more than $1.5 trillion per day. The Clearing House Payments Company still maintains the New York Clearing House Association — now called the Clearing House Association — as a forum that publishes position papers on issues that are important to the banking industry and the owner banks.

CUSIP

CUSIP numbers started being assigned in 1968, when the ABA outsourced the key assignment and distribution business to Standard & Poor's (owned by McGraw-Hill since 1966). They were given an exclusive contract to operate the CUSIP Service Bureau for the American Bankers Association.

The first six CUSIP symbols form a key called *issuer number* (symbols 1–3 must be numbers; symbols 4–6 may be numbers or letters). The next two symbols form a suffix known as the *issue number* (symbols 7 and 8 can be numbers or letters). Common stock has the suffix 10; other equity issues (such as preferred stock, warrants) are assigned higher numbers. Fixed income products start with an A1 or AA as the suffix (and continue to ZZ).

Box 5-4
The American Bankers Association

The American Bankers Association was started in St. Louis, Missouri in January 1875, by two bank cashiers (James T. Howenstein of the Valley National Bank and Edward Cruft Breck of the Exchange Bank). Their inspiration for an association of cooperating banks was apparently the result of the Woman's Suffrage movement (in 1875, Virginia Minor, the suffrage leader of St. Louis, successfully brought the issue of suffrage before the U.S. Supreme Court).

On May 24, 1875, 16 bankers across the country accepted Howenstein's invitation to meet in New York City at Barnum's Hotel. At the next meeting in July in Saratoga Springs, New York, 349 bankers from dozens of states and U.S. territories formed the American Bankers' Association.

Some of the initial problems that the ABA addressed concerned the reliability and safety of physical delivery of money, checks, and other financial securities. In 1894, the ABA Standing Protective Committee hired the Pinkerton National Detective Agency to monitor professional criminals; one of Pinkerton's successes was the elimination of the "Wild Bunch" gang (whose members included George "Butch" Cassidy and Harry Longbaugh, the "Sundance Kid").

During this time, the ABA and other representatives met to discuss the problem of clearing checks across the country. The ABA Clearing House Conference Committee was appointed in 1905 to solve the problem. This group created a Numerical Committee (with team members W. G. Schroeder, C. R. McKay, and J. A. Walker) to devise the system that associates a unique number to each bank. The team's "Universal Numerical System" (now called the ABA Routing Number) was approved by the ABA Executive Council in May 1911.

Also in 1911, the ABA set up a Currency Commission (to work with Senator Nelson Aldrich, chairman of the U.S. National Monetary Commission) to help organize a National Reserve Association. In 1913, the National Reserve Association became known as the Federal Reserve System.

The ninth symbol is the checksum digit. The CUSIP checksum scheme uses the Luhn algorithm; because the number of CUSIP symbols is an odd number, the first eight symbols are multiplied by the weights given successively as 1-2-1-2-1-2-1-2. In order to transform letter symbols into numbers for the checksum algorithm, A is mapped to number 10, B to number 11, C to 12, . . . , and Z to 35.

For example, for 36960410 (General Electric issue number is 369604; the 10 suffix denotes the stock), the weighted sum is 27 (Figure 5-7) and the checksum is $10 - \text{mod}(27, 10) = 3$. The formulas are shown in Figure 5-8.

SEDOL

The London Stock Exchange keeps track of over 400,000 global securities. Their seven-symbol database key is called the Stock Exchange Daily Official List (acronym: SEDOL); each SEDOL key is registered and distributed by the Exchange (not a third party). The seventh checksum digit is computed with an algorithm similar to the ABA algorithm, but with different weights.

SEDOL symbols consist of numbers 0–9 and letters (B–Z, excluding vowels). The first symbol is always a SEDOL letter; symbols 2–6 can be either numbers or letters; the last symbol is a number (the checksum). Unlike ABA numbers, groupings of SEDOL

	L	M	N	O
22	**8 Digit**			**Single**
23	**Number**	**Weight**	**Product**	**Digits**
24	3	1	3	3
25	6	2	12	3
26	9	1	9	9
27	6	2	12	3
28	0	1	0	0
29	4	2	8	8
30	1	1	1	1
31	0	2	0	0
32			Sum Single Digits S:	27
33			10-mod(S,10) :	3
34		**9 Digit**		
35		**CUSIP:**	369604 10 3	

FIGURE 5-7

	L	M	N	O
22	**8 Digit**			**Single**
23	**Number**	**Weight**	**Product**	**Digits**
24	3	1	=L24*M24	3
25	6	2	=L25*M25	=1+2
26	9	1	=L26*M26	9
27	6	2	=L27*M27	=1+2
28	0	1	=L28*M28	0
29	4	2	=L29*M29	8
30	1	1	=L30*M30	1
31	0	2	=L31*M31	0
32			Sum Single Digits S:	=SUM(O24:O31)
33			10-mod(S,10) :	=10-MOD(O32,10)
34		**9 Digit**		
35		**CUSIP:**	369604 10 3	

FIGURE 5-8

symbols have no meaning: the Exchange simply allocates SEDOL symbols sequentially. In the SEDOL checksum scheme, the first six symbols are multiplied by the weights given successively as 1-3-1-7-3-9. In order to transform the nonvowel letter symbols into numbers for the checksum algorithm, B is mapped to number 11, C to number 12, D to 13, . . . , and Z to 35, according to Figure 5-9.

Figure 5-10 shows an example showing the checksum algorithm for SEDOL symbol B1F3M59, with formulas shown in Figure 5-11.

ISIN

Stocks, bonds, and other securities not only depend on the issuing company or agency, they also depend on the country in which they are issued. Who issues the keys for international financial databases?

The Association of National Numbering Agencies (ANNA) was established in 1991 to address this question in order to develop "an International Securities Identification Number (ISIN) in a uniform structure for use in any application in the trading and administration of

B	C	D	F	G	H	J	K	L	M	N	P	Q	R	S	T	V	W	X	Y	Z
11	12	13	15	16	17	19	20	21	22	23	25	26	27	28	29	31	32	33	34	35

FIGURE 5-9

	W	X	Y	Z
71		Num.		
72	6 Symbols	Equiv.	Weight	Product
73	B	11	1	11
74	1	1	3	3
75	F	15	1	15
76	3	3	7	21
77	M	22	3	66
78	5	5	9	45
79				
80			Sum Products	161
81			10-mod(S,10)	9
82			SEDOL:	B1F3M5 9

FIGURE 5-10

	W	X	Y	Z
71		Num.		
72	6 Symbols	Equiv.	Weight	Product
73	B	11	1	=X73*Y73
74	1	1	3	=X74*Y74
75	F	15	1	=X75*Y75
76	3	3	7	=X76*Y76
77	M	22	3	=X77*Y77
78	5	5	9	=X78*Y78
79				
80			Sum Products	=SUM(Z73:Z78)
81			10-mod(S,10)	=10-MOD(Z80,10)
82			SEDOL	B1F3M5 9

FIGURE 5-11

securities in the international securities industry." The ANNA ISIN standard is maintained by the International Standards Organization (ISO) as ISO 6166. ANNA also certifies each individual national numbering agency (NNA) that is responsible for issuing an ISIN in each country. In the United States, the ISIN is the CUSIP Service Bureau of Standard & Poor's; in the United Kingdom it is the London Stock Exchange.

The first two symbols of an ISIN are two letters that correspond to the official country code (based on the ISO 3166-1 country code standard). This country code is similar to that used by top-level Internet domain names (i.e., US for the United States or GB for the United Kingdom). The next nine symbols are called the national securities identifying number (NSIN), issued by the country's NNA. (If the NSIN has less than nine symbols, then zeros are inserted in front of the number so that the full nine spaces are used.) The last (ninth) checksum digit is computed according to Luhn's algorithm. Note that even though ISO 3166 also identifies country code numerical equivalents (i.e., 840 for the United States or 826 for the United Kingdom) that are consistent with those used by the United Nations Statistical Division, the ISIN checksum algorithm is similar to the CUSIP computation: A is mapped to number 10, B to number 11, C to 12, ..., and Z to 35. Because the number of symbols is even, the Luhn algorithm specifies the weight for the checksum computation as 2-1-2-1-2-1-2-1-2-1-2.

CINS

The CUSIP international numbering system (CINS) was developed by Standard & Poor's and Telekurs (USA) as an international extension of the CUSIP numbering system. CINS numbers are based on a six-digit issuer number and a two-symbol issue number. The first symbol of the issuer number is a letter (from A to Z, excluding I, O, Z) denoting a country or geographic region (i.e., A is Austria, X is Europe-Other). The last (ninth) digit is the checksum computed according to Luhn's algorithm.

Telekurs (USA) is a wholly owned subsidiary of Telekurs Financial. Telekurs Financial started in 1930 as Ticker AG, a financial information vendor for Swiss banks. In 1962, Ticker AG renamed itself Telekurs; by this time it had developed a global systems infrastructure for financial information. Today, Telekurs Financial is owned by over 350 Swiss banks and stock exchanges, and the Telekurs database contains information on almost two million financial products.

Telekurs Financial is also the NNA responsible for maintaining the Swiss Registrar of Securities and issuing Swiss Valor numbers for security identification. The Swiss Valor numbers helped automate the Swiss Stock Exchange, a fully electronic exchange set up in 1996 that merged the traditional floor systems at Geneva (founded in 1850), Zurich (1873), and Basle (1876).

5.2. Other Identifiers in Financial Databases

Most financial transactions utilize brokers and clearing organizations: how are these market participants represented? Can we identify individual brokers or traders who issue or receive quotes or orders? Is there a way to keep field names consistent among exchanges, clearing houses, market data vendors, market participants, and traders so that data can be exchanged easily?

Identifying Market Makers

In the 17th century Amsterdam Stock Exchange, market participants were known to each other or could be verified by a personal contact. As trading floors got crowded, badge numbers were issued by the exchanges that would correlate to a company identifier.

Today, identifiers for equity and bond (municipal and corporate) market participants are assigned by the National Securities Clearing Corporation (NSCC), a subsidiary of The Depository Trust & Clearing Corporation (DTCC). Each NSCC member is assigned a four-digit number, referred to (by different exchanges, market makers, and vendors) as either the

> Market Maker Identifier (MMID)
> Market Participant Identifier (MPI)
> Market Participant ID
> NSCC Clearing Number
> Buy or Sell Clearing Member
> Broker Number
> Broker ID
> MP ID
> Executing Broker Symbol
> Clearing Number

The NSCC also assigns a ticker-like symbol to clearing members as well. The NSCC member directory provides several sorted lists of firms with their symbols and MMIDs.

Large financial firms may have subsidiary clearing corporations, these are assigned their own MMID. For example, three of the many Merrill Lynch clearing identifiers are

Merrill Lynch Professional Clearing Corporation	MMID 0551; Symbol PRO
Merrill Lynch, Pierce, Fenner & Smith Inc.	MMID 0161; Symbol M
Merrill Lynch Professional Clearing Corporation #2	MMID 0561; Symbol BUL

All NYSE and Nasdaq (and other equity exchange) quotes and trades are identified by an MMID field.

For electronic exchanges and markets, other market maker identifiers can be provided. For example, Nasdaq systems identify a workstation or terminal identifier in their quote and order systems by a 12-digit alphanumeric code.

Identifying Brokers

The MMID identifies firms for the purposes of quotes, orders, clearing, and settlement.

Information about brokers is contained in the *Central Registration Depository* (CRD), a database that now contains information on almost 900,000 registered entities (including over 6000 firms). The database is maintained by NASD Regulation, Inc. (NASDR), the regulatory subsidiary of the National Association of Securities Dealers (NASD). Brokerages, brokerage offices (also called *branch offices*), and state-registered brokers and dealers (called *registered representatives*) are assigned a CRD number. On a corporate level, these identifier numbers are used to correlate information about brokerage firms and offices. On an individual level, the registered representative (RR) CRD number is associated with records of career events, examination grades, and disciplinary hearings. The CRD is also used by the SEC, exchanges, and state securities regulatory authorities (usually involving registering and licensing) and is available on the Web as Web CRD.

CRD numbers are usually between 6 and 7 digits (i.e., 123345 or 1234567). For example, some of the many Merrill Lynch offices with their CRD numbers are

Merrill Lynch, Pierce Professional Clearing Corp.	16139
Merrill Lynch Government Securities Inc.	19693
Merrill Lynch, Pierce, Fenner, & Smith Inc.	7691
Merrill Lynch Alternative Investments LLC.	105067
Merrill Lynch Asset Management (UK)	107059
Merrill Lynch Investment Managers LP.	105068
Merrill Lynch Investment Managers, LLC.	108928
Merrill Lynch Trust Company	108469

Since 2001, the SEC also maintains an 8-digit *investment adviser registration depository* (IARD) number (also called an SEC Number or 801 Number) for SEC-registered investment advisers. Development of the IARD was modeled after the CRD; it is a joint effort by the SEC and the North American Securities Administrators Association (NASAA). Like the CRD, the IARD was built and is maintained by the NASDR.

Box 5-5
North American Securities Administrators Association (NASAA)

The NASAA was organized in 1919; it is the oldest international organization focused on broker licensing and investor protection. The NASAA is a voluntary association of state, provincial, and territorial securities administrators in all 50 states, the District of Columbia, Puerto Rico, Canada, and Mexico. Currently, the NASAA is investigating procedures to monitor or prevent email securities fraud.

To be a registered broker, an applicant has to pass the NASD Series 7 examination. This test makes sure that the broker knows securities regulations, trading procedures involving margin requirements and options, and clearing and settlement procedures.

Brokerage licenses are governed by state agencies. Before 1984, in order to be registered and licensed, brokers had to send a form, a picture, and a fee to each state. The CRD was developed to speed up this process. It was a collaborative effort between the NASD and the NASAA in order to provide applicants with an efficient state licensing procedure. After 1984, only one form needed to be filed with the CRD automated registration system; data would then be filed electronically to every state.

The CRD number is a database key of every person acting as a broker or broker dealer. It maintains information on their location, their branch offices, and their branch managers. Information about complaints, arbitrations, or regulatory actions can help regulators monitor the financial industry.

The NASAA also developed additional certification exams such as Series 63, Series 65, and Series 66. Series 63 (Uniform Securities Agent State Law Examination) is a test in state law. The Series 65 (Uniform Investment Adviser Law Examination) is required in some states and by some firms. It further tests knowledge of state laws related to securities registration, the 1940 Investment Adviser's Act, and what can be placed in pension funds. Series 66 (Uniform Combined State Law Examination) combines Series 63 and Series 65. Passing the NASD Series 7 is a prerequisite to be a Series 66 registered investment adviser.

All IARD numbers start with an 801-. Here are IARD numbers for the Merrill Lynch advisers in the aforementioned list:

Merrill Lynch, Pierce, Fenner, & Smith Inc.	801-14235
Merrill Lynch Alternative Investments LLC.	801-35676
Merrill Lynch Asset Management (UK)	801-31780
Merrill Lynch Investment Managers LP.	801-11583
Merrill Lynch Investment Managers, LLC.	801-56972
Merrill Lynch Trust Company	801-55309

Individual exchanges also have their own registration rules in order to keep track of market participants. For example, the New York Stock Exchange specifies that market participants must provide a numerical identifier unique to each of its locations to identify branch offices. This *NYSE branch code number* can be up to 15 alphanumeric digits.

Many regulatory and compliance systems require CRD, MMID, and IARD identifiers in order to assess whether markets are fair and orderly and to determine if any rule violations occurred. The NYSE *Audit Trail* system and Nasdaq *Order Audit* Trail System (OATS) are examples of exchange applications that analyze time-sequenced databases of quotes, orders, and trades so that events and actions can be reviewed at a market maker level.

On the transaction level, exchanges, market makers, and brokers can also provide data that identify individual buyers and sellers (by name, address, account number, and tax identification numbers such as EIN or SS). For several decades, the SEC would request this information by mailing special forms (known as *blue sheets* because of the color on which the forms were printed) to market makers and brokers. Before the 1980s these would be processed manually and mailed back to the SEC. Today, electronic blue sheets are database tables whose fields list SEC specified transaction details of all buyers or sellers for a given security during a given time period. These blue sheets are required to be submitted to the SEC within 10 days of a request.

The Meta Data Approach to Identifying Fields: ISO 15022

One database system may use the following 10-field names in a table:

Name Price Coupon% Maturity Yield Rating Frequency Coupon$ Date Type CUSIP

Another system may have the same information in a table but with different field names:

PRD PR CP MT YLD RTNG FRQ CPDT TYP CUSIPNUM

A third system may have the same information in several tables but with different field names. Finally, a fourth system may only have partial information. The only way to use these databases together is to utilize either a universal database standard or to have detailed knowledge about the database field names — data about data (also known as *metadata*) — so that we can develop translation procedures that use information in one table from one source in another table from another source. Both approaches are used in the financial industry. The metadata approach is discussed in this section. An approach based on universal standards [currently based on different representations written in extensible markup language (XML)] is discussed in Chapter 9.

ISO 15022 is a standard that specifies the minimum amount of information required to document each field in a financial database. In this specification, each database field is described by several "meta-fields" of information. Some of the metadata used to describe each database field include:

1. Name of the field.
2. Definition of the discrete data field or class of generic data fields.
3. Field type.
4. Format of data.
5. Valid values (e.g., a number between 1 and 99; a list of symbols or words). All the registered symbols together with their meaning, usage, and status should be given.
6. An example of the use of the field.
7. Rules on how and when to use data in the field.
8. When the field was created.
9. When the field was last updated.
10. History of the field; whether it replaces another field.

11. Where the field is used.

12. A list of ISO synonyms or equivalents for the data field.

13. Status.

14. Specific values (e.g., symbols or code words) that may be removed at a future date.

This metadata can be used to build applications involving queries to multiple databases of different structures or different vendors. The databases could also be *heterogeneous*, they support different data representations, different query languages, and different data models. For example, some financial database providers may structure their financial data as a set of tables, as in the spreadsheet approach (modeling a database as a set of tables is called a *relational* model). Figure 5-12 shows a schematic diagram where the financial database is structured as a hierarchy.

For example, this very simple hierarchy shows an owner, identified by an SSN and zero or more EINs having multiple brokers. Brokers can be responsible for one or more accounts. Figure 5-13 shows that another way of structuring a financial database is as a *network*. This network also indicates that owners can have joint accounts with other owners. In practice, hierarchy or network database structures may end up being implemented as tables (or any other convenient or useful data structure) supported by a database management system (DBMS). Much of the time spent in designing and building a financial database system is spent mapping procedures (specified by programming languages) to database fields (specified by a DBMS) so that system users can efficiently query and manipulate data in a robust way. *Data modeling* is concerned with representing and organizing, in an abstract way, data for a database. Data modeling languages, like all other languages, have a syntax, semantics, and pragmatics. (Only a very brief syntax, pictorially representing the structure, has been shown in these diagrams.)

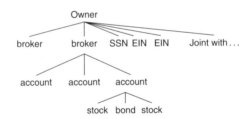

FIGURE 5-12   Schematic of a financial database structured as a hierarchy.

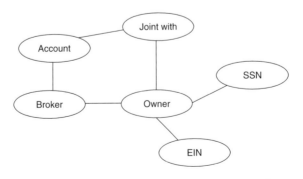

FIGURE 5-13   Schematic of a financial database structured as a network.

5.3. Exchange Ticker Symbols

Most financial products already had standard identifiers before the adoption of standard CUSIP identifiers in 1968. These identifiers were not necessarily unique, as they were issued by different exchanges.

Exchange-issued financial product identifiers grew out of the abbreviations used by telegraph operators. Morse code transmission was time-consuming and operators quickly developed a sublanguage to increase information throughput. For example, an operator could begin a transmission with GM ("good morning"), CFM ("confirm") a price, and terminate with a CUL ("see you later"). Today many of these codes survive in the Internet slang found in online chat rooms. Some of the telegraph abbreviations became so important that they became standardized for communication control purposes (especially when the telegraph technology became wireless). For example, in 1912, international maritime telegraph operators standardized a set of abbreviations for control messages. The abbreviations were three-letter sequences beginning with the letter Q (hence it is called *Q code*). For example, a transmission of QRS was a message to the other operator to "please transmit more slowly."

The stock ticker, essentially a receiving telegraph hooked up to a noisy impact printer, was used 100 years before the first CUSIP number. Tickers were used to receive quotes that telegraph operators transmitted from the New York Stock Exchange and the New York Gold Exchange. How were stock prices transmitted? Operators would abbreviate the most frequently traded products with single letters; more frequently traded products would have more letters. These *ticker symbols* (also called stock symbols or exchange symbols) uniquely identify the product.

Today, stock exchange traded ticker symbols have an associated CUSIP or ISIN identifier. However, there are other ticker symbols that do not have CUSIPs or ISINs because they are exchange traded contracts — not products issued by an issuer. These ticker symbols are associated most commonly with futures and options contracts. Recall that according to Joseph de la Vega, much of the activity occurring 400 years ago at the Amsterdam Stock Exchange was concerned with the buying and selling of these contracts, where the advantage over an outright purchase of the product was (and is) that money does not have to be tied up; essentially product is purchased with credit.

NYSE, AMEX, and Nasdaq Symbols

Telegraph-derived symbology survives on the NYSE today: NYSE ticker symbols can be a single letter (T for American Telephone & Telegraph, or AT&T: founded by Alexander Bell in 1876, now merging with SBC); two letters (GE for General Electric, founded in 1892 by Thomas Edison and others); three letters (IBM for International Business Machines; the 1911 Computing-Tabulating-Recording Company known as C-T-R, which renamed itself in 1924 under the aegis of Thomas Watson). When a company applies for listing at the NYSE, it can submit three choices for its ticker symbol for NYSE approval.

The NYSE also runs the largest U.S. centralized market for exchange traded bonds issued by U.S. and foreign corporations, the U.S. government, foreign governments, municipalities, and international banks (almost 1500 issues by 400 issuers). Bonds have coupons and maturity dates in addition to issuer name; the NYSE bond ticker symbols reflect these. Usually the bond ticker is the stock ticker appended with a space and the maturity year or other unique characteristic.

For example,

T 06 is the NYSE ticker for a bond issued by AT&T with 7 1/2% coupon and maturity date 06/01/06 (CUSIP: 001957AP4011)

HON ZRA05 is the NYSE ticker for a zero coupon bond issued by Honeywell INTL that matures on 8/1/05 (CUSIP: 438516AG1011)

and US NOV15 is the NYSE ticker for a U.S. Treasury Bond with 9 7/8% coupon that matures on 11/15/15 (CUSIP: 912810DT2001)

Note that the issuer of the last bond is the U.S. government — it is not a stock and does not have a ticker symbol.

Stocks trading on the American Stock Exchange typically have a three-letter ticker symbol (CUB is the ticker symbol for Cubic Corporation). Nasdaq-traded stocks always have four letters (INTC is the ticker symbol for Intel Corporation).

There are some exceptions. NYSE issues symbols of four or more letters, such as BRKA and BRKB, for Berkshire Hathaway class A and B shares, respectively. Foreign companies whose American depository receipts are traded have a Y as the last letter; e.g., RTRSY is the Nasdaq ticker symbol for Reuters Group PLC, a United Kingdom company. Other special codes are specified by the respective exchanges. Sometimes different data vendors distinguish these symbols with special separators, e.g., BRKB is also reported by some market data vendors as BRK.B, BRK-B, BRK'B.

Some companies that either refuse to list with NYSE, AMEX, or Nasdaq or are unable to meet the financial listing requirements may be traded among market makers on the *over the counter* (OTC) market. This practice of trading nonexchange listed products actually goes back to 1904 with the National Quotation Bureau system that linked market makers across the United States; trades for nonexchange companies were recorded on pink (or yellow) sheets of paper. Symbols are typically four letters; however, some data vendors will sometimes attach a PK suffix. For example, BSSM and BSSM.PK both denote the OTC traded Berkshire Asset Management. In 1999, a Web-based electronic quotation service called pinksheets.com was introduced for OTC pink sheet stocks.

Exchange-Traded Futures Contracts

A *forward contract* is an agreement to buy or sell a product at a certain *delivery price* for future delivery at some time T in the future. A *futures contract* is a forward contract that is traded on an exchange. (Recall that exchange-traded products reduce clearing and settlement risk: just because two parties have an agreement, it does not mean that both sides will honor the terms.) The last trading day of the contract is also called the *expiration date* or *maturity date* and is usually several days before the delivery date.

Today, in the United States, futures exchanges include the Chicago Board of Trade (CBOT, established in 1848), the Chicago Mercantile Exchange (CME, established in 1898), the Kansas City Board of Trade (KCBOT, established in 1856), the New York Board of Trade (NYBOT, established in 1870), and the New York Mercantile Exchange

Month	Future
January	F
February	G
March	H
April	J
May	K
June	M
July	N
August	Q
September	U
October	V
November	X
December	Z

FIGURE 5-14   Month codes for U.S. futures contracts.

(NYMEX, established in 1872). Newer all-electronic exchanges include the Chicago Board Option Exchange (CBOE), Futures Exchange (CFE), and OneChicago (owned jointly by the CBOE, CBOT, and CME; specializing in futures on individual stocks and narrow-based indexes).

Futures contract symbology requires a name for the underlying product and a delivery date. The actual delivery month, day, and year must be specified in the actual contract or in a delivery and settlement schedule. For example, according to the CME, the last day of trading for the S&P 500 future is "The business day immediately preceding the day of determination of the final settlement price (normally, the Thursday prior to the 3rd Friday of the contract month)."

Futures ticker symbols may differ among market data vendors. Futures trading on the same exchange but in different areas (either the floor "pit" or the electronic matching system) may also have different ticker symbols.

Figure 5-14 shows how months are represented by letters for U.S. contracts. Year codes may have all four digits of the year or just the last digit. For example, the NYMEX heating oil futures contract with delivery date in January 2004 has ticker symbol HOF4; NYMEX January Gold has ticker GCF5; and CBOT January gold has ticker ZGF05. Other vendors might display these three tickers as HO2004F, GC2005F, ZG2005F.

The contract specification provides meaning to the quoted price. For example, NYMEX crude oil is quoted in cents per barrel; one contract is for 1000 barrels. The CME S&P 500 futures contract is quoted in values of an index; one contract is worth $250 times this index.

Many traders graph futures prices in a way similar to the yield curve. The *nearby contract* is the contract whose last trading date is closest to the current date. If prices are lower for contracts that mature further in the future and contract prices are lower for contracts nearer the present, then the underlying product is said to be in *backwardation*. *Contango* (sometimes called a normal market) occurs when prices are higher for contracts that mature further out in the future and lower for those contracts that are nearer the present. Contango is the opposite of backwardation. In other words, if futures prices decrease in time, then the market is in backwardation, whereas if futures prices increase in time, then the market is in contango. (These terms, originating in trader slang, were in use by the1800s.)

Box 5-6

Futures Exchanges: Physical Delivery vs. Cash Settlement

Futures exchanges that specialized in agricultural commodities started appearing in the United States after the completion of the Erie Canal system. What became the most popular exchange was established in 1848 as the Board of Trade of the City of Chicago, now known as the Chicago Board of Trade (CBOT).

Trading in futures contracts increased due to the spread of railroad networks and the improved post-Civil War economic conditions. The advances in Morse telegraph telecommunications also led to the development of popular derivatives markets, such as the Public Grain Exchange, whose products were linked to the prices of the futures contracts traded on the CBOT. However, unlike a futures exchange in which the holder of a contract settled with actual delivery of the underlying product (i.e., a delivery of 5 tons of wheat), these exchanges settled in cash, based on the difference between the contract price originally paid and the actual price several months in the future. The cash-settled markets (disparagingly called bucket shops by regular exchanges because order tickets were placed in buckets) were even used by some CBOT members.

The CBOT wanted to eliminate these cash-settled exchanges. From the CBOT perspective, bucket shops were stealing market quotes; no data usage fees were paid to the CBOT. Furthermore, they argued that the bucket shops were also stealing customers from the CBOT. Consequently, in the 1880s, the CBOT stopped providing quotes to these exchanges.

The bucket shops, together with several telegraph companies, initiated lawsuits against the CBOT in 1884 to allow them access to the market data: from their perspective, the bucket shops were competing exchanges. The CBOT argued that cash settlement implied that bucket shops were gambling casinos. In 1915, the U.S. Supreme Court ruled in favor of the CBOT. The court ruled that cash-settled futures contracts that did not offer physical delivery were a form of gambling: futures contracts must include specific conditions for the delivery of goods. The effect was that cash-settled derivatives exchanges were outlawed, until 1982.

The 1929 crash was an impetus behind the public desire for market regulation. In 1934, the Securities and Exchange Commission (SEC) was established to regulate the securities markets (including stocks, bond, and stock options). In 1936, the Commodity Exchange Authority (CEA) was established (as part of the U.S. Department of Agriculture) to regulate traders directly and to restrict futures. In 1974 Congress passed the Commodity Futures Trading Act, which established the Commodity Futures Trading Commission (CFTC).

In spring 1981, John Shad (chairman of the SEC) and Philip Johnson (chairman of the CFTC) met to discuss the issue of cash-settled contracts. The result of the meeting, now called the Shad–Johnson Accord, partially reversed the Supreme Court 1915 decision on cash-settled contracts. They agreed that trading cash-settled futures was different from gambling after all.

The Accord (after validation by four congressional oversight committees) established the legality of trading and settling futures contracts in cash as long as the value of the futures contract was computed from an index derived from a set of securities (i.e., like the Standard & Poor's 500 index). The trading and settling of futures contracts in cash were still illegal for futures based on a specific individual security or an index computed from a small set of securities.

In December of 2000, Congress passed the Commodities Futures Modernization Act (CFMA) that did away with this prohibition. The trading of futures contracts based on a single stock (as was done in Amsterdam in the 17th century) was now legal in the United States. November 8, 2002 was the first trading date for "single stock futures." These futures contracts came under the joint regulation of the CFTC and SEC.

For example, on August 16, 2004, the futures prices for crude oil are as follow:

Expiration	OPEN	HIGH	LOW	SETTLE	CHG	LIFETIME HIGH	LOW	OPEN INT
Sept	46.6	46.91	45.95	46.05	−0.53	46.91	27.95	125,479
Oct	46.03	46.38	45.55	45.69	−0.34	46.38	23.75	171,040
Nov	45.58	45.9	45.2	45.29	−0.32	45.9	24.75	62,171
Ja05	44.29	44.55	44.22	44.17	−0.23	44.55	23.25	29,880

The prices decrease: crude oil is in backwardation. The futures prices for gold are as follow:

Expiration	OPEN	HIGH	LOW	SETTLE	CHG	LIFETIME HIGH	LOW	OPEN INT
Aug	399	403	399	402.9	4	433	324.7	738
Oct	401.6	405	399.2	403.8	4	432	332	19,687
Dec	401.9	406.4	400.7	405.2	4.1	436.5	290	144,615
Fb05	404.4	406	404.4	406.7	4.1	435	331.5	9,272

The prices increase: gold is in contango. The futures prices for Treasury bonds are as follow:

Expiration	OPEN	HIGH	LOW	SETTLE	CHG	LIFETIME HIGH	LOW	OPEN INT
Sep	111-06	111-09	110-11	110-24	−19	114-30	101-24	555,070
Dec	110-01	110-01	109-06	109-17	−19	113-07	100-24	40,713

The prices decrease: Treasury bonds are in backwardation.

Exchange-Traded Options Contracts

An option contract provides the bearer with the right, but not the obligation, to buy or sell a product at a certain price X within a certain time T. The time T is called the maturity or expiration time of the option. Suppose the product has price P at time T. At time T, the value of a *call option* (giving the right to buy) is

$$P - X \quad \text{if} \quad P > X$$
$$0, \quad \text{otherwise}$$

In MuPAD and other computer algebra systems, this value is expressed with the max function: the max function is defined as

$$\max(A, B) = A \quad \text{if} \quad A >= B$$
$$\max(A, B) = B \quad \text{if} \quad A < B$$

So the value of value of a call option at maturity is expressed as

$$\max(P - X, 0)$$

At maturity time T, the value of a *put option* (giving the right to sell) is expressed by

$$\max(X - P, 0)$$

Let $p(t)$ be the price of a product at time t, where t is any time before and up to maturity time T. A call option is *in the money* if $p(t) > X$; otherwise it is *out of the money*. A put option is *in the money* if $p(t) < X$; otherwise it is *out of the money*. If the strike price equals the current price then an option is *at the money*.

If the option contract specifies that the holder of the option is allowed to execute the option (buy buying if a call, and selling if a put) precisely at time T (or, more realistically, on a particular day or hour), then the option is called a *European-type* option. If the option contract specifies that the holder of the option is allowed to execute the option at any time prior to and including time T, then the option is called an *American-type* option. There may be other contract variations as well that specify other option types.

By 1934, equity options were declared legal; trading options was regulated by the SEC. However, there was little interest in trading options. There was no options exchange so all trades were done *over the counter* by a network of market makers via telephone and paper. There was not even a standard options contract that could be used across all market participants.

In the 1960s, the CBOT proposed establishing an exchange and clearing corporation that would trade and settle standardized options. After several years of development and legal work, the CBOT created the Chicago Board Options Exchange (CBOE) and the Options Clearing Corporation (OCC). Standardized American call options on 16 stocks began trading on April 26, 1973.

By 1975, listed stock options were being traded at the American Stock Exchange (AMEX, now owned by Nasdaq), the Pacific Stock Exchange (PCX), and the Philadelphia Stock Exchange (PHLX). Today, the collection and distribution of options market data are regulated by the Options Price Reporting Authority (OPRA). OPRA participating exchanges include AMEX, PCX, and PHLX, as well as the CBOE, the Boston Options Exchange (BOX: affiliated with the Boston Stock Exchange), and the International Securities Exchange (ISE: located in New York). Technology infrastructure for OPRA is provided by the Securities Industry Automation Corporation (SIAC), which is jointly owned by NYSE and AMEX.

OPRA standardized option ticker symbols require a symbol for the underlying product (called the *root symbol*), a maturity date, and a strike price. All these are assigned by the exchange or market data vendor. The root symbol is not necessarily the same as the underlying stock ticker symbol. For example, Intel has Nasdaq ticker symbol INTC; in 2005, its option ticker symbols include NQ, VNL (for options that expire in 2006), and WNL (for options that expire in 2007). Note that VNL and WNL are options having maturity over 1 year, which are called Long-term Equity Anticipation Securities (*LEAPS*).

Figure 5-15 shows how strike prices are mapped into letter codes according to the OPRA *strike price table*. OPRA calls the letters U–Z "nonstandard price codes" because they may change at some future time.

In general, option expiration dates are contract and exchange dependent. Stock option contracts typically expire on the "Saturday immediately following the third Friday of the expiration month." The expiration months are also used to distinguish between calls and puts.

Figure 5-16 shows the *expiration month table*, which specifies how the OPRA standard maps expiration months into letter codes. For example, suppose we have a call option and a put option for GE; both expire in December with the strike price of $37.50:

On the AMEX, the ticker is GELU for the call and GEXU for the put.
On the CBOE, the ticker is GE LU for the call and GE XU for the put.
On the ISE, the ticker is .GE LU for the call and .GE XU for the put.

Code	Strike Prices				
A	5	105	205	305	...
B	10	110	210	310	...
C	15	115	215	315	...
D	20	120	220	320	...
E	25	125	225	325	...
F	30	130	230	330	...
G	35	135	235	335	...
H	40	140	240	340	...
I	45	145	245	345	...
J	50	150	250	350	...
K	55	155	255	355	...
L	60	160	260	360	...
M	65	165	265	365	...
N	70	170	270	370	...
O	75	175	275	375	...
P	80	180	280	380	...
Q	85	185	285	385	...
R	90	190	290	390	...
S	95	195	295	395	...
T	100	200	300	400	...
U	7.5	37.5	67.5	97.5	...
V	12.5	42.5	72.5	102.5	...
W	17.5	47.5	77.5	107.5	...
X	22.5	52.5	82.5	112.5	...
Y	27.5	57.5	87.5	117.5	...
Z	32.5	62.5	92.5	122.5	...

FIGURE 5-15   OPRA strike price table: letter codes for strike price.

Month	Call	Put
January	A	M
February	B	N
March	C	O
April	D	P
May	E	Q
June	F	R
July	G	S
August	H	T
September	I	U
October	J	V
November	K	W
December	L	X

FIGURE 5-16   OPRA expiration month table: letter codes for expiration months.

Note that some market data vendors may represent the call and put with a suffix letter, namely GELU.X and GEXU.X. Other market data vendors may dispense with the strike price table and write the strike price directly in the ticker symbol. For example,

GELU can be denoted by GE DEC37.50 C
GEXU can be denoted by GE DEC37.50 P

Option Payoff Diagrams

Options are sometimes analyzed with payoff diagrams, which are graphs that show the value of the option at maturity over a range of product values. For example, suppose

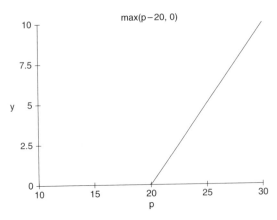

FIGURE 5-17   Payoff diagram for a call option (strike price $X = 20$).

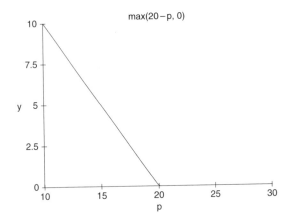

FIGURE 5-18   Payoff diagram for a put option (strike price $X = 20$).

a call option has strike price $X = 20$, and at maturity, the underlying product price can range from 10 to 30. In MuPAD, the payoff diagram (see Figure 5-17) is charted with

- `plotfunc2d(max(p-20,0),p=10..30)`

A payoff diagram for a put with strike price $X = 20$ is generated in MuPAD (Figure 5-18) with

- `plotfunc2d(max(20-p,0),p=10..30)`

Payoff diagrams and some put–call option relationships are summarized in Figure 5-19.

Portfolios (or packages) of options are used to model different types of payoff contingencies. Some option portfolios are given colorful names (such as straddle, strip, strangle, butterfly). For example, an option payoff diagram for a straddle with $X = 20$ is given by

- `plotfunc2d(max(20-p,0) + max(p-20,0),p=10..30)`

This and other option portfolios are shown in Figure 5-20.

Contract	Value at intermediate time t	Value at maturity time T
(Underlying) Asset price $p(t)$ at time t.	Market price $p(t)$	$P = P(T)$
Call Option: Contractual Right (not obligation) to buy Asset at price X at, or before time T. (European option: buys asset *only at* time T.)	Market price *call (t)*	$call(T) = \max(P - X, 0)$
Put option: Contractual Right (not obligation) to sell Asset at price X at, or before time T. (European option: sells asset *only at* time T.)	Market price *put (t)*	$put(T) = \max(X - P, 0)$
Payoff Relationships (Put-Call-Parity) Note: $A = \max(A, 0) - \max(-A, 0)$	For American options: $p(t) - X$ $< call(t) - put(t)$ $< p(t) - X \cdot B(t, T)$ For European options: $call(t) - put(t)$ $= p(t) - X \cdot B(t, T)$	For American options: $P - X = call(T) - put(T)$ For European options: $P - X = call(T) - put(T)$

FIGURE 5-19 Call and put options.

Options on Futures

An option on a futures contract provides the bearer with the right, but not the obligation, to buy or sell a specific futures contract at a certain price X within a certain time T. For these contracts to make sense, the maturity date of the option must be less than the maturity date of the futures contract (otherwise the futures contract does not exist). In most cases, the maturity month of the option is the same as the delivery month of the futures contract; the actual maturity date of the option is several days before the last trading date of the futures contract.

Contract (no income; no expenses)	Value at maturity time T	Payoff Diagram
Straddle: Portfolio long 1 call and long 1 put; same maturity and same strike	$straddle(T) =$ $\max[p(T) - X, 0]$ $+ \max[X - p(T), 0]$	
Strip: Portfolio long 1 call and long 2 puts; same maturity and same strike	$strip(T) =$ $\max[p(T) - X, 0]$ $+ 2 \cdot \max[X - p(T), 0]$	
Strap: Portfolio long 2 calls and long 1 put; same maturity and same strike	$strap(T) =$ $2 \cdot \max[p(T) - X, 0]$ $+ \max[X - p(T), 0]$	
Strangle: Portfolio long 1 call (with strike X_C), long 1 put (with strike X_P); same maturity and $X_C > X_P$	$strangle(T) =$ $\max[p(T) - X_C, 0]$ $+ \max[X_P - p(T), 0]$	
Butterfly Spread: Portfolio long 1 call (with strike X_C), long 1 put (with strike X_P), short one call (with strike X), short one put (with strike X), $X_C < X < X_P$	$butterfly(T) =$ $\max[p(T) - X_C, 0]$ $+ \max[X_P - p(T), 0]$ $- \max[p(T) - X, 0]$ $- \max[X - p(T), 0]$	

FIGURE 5-20 Portfolios of options.

Exchanges can trade any type of option contract (as long as there is a demand) in addition to the standard or "plain vanilla" (in options jargon) American and European options discussed earlier. For example, NYMEX lists the following types of options on crude oil futures contracts:

> Calendar Spread Options
> Crack Spread Options
> Average Price Options
> Inventory Options

These are all described by their contract specifications.

Options on futures symbology require a symbol for the underlying futures contract (a product and delivery date), a maturity date, a strike price, and an indication as to whether it is a put or a call. The contract type is also necessary in the symbol if the exchange trades more than one type of option. Note that we only need to supply 1 month if we assume that the maturity month of the option is the same as the delivery month of the futures contract.

Some data vendors or exchanges represent their ticker symbols by Root Strike Month Year. For example, the February 2005 futures contract is CL G5; the February 2005 call option on the futures contract (with February delivery date) with strike price 40 can be denoted by CL 40B5. Some data vendors or exchanges use different symbols for these options, e.g., LO40G5.

One area of discrepancy is concerned with how the strike price is represented in the ticker symbol. Some exchanges or market vendors may reserve anywhere from two to six digits for a strike price. The option on future with a strike price of 40.125 could be represented as the ticker symbol CL040125B5.

Other market data vendors or exchanges may utilize a Strike Price Table as is utilized with stocks. Different tables would be needed for different increments for a published strike price: the exchanges specify these minimum increments in the contract specifications. For example, Figure 5-21 shows a Strike Price Table for contracts with increments of $0.25 (or $25, or $2.50, or $25, or $0.025, or...). This uses a number convention similar to the Babylonians (see Section 2.2; numbers (depending on the context of the contract) are $25*10^n$. So 1225 ($1225 or $12.25 or...) corresponds to JJ. Figure 5-22 shows a Strike Price Table for contracts with increments of $5 (or $0.50, or $0.05, or $50, or $5*10^n$). So 125 (or $1.25, or $125, or $12.5, or...) corresponds to AF.

Using Strike Price Tables can be problematic for most options on futures contracts, as strike prices become essentially unreadable and potentially ambiguous. Different strike symbols will mean different prices for different contracts. There are other ambiguities as well: for example, on the NYMEX, the specification for options on crude oil futures requires the following about exchange reported strike prices:

Twenty strike prices in increments of $0.50 (50 ¢) per barrel above and below the at-the-money strike price, and the next 10 strike prices in increments of $2.50

	0	25	50	75
1000	JA	JB	JC	JD
1100	JE	JF	JG	JH
1200	JI	JJ	KA	KB
1300	KC	KD	KE	KF
1400	KG	KH	KI	KJ
1500	LA	LB	LC	LD
1600	LE	LF	LG	LH
1700	LI	LJ		

FIGURE 5-21 Strike Price Table for contracts with increment of $25*10^n$.

	0	5	10	15	20	25	30	35	40	45	50	55	60	65	70	75	80	85	90	95
0		AF	BA	BF	CA	CF	DA	DF	EA	EF	FA	FF	GA	GF	HA	CF	IA	IF	JA	JF
100	AA	AB	AC	AD	AE	AF	AG	AH	AI	AJ	BA	BB	BC	BD	BE	BF	BG	BH	BI	BJ
200	CA	CB	CC	CD	CE	CF	CG	CH	CI	CJ	DA	DB	DC	DD	DE	DF	DG	DH	DI	DJ
300	EA	EB	EC	ED	EE	EF	EG	EH	EI	EJ	FA	FB	FC	FD	FE	FF	FG	FH	FI	FJ
400	GA	GB	GC	GD	GE	GF	GG	GH	GI	GJ	HA	HB	HC	HD	HE	HF	HG	HH	HI	HJ
500	IA	IB	IC	ID	IE	IF	IG	IH	II	IJ	AA	AB	AC	AD	AE	AF	AG	AH	AI	AJ
600	BA	BB	BC	BD	BE	BF	BG	BH	BI	BJ	CA	CB	CC	CD	CE	CF	CG	CH	CI	CJ
700	DA	DB	DC	DD	DE	DF	DG	DH	DI	DJ	EA	EB	EC	ED	EE	EF	EG	EH	EI	EJ
800	FA	FB	FC	FD	FE	FF	FG	FH	FI	FJ	GA	GB	GC	GD	GE	GF	GG	GH	GI	GJ
900	HA	HB	HC	HD	HE	HF	HG	HH	HI	HJ	IA	IB	IC	ID	IE	IF	IG	IH	II	IJ

FIGURE 5-22   Strike Price Table for contracts with increment of $5\,10''$.

above the highest and below the lowest existing strike prices for a total of at least 61 strike prices. The at-the-money strike price is nearest to the previous day's close of the underlying futures contract. Strike price boundaries are adjusted according to the futures price movements.

In this case, which table should be used: the 5 table or the 25 table? Rules are needed to clear this ambiguity. A strike price of $45 would be EF, but how is a strike of $45.50 represented without further assumptions?

For market surveillance and compliance purposes, the CFTC has specified a Strike Price Format for options contracts registered on eight exchanges. Strike prices are specified by a seven-digit symbol; the precision of the minimum strike price is left adjusted anywhere from 0 to 2 decimal places, depending on the option.

Figure 5-23 shows some examples of the CFTC Strike Price Format (we added the extra space to improve readability). In all cases, because of all the parameters needed in the contract, ticker symbols for options on futures are neither convenient nor standard as they are for equities or for equity options.

In practice, an industry of market data vendors has become the intermediary — the information broker — between exchanges and market makers and traders. The market

Exchange	Contract	CFTC Code	Sample Strike Price	7-digit Strike Price
CBOT	Corn	C	$2.60/bu	0000 260
	Dow Jones Ind.Av	11	9700 pts.	0000 097
	Treasury Bonds	17	104% of par	0000 104
CME	Canadian/US Dollar	C1	0.62 USD/CAD	0000 620
	S&P 500 Index	SP	1120 pts	000 1120
	NASDAQ 100	ND	1630 pts	0 163000
NYBOT	Cotton	CO	$.39/lb	000 3900
	Canadian/US Dollar	YD	1.585 CAD/USD	00 15850
NYMEX	Crude Oil	LO	$21.50/bl	000 2150
(COMEX Div.)	Gold	OG	$280/troy oz	0000 280
	Unleaded Gas	GO	$.65/gal	000 6500
	Electricity, COB	WO	$31/mwhr	000 3100
	Natural Gas	ON	$2.050/mmbtu	000 2050
KCBOT	Natural Gas	NG	$2.00/mmbtu	0000 200
MGE	Durum Wheat	X	$3.05/bu	0000 305
EUREX	Treasury Bonds	US	104% of par	0000 104

FIGURE 5-23   Examples of the CFTC strike price format.

data vendors build systems to identify and retrieve pricing data from exchange and market maker systems; their systems need to be consistent with different exchange and market maker formats and protocols (which are always being updated). The vendors transform exchange data into a more usable internal representation and then provide data in a form that is convenient to subscribers. In some sense, this is similar to what news organizations do: they collect news in one format from news sources (i.e., announcements, speeches, press releases, memos, text, hearings) and transform this news into a format that is convenient for subscribers (newspaper, radio, television, Web page, searchable database). Market data are a form of news.

As opposed to the situation that existed in the days of the bucket shops (when the CBOT accused the bucket shops of stealing data), exchanges charge the data vendors for access and the data vendors charge their customers for subscription services. Exchanges earn hundreds of millions of dollars from data access fees. One question is concerned with how these fees are split among exchanges. The traditional model bases revenues on trading volume: an exchange that trades more should get more fees. Other models are also being considered by the SEC as part of their Regulation NMS (National Market System).

The use of data intermediaries saves traders a tremendous investment in technology. However, this may change as financial technology standards become more universal. The market data business is consolidating; market data systems are being integrated more and more with trading and financial messaging systems, enabling "one-stop shopping" for their customers.

5.4.   Non-Exchange Traded Products and Portfolios

Financial products that are issued by a company or agency have CUSIP or ISIN identifiers. Some products may also have ticker symbols. Exchange traded contracts have ticker symbols but are not identified by CUSIP or ISIN, as they are not issued by a company or agency. Another set of financial products have neither issuer nor ticker symbol: these products are typically traded by individual institutional market makers among themselves (i.e., over the counter). Figure 5-24 summarizes the combinations.

This section briefly provides some examples of nonticker symbol products from a financial technology perspective; in practice, the names and unique identifiers are customized by in-house trading or vendor systems:

Identification	Traded on Exchange	Not Traded on Exchange
Identified by Issuer (i.e., CUSIP)	Exchange traded stocks, bonds, funds	Most bonds, loans (OTC)
Not Identified by Issuer (i.e., no CUSIP)	Exchange traded futures and options contracts	OTC options, swaps, other OTC contracts, private funds and companies

FIGURE 5-24   Product identification vs. ticker symbol.

Non-Exchange Traded Options

Financial engineers and legal experts can devise thousands of types of option contracts; it goes without saying that most of these are not exchange traded.

One interesting type of option is a binary option (also sometimes called a digital option). A binary call option with Strike Price X=20 pays off $1 at time T if $X > 20$ and 0 otherwise. Its payoff diagram (with a jump at X=20) is plotted in MuPAD with

- `plotfunc2d(Discont=FALSE, heaviside(p-20), p=10..30)`

The heaviside function (sometimes called the unit step function) is named after the British telegraphist Oliver Heaviside (1850–1925). It is usually defined as

$$heaviside(x) = 1 \quad \text{if} \quad x > 0$$
$$heaviside(x) = 0 \quad \text{if} \quad x < 0$$
$$heaviside(x) = \tfrac{1}{2} \quad \text{if} \quad x = 0$$

Despite its simplicity, it is a very useful function. Note that our regular "plain vanilla" option payoffs can be written in terms of the heaviside function because

$$max(X,0) = X^*heaviside(X)$$

Figure 5-25 shows the payoff diagrams for some binary options.

The SuperShare binary option represents a high payoff bet on the price of an asset: the payoff is

$$\$\frac{1}{d} \text{ if the asset price is between } X \text{ and } X+d \text{ at payoff time}$$

In MuPAD notation it is represented by

- SuperShare:=(P,X, d)−>(1/d)*(heaviside(P-X)-heaviside(P-(X+d)))

Box 5-7

SuperShares

If d approaches zero, the SuperShare buyer is essentially betting on the *exact price* of the asset to the smallest fraction of a cent; the payoff grows commensurably large, like a lottery ticket. However, by construction, the area of the rectangle (the payoff times the betting width) always equals 1. In the 1880s, Heaviside found similar behavior when he studied how voltage pulses propagate in the Morse telegraph. He called such a sharp increase and decrease in voltage an *impulse function*. Years later, Paul Dirac (1902–1984), a professor of mathematics at the University of Cambridge, used Heaviside's impulse to model how electrons jump from state to state.

A SuperShare with d close to zero has the property that the payoff times the betting width is always 1, even though the betting width may be infinitesimally small and the payoff may be infinitely big.

Contract	Value at maturity time T	Payoff Diagram
Binary Call	$bcall(T) = heaviside(P - X)$	
Binary Put	$bput(T) = heaviside(X - P, 0)$	
SuperShare: Binary Call (Strike X1) − Binary Call (Strike X2)	$sshare(T) =$ $(1/d)^*(heaviside(P - X)$ $- heaviside(P - (X + d)))$	
Binary Call − Binary Put	$bcall(T) - bput(T)$	
Binary Call + Binary Put	$bcall(T) + bput(T)$	

FIGURE 5-25   Payoff diagrams for some binary options.

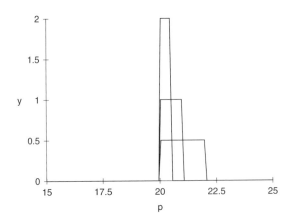

FIGURE 5-26   SuperShare payoff diagrams: strike price $X = 20$ with $d = 2, 1, 0.5$.

The SuperShare corresponds to the probability of betting that price of an asset will be in a certain price range. There is a payoff of $1/d$ if the price at maturity P is in the betting range between X and $X + d$; otherwise the payoff is zero. Note that as the betting range gets smaller (as betting width d decreases), the payoff increases in a way such that the payoff $1/d$ times the betting width d (the area of the rectangle) always equals 1. Figure 5-26 shows some SuperShare payoff diagrams with strike price 20 with $d = 2, 1, 0.5$. Note that the area under all these payoff graphs is 1.

The betting width d of the rectangle corresponds to the probability of the asset in the range. Because there is greater probability of an asset price being in a larger range than a smaller range, the payoff is smaller for a larger range but greater for a smaller range. For example, if the strike price is $20 and d is $0.01, then the SuperShare buyer is betting that the price of the asset will be between $20.00 and $20.01 at maturity. The SuperShare payoff in this case is $100.

Interest Rate Products

Many futures contracts for bonds and interest rates are exchange traded. These products help traders bet on the movement of bond prices or interest rates.

More general contracts such as swaps are not exchange traded. A *swap* is an exchange of periodic cash flows. It is a contract that stipulates that party A receives a payment rate (e.g., measured as a percentage or coupon against an agreed upon principal) of $a(t)$ a year and party B receives a payment rate of $b(t)$ a year. Suppose the payments continue for 5 years and there is no credit risk. The present value of the difference between the cash flows of party A and party B for a common principal P values the swap as

$$swap = P \cdot \sum_{t=1}^{5} [a(t) - b(t)] \cdot B(t)$$

If party B wants to exchange her payments with that of party A, B can buy the swap from A. After this transaction, party B receives $a(t)$ a year and A receives $b(t)$ a year plus the value of the swap. If party B wants to go back to the old payments at a later time, party B can sell the remainder of the swap back to party A.

Note that the value of each cash flow (or the value of the entire swap) can be positive, zero, or negative: it all depends on the rates $a(t)$ and $b(t)$. Also note that in general, payments can occur over arbitrary agreed-upon periods (yearly, semiannually, monthly, etc.).

For interest rate swaps, the values of $a(t)$ and $b(t)$ are either fixed throughout the contract or are based on a particular forward rate standard that is determined by the market.

Libor and Libid

One forward rate standard for swap rates was established by the British Bankers' Association (BBA). Their methodology is based on surveying lending and borrowing rates offered by a select set of reference banks. The BBA publishes standard rates across 15 maturities (overnight to 12 months) and nine countries (United States, United Kingdom, European Union, Denmark, Switzerland, Canada, Japan, Australia, and New Zealand).

Box 5-8

British Bankers' Association (BBA) and LIBOR

The BBA was set up in 1919 as a clearing organization for London banks. Foreign banks and British merchant banks were accepted into the BBA in 1972. By the early 1980s, the evolving money markets (especially markets involved with swaps) required recognized rate benchmarks and standards. The BBA was the natural standards organization: over 20% of all international bank lending and over 30% of all currency transactions take place in London.

BBA rates are set by a reference panel of 8 to 16 banks. The reference panel reflects the market: by country and by institution. Reference banks are selected on the basis of reputation, market activity, and expertise in handling a particular currency. By 11 AM London time, rates from the reference banks are submitted to the BBA and sorted. Rates from top and bottom quartiles are disregarded; for example, for quotes from 8 banks, the top 2 rates and bottom 2 rates are ignored. (Statisticians call this technique, used to eliminate statistical outliers, *winsorizing*. The eponym was created in the 1950s by the Princeton mathematician John Tukey in honor of the biostatistician *Charles Winsor*.) The rates in the middle two quartiles (i.e., the remaining 4 quotes for an 8 quote sample) are averaged: the resulting "fixing" is the BBA LIBOR rate. In most cases, the LIBOR day count basis is Actual/360.

The financial technology of LIBOR is managed by Moneyline Telerate: they collect data from reference banks, apply quality control tests, and calculate the fixing. Results are released before 12 noon London time to licensed financial technology information vendors (such as Reuters, Thomson Financial, Bloomberg) so that BBA LIBOR is seen simultaneously on hundreds of thousands of displays throughout the world. To ensure algorithm transparency, the rates from all reference banks are also published.

Since the adoption of the Euro currency in 1999, other standard rates for the money and capital markets in the Euro zone have been developed: *Euribor* and *Eonia*. Euribor (*Euro Interbank Offered Rate*) is the rate at which Euro Interbank term deposits within the Euro zone are offered by one prime bank to another prime bank. Eonia (*Euro OverNight Index Average*) is an effective overnight rate computed as a weighted average of all overnight unsecured lending transactions in the interbank market, initiated within the Euro area by the contributing reference banks. The Euribor and Eonia methodology is similar: one key difference is in the number of reference banks.

On each working day (by 11 AM Greenwich Mean Time), the BBA tabulates and statistically processes received data from the reference banks; by noon they publish the resulting floating rates on the Internet and through financial data vendors.

Dollar deposits in the BBA reference banks are called *Eurodollars*. A *Eurodollar deposit of maturity t* is a dollar-denominated zero coupon bond $L(t)$ held by a commercial bank outside the United States. [We reserve the symbol $B(t)$ to denote a zero risk zero coupon bond with default risk similar to that of the United States.] The rate that the bond earns interest — $RL(T)$ — is called the London Interbank offer rate — the LIBOR (or *Libor*) rate. LIBOR is the time-dependent rate at which banks lend Eurodollars to borrowers; the rate at which banks borrow from lenders is the London Interbank bid rate — the LIBID (or *Libid*) rate. Libor rates are correlated with Treasury rates; they are usually higher because the Libor rates are derived from commercial banks (which have a higher credit risk than the U.S. Treasury).

The relationship between Eurodollar deposits and LIBOR rates is similar to the bond relationships already defined. For example, for continuously compounded rates

$$RL(t) = -\frac{1}{t}\ln L(t)$$

There are a few more complications in translating between Libor and Treasury rates. Libor does not use the Treasury discount rate convention in its quotes (see Box 5-8). Also, Libor rates are simple period compounded interest rates with basis Actual/360, not Actual/365 as with the U.S. Treasuries.

Floaters

The technology for valuing a set of fixed cash flows was discussed in Chapter 4. How are cash flows valued when they might change from period to period?

Recall that for a sum of general continuous cash flows $c(t)$ that mature at time T, the Present Value (Section 4.1 and Box 4-7) is

$$CF = \int_0^T e^{-R(t)\cdot t}\cdot c(t)\cdot dt$$

Suppose the cash flow function $c(t)$ is set to be a combination of the spot rate $R(t)$, the rate-of-change (see Box 2-9) of the spot rate, and time t such that

$$c(t) = R(t) + t\cdot\frac{\partial R}{\partial t}$$

In MuPAD notation this is just

```
R(t)+t*diff(R(t),t)
```

It turns out that with this cash flow function, the present value of the total cash flows can be computed exactly. In MuPAD, we use the intlib (integral library) command and find that CF is

- ```
eval(intlib::changevar(hold(int)
(exp (-t*R(t))*(R(t)+t*diff(R(t),t)), t=0..T), u=t*R(t)))
```

$$1 - \frac{1}{\exp(T\ R(T))}$$

In mathematical notation, note that

$$CF = 1 - \frac{1}{e^{T \cdot R(T)}} = 1 - e^{-R(T) \cdot T} = 1 - B(T)$$

Recall (see the last formula in Box 4-7) that a bond is defined by its cash flows and final payment: its present value is

$$\text{bond} = P \cdot [CF + B(T)]$$

Therefore, a bond with coupon $c(t) = R(t) + t \cdot \frac{\partial R}{\partial t}$ has a present value that never changes:

$$\text{bond} = P \cdot [CF + B(T)] = P \cdot [(1 - B(T)) + B(T)] = P \cdot [1] = P$$

Surprisingly, this result is independent of the maturity time. Bonds with these kinds of coupons are called floating rate bonds (or floaters). The present value of a floater of principal $P$ is $P$. It also turns out that the expression for $c(t)$ is related to the forward rate. Look at the last formula in Box 3-12 for the forward rate $R(T, TA)$ from time $T$ to time $TA$: the same expression for $TA = T + h$ is

$$R(T, T+h) = \frac{R(T+h) \cdot (T+h) - R(T)}{h} = T \cdot \frac{R(T+h) - R(T)}{h} + \frac{h \cdot R(T+h)}{h}$$

The first term shows time $T$ multiplied by the rate of change (Box 2-9) of the spot rate. Note that for small time periods $h$,

$$\frac{R(T+h) - R(T)}{h} = \frac{\partial R}{\partial T}$$

In the second term the $h$ cancels out, so we get

$$R(T, T+h) = T \cdot \frac{\partial R}{\partial T} + \frac{h \cdot R(T+h)}{h} = T \cdot \frac{\partial R}{\partial T} + R(T+h)$$

As $h$ approaches zero, we see that $R(T, T)$ is the same as the expression for $c(T)$:

$$R(T, T) = T \cdot \frac{\partial R}{\partial T} + R(T) = c(T)$$
```

This is why $c(T)$ is sometimes called the (instantaneous) forward rate. This result is similar for cash flows under N-period compounding (Box 3-12). If $c(t)$ is set to the forward period rate, i.e.,

$$c(t) = R(t-1, t) = 1 \cdot \left[\frac{B(t-1)}{B(t)}\right]^{1/(t-(t-1))} - 1 = 1 \cdot \left[\frac{B(t-1)}{B(t)}\right]^{1/1} - 1$$

$$= \frac{B(t-1)}{B(t)} - 1 = \frac{B(t-1) - B(t)}{B(t)}$$

Then the present value of the cash flows is

$$CF = \sum_{t=1}^{T} \frac{B(t-1) - B(t)}{B(t)} \cdot B(t) + B(T) = \sum_{t=1}^{T} (B(t-1) - B(t)) + B(T)$$

Note that the cash flow summation "telescopes" — subsequent terms cancel:

$$CF = (B(0) - B(1)) + (B(1) - B(2)) + \cdots + (B(T-1) - B(T)) = B(0) - B(T) = 1 - B(T)$$

so that the present value of the bond again is

$$\text{bond} = P \cdot [CF + B(T)] = P \cdot [(1 - B(T)) + B(T)] = P \cdot [1] = P$$

Example: Valuing Floaters

Let us see how this works for the term structure specified on July 21, 2004 (Figure 4-7). Figure 5-27 shows values of the zero coupon bond (derived from the Treasury strips), values of the floating rate coupon (derived from the 1-year forward rates), and the sum of the cash flows up to time T for July 21, 2004.

For example, for the first payment period on August 15, 2004, the coupon is the forward rate of the previous period (0.0625%); the sum of cash flows is just 0.999375*0.0625% = 0.000625; we add this to the present value of the zero coupon bond having maturity August 15, 2004; the result is

$$0.000625 + 0.999375 = 1.0$$

Period	Date	Time (years) T	B(0,T)	1-Year Forward	Coupon t	CF: Sum of Cash Flows	CF + B(0,T)
0	7/21/2004	0	1	0.0625%			
1	8/15/2004	1.068493151	0.999375	2.2705%	0.0625%	0.000625	1.00
2	8/15/2005	2.068493151	0.9771875	3.3377%	2.2705%	0.0228125	1.00
3	8/15/2006	3.068493151	0.945625	4.3448%	3.3377%	0.054375	1.00
4	8/15/2007	4.071232877	0.90625	4.2790%	4.3448%	0.09375	1.00
5	8/15/2008	5.071232877	0.8690625	5.2612%	4.2790%	0.1309375	1.00
6	8/15/2009	6.071232877	0.825625	5.3429%	5.2612%	0.174375	1.00
7	8/15/2010	7.071232877	0.78375	5.6000%	5.3429%	0.21625	1.00
8	8/15/2011	8.073972603	0.7421875	5.6025%	5.6000%	0.2578125	1.00
9	8/15/2012	9.073972603	0.7028125	5.5869%	5.6025%	0.2971875	1.00
10	8/15/2013	10.0739726	0.665625	7.7390%	5.5869%	0.334375	1.00
11	8/15/2014	10.0739726	0.6178125		7.7390%	0.3821875	1.00

FIGURE 5-27   Value of floater on July 21, 2004.

as expected. For the second payment period (August 15, 2005), the coupon corresponds to forward rate of 2.2705%; the sum of cash flows are

$$0.999375^*0.0625\% + 0.9771875^*2.2705\% = 0.0228125.$$

We add this to the present value of the zero coupon bond having maturity August 15, 2004; the result is

$$0.0228125 + 0.9771875 = 1.0$$

as expected.

In practice, the forward rate for the coupon depends on the future term structure: as time advances, payment is computed from the actual 1-period forward rates. However, the structure of the "telescoping coupon" sum still guarantees that the present value of the floating rate bond will remain at P.

For example, let us move the calendar to August 5, 2004 and compute the value of the floating rate bond based on the August 5, 2004 term structure. The results are shown in Figure 5-28.

Here, for the first period on August 5, 2004, the coupon is a forward rate of the previous period (0.03125%); the sum of cash flows is just $0.9996875^*0.03125\% = 0.0003125$. We add this to the present value of the zero coupon bond of maturity August 15, 2004 and get

$$0.0003125 + 0.9996875 = 1.0$$

as expected. For the second period, the coupon corresponds to a forward rate of 2.0740%; the sum of cash flows are

$$0.020625 + 0.979375 = 1.0$$

as expected. In both cases, the present value of the floating rate bond sums to 1, even though the coupons are different (because they are computed from different term structures).

Floating rate bonds can be constructed and issued by governments, agencies, and corporations subject to different currency and credit limitations. For example, a floating rate bond based on the term structure of Eurodollar deposits of maturity t, which are dollar denominated zero coupon bonds, denoted by $L(t)$, is

$$\text{float} = \sum_{t=1}^{T} c(t) \cdot P \cdot L(t) + P \cdot L(T) = P$$

Date	Time (years) T	B(0,T)	1-Year Forward	Coupon t	CF: Sum of Cash Flows	CF + B(0,T)
8/5/2004	0	1	0.0313%			
8/15/2004	0.024657534	0.9996875	2.0740%	0.0313%	0.0003125	1.00
8/15/2005	1.068493151	0.979375	3.2619%	2.0740%	0.020625	1.00
8/15/2006	2.068493151	0.9484375	4.2239%	3.2619%	0.0515625	1.00
8/15/2007	3.068493151	0.91	4.2607%	4.2239%	0.09	1.00
8/15/2008	4.071232877	0.8728125	5.0395%	4.2607%	0.1271875	1.00
8/15/2009	5.071232877	0.8309375	5.2236%	5.0395%	0.1690625	1.00
8/15/2010	6.071232877	0.7896875	5.4234%	5.2236%	0.2103125	1.00
8/15/2011	7.071232877	0.7490625	5.5947%	5.4234%	0.2509375	1.00
8/15/2012	8.073972603	0.709375	5.5323%	5.5947%	0.290625	1.00
8/15/2013	9.073972603	0.6721875	7.5500%	5.5323%	0.3278125	1.00
8/15/2014	10.0739726	0.625		7.5500%	0.375	1.00

FIGURE 5-28   Value of floater on August 5, 2004.

with a cash flow rate

$$c(t) = \frac{L(t-1) - L(t)}{L(t)}$$

Valuing Swaps with Floating Rate Bonds

Note that the value for an interest rate swap can be simplified by using the telescoped value for the floating rate cash flows. For example, if the swap involves exchanging a 4% fixed payment rate for a floating payment for the next 5 years, the present value is

$$\text{swap} = 4\% \cdot P \cdot \sum_{t=1}^{5} B(t) - CF = 4\% \cdot P \cdot \left(\sum_{t=1}^{5} B(t) \right) - P \cdot [1 - B(5)]$$

Figure 5-29 shows an example using the July 21, 2004 term structure with principal $P = \$1$. The value of the swap is about \$0.057. Note that the total value of the floating payments, $1 - B(5) = (1 - 0.8690625)$, is 0.1309375.

In many cases, the fixed rate is adjusted to make the purchase value of the swap equal to zero. In our example, this amounts to finding a constant value r such that

$$\text{swap} = r \cdot P \cdot \left(\sum_{t=1}^{5} B(0, t) \right) - P \cdot [1 - B(0, 5)] = 0$$

so

$$r = \frac{[1 - B(0, 5)]}{\sum_{t=1}^{T} B(0, t)} = 2.787\%$$

In the jargon of swaps, a swap priced at zero is called a *par swap* and the fixed rate r is called the *par swap rate*. Note that the present value of the swap changes in time; the present value is different tomorrow because tomorrow's term structure is different from today's term structure.

Products of Products

A portfolio is a financial product that consists of a set of component products; the goal of the set is to satisfy some financial objective. A portfolio can denote a client's entire

Time (years) T	B(0,T)	1-Year Forward	Coupon t	Fixed (4%) Disc. Payments	Float Disc. Payments	Fixed-Float
0	1	0.0625%				
1.068493151	0.999375	2.2705%	0.0625%	0.039975	0.000625	0.03935
2.068493151	0.9771875	3.3377%	2.2705%	0.0390875	0.0221875	0.0169
3.068493151	0.945625	4.3448%	3.3377%	0.037825	0.0315625	0.0062625
4.071232877	0.90625	4.2790%	4.3448%	0.03625	0.039375	-0.003125
5.071232877	**0.8690625**	5.2612%	4.2790%	0.0347625	0.0371875	-0.002425
			Sum	**0.1879**	**0.1309375**	**0.0569625**

FIGURE 5-29   Present value of a swap.

holdings in a brokerage account. Conversely, client's holdings can be broken up into a set of separate portfolios in separate accounts. A portfolio of portfolios is a portfolio.

Mutual funds and exchange traded funds (ETFs) are portfolios that have CUSIP or ISIN identifiers. Hedge funds operate under different regulations (e.g., they may be set up as limited partnerships outside of a country's jurisdiction). All ETFs have ticker symbols; some mutual funds have ticker symbols. *Closed-end* mutual funds operate like investment or holding companies; many of these, such as Adams Express (ADX), trade on the NYSE. Other mutual funds may have a Nasdaq ticker symbol such as FMAGX for Fidelity Magellan.

Private funds (like private clubs, open only to a restricted set of investors) that are not registered with the SEC do not require a CUSIP. Sometimes these private funds are called hedge funds; because they are not registered, they are not subject to the scrutiny of many SEC regulations. (Many well-known companies are private, e.g., the market data vendor Bloomberg L.P.) However, funds consisting of hedge funds can be registered and have a CUSIP.

There are two primary degrees of freedom in portfolio building: product selection (i.e., which product?) and product weighting (how much of it should I own or sell short?). Portfolio building is difficult, which is why to a certain degree it has been outsourced to companies such as Standard & Poor's and Dow Jones. Indices such as the S&P 500, the Dow Jones Industrial Average, and the Goldman Sachs Commodity Index correspond to a selection of financial products from a universe, together with a set of weightings.

Portfolio selection is concerned with building a portfolio component set from a universe of potential products. Some questions that should be considered when selecting component products include the following:

1. Does the product universe satisfy the financial objectives for the portfolio?
2. Should the portfolio component set have a fixed size?
3. Are industry or product sectors significant?
4. Is the product traded actively?
5. Is the product a significant economic indicator?
6. Is the ownership of the product concentrated?
7. Is the product easy to trade at efficient and fair spreads (liquidity)?

Other questions should also be considered when removing component products:

1. How should product mergers, acquisitions, and consolidations be handled?
2. For issued products (stocks, bonds), how should bankruptcy, restructuring, and spinoffs be handled?
3. Does the product no longer meet the selection current criteria for inclusion?

There are several types of weighting schemes. *Price weighting* consists of buying an equal number of shares or contracts of each stock in the portfolio component set. For example, a price-weighted portfolio of set {GE, IBM, T} could have 300 shares of GE, 300 shares of IBM, and 300 shares of T. Note that the higher the price, the more weight the component has in the portfolio component set. Also note that price weighting only makes sense if the underlying products are all the same type, i.e., only stocks, only bonds, or only futures contracts.

Equal weighting gives each product in the portfolio component set equal financial representation. The equal weighting method requires knowing a total initial amount of capital P that is available for the products. We then divide that amount by the product or contract price to get how many shares or contracts to buy. So, for example, an equal-weighted $90,000 portfolio given the portfolio component set of {GE, IBM, T} would have $30,000 invested in GE, $30,000 invested in IBM, and $30,000 invested in T. Equal weighting methods can be applied to different product types, i.e., a $90,000 portfolio could invest $30,000 in equities, $30,000 in bonds, and $30,000 in futures contracts.

Box 5-9

Computing Portfolio Weights

Price weighting is a special case of *criteria weighting*. Suppose we have an observable quantity $c(s)$ that we can assign to each of N products in the portfolio component set. [One example of this for equities is market capitalization — $c(s)$ is the share price multiplied by the number of outstanding shares for stock s. Market capitalization for public companies is reported by market data vendors.]

First, compute the total $c(s)$ for all products in the portfolio component set:

$$C = \sum_{s=1}^{N} c(s)$$

The second expression (with absolute value) is sometimes used if we are allowed to have negative weights (i.e., we are allowed to sell short). Then the portfolio weight for each product s is:

$$w(s) = \frac{c(s)}{C}$$

Note that the weights all sum to 1. For example

$$\sum_{s=1}^{N} w(s) = \sum_{s=1}^{N} \frac{c(s)}{C} = \frac{1}{C} \cdot \sum_{s=1}^{N} c(s) = \frac{C}{C} = 1$$

The weights correspond to fractional percentages. So, given a portfolio of P dollars, we invest $w(1)^*P$ in product 1, $w(1)^*P$ in product 2, ..., $w(N)^*P$ in product N. For example, suppose our Portfolio Component Set {GE, IBM, T} has $c(1) = 8$ for GE, $c(2) = 2$ for IBM, and $c(3) = 10$ for T. Then $C = 20$ so we invest 40% of our money in GE, 10% in IBM, and 50% in T. The exact number of shares to purchase is usually rounded up or down: for example, if an asset is priced at X dollars per share and we need to buy Y dollars worth, the number of shares we need is the integer value of Y/X. Similar purchasing rules apply for contracts and bonds.

The S&P 500 index uses market capitalization as a criteria weighting. There also might be special constraints for short sales (i.e., negative weights). In practice, as share prices increase and decrease, the number of shares for each product has to be periodically adjusted (by purchases and sales) to reflect the portfolio weights. This activity is called *rebalancing*.

5.5. Notes and References

Quotes from Sumerian and Babylonian financial texts are from
[0.1] Karen Rhea Nemet-Nejat. *Cuneiform Mathematical Texts as a Reflection of Everyday Life in Mesopotamia*. American Oriental Society, 1993. ISBN 0940490757.

General References

See the general technology references in Chapter 1 for a discussion of databases and database management systems.

Symbology: Identifying Issuers and Owners

The Financial Information Services Division (FISD) of the Software and Information Industry Association (SIIA) is an association of exchanges, market data vendors, specialist data providers, brokerage firms, and banks concerned with the distribution, management, administration, and use of market data. One of their main concerns is symbology and security identification. Their reports and documents can be found at
[1] http://www.fisd.net/symbology/

The American Bankers Association is one of the major banking associations in the United States. One of their products, the routing number, is described at
[2] http://www.aba.com/Products/PS98_Routing.htm

The ABA routing number Registrar at TFP is
[3] http://www.tfp.com/aba.html

A history of the Internal Revenue Service (IRS) is at
[4] http://www.irs.gov/irs/

A description of Employer Identification Numbers is in the IRS brochure
[5] Understanding Your EIN (available at http://www.irs.gov/pub/irs-pdf/p1635.pdf).

The CUSIP Service Bureau, operated by Standard & Poor's for the American Bankers Association, is at
[6] http://www.cusip.com/

Information about SEDOL at the London Stock Exchange is at
[7] http://www.londonstockexchange.com/en-gb/products/informationproducts/sedol/

Other Identifiers in Financial Databases

The NSCC Member Directory listing "clearing numbers" is available at
[8] http://www.nscc.com/directory/

The rationale for the CRD, described by the SEC, is at
[9] http://www.sec.gov/answers/crd.htm

Some of the technology issues of interest to stockbrokers, financial planners, branch managers, registered advisors, and other financial professionals are described in *Registered Rep.*, a trade magazine published by Primedia, available at
[10] http://www.registeredrep.com/

The blue sheets specification lists the required data fields concerning all customers and proprietary transactions. All brokers and dealers must submit blue sheets to the SEC upon request. The specification is described in
[11] NASD Notices to Members 2001 01-60. New Requirements For Electronic Blue Sheets Submissions. Available at http://nasd.complinet.com/nasd/display/display.html?rbid=1189&element_id=1159001770

The history of the U.S. Securities and Exchange Commission from 1929 to the present (including archival papers, photos, and oral histories) is at the virtual museum
[12] http://www.sechistorical.org/

Exchange Ticker Symbols

The Q codes are a set of three-letter Morse code words — beginning with a Q — that were developed in 1912 to facilitate international maritime communication. Other Morse code abbreviations and a description of the current equivalent Internet slang can be found at
[13] http://en.wikipedia.org/wiki/

The Nasdaq "stock symbol" code is a unique four- or five-letter symbol assigned to a Nasdaq security. Rules denoting the fifth letter are described at
[14] http://www.nasdaq.com/reference/glossary.stm

The NYSE stock master file contains symbol, company name, CUSIP number, and other information. "Symbols" used to describe NYSE bonds are listed at
[15] http://www.nysedata.com/bondsymbols/

In 1872, a group of Manhattan dairy merchants got together and created the Butter and Cheese Exchange of New York. Ten years later, they included eggs, dried fruits, canned goods, and poultry and became the New York Mercantile Exchange. In 1933, the National Metal Exchange, the Rubber Exchange of New York, the National Raw Silk Exchange, and the New York Hide Exchange merged to form COMEX (Commodities Exchange). NYMEX and COMEX merged in 1994 into NYMEX. The "designated codes" for NYMEX and COMEX contracts are at
[16] http://www.nymex.com/cc_main.aspx

In 1848, 82 Chicago merchants founded the Chicago Board of Trade (CBOT). Their "futures codes" are listed at
[17] http://cbot.com/cbot/pub/page/0,3181,932,00.html

In 1998, the Coffee, Sugar & Cocoa Exchange (founded in 1870 as the Coffee Exchange of the City of New York) and the New York Cotton Exchange (founded in 1882) merged into the New York Board of Trade (NYBOT). Products now include futures and options for frozen concentrated orange juice (FCOJ), ethanol, currency cross rates, and various indices for equities and commodity futures. Their symbols are listed at
[18] http://www.nybot.com/library/newspecsglance.htm

In 1856 a group of Kansas City merchants (knowing that they were located in one of the most productive wheat-growing regions of the world) founded the Kansas City Board of Trade (KCBOT). They trade futures and options on wheat, and stock indices. Their symbols are at
[19] http://kcbot.com/symbols_trading_hours.html

The Chicago Butter and Egg Board was founded in 1898; it became the Chicago Mercantile Exchange (CME) in 1919. The CME created the first financial futures contracts (on

foreign currencies in 1972) and set up the first modern cash-settled contracts (Eurodollar futures in 1981). The GLOBEX electronic trading system (introduced in 1992) now is available 23 hours a day for 5 days a week. In 2002, the CME also became the first publicly traded U.S. financial exchange (traded on the NYSE). The most interesting CME product codes are weather-related contracts: futures and options on futures that depend on temperature, time, and a city. Their product codes are at
[20] http://www.cme.com/trading/res/cch/cmeprdcode2439.html

In 1973, CBOE was founded as first U.S. options exchange for equities. Today the CBOE offers products based on market indices, interest rates, and portfolios (i.e., options on Exchange Traded Funds) and single stock futures. Their futures symbology is at
[21] http://www.cboe.com/DelayedQuote/QuoteHelp.aspx

While many vendors have chosen to adopt the codes used by the Exchange, some vendors use their own symbols. One example of vendor symbology is the system used by Bridge/CRB (formerly known as the Commodity Research Bureau).
[22] http://www.crbindex.com/online/crbcharts/symbology.htm

Options Price Reporting Authority (OPRA) is a national market system plan that regulates the collection and distribution of options market data. OPRA strike price tables (Figure 5-15) and expiration month table (Figure 5-16) are from the
[23] Data Recipient Interface Specification. Securities Industry Automation Corporation, 2005 (available at http://opradata.com/).

One regulatory function of the Commodity Futures Trading Commission (CFTC) is to protect market participants from fraud, manipulation, and other practices related to the sale of commodity and financial futures and options. These markets include Chicago Board of Trade; Chicago Mercantile Exchange; New York Board of Trade; NYMEX and COMEX contracts at the New York Mercantile Exchange; Kansas City Board of Trade; Minneapolis Grain Exchange; and Eurex U.S. For regulatory submission, the CFTC Futures Exchange Commodity Codes and Strike Price Format, maintained by the CFTC Division of Economic Analysis (DEA) — now the Division of Market Oversight (DMO) — are summarized at
[24] http://www.cftc.gov/dea/deacodes.htm

The words "contango" (probably derived from trader slang for *contingent*) and "backwardation" (probably derived from trader slang as a noun form of *backward*) were seen in
[25] Charles Castelli. *The Theory of Options in Stocks and Shares*. Matheison, London, 1877.

For a history of futures in the U.S. (Box 5-6), see
[26] Joseph Santos. "A History of Futures Trading in the United States." *EH.Net Encyclopedia* (edited by Robert Whaples), August 10, 2004 (available at http://eh.net/encyclopedia/?article=Santos.futures).

Non-Exchange Traded Products and Portfolios

The British Bankers' Association (BBA) is the leading trade association in the banking and financial services industry, representing banks and other financial service firms operating in the United Kingdom. It has approximately 250 members. BBA LIBOR is defined at
[27] http://www.bba.org.uk/

Binary options are described in many places. A good source is
[28] Paul Wilmott, Sam Howison, Jeff DeWynne. *The Mathematics of Financial Derivatives: A Student Introduction.* Cambridge University Press, Cambridge, 1997. ISBN 0-521-49789-2.

The first floating rate bond was introduced by Citicorp (formerly the First National City Corporation)
[29] http://www.citigroup.com/citigroup/corporate/history/citibank.htm

Swap computations are described in
[30] Robert Jarrow. Stuart Turnbull. *Derivative Securities.* South-Western College Publishing. Cincinnati, 1996. ISBN 0-538-84255-5.

5.6. Discussion Questions

1. Why have different symbology conventions developed over the past 150 years?
2. The International Standard Book Number (ISBN) is a unique identifier for books. It was created in the United Kingdom in 1966. What are the similarities and differences between the ISBN and the ABA routing number? Does ISBN use a Luhn algorithm?
3. Discuss how easy it is to make up a social security number for use as an identifier.
4. Why are there only 14 symbols in the standard MICR font?
5. What is the rationale for the letters used to denote contract months for futures contracts?
6. In 1915, cash settlement of a futures contract was declared similar to gambling by the U.S. courts. Why is cash settlement not considered gambling today?
7. Discuss the rationale for strike price tables for options on futures contracts. Could these tables be simplified with different technology?
8. How are swaps and other nonexchange traded products identified by market data systems? Is there consistency across vendors? Why?
9. How has increased market regulation led to the standardization of name and price conventions?
10. The NSCC member number is called by different names in different organizations. Can this cause problems that could be blamed on technology?
11. Explain how you can approximate the payoff of a SuperShare by a portfolio of options.
12. Which came first: floating rate bonds or adjustable mortgages?
13. Show how the specifications of many mortgages can be viewed as options.
14. Can any customized financial product be given a standard name?

CHAPTER ◆ 6

Physical Aspects of Financial Networks

All of you people keep producing devices where the letters and numbers are much too small for me to read, and the buttons are too small for my big fingers . . . The products are designed by engineers who think too much of their own brilliance and too little about what customers need. . . . If there's one thing I worry about in my organization, it's that we're going to think that we're smarter than these other people are.

—Remarks by Michael Bloomberg from his keynote address at the 30th Annual Consumer Electronics Show in Las Vegas (January 1997)

6.1. Financial Network Infrastructures

In April 2003, three U.S. government agencies (the Board of Governors of the Federal Reserve System, the U.S. Treasury, and the Securities and Exchange Commission) issued a joint paper concerning business continuity practices for financial organizations, especially those involved with clearing and settlement. The main points concerned the reliability and backup of financial infrastructures involving networks of transportation, computer, communications, water, and electric power systems.

Some network nodes (also referred to as points or stations) can be regarded as sources or producers of power — the ability to do some kind of work in a unit of time. This includes generators and substations (for electric power), computer servers (for computational power), Internet and telephone access points (for telecommunications), pumps (for water), and commuter railroad stations (for employees). Other nodes can be regarded as users or consumers of power. Network node connections denote a delivery or transmission of power from producer to consumer, including electrical power lines, fiber optic cables, water and steam pipes, railroad tracks, highways, and subways.

Critical Services and Disaster Recovery

What are the recovery requirements after a disruption to financial infrastructure networks? How does this affect pending transactions for clearing and settlement times? The joint paper addressed these questions by making four recommendations for firms involved with "critical markets," i.e., federal funds and government securities; foreign exchange and commercial paper markets; U.S. government and agency securities; and corporate debt and equity securities:

1. Firms must identify what clearing and settlement activities it does for critical markets.

2. Financial firms must determine and specify recovery times and work resumption objectives. In particular, "core" clearing and settlement organizations should develop the capacity to recover and resume clearing and settlement activities within 2 hours after a disrupting event. Firms that play "significant" roles should strive to achieve a 4-hour recovery time.

3. Financial firms should maintain geographically dispersed network resources to meet their recovery and resumption objectives. Backup arrangements should be as far away from the primary site as necessary to avoid being subject to the same set of risks as the primary location. Backup sites should not rely on the same transportation, telecommunications, water supply, and electric power infrastructures used by the primary site. A preliminary draft suggested that backup sites be located between 200 and 300 miles away from primary sites.

4. Financial firms should routinely test their recovery and resumption arrangements in order to ensure network connectivity and capacity. They should test backup arrangements with major counterparties and customers and test the integrity of all data transmissions.

Note that many 21st century physical networks are merging in functionality:

- **Electric power utilities can provide computer and communication services**
  Internet connection can be enabled within the electric power grid via the Power Line Communication (PLC), or Broadband over Power Lines (BPL) protocols. (This has led to the development of the HomePlug Internet standard.)

- **Media companies can provide computer and communication services**
  The coaxial cable used in cable television can be used for Internet connections.

- **Power and media companies can provide telephone service**
  This service is enabled by the Voice Over IP (Internet Protocol) standards. Many financial organizations are using VOIP as backup to regular telephone service (or vice versa).

It may also be possible to use the pipes in the water supply or sewerage grid as backup transmission lines for Internet connection.

Payment for Financial Network Services

Most financial network infrastructures consist of separate networks, privately built or leased from third parties, that provide network services to customers who prepay, pay periodically, pay by use, or pay indirectly (through advertising or other arrangements).

For example, utility companies (electricity, water, telephone, toll roads, computing services, taxi) charge by use (measured in time, kilowatt hours, message units, mileage, or computing cycles); Internet service providers and many market data vendors charge by subscription (i.e., a fixed rate per month, regardless of use).

Box 6-1
Financial Technology of Business Continuity: Transmission Lines and Power

Business continuity is an important aspect of financial technology that is closely monitored by the SEC and other organizations. Financial business continuity relies on the ability to transmit power to run computers and telecommunications systems. Electricity-based systems also must be continually cooled, as normal internal electrical resistance induces overheating in equipment. To prevent systems from simply burning out, fans and air conditioners must also be included in network infrastructure recovery.

For example, on August 14, 2003, the electric power network failed in the northeast (at 4:10 PM, after the close of the markets). On request, emergency diesel-fueled electric generators were supplied to financial customers by Consolidated Edison (Con Ed), the local utility. At the American Stock Exchange (AMEX), the generators were installed and electric power was returned within 6 hours (1:00 AM) of the failure. However, even though the computer systems were ready, the cooling systems were not: AMEX, like many buildings in lower Manhattan, purchased steam from Con Ed in order to separately power their air-conditioning systems. This time the steam transmission network also failed; steam was not available. The AMEX needed to install a portable steam boiler to power the cooling systems for the automated trading systems.

Nasdaq calls their backup "N-plus-two reliability," i.e., the system has a backup system and the backup has a backup. The Nasdaq floor exists virtually in hundreds of computers in Trumbull, Connecticut. Nasdaq gets electric power from two separate stations located at the opposite ends of Trumbull. If this power fails, a Nasdaq backup diesel generator will automatically activate. If this generator fails, a second Nasdaq diesel generator will activate. If the second backup fails, a third Nasdaq diesel generator will activate. (Nasdaq has also arranged that their backup generators have a refueling priority just below the refueling priority of the local hospitals.) The system is designed to transfer smoothly among power sources, without voltage or current fluctuations, using a backup power supply of 66 tons of batteries. There are two other battery backups, each with 66 tons of batteries. (All Nasdaq systems can run solely on batteries for 15 minutes.) There are also two backups for the cooling system: a backup cooling pump can take over if the primary cooling system fails and a secondary backup can be used if the first backup cooling system fails.

Nasdaq has also built a complete backup facility hundreds of miles away in Rockville, Maryland. Both sites run a few hundred Hewlett-Packard (formerly Tandem) NonStop processors. A few multi-processor NonStop systems are used to switch quotes or orders to the Nasdaq application servers, including trading systems and online trade comparison and reporting applications. The Rockville backup was used in 1995, when a squirrel supposedly shut down Nasdaq Trumbull. In 1995, the switch-over time to a fully functional Nasdaq Rockville was about 30 minutes.

In the financial community, payment is frequently arranged in terms of *soft dollars*. The SEC has defined soft dollar practices as "arrangements under which products or services *other than execution of securities transactions* are obtained by an adviser from or through a broker–dealer in exchange for the direction by the adviser of client brokerage transactions to the broker–dealer." The buy side (brokerage clients) has an incentive to use sell side brokers that arrange profitable soft dollar terms to pay for products or services (such as delivering timely market data, analysis, and equipment); the brokers in turn could recoup their soft dollar expenses through higher commission rates on the buy-side orders. The SEC requires the buy side to disclose (to buy-side clients) any soft dollar arrangements (with buy-side brokers), especially when any buy-side investment adviser receives research, products, or other services as a result of deciding which broker to use. The value of soft dollar purchases has been estimated by the SEC to total over $1 billion.

The U.S. Congress provided a rationale for soft dollar arrangements when they abolished fixed commission rates in May 1975. Their goal was to protect the institutional buy side from claims that they violated their fiduciary responsibilities (i.e., to their investing clients) in cases where the buy side would pay higher commission rates in exchange for research and order execution.

Box 6-2 summarizes a 1998 SEC survey of soft dollar charges. Many of the categories relate to or depend on network infrastructure services dealing with transportation, computer, communications, water, and electric power.

Box 6-2

Soft Dollar Expenses

(From the SEC Inspection Report on the Soft Dollar Practices, September 22, 1998)

Category	Example
Accounting fees	Year-end financial audit of investment partnership
Association fees	Memberships and annual dues
Cable television	Local cable TV, pay TV, news
Commission rebates	Cash returned or expenses paid for a plan or fund
Computer hardware	Monitors, printers
Computer software	Software maintenance and support
Conferences/seminars	Conference fees, virtual (Internet) conferences
Consulting services	Investment advisory services, modeling, analysis
Courier and postage	Messenger service, overnight express delivery
Custodial fees	Payment to lower expenses of accounts
Electronic databases	Market, credit, earnings data; models and computation
Employee salary/benefits	Salary, insurance policy
Execution assistance	On-line quote systems
Industry publications	Magazines, newspapers, journals
Legal fees	Retainer, research bills
Management fees	Investment adviser fees, pension consultant fees
Miscellaneous expenses	Dinner, parking, limousine, concert tickets, radio station
Office equipment/supplies	Fax, furniture, staples, water, VCR, copy machines
On-line quotation/news	Market data, analytics, yields, risk computations
Portfolio management software	Portfolio modeling, allocation, and computation
Rent	Physical office space
Research/analysis reports	Statistical processing and reporting, trade and risk alerts
Telephone expenses	Mobile phone, pager, connections to on-line services
Travel expenses	Hotel accommodations, airfare
Tuition/training	Courses, books for courses, computer training
Utilities expense	Electricity bills

Financing Network Services

There is a correspondence between the technology of finance and the finance of technology related to network infrastructures. Innovation in delivering documents, commodities, market data, or other information demands capital. Technology entrepreneurs, inventors, and investors require compensation and protection for their investment. The engine that drives the acquisition of capital and reward of compensation is fueled by intellectual property laws — these laws give inventors the right to own and make money from their inventions. Different laws give different rights, ranging from protection from copying to giving an inventor a government monopoly for the invention.

Box 6-3
Who Owns the Quotes? Who Owns Market Data?

Exchanges produce market data. The "ownership" of market data was initially addressed in 1884 with the bucket shop lawsuits, concerning whether cash-settled products (virtual delivery) were or were not gambling (see Box 5-6). Later Supreme Court "ticker cases" from 1905 to 1926 ruled that quotations are property: an exchange may keep them or communicate them to others. For example, in the 1905 Board of Trade v. Christie Grain & Stock Co., the court compared an exchange's collection of quotes to a trade secret.

The SEC continues to clarify the conflicts between quote ownership and public access to quotes. For example, in 1975 the SEC requested that the national securities exchanges "eliminate any rules or practices that restricted access to or use of any quotation information disseminated by the exchange." Their rationale was that restrictions on dissemination of quotes reduce the efficiency of the market: the market must reflect *all* available information dealing with a security. This includes quote information, which represents the judgment of market professionals concerning buying and selling interest (measured by the size of the orders and price levels). However, the SEC stated that its public access objective is compatible with allowing exchanges to charge "reasonable fees" for quotes and other market data. Moreover, the exchanges are "the most appropriate bodies to collect, process, and make available consolidated, real-time quotation data."

Revenues derived from market data fees are an important source of exchange income. Here are some 2003 statistics for the world's largest stock markets.

Exchange	Market data revenues ($ millions)	Trading volume ($ trillions)	Market capitalization ($ trillions)	Market data revenue per trading volume
NYSE	$172	$10	$11	17.73
Nasdaq	$147	$7	$3	20.70
Tokyo	$60	$2	$3	28.57
London	$180	$4	$3	50.00
Euronext	$109	$2	$2	57.37
Deutsche Bourse	$146	$1	$1	112.31

For the U.S. exchanges, market data revenues represent approximately 20% of an exchange's total revenues.

In the 19th century, entrepreneurs, inventors, and investors took advantage of these laws to finance and develop the technology of railroad and "electromagnetic" telegraph and market data ticker networks.

These investments had a feedback effect: investors and the financial markets were one of the major users of delivery technology. The demand for new delivery and communication networks led to improvements in the financial technology of the markets, which in turn led to a greater demand for financing technology. Any solution to the problems of discovering arbitrage opportunities, timely news delivery, and communication of orders that would be faster, less expensive, more convenient, of higher quality, and of higher quantity to existing solutions would have an immediate set of users.

Intellectual Property Laws and Financial Networks

Intellectual property (IP) refers to the right to own and make money from inventions or creative work. This right is mandated in Article I, Section 8 of the U.S. Constitution, where Congress is given the power to "promote the Progress of Science and useful Arts" by passing laws that give authors the exclusive right to their works for a limited period of time. The following laws protect intellectual property.

Patents

A patent is a 20-year grant, issued by the Patent and Trademark Office, that gives an inventor a kind of monopoly. It is "the right to exclude others from making, using, offering for sale, or selling" the invention in the United States and also prevents others from importing the invention into the United States. Note that what is granted is not the right to make, use, offer for sale, sell or import, but the right to exclude others: this right is often contested in the courts.

Box 6-4
Caveats and Provisional Patents

A *caveat* was a preliminary patent application in which an inventor claims one or more potential inventions without presenting the detail that is required in a regular patent application. Caveats establish priority: if another inventor files a patent application on a similar invention within 1 year of the caveat, the patent office notifies the holder of the caveat and gives the caveat holder 3 months to submit a regular patent application. A caveat could be renewed annually.

Congress abolished the caveat application in 1910. However, since June 8, 1995, the United States Patent and Trademark Office (USPTO) has offered inventors something similar: the option of filing a *provisional application* for a patent. The provisional patent application lets applicants file "without a formal patent claim, oath or declaration, or any information disclosure (prior art) statement" in order to provide "the means to establish an early effective filing date in a non-provisional patent application." It also allows use of the term *patent pending*.

A provisional application for patent expires 12 months from the date that the provisional application is filed. The 12-month pendency period cannot be extended: an applicant who files a provisional application must file a corresponding nonprovisional application for patent within 12 months in order to benefit from the earlier filing of the provisional application.

Box 6-5

Abstract of U.S. Patent 6,061,663 (Nasdaq, May 9, 2000) for Index Rebalancing

A computer system, including a processor and a storage device storing a computer program product for rebalancing a capitalization weighted stock index, is described. The computer program includes instructions for causing a computer to classify stocks in the index as a large individual stock if a stock has a capitalization weight above or equal to a first threshold or as a small individual stock if the stock has a capitalization weight below the first threshold. The computer program causes the computer to scale down the large individual stocks by an excess capitalization weight of the large stocks and distribute an aggregated excess capitalization weight of the large individual stocks over the capitalization weights of the small individual stocks. An iterative redistribution of excess capitalization over all small individual stocks can be used to provide for less than proportional distribution of excess capitalization to very small capitalized stocks. The index rebalancing software retains a capitalization weighting characteristic while permitting the index to conform to generally accepted accounting, economic, and tax standards. Index rebalancing is accomplished while maintaining the original relative position of stocks and reducing the market impact of rebalancing on the small individual stock group.

What makes an invention unique must be disclosed to the patent office. Examples of patented inventions or processes include the telegraph, the ticker, and a computer program for determining the number of shares to buy or sell in a stock index weighted by market capitalization (see Box 6-5; see Box 5-9 for an outline of such an algorithm).

For example, according to the USPTO, from 1976–2006:

- Bloomberg has 12 patents covering flat panel and multipanel computer displays, telephone handsets, and a computer keyboard.
- Citicorp has 44 patents covering authentication, magnetic strips (including credit cards), and computer displays (for automated teller machines).
- Merrill Lynch has 35 patents covering computer server architectures, networks, Web services, cash management, and trading.
- Nasdaq has 3 patents covering transaction processing, report generation, and computing a capitalization weighted stock index.
- NYSE has 2 patents covering computer displays.

Copyright

A copyright gives its owner the exclusive right to "copy" a work. For works made for hire, this right lasts the shorter of 95 years (from creation date) and 120 years (from published date). This includes the rights to reproduce, to prepare derivative works, to distribute copies, to perform, or to display the work publicly. Published works such as art, software, and technical drawings can be copyrighted, including news and market data.

Trademark

A trademark is a word, name, symbol, or device used to indicate the source of origin of a product in order to distinguish the product from others. A service mark is a trademark for services. Both can last forever if they are used continuously. The Standard and Poor's 500 (S&P 500), first used in 1940, is a trademark and service mark (recorded in the U.S. Patent and Trademark Office as serial number 73673838, registration number 1521758).

License

A license agreement is a legal contract between an owner and a user of intellectual property, such as trademarks, patents, or copyrights. A license agreement grants to the user (the licensee) the right to use the intellectual property under certain conditions, such as payment of royalty fees, time frame provisions, conditions of reproduction, or manufacture. Many licenses (especially software) specify a limited warranty to protect the owner from a user's lawsuit in the event that the intellectual property does not work as expected.

6.2. Origins of Electronic Financial Communication Networks

In 1837, the *Journal of Commerce* (the business newspaper established by the Tappan brothers; see Box 4-5) started publishing articles about the American telegraph. The inventor was Samuel Morse, a professor of Literature of the Arts and Design at the University of the City of New York (now New York University) who was also a candidate for New York City mayor in the 1836 election (professor Morse ran under the Native American Democratic Association; he ran again in 1841). The *Journal* previously published several articles relating to the European development of telegraphs based on electricity. Apparently, these articles inspired Samuel Morse to announce his invention.

The Intellectual Property of the American Electromagnetic Telegraph

Morse applied for a *caveat* on September 28, 1837 to protect his work. Between then and April 7, 1838 (when Morse applied for the full patent), Morse put together a design team of professors and students to build and demonstrate a working prototype and awarded them shares in a future company that would own the patents. On June 20, 1840, Morse was awarded U.S. patent 1647, for "A new and useful improvement in the mode of communicating information by signals by the application of electro-magnetism." This was followed by U.S. patent 3316 (October 25, 1843) for "A method for introducing wire into metallic pipes," which specified a method for making telegraph wire.

The annual report of the commissioner of patents for 1843 devoted a large discussion on the potential of the telegraph (see Box 6-6). Morse's intent was to license his patents to manufacturers of telegraph equipment and builders of telegraph network lines. The initial partners in the venture was Morse (nine shares); geology professor Leonard Gale (one share); student Alfred Vail, whose father owned the Speedwell Ironworks of Morristown, New Jersey (two shares); and Maine congressman Francis Smith, former chairman of the House Committee on Commerce (four shares). Maine was strategically located between the news ships that docked in Halifax and the market centers in New York and Boston.

Box 6-6

Excerpt from the Review of the 1843 Patents (by U.S. Patent Commissioner Henry Ellsworth)

In effecting the transmission of intelligence by the telegraph, the artificial magnet . . . created by electricity sets in motion an apparatus which gives on paper certain characters representing letters of the alphabet. Communications are thus recorded, either by day or night, on a revolving cylinder, without even superintendence, and may be transcribed at leisure.

The medium employed is simply a copper wire, insulated and extended on posts, at an expense not exceeding $150 per mile. It is confidently believed that proprietors will thus connect their dwellings with the places of their mechanical operations. . . . The same posts, too, would answer for many lines of communication. Each wire, however, must be insulated; and, strange as it may seem, if two wires are placed horizontally, at some distance apart, and one is charged, a similar effect will be produced on the other.

Experiments already made, in England and on the continent, leave no doubt of its practicability; and this will, ere long, be further tested on the railroad route between Washington and Baltimore. The advantage of this mode of communication must be obvious. . . . The East and the West, the North and the South, can enjoy the earliest intelligence of markets, and thus be prepared against speculators. Criminals will be deterred from the commission of crimes . . . for the mandate of justice, outrunning their flight will greet their arrival at the first stopping place.

Morse initially assumed that the electromagnetic telegraph would be under government control, like the European Chappe telegraph system. After the Washington–Baltimore test, Morse offered the telegraph patent rights to the U.S. Post Office for $100,000, but they refused. Consequently, in 1845, Morse found private investors to fund the Magnetic Telegraph Company (capitalized at $15,000) that would initially provide real-time communication between Washington and Baltimore. Within a year, the network had stations in the major U.S. financial centers (Philadelphia, New York, and Boston); by 1848 it reached New Orleans and linked Maine to St. John (across the Bay of Fundy from Halifax).

Morse reissued patent 1647 (see Box 6-7) on January 15, 1846 and again on June 13, 1848. Patent 6420, "improvement in electric telegraphs" was issued on May 1, 1849. These patents had to be defended in court at least 15 times (including lawsuits between the partners).

One significant aspect of the Morse telegraph was stated in Claim 7: at the receiving end, the Morse register (Claim 1) would leave marks looking like a "dot" or a "dash" on a moving paper tape (a device specified in the "Morse Register"), depending on how long the sender held down the transmitting key (which completed the circuit and sent a voltage to the receiver). The dictionary alluded to in Claim 9 specified the precise meaning of a sequence of dots and dashes (now called Morse code). After reception, the tape would be read and translated into a message. Morse and Vail observed that a message could be transmitted just by listening to the clicking sounds made by the register: waiting for the marks to appear on the moving tape actually slowed things up. Using the "Morse sounder" increased transmission to about 20 words per minute from about 5 words per minute.

Box 6-7

Excerpts from U.S. Patent Number 1647 (9 pages; June 20, 1840): Improvement in the Mode of Communicating Information by Signals by the Application of Electro-magnetism

I . . . Samuel F.B. Morse . . . have invented a new and useful machine and system of signs for transmitting intelligence between distant points by the means of a new application and effect of electro-magnetism in producing sounds and signs, or either, and also for recording permanently by the same means, and applications, and effect of electro-magnetism, any signs thus produced and representing intelligence, transmitted as before named between distant points; and I demonstrate said invention the "American Electro-Magnetic Telegraph," of which the following is a full and exact description. . . . What I claim as my invention, and desire to secure by Letters of Patent is as follows:

1. The formation and arrangement of the several parts of mechanism . . . constituting the . . . two signal levers, and the register lever, and alarm lever . . .

2. The combination of the mechanism constituting the recording-cylinder . . .

3. The use, system, formation, and arrangement of type, and of signs, for transmitting intelligence between distant points by the application of electro-magnetism and metallic conductors . . .

4. The mode and process of breaking and connecting by mechanism currents of electricity or galvanism in any circuit of metallic conductors . . .

5. The mode and process of propelling and connecting by mechanism currents of electricity or galvanism in and through any desired number of circuits of metallic conductors from any known generator of electricity or galvanism . . .

6. The application of electro-magnets by means of one or more circuits of metallic conductors from any known generator of electricity or galvanism to the several levers in the machinery . . . for the purpose of imparting motion to said levers . . . and for transmitting by signs and sounds intelligence between distant points and simultaneously to different points.

7. The mode and process of recording or marking permanently signs of intelligence transmitted between distant points, and simultaneously to different points . . .

8. The combination and arrangement of electro-magnets in one or more circuits of metallic conductors with armatures of magnets for transmitting intelligence by signs and sounds, or either, between distant points, and to different points simultaneously.

9. The combination and mutual adaptation of the several parts of the mechanism and system of type and signs with and to the dictionary or vocabulary of words as described in the foregoing specification.

Demand for Real-Time Messages

Each Morse telegraph patent had a lifetime of 20 years (the last one expired in 1869). During that time, the Morse telegraph network grew from nothing to a set of competing infrastructures of wires, poles, and batteries that would link every city in the

---

Box 6-8
Telecommunication Networks: Existing Technology

In the 1830s, financial news from Europe was delivered by ships that arrived at New York ports. The state of the art in news reporting technology was for each newspaper to send a rowboat to the ships in dock to pick up newspapers and financial data; the content would then be delivered to the New York newspaper reporters.

The *Journal of Commerce* management team understood the value of immediate delivery of news and market data. At the same time, their business charter required them to be strict Sabbath observers: there was to be no printing, reporting, or publishing work "between 12 P.M., Saturday, and 12 P.M., Sunday." They satisfied these requirements by purchasing fast "news schooners." Two schooners (the first one was named the *Journal of Commerce*) constantly traveled up and down New York Harbor (a few miles out on the Atlantic Ocean), searching for ships from Europe that they could meet before they would arrive in New York. The news schooners would then relay news using a Chappe marine telegraph to a base on a hill near Sandy Hook (New Jersey); Sandy Hook would telegraph to the hill on Staten Island, and Staten Island would telegraph to the Battery (downtown Manhattan). Runners would deliver the message to the *Journal* office; activity would be suspended in order to determine whether an "extra" edition needed to be printed.

By 1833 the *Journal* expanded their network to include a "pony express" service between Philadelphia and New York, initially consisting of eight relays of horses. The network subsequently expanded to Washington. The network worked so well that the *Journal* had the news a day in advance of the U.S. government network. Competition forced the other New York newspapers to purchase news schooners and Chappe telegraphs. The *New York Herald* also set up a pigeon network between New York City and Albany to get the edge on announcements from the governor of New York.

In 1838, Samuel Cunard of Halifax (Canada) formed the British and North American Royal Mail Steam Packet Company (later becoming Cunard Steamships Limited) and won the rights, under contract with the British Admiralty, to be the royal mail carrier. Cunard ran a trans-Atlantic shipping service between Liverpool and New York (alternating with Boston) with a stopover in Halifax. By this time the newspapers and "private speculators" sent their news schooners to meet the Cunard ships far out at sea. The Liverpool to New York trip averaged 12 to 13 days; the news schooners would meet the ships as far as 50 miles out at sea and reporters would send pigeons back to Boston or Halifax with a rolled up summary of news.

United States. Many of the early investors in Morse telegraph companies were express and railroad companies; investors were also customers. For example, John Butterfield obtained Morse patent rights in 1845 and formed the New York, Albany, and Buffalo Telegraph Company. (Butterfield later founded American Express and Wells, Fargo & Company; see Box 1-4).

Because wires were cut easily (by accident or by intention), Morse telegraph networks were initially regarded as being less secure and less reliable than wireless Chappe networks or wireless pigeon networks. One solution was to have Morse telegraph lines follow railroad tracks, which lowered development costs, simplified construction and maintenance, and increased network security. Because of this, railroad companies were Morse telegraph users (for train scheduling and track allocation) as well as host providers for Morse telegraph services (a majority of Morse telegraph stations were located at railroad offices).

Two events helped spur the investment in the Morse telegraph network: the Mexican–American war (1846–1847) and the potential war between Great Britain and the United States over ownership of the Oregon territories. The Mexican–American war was the first war featuring real-time news reporting. Reporters from the New York newspapers would dispatch stories via pony express to the nearest Morse telegraph station: news would reach headquarters and major media outlets in hours instead of weeks. A similar method was in place for capturing the news from London; by the 1840s a Cunard ship arrived at Halifax about once a week.

An important Morse telegraph gap was between Halifax and to the Morse telegraph station at Saint John (across the Bay of Fundy). It was reported that several Wall Street speculators arranged a private pony express system to close the gap in order to take advantage of the arbitrage between London and New York. This led David Hale and Gerard Hallock of the *Journal of Commerce* to propose a news association that would share the expense of a Bay of Fundy steamer, a pony express service, and the cost of the Morse telegraph network. In 1848, the *Journal* and five other New York newspapers formed the Harbor News Association; it soon renamed itself the New York Associated Press (AP), and Gerard Hallock was declared the first president. According to George Mullane (1914), the association

> bound themselves to furnish funds necessary for carrying out the enterprise. The chief object of this newspaper movement was the protection of the commercial interest of New York, in respect to furnishing at the earliest possible date the state of the European markets.

The entire AP enterprise focused around a 3000 word summary of the news (note that the "news" was at least 12 days old, due to the latency of the shipping speeds). The AP news summary was carried to a pony express rider as soon as the Cunard steamship arrived at Halifax; the rider sped to Victoria Beach and delivered it to the AP-chartered steamship. The steamship raced across the Bay of Fundy to the Saint John Morse telegraph station, where it was immediately transmitted to Boston and New York. At these centers, the summary was typeset for subscribing newspapers. Investors continually sponsored Morse telegraph companies and lines to eliminate communication gaps. The Morse telegraph gap between St. John and Halifax was eliminated on November 15, 1849.

By 1851 (11 years after the first Morse patent) there were over 50 separate U.S. Morse telegraph companies. Dozens of new companies went out of business or were consolidated as the networks grew exponentially. By 1856, 14 companies located in the western United States (at the time, this meant west of the city of Buffalo) merged into the Western Union Telegraph Company. Further consolidations gave rise to a set of agreements (1857) among the six largest companies called the Treaty of the Six Nations (American Telegraph, Atlantic & Ohio, New York, Albany & Buffalo, Western Union, New Orleans & Ohio, and Illinois & Mississippi). American Telegraph bought the remaining Morse patent rights and the rights of other telegraph inventors in 1861. By 1866 Western Union merged with American Telegraph and controlled 90% of U.S. telegraph traffic.

Payment for Electronic Messages

Morse telegraph companies made money by charging by a message-based pay-per-use model: in 1846, the fee was $2.50 for a 10 word message — a "telegram" — covering a 100-mile distance (exclusive of address and signature). This is worth about $500 today (based on the unskilled wage rate). Without discount or allowing for long distance premium, the weekly 3000 word AP summary would be worth today about $150,000. These earnings could be distributed quickly as dividends to corporate investors. Competition and improved technology reduced these rates. The price of a 10 word message from New York to Chicago was $2.05 in 1866. By 1884, the cost of a 10 word message between any two cities in the continental United States was $1.00 (still about $116 in 2003, based on the unskilled wage rate).

The financial services industry helped make the telecommunications business very profitable. In April 1856, at a talk to potential investors at the American Geographical and Statistical Society, Marshall Lefferts, president of the New York and New England Telegraph Company (who soon became the chief engineer of the American Telegraph Company, then president of the Gold & Stock Reporting Company, and finally the first president of Western Union), classified the Morse telegraph messages between New York and Boston (exclusive of the press) during November 1855 as shown in Figure 6-1.

Of these 20,400 messages per month, about 57% were related to finance and commerce and about 18% were related specifically to financial markets. Even if each message was the minimum 10 words, at $2.50 per 10 word message, this monthly income amounts to $51,000 (about $8.1 million in 2003, based on the unskilled wage rate). Lefferts claimed that New York newspapers spent another $5000 per month (collectively) on Morse telegraph service. Presumably this included the $750 for the weekly 3000 word AP summary from Cunard.

This availability of the Morse telegraph to anyone who can afford a telegram had a dramatic effect on the financial markets. Many arbitrage opportunities that were available only to very wealthy speculators who can afford their own networks were eliminated, especially those between London and New York. The price of delivering real-time financial information, news, prices, and orders dropped by orders of magnitude; moreover, financial news that was valuable just a few months ago became commonplace and was reported, like today, in daily newspapers. For example, in 1852, even 17-year-old telegraph operator Andrew Carnegie was able to buy and profit from NYSE listed stock (see Box 6-9).

One effect was that markets became more efficient: prices became uniform and dependent on the large market centers as the financial technology became more accessible and affordable.

for freighting and shipping	3130
on general mercantile matters	2140
for reports of markets	2020
for making appointments	1930
for instructions (money & notes)	1692
for buying goods	1608
for social occasions	1320
for selling goods	1050
in cipher	750
for railroads	644
relating sickness	374
relating deaths	228
miscellaneous	3514

FIGURE 6-1   Classification of telegraph messages (Marshall Lefferts: 1855).

Box 6-9
Andrew Carnegie and the Morse Telegraph

Andrew Carnegie (1835–1919) started his career as a Morse telegraph messenger at the age of 14 at the Pittsburgh division of the Pennsylvania Railroad. By the time he was 17, Carnegie was the personal Morse telegrapher to Thomas Scott, the superintendent of the western division of the railroad. From Carnegie's autobiography:

> My pay was now $35 a month and I was employed where I could see the importance of the railroad and the telegraph to economic life. I was 17 years old but knew that my future was in the opportunities that Mr. Scott had presented. . . . Tom Scott also introduced me to the fine art of investing. He advised me to buy shares in the Adams Express Company but lacking funds, I asked my Mother for a loan. She mortgaged the home and I invested $500; but soon Adams Express was prospering and the dividends amounted to $1,400 per year. I then invested in the Woodruff Palace Car Company (later to be merged with George Pullman's sleeping car company); bought shares in Andrew Kloman's iron foundry; shares in telegraph and oil companies; and in the Keystone Bridge Company. By age 28, my total income was $48,000 a year, including my $2,800 salary from the Pennsylvania Railroad.

Carnegie's experience with the railroad led him to invest in the steel production of railroad tracks, using the new Bessemer technology. The railroad companies also helped finance the venture. In 1901, he sold his Carnegie Steel Corporation, the largest steel manufacturing company in the world, to J.P. Morgan for $480 million (about $50 billion in 2003, based on the unskilled wage rate).

Network Consolidation

In 1856, Lefferts proposed extending the telegraph networks directly to Europe, thus finally closing the "killer gap" and eliminating the 12-day network latency. His appeal was to create a global financial system:

> With a submarine cable joining Europe and America, our merchants would hold "high change" indeed — discussing the day's transactions with the cities of London, Vienna, and Paris. A sale of "Illinois Centrals," or New York sixes, made in London at 5 P.M. will be discussed at the New York board at 12 o'clock. Or a message sent from New York to San Francisco at 12 o'clock, will reach its destination at a quarter before nine in the morning of the same day; and a message from New York at 12 o'clock will reach St. Louis at eleven. This all seems strange, and it becomes necessary to pause and reflect before it can be realized as truth. But truth it is; and "old father Time," hour glass and all, is completely beaten.

Despite the relatively poor understanding of electricity at the time, the first trans-Atlantic cable (between Ireland and Newfoundland) was deployed for telegraph service on August 4, 1857 (it broke down about 1 month later during the financial "panic of 1857").

Financial markets consolidated just as the telegraph companies consolidated. The elimination of arbitrage reduced the importance of hundreds of local markets and exchanges. By 1910, 90% of all U.S. bonds and 66% of all U.S. stocks were traded on the New York Stock Exchange.

The technology feedback effect also increased the universe of traders and stockholders. An increased universe of traders meant that it was easier for buyers to meet sellers: this "market liquidity" increased with the availability of telegraph communication. Increased liquidity and market participation induced an increase in the total amount invested in the market, leading to more investment and more demand for financial information and financial technology.

The Morse Telegraph as an Internet

In the 1850s, the maximum single-wire range for Morse telegraph communication was about 100 miles. As with the Chappe telegraph, repeaters had to be used for longer distances. The Morse patent (see Claim 6 and Claim 8) proposed using repeaters (implemented as automatic electromechanical relays) to enable transmission from sender to receiver without intervening human operators. Compared to the Chappe telegraph, network latency (see Section 1.5) was reduced by orders of magnitude, even though both the Morse telegraph and the Chappe telegraph transmitted individual symbols at the speed of light.

Note that at routing points, human operators still had to translate the message, parse out address and routing information, determine the best routing path, and retelegraph the message along the appropriate line so that the message can be routed through to other intermediate stations and ultimately to the destination station. Like the Chappe telegraph, the early Morse telegraph operators performed a task manually that is done by today's Internet routers.

Telegraph network latency increases with the number of routing hops and the length of the message: longer messages have longer latency. The latency in the Morse telegraph network was still much less than the latency in the Chappe telegraph, where transmission rates along a 100-mile (through 10 optical repeaters) distance was about one letter per minute. The Morse sounder further reduced network latency from about 12 seconds per word to 3 seconds per word.

Professionally, a Morse telegraph operator performed tasks that were similar to today's software engineer and network engineer. At a minimum, a Morse telegraph operator was a highly paid technologist whose primary task was to translate a high-level language (i.e., English) into a low-level representation (i.e., Morse code) and back again.

Reconstructing received code was much more difficult than transmitting: operators had to train their ears in a "noisy domain" (due to poor insulation and crashes, which resulted in misspellings, missing words, missing sentences) as the 1907 complaint to Western Union shows (Box 6-11).

Thomas Edison said that receiving operators often had to make up 20% of the text and had to interpolate messages based on context. Good operators had to be constantly aware of current news events and price movements in the primary markets.

Early Examples of Virtual Delivery: Fedwire

By 1864, Wells, Fargo & Company was using the telegraph to enable the transfer and virtual delivery of money. Such "wire transfers" became a product offered by Western

---

Box 6-10
Latency in Financial Communication Networks

The April 2003 interagency paper on financial network infrastructures (Section 6.1) was criticized for suggesting that there be a minimum distance of 200 to 300 miles between primary and backup centers. Many financial firms stated that maintaining a continuous real time backup more than 100 miles away was beyond the state of the art, even using fast (several gigabit per second) fiber optic technologies. For example, one of the most common data transfer protocols used (called fibre channel) has a distance limit of about 100 miles, about the same limit between stations as the original Morse telegraph network.

The reason for this is due to network latency. Financial data transfer networks based on Internet technology require repeaters and routers. In the current protocols, data are distributed into chunks (called packets or frames); because each packet is sent *reliably* between routers, there are acknowledgements sent between stations for each chunk transmitted (this is similar to the Chappe telegraph, where each symbol was sent reliably). In general, the smaller the packets, the larger the latency (because of the acknowledgments sent between stations for each packet). Latency is also affected by the speeds of the processor (the address parser and translator) in each router, as well as the speeds of the processors controlling the storage units in the sending and receiving computers (the so called buffer-to-buffer latency). For example, a tape drive storage unit stops while waiting for data; latency becomes worse while waiting for the tape drive to restart (disk drives are faster but are still regarded as a bottleneck). In any case, latency increases with the number of routing hops and the length of the message.

One solution is to change the protocols by reducing the number of message acknowledgments or by increasing the size of the message chunks. Such asynchronous techniques transmit more data across larger distances and minimize the latency effects of acknowledgments; the tradeoff is the possibility of reduced reliability and data integrity.

Union in 1871. At that time there were actually several "foreign exchange" rates across regions in the United States that governed commercial and banking payments. The different regional exchange rates for the dollar depended on physical delivery costs and interest expense (due to network latency).

One of the first technology projects of the newly formed U.S. Federal Reserve System (1913) was to create a standard money transfer network. By 1918, the Federal Reserve set up a secure telegraph network connecting the 12 Federal Reserve Banks, the Federal Reserve Board, and the United States Treasury. The network, called *Fedwire*, was based on leased public telegraph lines. Member banks could transfer funds and update account records for free instead of paying for the physical delivery of cash or gold to counterparties. Fedwire also eliminated the interest expense due to a long wait for physical delivery.

The Federal Reserve also set up the Gold Settlement Fund — a netting system where commercial banks could settle accounts with the help of their local Reserve Banks and Fedwire transfers. Balances could be settled by simply updating database records via "book-entry transfers" posted to accounts that member banks held at the Federal Reserve. Physical delivery of gold or paper currency became unnecessary (just as paper checks are unnecessary in the post Check-21 era — see Box 5-2).

Box 6-11
A Complaint to Western Union

July 21, 1907

General Manager
Western Union Telegraph Office
931 Chestnut Street
Philadelphia

Dear Sir:

Enclosed is a message I received from New York nearly a fortnight ago so carelessly transmitted that I intended at the time to complain of it but forgot it.

Whether the fault lay in the transmitter in New York misreading the message or in the receiver here is not certain, but I incline to the latter for the reason that in all cases the mistake in the letter appears to have been resulted from the inattention of the receiving ear to certain dots and dashes constituting the letter he was taking. Thus in my name he recorded only one dot instead of two. In "ceased" he lost two dots from the "r" making it an "e." He took a dot for a dash in "o" making it on "a," & he skipped the second "s" from inattention. To make "HAE" out of "bar" he made four dots out of a dash and three, and lost two of the three dots of the "r." Similarly, he made an "n" out of a "v" by not hearing two dots of the latter.

It is irresponsible for me to say whether the fault was a bad writer or a careless reader or both, but the fact is that it is not a creditable example of telegraph efficiency.

Very truly,

Persifor Frazer

Fedwire still provides real-time settlement for fund transfers: transactions are processed as entered and they are settled individually. In contrast with Fedwire, securities processing on Wall Street was primarily a manual enterprise until the 1970s. The essential procedure was as follows:

1. A customer (buyer or seller) delivers an order to a broker at a registered representative branch office.

2. A messenger at the registered representative branch office carries the order to the firm's order desk.

3. A messenger at the firm's order desk carries the order to the firm's trading booth on the exchange trading floor. The trading booth creates a paper order ticket.

4. On the floor, a firm representative (the floor broker) carries the order ticket to the market maker for the particular stock at a special location on the trading floor (the specialist).

5. The specialist either personally executes the order or executes the order with another trader in the crowd. If the order was not executed, the specialist writes an entry into an order book for future execution. The order may be good for the entire day, good for the entire month, or good forever (until canceled), depending on instructions received.

The customer had to be notified if the transaction was executed. The reporting procedure was the same steps in reverse.

In many cases, the patented innovations introduced by the Morse telegraph (and telephone in the 1880s) replaced physical delivery by virtual (electronic) delivery in steps 1–3. However, many Wall Street offices still relied on speaking tubes for office-to-office messages, high-pressure pneumatic pipes to transfer small documents under the streets from building to building, and carriers for the delivery of large documents.

During the 1960s, the entire procedure broke down with the increase of orders. By April 1968, the exchanges were forced to shorten trading hours so that brokerage firm back offices could handle the paper backlog. The usual situation was described in Michael Bloomberg's autobiography (Box 6-12).

Box 6-12
Sorting, Stamping, and Updating

Michael Bloomberg's first job on Wall Street (June 1966) was in the "back office" of Salomon Brothers. Every afternoon, stock and bond certificates were physically carried to banks as collateral for overnight loans; these would be carried back every morning and checked back into inventory. Bloomberg's job was to help the inventory check-in procedure by counting the securities by hand and sorting them alphabetically.

His second job was on the Salomon trading floor dealing with electric and gas company bonds (a "front office" job at the "utilities desk"). From Bloomberg's autobiography:

> After a partner signed each transaction ticket (big trades got both partners' signatures), I stamped them with a consecutive number and updated our records. The tickets then went zipping down the conveyor belt to the Back Office from whence I had just escaped. At last I had become an integral part of capitalism. Stamping and updating: I was so glad I'd gone to graduate school!"

Ultimately, this prompted exchanges to develop better electronic systems for transmitting market data, for order processing (delivery and execution), and for the presettlement comparison of trades.

The Morse Social Network

Among some circles, it is customary to sneer at the scientific background of Samuel Morse: he was trained as a portrait artist, not as an engineer or technologist: he was not an academic expert in electromagnetism. Nevertheless, in his time the gap between art

Box 6-13
The Morse Social Network

Samuel F. B. Morse (1791–1872) wanted to be a classical artist (a painter and sculptor), yet he graduated Yale with a major in chemistry in the class of 1810. His father, Jedidiah Morse (1761–1826), known as the "father of American geography" because of his best-selling geography books (including the 1784 *Geography Made Easy*), was also a publisher: his magazine *The Panopolist* (started in 1805 and renamed *The Missionary Herald* in 1843) remained in business until 1951.

The Yale class of 1810 included the Ellsworth twins, Henry (1791–1858) and William (1791–1868). Their father, Oliver, was a senator from Connecticut and Chief Justice of the U.S. Supreme Court (1796–1799). William became a law professor, judge, and governor of Connecticut (1838); he was an expert on intellectual property and was responsible for drafting the fundamentals of U.S. copyright laws. Henry became the U.S. Commissioner of Patents from 1836 to 1848. Henry's son Henry William (1814–1864) became one of Samuel Morse's patent attorneys (1850).

Morse was no stranger to intellectual property law. Artists made money by acquiring portrait commissions and by owning copyright; these allowed them to sell miniature versions of the larger paintings. Among the more famous paintings by Morse were his 1819 portrait of U.S. president James Monroe; his 1822 painting of the Capital Rotunda that included over 80 portraits of members of Congress and the Supreme Court; and his 1826 portrait of Lafayette (commissioned by New York City for $1000). Morse also was awarded his first patent at age 26 (for a manually powered piston driven water pump), filed jointly with younger brother Sidney in 1817.

Sidney Morse graduated Yale in 1811, studied law, and became a newspaper reporter and publisher. The first newspaper he cofounded, *The Boston Recorder*, became the third largest newspaper in Boston within a year of its first issue (January 3, 1816). In 1823 Sidney (and a third brother, Richard) came to New York to start their second newspaper, the *New York Observer*. Samuel also came to New York during that time, where he set up a portrait studio near the corner of Wall Street and Broadway, not far from the *Observer* offices and the New York Stock Exchange.

In 1825, Sidney merged the *Recorder* with the *Boston Telegraph*, founded in 1824 by Gerard Hallock (1800–1866). After the merger, Hallock joined the Morse brothers in New York in 1827 and became a co-owner and editor of the *Observer*. During this time, Samuel Morse founded and became first president of the *National Academy of Design* (1826).

Morse brothers also acquired a controlling interest in the *Journal of Commerce* from the Tappan Brothers (see Box 4-5); Arthur Tappan was more interested in politics and philanthropy (and at a later time, Lewis was more interested in credit reporting). Samuel Morse wrote the business plan for the new *Journal*. In February 1828, Samuel Morse sold the New Haven house that belonged to his late father Jedidiah to Arthur Tappan, which allowed Tappan to commute (weekly) to New York City. Later in 1828 the Morse brothers, Hallock, and David Hale (1791–1849), also from Boston (a nephew of the American patriot Nathan Hale) bought out the rest of Arthur Tappan's interest and became part owners (with Lewis Tappan) of the *Journal of Commerce*. Samuel Morse was a contributor to both newspapers, writing mostly about art and politics.

In 1848, David Hale and Gerard Hallock helped organize the Associated Press to share the expense of a Morse telegraph network among several New York newspapers: Gerard Hallock was the first president.

and technology was much smaller than it is today. During the 20-year lifetime of the Morse patents, institutions offering instruction in the "many practical arts" (*poly techne* in Greek) were being founded: Brooklyn Polytechnic Institute (now Polytechnic University) in 1854; Massachusetts Institute of Technology in 1861; the Rensselaer School, renamed Rensselaer Polytechnic Institute in 1861.

However, it was probably because of Morse's background and the utilization of his social network that his version of the telegraph proved to be the most popular one on the market. Other electronic telegraph models by Wheatstone (based on moving needles) and others were more difficult to use. The Morse social network of influential people in finance, the news media, and politics, derived from his portraits of the same people, helped enormously in forming technology and legal teams, in raising capital, and in acquiring high-profile (and high-paying) users for his service. In some sense, publishing was also the family business; from his brothers, he was familiar with the rewards of supplying real time news and market data.

6.3. The Technology of Virtual Delivery

Since the 1840s, the trend in financial network services is to replace physical delivery with virtual delivery. The way to do this is, according to Claim 3 of U.S. Patent 1647, is by "transmitting intelligence between distant points by the application of electro-magnetism and metallic conductors." Systems using "electromagnetism" (today called electronic systems) enable virtual delivery of financial information — messages and orders — that can be encoded in voltages. Delivery time is a function of network latency.

Today, the elimination of physical delivery, paper, or human involvement in financial processing is sometimes called *straight through processing* (STP).

Basic Properties of Electronic Systems

The first electronic signaling system built in the United States was a prototype developed by Benjamin Franklin. The single wire network traversed the Schuylkill River in Philadelphia in 1748 (the same year that Franklin wrote that "Time is Money" and "Credit is Money"; see Box 2-2). Franklin sent a signal across the river that ignited a container of alcohol. The significance was that a message was transmitted that was based on a different technology from that of the Chappe telegraph, signal flare, or sound.

Franklin chose to use the word *current* to describe the carrying of *charges* in a manner similar to his use of the word *currency* in his essays on paper money: the paper currency carries monetary charges (debits and credits). Electricity likewise carries debits and credits — called by Franklin *positive* and *negative*. Money, like electricity, flows like a current in either a net positive or a net negative direction. According to Franklin's model, if electricity (and cash) flows like a liquid in a pipe, then the amount of current flowing in the pipe, the resistance or friction to the flow by the pipe, and the fluid force or pressure in the pipe should be measurable.

Before the 19th century, the only way to generate electricity was by rubbing certain materials together, such as silk, glass, amber, and fur (*electron* is Greek for *amber*), generating what is called *static electricity*. Generation relied on inefficient physical (mostly manual) means but it was discovered that charges can be stored in specially constructed devices, now called *capacitors* and then called Leyden jars. Electrical generation based on friction is the basis of today's commercially available *triboelectric generators*.

The ability of a Leyden jar or capacitor to store electricity is measured by its *capacitance*. The unit of capacitance, the farad, is named after Michael Faraday (1791–1867). In 1748, Franklin coined the word *battery* to refer to a set of charged capacitors, apparently associating the sudden painful electric shock of an accidental discharge with the legal definition of battery as "the willful or intentional touching of a person against that person's will by another person, or by an object or substance put in motion by that other person."

Batteries

Electricity can be generated by chemical processes. This was demonstrated by Alessandro Volta (1745–1827). His battery (1800) was a container cell containing sulfuric acid covering zinc and copper rods. The chemical reaction produced a current; the by-product was hydrogen gas. Because there were no cycles or oscillations in the strength or direction of the current, it is said that batteries produce *direct current* (DC).

Today's unit of electric "pressure" — an amount of work that a charge performs by moving between two points — is called a *volt*. Using the analogy of a liquid flowing through a pipe, differences in pressure (called a *potential difference*) induce a force (called *galvanism* in the Morse patents, and now called the *electromotive force*) that "pushes" charges from one point to the other.

The unit of current (an amount of charge flowing per second) is called the *amp*, named after André-Marie Ampère (1775–1836). The product of voltage times current is *power* (i.e., $P = I \cdot V$), where I is the current and V is the voltage. Power is defined as the rate of doing work: the amount of work performed in a unit of time. The unit of power is the *watt*, named after James Watt (1736–1819).

Box 6-14

Grove Cells, Fuel Cells, and Batteries for Financial Systems

Modern batteries and fuel cells are an important component for backup or alternative power in financial infrastructures (witness the 66 tons of batteries used at Nasdaq). They trace their origins to British inventor Sir William Grove (1811–1896). Grove's fuel cell consisted of two platinum strips immersed in tubes containing hydrogen, oxygen, and sulfuric acid. The chemical reaction produced a voltage between the strips. At the time, Grove proposed replacing the coal and wood used as energy sources with hydrogen.

Grove's nitric acid model, using zinc, platinum, nitric acid, and sulfuric acid, became the favorite battery for the early telegraph (the first Morse Washington–Baltimore line used five Grove cells). Each cell was able to generate about 12 amps of current at 1.8 volts. One rule was to use one Grove cell per 20 miles between repeaters.

The nitric acid Grove cells were noisy: the hissing acid produced nitric dioxide as a toxic by-product. Safer batteries produced half the voltage. Among the less toxic generators was the Daniell cell, named after John Daniell (1790–1845); it was based on zinc, copper, and copper sulphate. The first transatlantic cable was powered by 400 Daniell cells. In 1886, Western Union used 12,500 cells in their New York offices.

Resistance

Using the analogy of a liquid flowing through thin and thick pipes, long thin wires have greater friction or resistance to a current than short fat wires. The *resistance* (R) is the ratio of potential difference to the current (i.e., $R = V/I$). The unit of resistance is the ohm, named after Georg Ohm (1789–1854). Consequently, the power dissipated through a resistor is

$$P = I \cdot V = I^2 \cdot R = V^2/R.$$

Resistance increases in proportion to the length of a wire and decreases in proportion to the cross-sectional area of the wire: long wires have bigger resistance than short wires, and thick (heavier) wires have less resistance than thin wires. The best conductors (silver, copper, gold, aluminum) have smaller resistance per unit length (resistivity); the best insulators (quartz, glass, rubber) have larger resistivities. This is the principle behind the ordinary incandescent light bulb: a high current transmits power through a thin (high resistant) wire, which becomes white hot.

For electric transmission applications heat must be dissipated to prevent the wires from burning out. One 19th century solution that is still used today is to place such electrical components in (nonflammable) *insulating oil*. The oil must be circulated and cooled to remove the heat. A more modern solution to reduce resistance is to miniaturize all components, as wires operating over shorter distances will generate less heat (and require fewer cooling units) than longer wires.

In any case, the resistance in the wire increases with its length, thereby decreasing the strength of the voltage. Transmitting weak voltages over large distances requires amplifiers or repeaters. This was known in the Chappe telegraph (using a telescope as a signal amplifier and the relay stations as repeaters) and known in the Morse telegraph (using the electromechanical repeater).

Combining Voltage and Current Sources

Voltages add when batteries are connected in series; currents add when batteries are connected in parallel (sometimes called *shunt*). If batteries are connected in series, then pressure (voltages) is added and the current remains the same. If batteries are connected in parallel, then pressure (voltage) remains the same but the currents are added. The situations are shown in Figure 6-2.

Other series–parallel relationships are as follow.

For components connected in series:
   Voltage adds: $V = V1 + V2$
   Current is the same through all components connected in series
   Resistance adds: $V = R1 + R2$
   Capacitance combines according to $1/C = 1/C1 + 1/C2$

For components connected in parallel:
   Voltage is the same across all components connected in parallel
   Current adds: $I = I1 + I2$
   Resistance combines according to $1/R = 1/R1 + 1/R2$
   Capacitance adds: $C = C1 + C2$

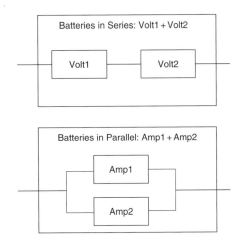

FIGURE 6-2   Relationships for series and parallel series.

Note that if the voltage is high enough, only one wire is needed to transmit electricity. This was observed in Franklin's demonstration. The "return circuit" is the *ground* (also called the *earth return*). The ground return reduced the expense to build most telegraph lines by 50%. Most of the early telegraph and telephone circuits were ground return. Ground return (direct current) electric power transmission is still used by the New York City subway system: power is transmitted through the "third rail" and the circuit is completed using ground return.

Magnets and Alternating Currents

Electricity creates magnets. Charges moving in a wire (a current flow) induce a magnetic field around the wire: a magnet is attracted to the wire. This was demonstrated in 1820 by Hans Ørsted (1777–1851).

The effect can be increased if the wire is coiled (i.e., wrapped around a cylinder) and if more current flows through the wire; the effect is reduced with the increased length of the wire. In other words, if I amps flow through a wire of length X with N coils, then the strength of the magnetic field B increases according to

$$B = \frac{N \cdot I}{X}$$

The coil is called an *electromagnet* or an *inductor*. If the coil wraps around or near a compound such as iron, cobalt, or rare earth metals, then the strength of the resultant magnetic field increases still further. When the current is shut off, these materials retain some magnetic properties: these materials are called *ferromagnetic*.

The ability of an inductor to store magnetism is measured by its *inductance*. The series-parallel relationships for inductance are

Inductance in series adds: $L = L1 + L2$
Inductance in parallel combines according to $1/L = 1/L1 + 1/L2$

The unit of inductance, the henry (H), is named after the American physicist Joseph Henry (1797–1878).

In 1831, Faraday showed that electricity can be generated by moving magnets. A magnet moving in or near a coiled wire induces a current in the coiled wire, which implies that a voltage is produced by a magnetic field that changes in time and space. Conversely, instead of moving the magnet in or around a coil, we can move a coil in or around a magnet: a coiled wire moving (i.e., that changes position in time and space) in or near a magnetic field induces a current in the coiled wire. The induced voltage flows in a direction that opposes the changing magnetic field; this was observed by Heinrich Lenz (1804–1865) in 1833.

The voltage generated increases according to the number of coils and the (changing) strength of the magnetic field due to motions. Stronger magnets also produce stronger voltages. If the coil is attached to a rotating wheel (i.e., on a bicycle spoke) that rotates in a magnetic field, then a regular periodic alternating current is induced in the coil. As the wheel spins, the spoke and coil first get closer to one pole of the magnet. The induced voltage starts in one direction, peaks (at the closest point to the magnet's pole), and decreases. As the spoke and coil approach the opposite pole of the magnet, the voltage starts flowing in the opposite direction; it weakens after it passes the closest point of this magnetic pole. After a full revolution of the wheel, the cycle repeats.

The current flows like a wave in alternating magnitude and direction (positive or negative). The number of cycles per second that the wheel makes defines the *frequency* of the current. Frequency is the number of times a periodic event occurs (like a single cycle of the wheel) per unit time. For electronic systems, a frequency measured in events (or cycles) per second is called a Hertz (abbreviated Hz), named after Heinrich Hertz (1857–1894). Other frequency units are revolutions per minute (RPM), beats per minute (heartbeats), or dollars per year (annual interest rate). Note that the units of frequency and the units of *interest rate* (i.e., a payment event per time) are similar.

If another coiled wire is attached to a spoke on the same wheel, then current flows in it with the same frequency; however, because the spokes are displaced, the voltage waves are out of *phase*: the maximum (and minimum) levels are regularly lagged in time from each other. For example, four coils placed on the bicycle wheel at the 12, 3, 6 o'clock, and 9 o'clock spoke positions generate a four-phase *alternating current* (AC); each phase is separated by 90° (with respect to a 360° circle). In the interest rate scenario, phase can be seen with regular yearly interest rate payments that occur at different payment dates (i.e., a coupon payable on March 1st is 30 days out of phase with another coupon payable on March 30th).

In an electric generator, the rotating wheel could be powered by a waterfall, wind, tides, or an engine (which can be powered by burning coal, gas, diesel fuel, or nuclear power). Today, most electric power plants generate three-phase AC (with each coil separated by 120°); voltages for large generators reach 765,000 volts. Conversely, if alternating current is supplied to the coils on the wheel in the correct phase, then the coils will be alternatively magnetized and demagnetized. Each magnetic coil will be successively attracted and repelled by the surrounding permanent magnets and the result will cause the wheel to move. The result is a polyphase AC induction motor.

Properties of Alternating Current (AC)

The voltage amplitudes in alternating currents can be changed by a transformer. For example, suppose two coils are connected such that the left coil is connected to an AC source and the right coil is not connected to a current source. The current (moving charges) in the left coil creates a magnetic field; because the current is alternating, the magnetic field is alternating as well. This changing magnetic field thus creates a current in the right coil.

The voltage in the right coil is proportional to the number of coils in the left and right wires. If VL and VR are the voltages of the left and right wires and NL and NR are the number of coil windings in the left and right coils, then

$$\frac{VL}{VR} = \frac{NL}{NR}$$

Depending on the values of NL and NR, low voltage is *stepped up* (i.e., amplified or magnified) to high voltage or high voltage is *stepped down* to low voltage. For example, if the right coil has 100 times more windings than the left coil, the voltage in the right coil is stepped up to 100 times the voltage in the left coil. The wires have resistance and the currents are transformed via the $R = V/I$ relationship. For high power transformers [where $P = I \cdot V$ is greater than 1000 watts (1 kilowatt)], the resistance generates heat so the entire transformer system is usually placed in insulating oil.

Electrical power generation and transmission only became practical with the acceptance of AC and the development of the transformer in the 1880s.

It turns out that alternating currents can demagnetize previously magnetized ferromagnetic materials. This is important: maintaining two states — magnetized and demagnetized — is the basis of most magnetic memory devices. All magnetic recording media consist of a ferromagnetic material that is spread on tape (as in magnetic tape, cassettes, or the back of credit cards) or rotating material (magnetic disk drives, drums, floppy disks, or hard disks).

Inductors and Capacitors Act Like Filters

Capacitors block DC voltages but let AC voltages pass through, whereas inductors block AC voltages but let DC voltages pass through. When used together, inductors and capacitors can "tune" a circuit to select a range (a band or channel) of voltage frequencies that can be passed or blocked. The effective range of allowed frequencies is called the *bandwidth*. More rigorously, the bandwidth (filter or half-power bandwidth) is the frequency range at which the power drops to one-half, corresponding to a voltage drop of about 71%. For example, the telephone network was originally designed to support a bandwidth of 3000 Hz (from a low tone of 400 Hz to a high tone of 3400 Hz; all other frequencies are filtered out).

Note that power ratios are specified in a logarithmic scale called a *decibel*. The decibel (abbreviated by db) scale was proposed in 1923 by engineers from Bell Telephone Laboratories to honor Alexander Graham Bell (1847–1922). The decibel scale can be used to describe any power ratio. The convention is

$$\text{db ratio} = 10 \cdot \log_{10} \frac{P1}{P2}$$

A 2:1 power ratio is about 3 db; a 10:1 power ratio is 10 db; and a 1000:1 power ratio is 30 db.

AC Allows the Transmission of Multiple Voltages at the Same Time

In the Morse telegraph, it was observed that two different messages can be sent on the same wire at the same time, as long as the batteries at either end are out of phase (i.e., the current flowed from left to right on one transmitter, and from right to left on the other transmitter.)

Information "intelligence" can be encoded with voltage phase and magnitude. Sending information at the same time in both directions is called *duplexing*. Voltage phase (or polarity) can be transmitted by first connecting the wires to the terminals of a battery and then switching the wires to send a voltage with opposite polarity. On the receiving end, the different voltage polarities could be detected by a magnetic needle (like a compass) at the farther end; depending on the polarity, the needle would point one way or the other. Such current reversals were used on very long lines such as the 1857 Atlantic cable.

Multiplexing, the ability to combine two or more communications on a single channel, is an important property of modern communication systems. Edison's 1874 invention of the *quadruplex repeater* enabled two telegraph operators to simultaneously transmit and receive messages on the same single (ground return) telegraph line. His patent (U.S. Patent 209,241, filed March 23, 1875) for "Improvement in Quadruplex-Telegraph Repeaters" helped Western Union save $20 million (in 19th century dollars) in wiring costs (according to Edison's biographer). One of Bell's earliest patents was in using multiple frequencies to send multiple messages in the same wire (see Box 6-15). Figuring out how to build better multiplexers and demultiplexers was, and still is, big business: multiplexing helps reduce network implementation costs. Better multiplexers also helps increase profits because more messages can be transmitted and received at the same time; more message volume means more profits.

Multiplexers, along with repeaters, routers, and amplifiers, are now a necessary requirement for modern wired and wireless (radio and optical) communications networks.

6.4.   Market Data Technology: From Ticker to Consolidated Tape

At a minimum, market data contain a time series record of *transactions* (recording the last or most recently executed sale of a given quantity of a product) and a time series record of *quotes* or *quotations* (specifying the buyers and sellers and what they would offer for a given quantity of a product at a specified price). Today, market data are treated as a commodity: different markets charge different fees for access to transaction and quote data. In the United States, regulations about market data ownership, fees, and structure are under the jurisdiction of the evolving SEC plans for the National Market System (NMS).

A *ticker* is a device that records and broadcasts data (originally only transaction data) in real time as they occur at a market. It was originally a telegraph system where market data were telegraphed to a special printing telegraph. The printing telegraph is automatically fed a paper tape; it generates a *market data feed* or *tape feed* as it prints data on a paper tape. The ticker tape terminology survives today.

Price Reporting with Quote Boards and Indicators

Before the 1860s, it was common practice to write transaction and quote data on large blackboards that were visible to market participants on an exchange floor. Some wealthy

---

Box 6-15

Western Union vs. AT&T: The Competition for Financial Networks

On February 27, 1875, Boston attorney Gardiner Hubbard organized the Bell Patent Association, named after Alexander Graham Bell (1847–1922) an elocution teacher and telegraph inventor. Hubbard (Bell's father-in-law) owned 60% of the association. Bell's first patent (April 6, 1875: 161,739) specified a technique now called frequency division multiplexing: messages were sent as different voltage oscillations on a single wire. Receivers were "tuned" to the originating oscillation: other messages were filtered out. Bell also noticed that energy from voice or other sounds can vibrate a magnet to change the resistance in a wire. This caused a DC voltage to oscillate in the same way; at the receiver, the sound waves could be reconstructed with a similar device (now called a loudspeaker). This is Claim 5 of US patent 174,465 (March 7, 1876, "Improvement in Telegraphy"). A third patent (June 6, 1876: 178,399) showed how to transmit voice over telegraph lines. Bell's "telephone" was demonstrated at the 1876 Philadelphia Exposition (the 100th year birthday party for the US). The telephone transmitted low quality voice for short distances.

Western Union thought that the big profits were in using the telegraph to transmit financial data and in maintaining a long distance telegraph monopoly: they were not interested in Hubbard's offer of patents (for $100,000). However, it turned out that Wall Street brokers preferred the privacy of direct telephone conversation to telegrams (which involved telegraph operator intermediaries). Brokers started installing telephones and the renamed Bell Telephone Company had 778 subscribers by 1877. Telephones were leased; not sold.

Next year Western Union formed the American Speaking Telephone Company (hiring Thomas Edison). Bell launched a patent lawsuit against Western Union in September 1878. They settled in November 1879: Bell kept the telephone and Western Union kept the telegraph and market data business. Western Union gave up its telephone rights, patents, equipment, and telephone subscribers; Bell agreed to route received telegraph messages to Western Union, to pay Western Union a 20% royalty on telephone licenses for the next 17 years, and to not use the telephone for "*transmission of general business messages, market quotations, or news for sale or publication in competition with the business of Western Union.*" After the expiration of the 17 year period, Bell expanded. There were no technology problems in sending telegraph signals ("data") over the telephone lines ("voice") at the same time: both voltages (sent at different frequencies) were effectively multiplexed. Quality was further improved by introducing a "twisted pair" of wires, instead of the single ground return. Long distance was extended with the addition inductors along the wires ("loading coils"). Bell became American Telephone and Telegraph (AT&T) in 1899. AT&T bought Western Union in 1909 but spun it off in 1913 to avoid US antitrust action (they kept the private leased line telegraph business).

---

traders who were able to afford to build or lease their own private Morse telegraph line would arrange for prices to be telegraphed to their offices. However, in most cases, market data would be delivered to traders outside the exchange by physical delivery messenger services. In either case, updating prices with chalk and eraser was error prone and induced confusion, especially in active markets.

In 1863 the New York Gold Exchange (located around the block from the New York Stock Exchange on New Street) hired Samuel S. Laws (1824–1921) to address these technology problems. Dr. Laws was a former professor of physics and a former college president (of Westminster College in Missouri). Laws may have been hired as the chief technology officer of the Gold Exchange, even though he graduated from Princeton as a theology major (he was a Presbyterian minister). Laws took several courses in electricity with physicist Joseph Henry and his resume listed him as having worked in a tool factory in his youth.

In 1866, as vice president of the Gold Exchange, Laws set up an inside–outside electronic display system. One display was above the trading floor of the Gold Exchange and the other was mounted on a window that faced New Street. The "gold indicator" display was similar to today's mechanical digital clocks. In operation, an official of the Gold Board would use a telegraph-like key to transmit voltage pulses to both indicators. Different voltage pulses would shift a geared dial to the appropriate price.

The system did not eliminate problems due to the delay, confusion, and mistakes that the street messengers made when, after viewing the prices displayed in the window from the street, they ran to their respective offices. Laws realized that the solution was to have identical gold indicators installed anywhere: a master transmitter from the Exchange would distribute the prices to *subscribers*, thus eliminating the human messengers. For backup and because of his distrust of the reliability of telegraph technology — the hydrogen-based Grove cells would sometimes explode — Laws also installed long lines of *speaking tubes* for short-range audio communication via voice.

In late 1866, Laws resigned from the Gold Exchange and patented a Gold reporting telegraph. Soon his service had 50 subscribers. The significant technology innovation of the Laws indicator was that receivers were not required to know Morse code, which appealed to wealthy traders, as well as traders who could not afford their own private lines.

Price Recording: Printing Telegraphs and Tickers

In 1867, Edward A. Callahan of the American Telegraph Company (probably a telegraph consultant to the New York Stock Exchange) created a different real time price reporting system that would create a permanent record. Instead of a display wheel, Callahan used a printing wheel and thus produced a kind of printing telegraph.

The system was originally called a clicker or ticker because of the sound of the impact printing. Instead of presenting a changing real time display, the new system created a permanent record of real time transactions. This combination of real time display with a permanent price record created an audit trail of data for traders, news reporters, and regulators. The New York Stock Exchange was one of the 100 initial subscribers.

Callahan's ticker was able to print abbreviations of stock names (now called *ticker symbols*) as well as prices. To increase reliability and to assuage the distrust of the new technology, Callahan used several insulated wires (costing 40 times as much as bare wires) to prevent short circuits caused by mice, insects, and bugs.

By 1869, the Gold Indicator Company had 300 subscribers. Laws hired a 21-year-old telegraph operator named Thomas Edison to keep the central system from crashing at the salary of $300 per month (almost $31,000 per month in 2003, based on the unskilled wage rate; this amount is similar to Wall Street consulting rates for top programmers in the late 1990s). Maintaining a subscription-based financial technology enterprise was very stressful, as Edison related in his autobiography:

On the third day of my arrival . . . the complicated general instrument for sending on all the lines, and which made a very great noise, suddenly came to a stop with a crash. Within two minutes over three hundred boys — a boy from every broker in the street — rushed upstairs and crowded the long aisle and office, that hardly had room for one hundred, all yelling that such and such a broker's wire was out of order and to fix it at once. It was pandemonium, and the man in charge became so excited that he lost control over all the knowledge he ever had. I went to the indicator, and, having studied it, thoroughly knew where the trouble ought to be, and found it. . . . Doctor Laws appeared on the scene, the most exited person I had seen. He demanded of the man the cause of the trouble, but the man was speechless. I ventured to say that I knew what the trouble was, and he said "Fix it! Fix it! Be quick!" . . . In about two hours, things were working again. . . .

Edison helped Laws file additional patents (they both tried to match the competition by developing their own printing telegraph ticker). Laws soon retired and sold his patent rights of his "Gold indicator and stock printer" to the newly formed Gold & Stock Telegraph Company. (During his retirement, Laws took advantage of the availability of higher education in New York. He first earned a law degree from Columbia University in 1870 and then he earned an M.D. from Bellevue Hospital Medical College in 1875. In 1876, Laws returned to Missouri and in 1893 he returned to his original field and became a professor of apologetics at the Presbyterian Theological Seminary in Columbia, South Carolina.)

Box 6-16

Excerpts from U.S. Patent 96567, Improvement in Printing Telegraph Apparatus, November 9, 1869 (Thomas A. Edison, Assignor to Samuel S. Laws)

This invention relates to certain improvements in that class of instruments for which Letters Patent were granted to S.S. Laws December 31, 1867 and March 24, 1868 and also described in an application for a patent filed by said S.S. Laws in the Patent Office on January 4, 1869. . .

. . . The strip of paper . . . is carried through the platen and the type wheel by the feed mechanism. A roller presses the strip of paper against one of the serrated rims or flanges of the feed wheel, and as the platen lever oscillates by the combined action of its electro-magnet and its detaching spring the ratchet of the feed drum acts against the click and receives an intermittent rotary motion so that for each oscillation of the platen lever the strip of paper is moved a sufficient distance to make room for a subsequent impression. . . . the letters and characters printed on the strip of paper are not at all concealed by it while the strip passes through the feed mechanism, and said printed characters remain open to view from the time when they have been printed.

Ticker Innovation, Improvement, and Standardization

The Gold & Stock Telegraph Company was jointly owned by American Telegraph and Western Union; it was headed by Marshall Lefferts (see Section 6.2 and Figure 6-1).

Lefferts hired Franklin Pope as superintendent (chief technology officer) of Gold & Stock; Pope was a telegraph operator who worked with Lefferts at American Telegraph during the Civil War and was the author of the classic 1869 text *The Modern Practice of the Electric Telegraph* (it eventually went through 15 editions).

In 1869, Pope and Edison resigned from Gold & Stock Telegraph to start (in the summer) a consulting company with offices at 78 Broadway. Pope and Edison created two companies, which were eventually bought out by Gold & Stock: the Financial & Commercial Telegraph Company and the American Printing Telegraph Company. Among their inventions was a system of printers designed explicitly for gold and sterling currency exchange (intended for importers and foreign exchange brokers). Their currency subscription service was priced lower than the regular gold and stock subscription service. They also built and equipped private telegraph lines on the side.

Lefferts also funded Edison with the goal of producing a "universal ticker" that could be used on an international scale: Lefferts believed that the New York ticker market was already too fragmented and saturated; however, there was an opportunity to make a standard ticker for the European exchanges. Edison's system interface design required extreme operational simplicity because "they did not have the experts we had in New York to handle anything complicated." Approximately 1200 of these universal tickers were installed in the United States and Europe. Subscribers generally paid $100 per machine and $25 per week for the service. Wherever possible, machines were leased and not sold. This business model for market data systems and terminals continues to this day.

Today, Edison's design ideas would be called "object oriented." The system was based on standard parts that had standard interfaces that simplified interchangeability. [Edison liked to say that there are three types of interchangeability: (1) the parts fit, (2) they will "almost" fit, and (3) they do not fit, and can never be made to fit.]

Edison later sold his rights to the ticker to Lefferts and Gold & Stock for $40,000. Pope split from Edison after a few years and rejoined Gold & Stock in 1875 as a patent expert. (Western Union absorbed Gold & Stock in 1881.) In the 1880s Pope became an independent consultant and patent attorney (supposedly the highest paid in the country). He later became president of the American Institute of Electrical Engineers, the forerunner of the Institute for Electrical and Electronic Engineers (IEEE). In 1895 he was tragically killed in an electrical accident during a storm.

Teleregister's Quote Boards

The exchange telegraph-based ticker lines were able to transmit about 80 10-symbol words per minute. The ticker tape would move from left to right (with the most recent trades printed on the left). A display would be encoded on a tape such as

... IBM 4S 651/4 T 2S 291/8 ...

This reports in real time that the last transaction (purchase or sale) of International Business Machines (ticker symbol IBM) was 400 shares at $65.25 per share. This ticker tape also shows that the previous trade was for 200 shares of AT&T (ticker symbol T) at $29.125 per share.

Box 6-17

New York Stock Exchange Technology in 1885: Excerpts from Harper's Magazine, Vol. LXXI, No. 426

After its establishment at the Tontine Coffee House, by 1820 the New York Stock and Exchange Board met at Samuel Bleeker's newspaper offices at 47 Wall Street. They kept moving to different spaces due to fires and epidemics until they settled at their current space on Broad Street in 1863. Prospective exchange members had to be nominated by existing members. Nominators had to state that they knew the nominee more than 12 months and that the nominee had good credit (and knew the names of the creditors). Nominators also declared that they would accept a personal uncertified check from the nominee for $20,000. In 1885, the initiation fee was $20,000 and the membership fee was $32,500. The exchange had two different types of auctions (in the Bond Room and the Board Room):

Government, State, and Railroad bonds, bank stocks, and other securities are called twice a day in the Bond Room — at 11 AM and 1:45 PM. . . . In the Board Room: the gavel announces at 10 AM open for business; a dozen blending thunderstorms break lose. . . . In the Bond Room comparative order reigns. . . .

Sales are for cash (delivery same day) or regular way delivery on 3, 10, 30, 60 days. . . . All securities sold are actually delivered; all securities bought are paid for on delivery; all borrowed stock is returned; all borrowed money is refunded. There are few exceptions to these rules. In case of default the stocks involved are publicly bought or sold, . . . the contracts closed, and the differences paid. . . . The vaults under the building are among the strongest in the world and contain 1032 safes for securities.

Between the Board and Long Room are telegraphic and telephonic instruments. . . . Notifications of sales as they occur are made by 24 quotation clerks, who are also telegraph operators, and send the news by "sounders" to the main offices of the Western Union and Commercial Union Telegraph Companies. Thence the news is sent by "transmitter" from each office to over the tickers, of which there are many hundreds in and out of the city, in the offices — private, in hotels, club rooms, etc. — of their patrons. There, agents, speculators, and investors watch the fluctuations as they follow, and intelligently issue orders to their brokers. Boston, Philadelphia, and other cities are thus in instantaneous communication with the New York market.

. . . Stock-brokers also establish private telegraph codes between themselves and clients, codes in which certain names stand for names, phrases, numbers, etc.

Four telegraph companies — the Western Union, Baltimore and Ohio, Bankers' and Merchants' and Mutual Union — receive and deliver messages of the Stock Exchange by public wires, and also by about 100 private ones owned by different persons. On one day in the space of 5 hours, 5727 telegrams were received from or dispatched to various parts of the country; and 1904 messages were sent by messengers to people in the neighborhood of the building.

Brokers typically subscribed to one or more ticker feeds. Information processing also involved *tapewatchers* — individuals trained to remember recent prices for the more popular stocks. A tapewatcher served as the market database: on request, a tapewatcher could simply pick up the tape and execute a sequential search for a specific transaction.

By 1913, telegraphy was fully automated: the Teletype Corporation (founded 1906; merged into AT&T in 1930) merged a typewriter (the QWERTY keyboard was standardized in the 1870's) with a Morse register. The Teletype machines represented symbols by a sequence of 5 voltage pulses (the 5-bit Baudot code) instead of Morse code, and transmitted almost 9 symbols per second (9*5=45 pulses or bits per second). In the 1920's German teletypewriters used telephone numbers as "addresses" for automatic messages routing. This routing system was called *Telex*. AT&T built a competing Teletype Wide-Area Exchange (called *TWX*). Both systems evolved into a global network of millions of users.

The first innovation in broadcasting market data since the deployment of Edison's ticker by Western Union was the electronic quotation board, first built by the Teleregister Corporation (founded in 1928). These electronic black boards were similar to the schedule boards seen in railroad stations and airports. The Teleregister engineers figured out how to route the telegraphed output of the ticker to an electromechanical board that was able to display the last prices of 50 to 200 products. In some sense, the quote boards were similar to the original Laws indicator. Teleregister had about 700 subscribing brokerage offices in the continental United States.

Western Union soon purchased Teleregister, but spun it off in 1948. Over the next few years Teleregister developed some of the earliest computer applications, including the first online terminals for banks (1957). The initial computer-to-computer communication systems used the Telex and TWX protocols. By 1958, AT&T introduced the *Dataphone* service, capable of transmitting 1200 bits per second over telephone lines. Dataphone was initially developed to transmit radar telemetry data to the Air Force's SAGE Program air defense centers. A few years later, Dataphone was used to transmit financial data from market centers to the financial community.

Quotron and Ultronics

In 1960, Scantlin Electronics, Inc., founded by John R. "Jack" Scantlin (an electrical engineer from California), developed another system that automated the ticker tapewatcher. The innovation was in recording ticker feed data onto magnetic tape at a brokerage office; when the broker requested the last price of a particular ticker symbol, a second tape head was used to scan the tape in reverse. The scanned tape would loop in a large bin between the tape heads. When the given ticker symbol was found, it would print the results on a paper tape. If the tape scanner detected a "start of market" symbol, then there would be no reply and the tape would rewind. During the entire search process, market data would continue being received from the broker's ticker line and recorded on the tape. The system, called Quotron, registered 800 subscribers within 2 years.

Around the same time, Sydney "Sam" Azeez (1932–2000), a 27-year-old electrical engineer from Woodbine, New Jersey, left RCA and founded Ultronics in 1959 after he and his friends realized that existing ticker systems were not using the latest technology. Their 1961 system was based on a central computer "ticker plant" located near Philadelphia that redistributed prices to regional brokerage offices. Market data were distributed with the new AT&T Dataphone lines and stored at local brokerage offices on Ultronics magnetic drums (not tape). Because of the combination of storage with computation, brokers could obtain transaction prices as well as data derived from the trades, including (1) ticker symbol; (2) the previous day's closing price; (3) today's opening, (4) high, (5) low, and (6) closing prices; (7) the total accumulated shares traded (volume); (8) the net change from the previous trade; and (9) the exchange where the stock is traded. The distribution of market data from the ticker was now tied to algorithmic computation — *market analytics* — designed to help traders assess the market conditions.

These data and other market analytics were incorporated in the 1963 version of Quotron. That version was based on the CDC 160A computer, a system having two processors that shared a memory made up of 24,000 12-bit words. Like Ultronics, Quotron II used the AT&T Dataphone service to broadcast data to clients. [The CDC 160A was made by the Control Data Corporation, a company (founded in 1957) that made new transistor-based computers and related equipment for the military.] Instead of writing the ticker feeds onto magnetic tape (as in the first Quotron) or a magnetic drum (as in the Ultronics system), market data would be read directly into computer memory: the latency for recording and retrieval was reduced substantially. Scantlin designed a unique way of representing 10 significant pieces of market data: (1) ticker symbol; (2) the previous day's closing price; (3) today's opening, (4) high, (5) low, and (6) closing prices; (7) the total accumulated shares traded (volume); (8) the exchange where the stock is traded; (9) whether the stock declared a dividend (the "ex-dividend" indicator would be set before the market open); and (10) the tick indicator (+1 if the last price was an increase over the previous price, and 0 if the last price was a decrease). The encoding scheme involved five 12-bit words per stock, which was enough for 2700 stocks listed on the New York and regional exchanges. Quotron also included the best bid and asked for 1300 over-the-counter (OTC) stocks (that required an extra 12-bit word).

Teleregister, Bunker-Ramo, and Nasdaq

In the mid-1960s, the SEC started issuing recommendations to modernize the market for securities not listed on the NYSE or regional exchanges. Why can't dealer quotes and dealer-to-dealer trading be integrated electronically? Such "over the counter" trading fell under the regulatory aegis of the National Association of Securities Dealers (NASD), the nonprofit corporation established in 1939 under the amendments to the same laws that established the SEC (the 1934 Securities Exchange Act). NASD was responsible for implementing the recommendations of the SEC.

On July 8, 1964, Teleregister merged with the computer and electronics divisions of two defense contractors — Thompson Ramo Wooldridge (TRW) and Martin Marietta — to concentrate on commercial civilian applications of information processing. The resulting company, Bunker-Ramo, was based in Trumbull, Connecticut. One of the first Bunker Ramo contracts was with the NASD: to develop an electronic quote distribution system. The NASD Automated Quotations system— NASDAQ (or Nasdaq) — was demonstrated in 1969. Nasdaq started being used as a trading system on February 8, 1971 and became the world's first virtual market.

In 1976, the NASD purchased the Nasdaq system from Bunker Ramo (and organized it as a wholly owned subsidiary; today the Nasdaq Stock Market, Inc. is a public company with ticker symbol NDAQ). Nasdaq systems remained in Bunker Ramo's Trumbull location. These electronic systems influenced the SEC in forming its plans for the National Market System (see Box 6-18).

Box 6-18
National Market System Plans

Consolidated Tape Association and the Consolidated Quote Plan
On May 17, 1974 the Consolidated Tape (CT) Association (CTA) was organized under the aegis of the SEC (the CTA Plan) to oversee the collection, processing and distribution of transaction data. CTA include members from the American, Boston, Chicago, Cincinnati, New York, Pacific (with ArcaEx), and Philadelphia stock exchanges, the Chicago Board of Options Exchange and Nasdaq. Network A (also called Tape A or System A) contains CT data from all markets dealing with securities listed on the NYSE (these securities can be traded on NYSE, Nasdaq, or anywhere else). Tape A operations are administered by the NYSE. Network B (also called Tape B or System B) contains CT market data from non-NYSE listed securities. Tape B operations are administered by the American Stock Exchange.

On July 28, 1978 the SEC approved the Consolidated Quotation (CQ) Plan in order to enable the collection and dissemination of quotes. The CQ organization is similar to the CTA.

In the CT and the CQ, market data is electronically delivered to an SEC approved *Securities Information Processor* (SIP). For both Tape A and Tape B, the SIP is the Securities Industry Automation Corporation (SIAC). SIAC processes and broadcasts the market data to financial information vendors which then rebroadcast the data to their clients. The CT and CQ systems facilitate intermarket trading in exchange-listed securities: this Intermarket Trading System (ITS) enables a broker who is physically present in one market to execute orders (as principal or as agent for a client) in an ITS security at another market.

Unlisted Trading Privilege Plan
Nasdaq market data consists of the Nasdaq National Market (NNM), the Nasdaq SmallCap Market (SCM), and other non-exchange listed securities that are traded in the "over-the-counter" (OTC) market. Market data from these securities are covered by Nasdaq's Unlisted Trading Privilege (UTP) Plan, sometimes called Tape C or Network C. The UTP Quote Data Feed (UQDF) provides quotations from markets trading Nasdaq-registered securities. The UTP Trade Data Feed (UTDF) provides last sale transaction data. The UTP Plan includes the markets of the American, Boston, Chicago, National, Pacific (with ArcaEx), and Philadelphia stock exchanges, and Nasdaq. Nasdaq is the registered SIP for the UTP Plan.

OPRA Plan
The Options Price Reporting Authority (OPRA) System also has an SEC approved plan for "Reporting of Consolidated Options Last Sale Reports and Quotation Information" for the dissemination of market data for options contracts. The OPRA Plan includes the markets of the American, New York, Pacific, and Philadelphia stock exchanges, and the Chicago Board Options Exchange (CBOE). OPRA is a registered SIP: the CBOE provides administrative services and SIAC provides computer processing services.

Technology Competition and Consolidation

By 1984 there were over 70,000 Quotron terminals; another 70,000 were split between Ultronics and Bunker-Ramo.

Ultronics was acquired by GTE Sylvania in 1965. (GTE started out as Associated Telephone Utilities in 1926; after it went bankrupt it reorganized itself as General Telephone in 1934. After several decades of acquisitions of technology companies, GTE merged with Bell Atlantic to form Verizon in 2000.) In the 1980s, GTE sold Ultronics to Automatic Data Processing (ADP). (In 1949, Henry Taub, a 21-year-old accountant, founded Automatic Payrolls, Inc. to provide outsourced payroll processing services for businesses in northern New Jersey. It became Automatic Data Processing in 1958 to concentrate on providing outsourced "back office" processing — record keeping and related computing services — for financial firms and other businesses.)

Bunker Ramo continued developing financial technology systems. In 1974, they developed the first real time news retrieval system (through a joint venture with Dow Jones & Company Inc.). In 1975, they developed (with Bank of America) one of the largest on-line bank teller terminal systems, having over 9000 terminals in over 1100 branches. Bunker Ramo was acquired by Allied Corporation in 1981; in 1986 Allied sold Bunker Ramo to ADP.

In 1973, Scantlin Electronics renamed itself Quotron. In 1986, Quotron purchased Securities Industry Software (SIS), a company formed in 1981 as a consortium of brokerages to centralize securities processing within the securities industry. Later that year, Quotron was purchased by Citicorp for $680 million. After this purchase, Quotron lost its two largest brokerage customers because they naturally considered Citicorp to be their competitor: Merrill Lynch and Shearson Lehman soon signed up with Bunker Ramo (which that year became ADP).

Citicorp used its purchase of Quotron to help develop the technology behind their automated teller machines (ATM). In 1993, Citicorp sold the SIS part of Quotron to ADP; the following year, Citicorp sold Quotron's non-U.S. business to ADP and Quotron's U.S. business to Reuters.

By 1992, the most popular providers of market data and market analytics to buy-side and sell-side institutional customers were Bloomberg and Reuters. Bloomberg was founded in 1981 as a market data and analytics provider for bonds and other fixed income products — a market that was not as popular among vendors as equities as there were no bond exchanges: bond market data must come from bond dealers (such as Merrill Lynch).

Bloomberg's innovation was in the supply of computational power — in terms of compute-intensive financial analytics — in addition to supplying quotes, market data, and simple Quotron-like market analytics. For example, before Bloomberg, traders and analysts would access bond data and type it into specialized bond calculators. A trader using the Monroe Model 360 Bond Trader (released in 1979 at a cost of $1200) was able to compute a bond yield (see Section 4.2 and Box 4-3) in 15 seconds (today's PCs can compute at least a million yields per second). Computation improved with the availability of spreadsheet systems in the early 1980s, but data still had to be typed in or otherwise integrated. The Bloomberg system integrated data and computation (much of it precomputed) in a customer-located server. The result was a financial one-stop shopping system, initially delivered to users on a patented terminal and keyboard (now delivered on Internet-compatible platforms). Because of its high-end analytics, Bloomberg also charged higher monthly fees ($1200–$1500 versus about $500 for other market data vendors).

Bloomberg's first customer and investor (a 30%, now 20% owner) was bond dealer Merrill Lynch. Merrill helped Bloomberg evaluate additional products and delivery infrastructures (including portfolio management, messaging, news, corporate data, and order processing trading systems).

Box 6-19
Bloomberg on Bloomberg

In 1972, Bloomberg helped design the Solomon Brothers proprietary "bond page" (called the B-Page). His idea was to encourage the integration of data and procedures:

> We should remove Ultronics and install Quotrons. . . . Quotrons will work better and connect with our in-house computers directly from the desks. We'll have access to our trading records, be able to retrieve all the publicly available securities indicative data (ratings, call features, P/E ratios, and so on) instantly and effortlessly, and have our own electronic messaging system for fast, reliable internal communication.

By 1979, as head of information systems at Salomon, his vision was for a "firmwide computer system to facilitate cross-department cooperation and multiple product risk management."

From Ticker to National Market System

The technology successes of the Ultronics, Quotron, and Bunker Ramo systems inspired the SEC to create a National Market System. The basic system was initially set up with the 1974 Consolidated Tape and 1978 Consolidated Quote plans.

It is interesting to compare the technology problems of the early market data systems with those of today in order to see a possible evolutionary trend. The 19th and 20th century tickers were characterized by:

- **Proprietary network infrastructures**
  The market data vendors manufactured much of the component hardware themselves, from telegraph indicators to tickers, terminals, and keyboards. These components were protected by patents. Network communication devices and displays of data and analytics were also patented and copyrighted. Today, network protocol standards and interoperability seems more important than implementation standards.

- **Proprietary codes**
  The market data vendor delivery systems were based on leased lines (initially from Western Union and Dataphone; today from other telecommunication providers). Different vendors had different internal encoding schemes for representing prices and other information; these encoding schemes were optimized for the infrastructure of the particular market data vendor (e.g., the 12-bit word in Quotron systems) to speed the transmission and storage of large quantities of market data. Code standardization began with Morse code and has continued

through the evolution of message standards such as the public-domain Financial
Information eXchange (FIX) message standard.

- **Monopolistic pricing structures and soft dollar pricing arrangements**
  Proprietary protocols and infrastructures seem to encourage monopolistic
  economics as shown by the Western Union, AT&T, and Quotron histories: the
  vendors owned the networks. Using proprietary protocols and representations is
  also a characteristic of physical delivery systems, such as the pony express carriers
  and the news schooners. Other pricing structures (such as subscription agreements
  and soft dollars) let market data vendors and their customers recoup their
  investments in technology from the end user.

In some sense, the use of open standards encourages more competitive practices.
Proprietary architectures induce *lock-in* — the reluctance of a customer to change to
another vendor because of changing infrastructure costs and retraining. However, even
with standard infrastructures, protocols, and encoding schemes, market data technologists
must be aware of the following costs in order to be competitive:

- **Costs of intellectual property**
  Market data are owned by its creators: the exchanges and dealer associations.
  There are legal costs of interfacing with the owners of market data (negotiating
  contracts with separate organizations and exchanges). There are technology costs
  of interfacing with the owners of market data (building database adapters to
  different standard formats and organizational protocols).

- **Costs of building databases**
  There are high development costs associated with designing and implementing
  data systems (see Section 5.2), especially systems that change as different financial
  products are created and evolve. This involves simply deciding what to save and
  how to save it (e.g., how many tables, how many fields per table, how many
  indices for search and computation). The engineering costs for building a storage
  infrastructure remain high even with the reduced hardware costs for storage. This
  is especially true with new regulatory requirements (such as the Sarbanes Oxley
  regulations) that encourage financial firms to archive all communications.
  Maintenance and correction are also problems, as many market data vendors speak
  "dirty data," "data cleaning," and "data maintenance." This is the same "noisy
  domain" observed by telegraph operators. Some errors are due to model revisions
  or parameter reestimations. Cleaned market data, namely data that can be used to
  resolve disputes or to build sophisticated financial analytics, are called
  reference data.

- **Costs of integration**
  The costs of integrating market data, analytics, and news are reduced if there are
  standard representations for market data, analytics, and news. This includes
  standard displays, standard models, and standard analytics. Will customers want
  such standards or will they prefer looking for market data vendors who can
  provide them with a proprietary edge of their competitors? According to the
  current philosophy, integration is key (see Box 6-19).

Box 6-20
Financial Technology Standards and the Software & Information Industry Association

The Information Industry Association (IIA) was established in 1968 to represent companies involved in creating, distributing, and facilitating the use of information in print and digital formats. The IIA represents online content providers (many specializing in financial data).

In 1984, 25 firms founded the Software Publishers Association (SPA) to be the principal trade association of the software industry. The SPA represents software vendors and content on issues concerning the legal use of software. The SPA was known for its ongoing campaigns against piracy and antitrust issues. The SPA supported the Digital Millennium Copyright Act, the Internet Tax Freedom Act, the expansion of the H1-B visa, and tax credits for research and development.

The SPA and IIA merged in January 1999 to form Software & Information Industry Association (SIIA).

Standards and the Financial Information Services Division (FISD)
The FISD was formed in 1985 as an operating division of the IIA to be a forum for producers and consumers of financial information. Members include exchanges (equity, options, and futures), market data vendors, data providers, brokerage firms, news organizations, hardware and software vendors, and system integrators. Now part of the SIIA, the FISD is concerned with three main projects.

1. Market data business/commercial issues.
   The goal is to increase the efficiency of information dissemination and to reduce the overall costs of market data administration by promoting standardization in policies and processing for procurement and payment.
2. Market data definition language (MDDL).
   The goal is to develop a specification that enables the interchange of information necessary for the accounting, analysis, and trading of financial products. MDDL focuses on the development of a common format so that data can be efficiently passed from one system to another. MDDL supports a standard structural financial taxonomy that promotes a common understanding of data content and data relationships. Recent versions model equities, indices, mutual funds, and bonds (corporate, municipal, government, and agency).
3. Symbology and reference data.
   The focus is on information requirements for automating clearing and settlement by supporting standards initiatives such as ISIN assignment, access and usage; definition of the data elements required for unique security identification; development of an international business entity identification standard for risk management; and efforts involving straight-through processing.

6.5. Notes and References

The quote from Michael Bloomberg is from
[0.1] Ken Auletta. "Why does America's newest media mogul scare Dow Jones?" The New Yorker, March 10, 1997 (available on the Web).

General References

Note the following copyright disclaimer per Section 403 of the U.S. Copyright Act (Title 17 of the U.S. Code): the following material has been obtained from the public records of the United States Patent and Trademark Office: Box 6-5 (U.S. Patent Number 6,061,663: Nasdaq, May 9, 2000); Box 6-7 (U.S. Patent Number 1647: Samuel Morse: June 20, 1840); and Box 6-16 (U.S. Patent 96567: Thomas A. Edison, Assignor to Samuel S. Laws: November 9, 1869).

Financial Network Infrastructures

The joint paper concerning business continuity practices for financial organizations is
[1] Interagency Paper on Sound Practices to Strengthen the Resilience of the U.S. Financial System. Securities and Exchange Commission, Release No. 34-47638; File No. S7-32-02 (available at http://www.sec.gov/news/studies/34-47638.htm).

Some industry comments on the joint paper are discussed by
[2] Matt Migliore. "Wall Street Wins with New Recovery Plan: Regulators Temper Draft Strategy for U.S. Financial Systems." *Contingency Planning & Management*, Volume VIII, No. 4, May/June 2003 (available on the Web).

[3] Lucas Mearian. "Regulators issue disaster recovery guidelines." Computerworld, April 11, 2003 (available at http://www.computerworld.com/securitytopics/security/recovery/story/0,10801,80262,00.html).

The power blackout events described in Box 6-1 were reported by
[4] Ivy Schmerken. "Wall Street Goes Dark: Blackout 2003." *Wall Street & Technology*, October 3, 2003 (available at http://www.wallstreetandtech.com/story/currentIssue/WST20031003S0006).

A 1998 description of Nasdaq's backup is by
[5] Karlin Lillington. "Nasdaq: The World's Best Backup." *Wired News*, December 9, 1998 (available at http://wired-vig.wired.com/news/print/0,1294,16714,00.html).

Soft dollar practices described in Box 6-2 are from the
[6] SEC Inspection Report on the Soft Dollar Practices of Broker-Dealers, Investment Advisers and Mutual Funds. SEC Office of Compliance, Inspections and Examinations, September 22, 1998 (available at http://sec.gov/news/studies/softdolr.htm).

The control and ownership of market information (Box 6-3) is described in
[7] SEC Concept Release 34-42208: Exchange Control of Market Information and the Regulation of Market Information, December 10, 1999 (available at http://www.sec.gov/rules/concept/34-42208.htm).

The 2003 data in the table in Box 6-3 are from
[8] SEC Concept Release No. 34-50700: Concept Release Concerning Self-Regulation, November 22, 2004 (available at http://www.sec.gov/rules/concept/34-50700.htm).

U.S. Patents from 1790 (including U.S. Patent 1647 excerpted from Box 6-7) may be searched for and viewed at the U.S. Patent and Trademark Office at
[9] http://www.uspto.gov/

A description of caveats is at
[10] "The American Patent System." Thomas A. Edison Papers Project at Rutgers University. http://edison.rutgers.edu/paulpats.htm
A copy of all of Edison's patents are also available on this site.

Origins of Electronic Financial Communication Networks

Commissioner Ellsworth's annual report to Congress for 1843 (Box 6-6) can be found in its entirety, as well as other historical intellectual property records at
[11] Kenneth W. Dobyns. *The Patent Office Pony; A History of the Early Patent Office.* Sergeant Kirkland's Press, Reprint edition, August 1997. ISBN 1887901132 (available at http://ipmall.info/hosted_resources/patent_history.asp).

The life and times of Samuel F.B. Morse are described in
[12] Kenneth Silverman. *Lightning Man: The Accursed Life of Samuel F.B. Morse.* Alfred A. Knopf, New York 2003. ISBN 0-375-40128-8.

Pre-Morse telegraph financial technology for Market data is described by
[13] Greg Storey. "Thirty-Six Days Out of London: Ships and Foreign News in Pre-Telegraphic America." Chapter 1, *History of Maritime Journalism* (available at http://www.webandwire.com/storey1.htm).

Background on the *Journal of Commerce* and other newspapers is in
[14] James Sullivan (editor). "The New York Press and Its Editors." *The History of New York State.* Chapter 21, Lewis Historical Publishing Company, Inc., 1927 (available at http://www.usgennet.org/usa/ny/state/his/).

An eyewitness history of the events in New York City from 1816 to 1860 is by
[15] Charles H. Haswell. *Reminiscences of New York by an Octogenarian.* Harper & Brothers, 1896 (available at http://www.earlyrepublic.net/).

George Mullane's 1914 account of the Morse telegraph gap between St. John and Halifax (the Nova Scotia Pony Express) originally in the *Halifax Morning Chronicle* (January 1, 1914) is at
[16] http://www.newscotland1398.net/ponyexpress/ponyexdx.html

The financial impact of the telegraph (at rationale for the expense for a trans-Atlantic cable) is by
[17] Marshall Lefferts. "The Electric Telegraph; Its Influence and Geographical Distribution." *Bulletin of the American Geographical and Statistical Society*, Vol. II, New York, 1856 (available at http://atlantic-cable.com/Article/1856Lefferts/index.htm).

The material in Box 6-9 is from
[18] http://www.carnegie.org/

A history of the industry spawned by the Morse telegraph is by
[19] Tomas Nonnenmacher. "History of the U.S. Telegraph Industry." EH.Net Encyclopedia, edited by Robert Whaples. August 15, 2001 (available at http://www.eh.net/encyclopedia/?article=nonnenmacher.industry.telegraphic.us).

The material in Box 6-11 is from
[20] Professor Persifor Fraser. Letter of 1909. Persifor Frazier Papers. Courtesy of University of Pennsylvania Archives.

A history of Fedwire is described by
[21] Adam M. Gilbert, Dara Hunt, and Kenneth C. Winch. "Creating an Integrated Payment System: The Evolution of Fedwire." *Federal Reserve Bank of New York Economic Policy Review*, July 1997 (available at http://www.nyfedeconomists.org/research/epr/1997.html).

Michael Bloomberg's description of the 1966 Wall Street back office (Box 6-12) is from
[22] Michael Bloomberg and Mathiew Winkler. *Bloomberg by Bloomberg*. John Wiley, New York 2001. ISBN 0-471-20888-4.

Information about individuals in the Morse social network is from
[23] James Grant Wilson, John Fiske, and Stanley L. Klos (editors). *Appleton's Cyclopedia of American Biography* (6 volumes). D. Appleton and Company, New York 1887–1889 and 1999 (available on the Web at http://famousamericans.net/).

The Technology of Virtual Delivery

A review of basic electronics is available at many places on the Web. Another good source is
[24] Larry Wolfgang (editor). *Now You're Talking*. American Radio Relay League, Inc. (ARRL) Association for Amateur Radio, Newington, CT 2001. ISBN 0-87259-797-0.

A very readable technical history of the Morse and other telegraphs is by
[25] James B. Calvert. The Electromagnetic Telegraph (available at http://www.du.edu/~jcalvert/tel/morse/morse.htm).

Edison's inventions and their financial impact are decribed by
[26] Frank Lewis Dyer and Thomas Commerford Martin. *Edison: His Life and Inventions* (2 volumes). Harper Brothers, 1910 (second enlarged and revised edition in 1929). Both editions are available on the Web. At Project Gutenberg it is at http://www.gutenberg.org/etext/820. Dyer was one of Edison's patent attorneys.

A survey of the components of optical networks (optical repeaters, optical amplifiers, optical routers, and optical multiplexers) with a discussion on wavelength division multiplexing (WDM) is in the interview of Rajiv Ramaswami and Chunming Qiao conducted by
[27] Frederick Su. "All-optical networks may one day form national backbone." *OE Reports*, published by the International Society for Optical Engineering, No. 188, August 1999 (available at http://www.spie.org/web/oer/august/aug99/cover2.html).

Market Data Technology: From Ticker to Consolidated Tape

The technology that was used in the early tickers is discussed by Edison's former partner
[28] Franklin L. Pope. *Modern Practice of the Electric Telegraph* (first edition), Russell Brothers, New York, 1869; editions from 1872 to 1890 were published by D. Van Nostrand. (The 1881 edition is available on the Web at http://www.insulators.com/books/mpet/.)

A history of tickers (with pictures of working reproductions) is at
[29] http://www.StockTickerCompany.com

The description of New York Stock Exchange Technology in 1885 (Box 6-17) is from
[30] R. Wheatley. "The New York Stock Exchange." *Harper's Magazine*, Vol. LXXI, No. 426, 1885. Courtesy of Cornell University Library, Making of America Digital Collection (available at http://cdl.library.cornell.edu/moa/moa_browse.html).

Brief histories of Teleregister and Bunker Ramo are at
[31] William Mitchell. "The Genesis of NASA RECON." *Proceedings of the 2002 Conference on the History and Heritage of Scientific and Technological Information Systems* (edited by W. Boyd Rayward and Mary Ellen Bowden). American Society for Information Science and Technology and the Chemical Heritage Foundation, Medford 2004 (available at http://www.chemheritage.org/events/event-asist2002.html).

The Teleregister Magnetronic Bid-Asked Stock Quotation System, installed at the Toronto Stock Exchange in 1937 (as well as other systems such as the CDC 160), is described in
[32] Martin H. Weik. *A Third Survey of Domestic Electronic Digital Computing Systems.* Report No. 1115, Ballistic Research Laboratories, Aberdeen Proving Ground, Maryland, March 1961 (available at http://ed-thelen.org/comp-hist/BRL61.html).

A history of Quotron and its competitors is by
[33] Montgomery Phister, Jr. "Quotron II: An Early Multiprogrammed Multiprocessor for the Communication of Stock Market Data." *IEEE Annals of the History of Computing*, Vol. 11, No. 2, Summer 1989.

Descriptions of other computer systems described in this section can be found at
[34] William Aspray (editor). *Computing before Computers.* Iowa State University Press, Ames, Iowa, 1990. ISBN 0-8138-0047-1.

A presentation detailing the technology evolution from yield tables and Monroe calculators to Bloomberg was presented at the Panel on the Evolution of Technology in the Bond Market at the Bond Market Association Annual Meeting (April 2003) by
[35] Andrew Kalotay. Evolution of Technology in the Bond Markets (available at http://www.kalotay.com/articles/).

A history of software and services companies is maintained by the Software History Center. A history of ADP based on an interview with third founder Frank Lautenberg is at
[36] http://www.softwarehistory.org/preservation/frank_lautenberg.htm

Other descriptions of market data systems are at
[37] Barbara E. and John F. McMullen. "Screen Envy on Wall Street." *Digital Deli: The Comprehensive, User-Lovable Menu of Computer Lore, Culture, Lifestyles and Fancy* (Steve Ditlea, editor), Workman Publishing, New York, 1984. ISBN 0-89480-591-6 (available at http://www.atariarchives.org/deli/wall_street.php).

[38] Ivy Schmerken. Oh What Memories! *FinanceTech*, June 18, 2002 (available at http://www.financetech.com/featured/showArticle.jhtml?articleID=14702685).

The Financial Information Services Division (FISD) of the Software and Information Industry Association (SIIA) issues many reports on and for the market data industry. An interesting perspective is the report by
[39] Tee Williams. Death of a Thousand Cuts: Strategic Peril and Potential in the New Market Data Industry. Shriver Associates, 2003 (available at www.fisd.net/reports/20030521williams.pdf).

The quote in Box 6-19 is from [22].

6.6. Discussion Questions

1. Many compliance regulations, particularly the Sarbanes–Oxley laws, require the archiving and access of records for 30 years. How many systems (financial or otherwise) maintain hardware compatibility over these time periods?

2. A requirement for an archive is that it be tamper resistant. Compare a storage technology called Write Once Read Many (WORM) with writing records on a CD or DVD.

3. All networks need to be maintained. Describe how soft dollars maintain social networks.

4. Can an exchange or market dealer patent market data? How can market data be protected?

5. In his review of the 1843 patents, Commissioner Ellsworth (Box 6-6) stated that because of the electric telegraph, U.S. citizens will "enjoy the earliest intelligence of markets, and thus be prepared against speculators." Can the same claim be made about the Chappe telegraph?

6. In his review of the 1843 patents, Ellsworth alludes to a caveat filed by Sidney Morse, "the publisher of the New York Observer" for a process, called cerography, that used electric charges to print high-resolution images. Explain why this process is similar to laser printers.

7. Why did Morse award the Maine congressman 25% of the company?

8. Could the Internet come under some of the claims covered by U.S. Patent 1647 (Box 6-7)?

9. What is the latency caused by in Fibre Channel?

10. Does PayPal perform a similar service today as Western Union performed in the 19th century? What does Western Union do today?

11. How come fuel cell technology has changed so little in over 150 years?

12. What was the first "killer application" for the Bell telephone (see Box 6-15)?

13. On January 31, 2005, the Wall Street Journal reported that Yahoo will become a market data provider (instead of a market data reseller). What are the major similarities and major differences among the Edison ticker, the Teleregister quote board, Quotron, and a display of Yahoo quotes?

14. On February 16, 2005, the *Wall Street Journal* reported that a trading group "received an incorrect price quote from a third-party data vendor" that resulted in "$7 million in trading losses over a seven-second timespan." Who is liable for the error?

15. Some market data vendors time stamp their data with an "embargo time" or "release time" — the earliest time the data may be used — so as to enable the simultaneous release of information independent of distance. Discuss this from a technology and intellectual property perspective.

CHAPTER • 7

Orders and Messages

Some of the merchants, like the great financiers, do not visit the Exchange themselves but also give their orders to brokers. They do not think it appropriate to allow themselves to be upset by attacks, insults, and shouts... When the merchants come to know about an event which certainly will bring about a change in price, they turn to the brokers... they give their orders only to those who will not divulge their names before the order is carried out, for it seems to them that... the price might be changed before execution.

—Joseph de la Vega (1688)

I have been surprised to reflect how much of our business has to do with control devices. Control devices are devices which take our orders and pass them on to a machine in a language which the machine can understand. We ought to concentrate on these devices.

—From *The Tempter*, a novel by Norbert Wiener (1959)

He wanted to decide things, not study them.

—Sarah Ellison, describing Procter & Gamble CEO A.G. Laffley,
Wall Street Journal (June 1, 2005)

7.1. The Anatomy of Orders

An order communicates a decision that results from analyzing a situation. Like all communications, orders involve a language, which, in most cases, involves *acronyms*: abbreviations formed from the initial letter or letters of words. Many financial technology terms are described in terms of acronyms and acronyms of acronyms. The word *acronym* (from Greek from *acros*, top point, and *nym*, name, related to the word *acrostic*, came into the English language in the 20th century. Aside from ticker symbols and Q-codes, acronyms started being used during World War I in the military (e.g., AWOL). The use of acronyms became very popular during and after World War II, especially in technology (e.g., TV, RADAR, NATO).

For example, let us look at the orders and messages associated with a client communicating with a broker regarding IBM:

> Customer: Hi Sam. How is IBM today?
> Broker: Improving. The last trade was at $87.95.
> Customer: I want 200 shares for my IRA account. Could you get it for $87.50?
>   I'm here all day.
> Broker: OK Stacy . . . I will call you right back.
> Broker [to market maker]: Bill, I need 200 shares $87.50.
> Market maker: Done!
> Broker [to customer]: You got it, Stacy: 200 shares for $87.50.
> Market maker [to trading service]: Buy 10,000 IBM VWAP $86.50 work
>   10 minutes. . . .

There are several implicit assumptions in these three dialogs. In the first dialog (between the customer and the broker) the customer assumes that her order to buy 200 shares of IBM stock is good for the day or until she cancels her order; she also assumes that the broker will fill the entire order for 200 shares (and not come back with a partial fill, e.g., for 150 shares). These assumptions are also seen in the order in the second dialog (between the broker and the market maker). The third dialog (between the market maker and the Trading Service) asks that the order be "worked" to get the best price: the constraints are that the service has 10 minutes to purchase at most 10,000 shares of IBM and the VWAP (acronym for *Volume Weighted Average Price*) should be less than $86.75 per share. For example, 2500 shares at $86.00, 2500 shares at $87.00, and 5000 shares at $86.50 result in a VWAP of 10,000 shares of $86.50, as

$$2500^*\$86.00 + 2500^*\$87.00 + 5000^*\$86.50 = 10000^*\$86.50$$

Worked orders mean that partial fulfillment is also acceptable. Note that the orders in all three dialogs are conditioned on a price: these are all *limit orders*. An order that is unconditional on price is called a *market order*. For example

> Customer: I want 200 shares for my IRA account. Could you get it at
>   the current market price?

From the customer's perspective, a market maker's limit order corresponds to a quote.

Trading services use rules and algorithms to determine a best price and therefore a best set of orders from a variety of exchanges, networks, and markets using factors such as speed of execution, transaction costs, and identity of the contra side, as well as price and volume constraints. Orders can be dynamically canceled and resubmitted as market conditions evolve in a way that minimizes costs and maximizes opportunity. Negotiation can also be automated. Effective order management systems are key components of rule-based algorithmic trading strategies.

Orders should be reported to regulatory authorities *immediately* — legally, as soon as the firm accepts responsibility for the order and confirms the order with the customer. Because of clock synchronization specifications, this means in practice that most orders are reported within 3 seconds. On Nasdaq, executed trades (executions) must be reported within 90 seconds.

Order Characteristics, Properties, and Conditions

Order audit trails are reported for both exchanges (e.g., NYSE Audit Trail) and other markets (i.e., Nasdaq Order Audit Trail System: OATS) and provide an integrated record of orders, quotes, and executions. What is needed in order to fully specify an order for trading and regulation? There are essentially six basic order dimensions: for side, product, size, limit price, order duration, and routing. The details of these dimensions (with some financial industry abbreviations) are as follows:

1. Side: Is this an order to buy or sell?
   We need to indicate if an order is an instruction to buy or to sell shares of a security. Possible values are Buy *B*; Sell Long *SL* (i.e., sell if we already own it); Short Sale *SS* (i.e., sell if we do not own it: we need to borrow the shares and pay them back at a later time); and Short Sale Exempt *SX* (some short sales are not normally allowed by regulatory authorities; however, the exceptions are covered in this order type).

2. Product: What product is being bought or sold?
   We need to indicate the ticker symbol: a unique symbol for the market.

3. Size: How much (e.g., how many shares or contracts or bonds) do we need?
   The numerical conventions associated with size depend on the market or exchange.

4. Limit price:
   What are the constraints for limit orders? Are there associated stop orders? The *limit price* (specified by the customer) is the *maximum buy* or *minimum sell* price. (The numerical conventions associated with price depend on the market or exchange.) A customer can command that a limit order should or should not be displayed because, as de la Vega observed, customers may not want to "divulge their names before the order is carried out"; whatever the case, the "Limit Order Display Indicator" is No or Yes. The *stop price* is the price where an order becomes either a market order (if no limit price is specified in the order) or a limit order (if a limit price is specified in the order). The order is transformed once the price has been quoted by a market maker at or through the specified stop price. A *stop limit order* specifies both the *stop price* and the *limit price*.

5. Order duration: How long is this order in force?
   Certain "time in force codes" have been established for simple orders. For example, market orders are valid for execution only at the time of the current market price. An order good for the duration of the day — a Day Order *DAY* — is valid from the current time to the next market close. A Good Till Canceled order is valid until it is canceled by the customer. Good Till Date *GTD* orders are valid until the close of market on a specified date; Good Till Time *GTT* orders are valid until the specified time. Here, the numerical conventions associated with time and date depend on the market or exchange. A Good Till Month *GTM* order is valid until the last business day of the month in which the order was received.

6. Routing: Do I need to route the order to someone else?
   It may be necessary to specify whether the order needs to be routed to an exchange or market member firm (e.g., another broker or dealer), a nonmember firm, a trading network [such as an electronic communication network (*ECN*)], a trade execution system (such as Nasdaq's SelectNet or SuperMontage), or another exchange.

Supplementary information, used by most regulatory organizations and some algorithmic trading systems, includes the dimensions of market maker identification and order capacity:

7. Who am I? When was the order received (or sent)?
   These include the date and time the order was received, the market participant identifier (e.g., for Nasdaq, this is the four-character MPID of the member firm that received the order), and the unique identifier assigned to an order by the order receiving firm that is used to internally identify orders. For routed orders, we may require a time stamp recording the date and time the order was sent to another firm. Other identifying information includes the department or desk within a firm that originates an *intrafirm order* (a proprietary order originated by one member firm's department for execution by another department).

8. Capacity: What is my role in the order? For whom was this order for?
   Essentially order capacity indicates whether an order was carried out either for someone else or for my own account. An Agency Order *A* is an order where I act as an agent (i.e., broker) for someone else. A Principal Order *P* is an order for my own account. Another type of order, a Riskless Principal order, is where the buyer and seller pay the same price. Associated with capacity is the identity of the order originator. A Retail Order is an order received for an investor's account (this includes institutional orders); a Wholesale Order is an order from another broker or dealer; a Proprietary Order is an order placed by a firm for a proprietary account (i.e., their own trading account); and an Employee Order is an order received for the account of an employee (or associated person) of a member firm.

Trading services support more complex order types that can be built on simpler orders based on individual products. These orders are handled differently by the markets. The most well-known orders of this type include the following:

9. Block trade:
   A large order, usually defined as an order having a size of at least 10,000 shares (for equities) or having a value of at least $200,000 (for bonds).

10. Basket trade:
    A set (portfolio) of individual product orders with each size, side, and other order parameters specified — treated as a single order. The intent is to have each buy and sell order execute simultaneously.

11. Program trade:
    Either (i) a basket trade of 15 or more stocks from the Standard & Poor's 500 Index or (ii) any basket trade consisting of stocks from the Standard & Poor's 500 Index valued at $1 million or more. The intent is to have each buy and sell order execute simultaneously.

Order Details, Codes, and Parameters

For system implementation, the aforementioned characteristics, properties, and conditions are encoded in standard phrases that are used to name database fields.

New Orders

These orders originate from brokerage customers, exchange member firms, nonmember firms, or a department within a firm. Usually, information recorded for new orders is from the perspective of the firm that received the order. Information about the originating customer would be recorded by the first firm that received the order. Some information associated with a new order includes the following:

Order Receiving Firm Identifier
Order Receiving Firm's Order Receive Date
Order Receiving Firm's Order Identifier
If routed, the Routing (Sending Firm's) Identifier
If routed, the Routed (Sending Firm's) Order Identifier
Ticker Symbol
Buy/Sell Type
Size
Limit Price
Limit Order Display Indicator
Stop Price
Duration Time in Force Code
Expiration Date
Expiration Time
Instruction for modification (i.e., a Do Not Reduce/Do Not Increase Code)
Special Handling Codes
Receiving Terminal Identifier (if using an exchange system)
Receiving Department Identifier
Originating Department Identifier
Program Trading Indicator (Is the order part of an automated program trading strategy?)
Arbitrage Indicator (Is the order part of an automated program trading strategy?)
Order Cancel Time Stamp
Canceled Indicator

Identifying Routed Orders

Orders are routed whenever a market participant sends an order to another market participant (a member or nonmember firm, ECN, or execution system) for handling or execution. A routed order received by a market participant can view this order as a new order. For regulatory purposes, routing information should include the following:

Order Receiving Firm Identifier
Order Receiving Firm Order Received Date
Order Receiving Firm Order Identifier
Routed Order Identifier
Ticker Symbol Identifier
Routed to (Destination) Firm Identifier
Order Sent Time Stamp
Routed Shares Quantity

Box 7-1

Special Order Handling Commands, Instructions, and Acronyms

The following commands specify other common instructions to traders or market makers concerning orders, together with a common abbreviation.

ADD Add-On Order. An order modification: customer adds additional shares to an already executed order.

AON All or None. If an order cannot be filled in its entirety, the order should not be executed.

CNH Cash Not Held. Buy or sell as much as possible (given a specified dollar amount) over the trading day.

E.W Exchange for Physical Transaction. For a security covered by a futures contract: two parties simultaneously execute the futures contract and a security trade.

FOK Fill or Kill. Execute the entire order immediately; if unable, then cancel the order.

IOC Immediate or Cancel. All or part of the order must be executed immediately; do not bother about any shares left over.

LOO Limit on Open. If the open price is at or within the specified limit, then execute the order.

LOC Limit on Close. If the close price is at or within the specified limit, then execute the order.

MAO Market at Open. Execute the order at the opening inside quote of regular market hours.

MAC Market at Close. Execute the order at the closing inside quote of regular market hours.

MOC Market on Close. Execute the order at the closing last sale price of regular market hours.

MOO Market on Open. Execute the order at the opening print price of regular market hours.

MQT Minimum Quantity. Cancel the order if a specified minimum quantity cannot be executed.

NH Not Held. Use the "best judgment" as to the time of execution and the price.

OVD Over the Day. Break up an order into several partial executions. (The customer may specify the total number of executions.)

PEG ("Pegged") The customer limit price is determined by a specified formula.

RSV Reserved Size Order. If a customer has authorized the display of part of the full size of the order then the remainder is held (undisplayed) but will be displayed as the displayed part is executed.

SCL Scale. The order requires partial executions that are not more than a specified price increment apart (e.g., $0.05).

TS Trailing Stop. A Trailing Stop for a sell order increases the stop by a preset amount or formula as the price of the security increases. A Trailing Stop for a buy order decreases the stop by a preset amount or formula as the market price of the security decreases. If the Trailing Stop is triggered, the buy or sell order becomes either an executable market order or a limit order.

WRK Work. A command to use the "best judgment" as to the time of execution: full execution or partial executions are accepted.

Identifying Executed Orders

Executed orders can be filled fully or partially. For partial executions, information must be maintained to indicate the quantity of shares that remain and need to be executed. If an order was routed, only the firm that executed the order should report the execution. Separate executions of an order should result in separate execution records. Execution specifications should include the following:

Order Receiving Firm Identifier
Order Receiving Firm Order Received Date
Order Receiving Firm Order Identifier
Execution Time Stamp
Execution Quantity
Trader Terminal Identifier
Ticker Symbol
Leaves Quantity (any shares left over?)
Execution Price
Capacity

Canceling Orders

One of the most important commands is to cancel an order. A cancel command can be used to modify and replace orders during the day; depending on the market, the cancel command might also be used at a later date. Cancel commands are also used with partial orders to reduce the size (*cancel with leaves*) or to cancel cancellation all remaining shares of an order (*full cancellation*). If less than the entire order size is being canceled, a Cancel Type Code should indicate a partial cancellation. If a customer cancels a routed order, the firm that originally received the order should record the cancellation and communicate the cancellation to the firm to which the order was routed. An order is not canceled if the originating firm cancels the routing (not the order) — the order remains alive.

The simplest way to modify an order is to cancel the order and submit a new one (indicating that this new order is a replacement order). Modifications include changes to limit prices, stop prices, size, side, ticker symbol, time in force, or special handling. Note that an order modification is not guaranteed if the order was already executed.

7.2.   Order Processing Technology: From Q-Codes to FIX

In order to build automated systems that converse in a financial dialog (by understanding orders and executing trades), we require four computer systems implementing customer, broker, market maker, and trading service applications; the systems need to communicate with each other and record all the orders and executions in different databases and sending. All information should also be sent to systems at exchanges and clearing houses.

Our development task can be simplified if there is a standard communication protocol and a standard way of constructing messages that can be recognized across systems for the customer, broker, market maker, trading service, exchanges, and clearing houses. Such a standard language could also be used in place of human languages as well: trading across international markets could be accomplished as long as these markets agree to use the same communication protocols.

This was not done historically. We saw that ticker feeds and order management systems evolved from proprietary telegraph systems, based on their own proprietary modifications of Morse and other codes. The acceptance of the Internet is the catalyst for developing today's standard protocols.

Order and Message Protocol Standards

From a practical perspective, orders and messages from one entity to another entity consist of *content* (what the actual message is) and *control* (instructions on how the message is delivered); this is true today as it was with the Q-codes and semaphore from previous times. Today we also consider *markup* (instructions on how the message can be displayed). One way of showing how orders and messages are communicated across systems is shown in Figure 7-1.

Here, an order originates from a trader's (human or algorithm) decision-making process. The order or message is represented in some vendor-based order management or transaction system, which in turn represents it in a common financial message format such as the *FIX* (acronym for *Financial Information eXchange*) standard. Ultimately, these FIX messages are represented as standard information packets in some communication network, such as the TCP/IP Internet standard.

Note that the financial communication can be regarded from a peer-to-peer perspective. For example, at the highest level, a buy order is matched with a sell order. The next level specifies, for example, how order management systems interface with transaction or matching systems. This specification uses representations of the next lower level of a standard financial message protocol such as FIX. In older systems, these messages would be represented in a proprietary format (such as Quotron's proprietary 24-bit representation) or even earlier, as the hand signals used in a trading pit to signal to the crowd the buy signal or sell signal.

Finally, the actual communication is accomplished by considering packets and control at the communication network level. (Note that this level can be broken down further into several other levels to specify lower level communication processes.) In older systems

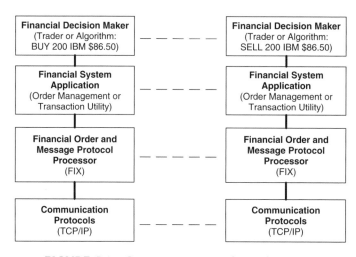

FIGURE 7-1   Communication of orders and messages.

this is the level of actual bit representations or of handshake authentication at the 17th century Amsterdam Stock Exchange.

In general, layered communication schemes are designed to use representations and services at the next lower level. In practice, this utilization is not strict: applications may use services at several lower levels (not just the next one).

Building TCP/IP-Based Communication Protocols

The most influential communication protocol scheme is the set of protocols that implement the Internet. It is sometimes called the *TCP/IP Protocol Suite*, acronyms for the *Transmission Control Protocol* (TCP) and the *Internet Protocol* (IP). TCP/IP can be used as a model for financial communication as well as an implementation technology. The TCP/IP Protocol Suite was first used in 1983 in the *Arpanet* (acronym for the *Advanced Research Projects Agency Network*), a computer network funded by an agency in the U.S. Department of Defense. (In 1989, the Internet split off from the Arpanet. In 1995 it was organized as a private nongovernmental network.)

IP manages services at a lower level usually called the *Network Layer*; and TCP manages services at the next higher level, usually called the *Transport Layer*. The transport layer provides services to the next higher level, called the *Application Layer*.

The low-level network layer service concerned with moving packets of data from a source to a destination is the Internet protocol. This network protocol uses the dotted quad decimal name and address conventions (discussed in Section 2.2) for computers and routers in the network; consequently, it is responsible for routing data packets from the source to the destination. Switching, routing, and congestion control do not use error detection or flow control; service is *unreliable*.

Another network protocol that manages simple network control is *ICMP* (acronym for *Internet Control Message Protocol*). One important function of ICMP is to send messages indicating whether a network computer host or router identified by a particular IP address can be accessed.

One of the most useful ICMP applications is *ping*: ping sends ICMP echo request messages (and receives echo response messages) to determine whether a host or router at a specific IP address is reachable; ping also reports how long it takes (usually in milliseconds) to send and receive long data packets from that address. Communication engineers routinely use ping to determine if a network is not well connected (i.e., if it is "dropping packets"). Ping can also be supplied with an Internet domain name; in this case, ping can also be used to determine if the service that translates domain names into IP addresses (the domain name server) is working correctly. Some other ICMP control messages look very much like the Chappe control messages. ICMP messages include the following:

- **Echo request and echo reply**
  Echo request is an ICMP message that sends a packet of data to the host and expects that data to be sent in return in an echo reply.

- **Destination unreachable**
  A router informs the sender that the destination IP address is not available.

- **Source quench**
  The router tells the sender to decrease the transmission rate.

- **Redirect message**
  The router tells the sender to reroute to a different IP address.

- **Information request and information**
  The sender asks the router for time or domain name information.

Protocols on the transport layer are concerned with reliability (ensuring that the messages from the source reached the destination); these protocols also ensure that data packets arrive and are assembled in the correct order. The transmission control protocol (TCP) is the transport layer service used for applications requiring a kind of "registered return receipt" *guaranteed error-free delivery*; if such guarantees are not needed, applications use *UDP* (acronym for *User Datagram Protocol*) transport layer service.

Transport layer protocols also provide identifiers for particular applications developed at the application layer, which is necessary so that the transmitter and receiver both know how to route the correct messages to the correct application.

One way to structure application identifiers is with a *socket*: a socket is the combination of an IP address, a transport protocol (e.g., either TCP or UDP), and a *port number*. If an IP address represents a street number, city, and zip code, then a port corresponds to a person living at that address; ports are used to address multiple recipients at the same location. Applications "listen" for information on their own designated ports; this enables the simultaneous utilization of several different communicating applications.

Most programming languages have libraries that implement sockets. For example, the following Java statement uses a socket library to specify a socket for a UDP application with port number 2689 at a server called inductive.com:

```
MySocket = new SocketMixin(this,"inductive.com",2689,"UDP")
```

In order for a client computer to communicate with the server, both the IP address (or server name) and the port number and protocol must be known to both client application and server application. In the implementation, socket programming requires client and server applications to try connecting or to wait for a connection; both utilize a "time out" to avoid an infinite wait if the connection is not established correctly. The programming pattern requires commands to be "wrapped" in an exception handler.

In Java, one implementation involving two client computers communicating on the same port to a server computer can be structured as shown in Box 7-2. The server waits for connections from two clients (the clients initiate the connections); after connection, the clients and server establish streams for input and output and wait for messages.

According to TCP/IP, UDP or TCP application port numbers can be defined as any integer between 1025 and 65,535 (the last number shows that port numbers are related to 16-bit values). TCP/IP reserves other port numbers for "standard" Internet programs; these ports are registered with *IANA* (acronym for the *Internet Assigned Numbers Authority*), the organization that keeps track of IP address and top-level names and Internet protocol identifiers.

TCP is designed to be *reliable* in that all messages reach their destination in the correct order. Financial transaction and messaging applications have this requirement. This insurance demands much network and computational overhead, implemented by different "hand-shaking" algorithms. For applications involving streaming (where data are "consumed" — read, heard, or viewed while it is being delivered), extremely fast arrival is more important than reliability. Examples of such applications include the delivery of

---

Box 7-2
Simple Socket Server

```
// ------ On Server -----------------------
// Wait for 2 clients to get connected to Server
try {    SocketonServer = new ServerSocket(PortNumber,"TCP");
         SocketConnection1 = SocketonServer.accept();
             Input1 = new InputStream(SocketConnection1.getInputStream() );
             Output2 = new OutputStream(SocketConnection1.getOutputStream());
         SocketConnection2 = SocketonServer.accept();
             Input2 = new InputStream(SocketConnection2.getInputStream() );
             Output2 = new OutputStream(SocketConnection2.getOutputStream());
         }catch(Exception e) {
             System.out.println("Unable to talk at port" + PortNumber + e);
             return;
}
// ------ On Each Client -----------------------
//       Open a socket to the server
try {    SocketonClient=new ClientSocket(PortNumber, IPAddress, "TCP");
         }catch(Exception e) {
             System.out.println("Unable to open port" + PortNumber);
             return;
}
// WAIT to Accept connections
try {    SocketConnection = SocketonClient.accept();
             Input = new InputStream(SocketConnection.getInputStream() );
             Output = new OutputStream(SocketConnection.getOutputStream());
         }catch(Exception e) {
             return;
}
```

---

market data (a missed packet will be probably made up by the next one in a fast-changing market), the delivery of audio (Internet radio) and video, and Internet telephony using voice over IP (VOIP).

Early protocols (deployed on the Arpanet in the 1980s) supported the following applications:

- Sending email from a client computer using *SMTP* (acronym for *Simple Mail Transfer Protocol*) on TCP port 25.
- Retrieving email from a server to a client using the *POP3* (*Post Office Protocol version 3*) on TCP port 110.
- Transferring files using *FTP* (acronym for the *File Transfer Protocol*) on two ports: TCP port 20 for data — the "data port" — and port 21 for control commands — the "control port."
- Synchronizing computer system clocks using *NTP* (the *Network Time Protocol* discussed in Chapter 4) on UDP port 123. Note that in time synchronization, extremely fast arrival is more important than reliability so UDP is used to implement NTP.

Box 7-3
Multiplex Communication Protocols and Their Acronyms

A trader views different web pages from the same site (same port, same host name, and same TCP protocol) using several "copies" (windows) of her web browser. She sees different content in different browser windows. At the site's web server, there is only one socket connection with the trader; from the perspective of the trader, there seems to be several different connections. *Different messages are multiplexed through the same socket.* Moreover, the trader's workstation may be part of a *local area network* (LAN) on the trading floor, with all workstations connecting to an outside network (such as the Internet) through a router. To a web server on the Internet, that single router is the source and destination for all messages. *Different messages are multiplexed through the LAN router.*

In most programming systems, a program can be cloned into several processes or tasks that seem to simultaneously execute. A (multitasking) computer operating system can launch different separate running instances of the program: the operating system then switches between each running instance (called a *process*) to give the appearance of simultaneous execution. Or, program segments that execute in parallel can be developed in some programming systems: these "threads of execution" (*threads* for short) carry less operating system overhead (in today's jargon, "threads are cheap and processes are expensive"). Messages can be multiplexed long as these threads or processes have unique identifiers. In the above socket example, uniquely identified threads can handle different input and output streams resulting from the single socket connection. Processes can support several threads. Depending on the underlying infrastructure, both threads and processes can execute on the same or on different computers; they can also communicate via socket-like conventions such as *Inter Process Communication* (IPC), *Remote Procedure Call* (RPC), or *Remote Method Invocation* (RMI). In the case of the trader viewing different web pages on the same site: there may be one process connected to one socket (with the web server) containing threads that communicate and control the other threads for each browser window. The host and client computer operating system controls how messages are multiplexed (on transmission) and demultiplexed (on reception) between threads or processes. IPC protocols also support *Grid* or *Utility computing*: computer networks configured to solve pieces of applications in a way that is more cost-effective than using a single large computer.

Multiplexing in a LAN works in a similar manner. By convention, hosted computers on the LAN use special "private" IP addresses (addresses beginning with 192.168.0.1 or 10.0.0.1). The LAN router has a private address and also has a public address provided by a network service (e.g., an Internet Service Provider – or ISP). When messages pass from the LAN to the public network, the source addresses on the message packets are translated from a private address to the public address. Depending on the *Network Address Translation* (NAT) technique, port addresses may be translated as well. The router controls how messages (IP address and port numbers) are multiplexed and demultiplexed between client computers connected to the LAN. These NAT techniques are used in reverse by programs (called *Firewalls*) that block messages from or to specified addresses and ports.

In some sense, email corresponds to a telegram where the Q-codes are replaced by SMTP and POP3 and the telegraph office is replaced by the server. Later protocols deployed on the Internet were designed to support the following:

- Browsing the Web using *HTTP* (acronym for the *HyperText Transfer Protocol*) on TCP port 80. This protocol was specified and first deployed in 1991 by Tim Berners-Lee (1955–).
- Internet telephone applications and voice over IP using MGCP (Media Gateway Control Protocol) on UDP port 2427 (developed by Cisco Systems, Inc. in 2003).
- Chatting (using a real time "instant messaging" service).

Instant messaging differs from email in that delivery is "instantaneous" and delivered right to the client, not to a server for download. Instant messaging corresponds to a private telegram service. Instant messaging protocols registered by IANA include Internet Relay Chat on TCP port 6667 (first specified for private networks in 1993 and first deployed on the Internet in 2000) and the America Online Instant Messenger (AIM) on TCP port 5190. AIM also owns the ICQ (an acronym pronounced "I seek you") instant messaging system. ICQ was deployed by Mirabilis Corporation on the Internet in 1996 (as a free client download); AOL purchased Mirabilis in 1998 for $287 million.

Real time messaging, in the form of telegrams, email, or today's instant messages, was always needed in the financial industry. For example, Bloomberg first offered Bloomberg Mail on its proprietary network in 1993; they now also offer Instant Bloomberg. Competitors Reuters and Thomson Financial deploy instant messaging systems that may be compatible or interoperable with other messaging systems, such as AIM, ICQ, Yahoo Messenger, Microsoft's MSN Messenger, and others. In any case, financial users of chat services must comply with the archiving and auditing rules set up by the SEC (as well as the Sarbanes-Oxley regulations).

By the early 1990s, users of TCP/IP services realized that TCP/IP was not adequate in protecting information from eavesdroppers (or wiretappers in the telegraph jargon) or message forgers (who would pretend they are the actual message sender or message recipient). The solution used in telegraphy, namely to send encrypted Morse code, was adapted for TCP/IP by Netscape Corporation in 1996.

Netscape's solution, called *SSL* [acronym for *Secure Socket Layer* also called *Transport Layer Security* (TLS)] squeezes an additional level between the application layer and the transport layer. SSL uses TCP services for reliable connections and also introduces additional hand-shaking algorithms that

- Prevent forging by authenticating sender and receiver by means of a third trusted party (using a technique called public key encryption)
- Prevent eavesdropping and securing privacy by encrypting data

From a programming perspective, instead of using libraries to create ordinary sockets, other libraries were made available for creating *secure sockets* (which to a programmer essentially behaves like an ordinary socket).

One difference is in port and protocol use; e.g.,

- Secure Web browsing uses the SSL implementation of the *Secure HyperText Transfer Protocol* (acronym: HTTPS) on TCP port 443.

- Secure email transmission from a client computer uses the SSL implementation of the Simple Mail Transfer Protocol SMTP on TCP port 465.
- Secure email retrieval from a server to a client uses the SSL implementation of the Post Office Protocol version 3, POP3, on TCP port 995.

The SSL solution is endorsed by most credit card vendors and financial institutions. Note that by construction, it only secures TCP services (not, for example, UDP or other services).

A few years later (starting in 1998), another solution was proposed that required securing the low-level network layer. This security solution, called *IPsec* (short for *IP security*), requires at least two specially built secure routers for the source and destination. By construction, IPsec can be used to secure UDP as well as TCP (and other message services). Both SSL and IPsec are used to build *Virtual Private Networks* (VPN). Note that beyond the IPsec routers, message traffic may be carried on a network vendor's infrastructure using standard (possibly insecure) protocols.

Box 7-4
SWIFT

The *Society for Worldwide Interbank Financial Telecommunication* (SWIFT) was founded in Brussels in 1973, initially supported by 239 banks in 15 countries with the goal of automating the telex — the printing telegraph-based routing system in use since 1935. (The original acronym was S.W.I.F.T.) SWIFT was set up as a financial industry-owned cooperative to supply secure, standardized messaging services and interface software.

Telex was used as the worldwide financial message among banks and other financial institutions and was neither reliable nor secure. The SWIFT goal was to make financial communication reliable in the technical sense: the message must get to the destination. After establishing a computer and communications infrastructure for a FInancial messaging Network (FIN), a common language for financial messages (known as FIN messages), and a set of naming conventions for banks and other institutions (SWIFT codes), SWIFT processed its first message in 1977. Messages were guaranteed to be received within 30 minutes. (SWIFT currently processes over 9 million messages a day from over 7600 members in 200 countries; transit time averages less than 20 seconds.)

The user community includes banks, brokers, dealers, investment managers, and supporting institutions involved with payments (clearing and settlement) and trade of securities and treasuries. For example, over 20 different exchanges and 40 different clearing settlement organizations [such as the NYSE and the Depositary Trust Clearing Corporation (DTCC)] use SWIFT for secure messaging services, connectivity, and common message standards.

In 2003, SWIFT implemented FIN by a reliable multivendor IPsec-based network called SWIFTNet. The Federal Reserve is planning to use SWIFTNet as a backup to the FEDNET network that supports Fedwire. The (New York) Clearing House also announced it would allow SWIFTNet access to its new proprietary TCP/IP network for CHIPS (the international Clearing House Interbank Payment System) and the domestic ACH (Automated Clearing House) systems.

The Financial Information eXchange (FIX) Protocol

The financial industry developed its own set of message protocols simultaneously with the development of TCP/IP messaging standards. The FIX protocol has become a standard for pre-trade financial messages (orders and quotes) and executions. It was initially specified in 1992 (before the Internet privatization) by Fidelity Investments and Salomon Brothers in order to facilitate electronic communication between the buy side and the sell side. FIX is designed to be independent of a particular communication infrastructure: it can be used on a telegraph as well as on TCP/IP-supported networks (e.g., the SWIFT *SWIFTNet FIX* Service provides FIX messaging to their user community). In many cases, FIX has been used as alternative to English or other human languages for international trading.

Fix messages support communication control and financial communication. In FIX terminology, these include the following:

- Administration and Control
  Heartbeat (to make sure the connection is alive)
  Logon
  Test
  Request to Resend
  Reject
  Message Sequence Reset
  Logout

- Financial Communication Applications
  Advertisements
  Indication of Interest
  News
  Email
  New Single Order Single
  Execution Reports
  Request to Cancel an Order
  Request to Cancel and Replace an Order
  Reject Request to Cancel an Order
  Order Status Request Allocation
  Allocation Acknowledgment
  New List Order (In FIX, Lists model collection of orders; lists are used to support basket trading, portfolio trading, and program trading)
  List Status
  List Execute
  List Cancel Request
  List Status Request

The syntax of FIX messages is very simple. A FIX message has the following three-part structure.

<MESSAGE HEADER> <MESSAGE BODY> <MESSAGE TRAILER>

Headers, bodies, and trailers contain *fields*; each field looks like

<tag>=<value>

Field tags are numbers. Field values can represent integers, decimal numbers, or character strings. Usually, fields can usually be in any sequence. In earlier versions (1994), FIX specified 24 different message types using about 100 tag fields; later versions (2003) specify almost 90 message types using 914 fields. FIX fields are separated by the (nonprinting) ASCII *Start of Header* (SOH) character represented on the keyboard as Control-A (binary: 00000001).

Here is a FIX message from one user (FIDEL) to another (SAL) representing FIDEL's interest in buying 100,000 shares of IBM at $85 (it is not an order):

```
 8=FIX.4.4
 9=41
35=6
49=FIDEL
56=SAL
34=100
34=1

23=201
28=N
55=IBM
54=1
27=100000
44=85.00

10=129
```

Note that the first grouping (seven lines) is the HEADER, the second group is the BODY, and third group is the TRAILER. (To help readability, we did not use SOH as a field separator.)

FIX syntax requires that the first, second, and third HEADER fields are 8, 9, and 35 tags; the FIX message TRAILER field is just 10=<value> where "value" is a checksum. The checksum is calculated by summing every character (byte); the checksum is this sum modulo 256. (The checksum is then represented by three ASCII digits (leading zeros may be necessary). FIX (optimistically) assumes messages are always delivered (this can be justified if TCP/IP is the underlying network infrastructure). FIX messages supply sequence numbers: consequently, FIX processors can detect errors if there is a problem in message sequencing.

Here is an annotated version of the FIX message:

8=FIX.4.4

Tag 8 identifies the startof a new message. The field value identifies the FIX protocol version. It is always the first field in the message and must never be encrypted.

9=41

Tag 9 is the Body Length tag:the length of the message body (in characters or bytes) that is used in the checksum computation. It is always the second field in the message and must never be encrypted. The message length in this message is 41 bytes.

35=6

Tag 35 denotes the MessageType field. It is always the third field in the message and must never be encrypted. Values for this field include:

0: Heartbeat
1: Test Request
2: Resend Request
3: Reject
4: Sequence Reset
5: Logout
6: Indication of Interest
7: Advertisement
8: Execution Report
9: Order Cancel Reject
A: Logon
B: News
C: Email
D: Order — Single
E: Order — List
F: Order Cancel Request
G: Order Cancel/Replace Request
H: Order Status Request
J: Allocation
K: List Cancel Request
L: List Execute
M: List Status Request
N: List Status
P: Allocation Acknowledgment

In our example, the value 6 is an *indication of interest* (IOI).

Private encrypted formats can be specified between sender and receiver; in this case, a U must be the first character in the value for the Message Type, i.e., U34 might translate to 6 for a specific sender–receiver pair.

49=FIDEL

Tag 49 denotes the Sender Identifier field. Here the identifier is FIDEL.

56=SAL

Tag 56 denotes the Receiver Identifier field: here it is SAL.

34=1

Tag 34 denotes the MessageSequence Number (incremented for each message except the heartbeat message) used to assess communication errors. Values range from 0 to 99999. This sequence number in this message is 1.

52=20050509-09:30:28

Tag 52 is the Sending Time. Here it is 9:30 AM (and 28 seconds) on 9 May 2005.

23=201

Tag 23 denotes a unique identifier for the message. Here it is message 201.

28=N

Tag 28 denotes a message transaction type.
Valid values include N, New; C, Cancel; and R, Replace.
The message here is a new message.

55=IBM

Tag 55 specifies that the ticker symbol is IBM.

54=1

Tag 54 denotes the Side of an order. Valid values include:

1: Buy
2: Sell
3: Buy minus
4: Sell plus
5: Sell short
6: Sell short exempt
7: Traded
8: Crossed

This message specifies a buy.

27=100000

Tag 27 denotes the numberof shares in numeric or a predefined relative size.Valid
values include range from 0 to 1000000000 and

S: Small (i.e., a "small" order)
M: Medium
L: Large

This message specifies 100,000 shares (a block trade).

44=85.00

Tag 44 denotes the price per share. Here it denotes $85.00.

10=129

Field 10 is the TRAILER: the value is the checksum.

An example of a buy order looks like this (where we used a space or new line for the ASCII SOH character):

8=FIX.4. 49=54 35=D 49=FIDEL 56=SAL 34=102 52=20050509-09:37:00
11=12347 21=3 55=MSFT 54=1 38=500000 44=67.00 40=5 10=124

Our annotation of this message is

35=D

The message type is D: a single order.

11=12347

Tag 11 is used to identify orders (assigned by the institution).

21=3

Tag 21 provides the special handling instructions for an order. Valid values include:

1: Private automated execution: no broker intervention.
2: Public automated execution: broker intervention is permitted.
3: Request to work the order for best execution.

Here the broker is told to work the order.

55=MSFT

Tag 55 specifies the ticker symbol.

54=1

Tag 54 indicates the side of order (here it is a buy).

38=500000

Tag 38 indicates the number of shares ordered (here it is 500,000).

44=67.00

Tag 44 indicates the price (here it is $67.00).

40=5

Tag 40 provides the order type. Valid values include:

1 = Market
2 = Limit
3 = Stop
4 = Stop limit
5 = Market on close
6 = With or without

7 = Limit or better
8 = Limit with or without
9 = On basis
A = On close
B = Limit on close

This message indicates a market order to be submitted at the close of the market.

FIX and FIX Markup Language (FIXML)

Telegraph messages encode content and control in short data packets in order to conserve the resources in the communication network. The current trend in message processing is to send more information — not less: markup information is typically encoded, as well as content and control. Markup includes *meta data* (information about data) that can be used to help the receiver process and understand the message.

One of the problems with FIX and other traditional protocols is the rigid structure mandated across version changes: protocol processors must be modified. However, markup languages are characterized by flexible formatting, simple structural rules, and somewhat improved readability (in a self-documenting manner).

FIXML, the markup language for FIX messages, has been proposed to simplify FIX messages across various platforms and versions. Here is a side-by-side comparison. Broker A sends a buy order to B for 50,000 shares of MSFT at $65. The FIX message is

8=FIX.4.4 9=54 35=D 49=A 56=B 34=102 52=20050509-09:37:00 11=123765 21=3
55=MSFT 54=1 38=500000 44=65.00 40=4 10=124

In FIXML the message looks like this:

```
<FIXML
    xmlns = "http://www.fixprotocol.org/FIXML-4-4"
    xmlns:xsi="http://www.w3.org/2001/XMLSchema-instance"
    xsi:schemaLocation=
    "http://www.fixprotocol.org/FIXML-4-4 F:\fixml-main-4-4.xsd"
    v="4.4"
    r="20030618"
    s="20040109">
    <Order
        ID="123765"
        Side="1"
        TxnTm="2005-05-09T09:37:00"
        Typ="2"
        Px="67.00">
      <Hdr
        TID="A"
        SID="B"
        SeqNum="102"
        Snt="2005-05-09T09:37:00"/>
      <Instrmt Sym="MSFT"/>
      <OrdQty Qty="50000"/>
    </Order>
  </FIXML>
```

At first glance, it looks like the FIX message has been wrapped around a redundant-looking syntax having delimited tags that look like this:

```
<tagname fields and values/>
```

Note that specific values are always surrounded by the (double) quote character. This is a general property of markup languages.

7.3. Markup Languages

The most popular markup language used today is Extensible Markup Language (XML), which is a text-based language that is specified and maintained by the *World Wide Web Consortium* (W3C). The first version of XML was released as a W3C recommendation in 1998.

XML is based on *Standard Generalized Markup Language* (SGML), a markup language used for defining other markup languages. SGML is maintained by the International Organization for Standardization as ISO 8879. It was first released in 1986.

Box 7-5 shows an example of a *Well Formed* XML document, contained in text file PlainNote.xml, that represents the content of a simple message.

Box 7-5
Well-Formed XML

```
<?xml version="1.0"?>
<!-- PlainNote.xml: A Database in XML. -->
<note>
        <to>Marie</to>
        <from>Stacy</from>
        <heading>Reminder</heading>
        <body>Don't forget to buy another 300 IBM!</body>
</note>
```

This plain note specifies the receiver (between the *to* tags), the sender (between the *from* tags), a summary (between the *heading* tags), and the content of the actual message (between the *body* tags). Tags contain meta-information if their labels are understandable; a good choice of tag names makes the document *self-annotating*, making document comments redundant. (In XML, comments consist of any text between <!- and - ->.) Tags have beginning and end delimiters (e.g., <to> and </to> delimit the value contained between them) that make it suitable for reading and parsing by humans and computer programs. (Sometimes the final delimiter can be abbreviated with />.) In some sense, XML parsing algorithms are very simple and efficient because of the strict insistence on start and end tags. There are many libraries that can search, query, and index XML documents.

XML, XSL, DTD, and XSD Acronyms

One problem with plain XML documents is that there is no instruction relating how it should be displayed. For example, when viewed in the Internet Explorer Web Browser, file PlainNote.xml is displayed in the indented form as shown earlier. Other utilities may display the content differently.

For some applications it is necessary to specify how to format or transform the content in an XML document for display or publishing purposes. A language called *Extensible Stylesheet Language* (XSL) provides such transformation rules. The first W3C XSL specification dates from 1999. Specific formatting rules are written in a file (sometimes called a *StyleSheet*) containing the XSL rules; in order to apply the rules, the XML document simply references the StyleSheet file.

A *Valid* XML document is a Well Formed XML document that conforms to a set of rules called a *schema*. There are several XML schema languages available. The oldest (dating from the 20-year-old SGML) XML schema language is the *Document Type Definition* (DTD) format. Another XML schema language is called *XML Schema Definition* (XSD) language (a W3C recommendation dating from 2001). Rules specifying the form for the content are written in a file containing the schema; in order to apply the rules, the XML document simply references the file.

For example, Box 7-6 shows that text file MyNote.xml has a reference to DTD file MyNote.dtd that contains syntax rules for the note as specified by the XML content: a note has a *to* field, a *from* field, a *heading*, and a *body*. File MyNote.xml also has a reference to StyleSheet MyNote.xsl that provides rules for a proper display of MyNote.xml in a Web browser.

Box 7-7 shows text file MyNoteToo.xml that has a reference to XSD document MyNoteToo.xsd and a link to the same *StyleSheet*. In either case, Figure 7-2 shows what the resulting XML document (for MyNote.xml or MyNoteToo.xml) looks like in a Web browser.

Box 7-6
XML with Reference to XSL and DTD

```
<?xml version="1.0" ?>
<!-- MyNote.xml: A Database in XML. -->
<!-- Includes Document Type Definition (dtd) and html Style Sheet (xsl) -->
<!DOCTYPE Collection SYSTEM "MyNote.dtd">
<?xml-stylesheet type="text/xsl" href="MyNote.xsl"?>
<!-- Here is the marked up Data: -->
<note>
       <to>Marie</to>
       <from>Kelman</from>
       <heading>Reminder</heading>
       <body> Don't forget to buy another 300 IBM!</body>
</note>
```

Box 7-8 shows the DTD text file MyNote.dtd that specifies the syntax rules. The syntax for DTD is derived from SGML. Box 7-9 shows the same rules in the XML Schema Definition (XSD), contained in text file MyNoteToo.xsd. The syntax for XSD follows the syntax for XML. Finally, Box 7-10 shows text file MyNote.xsl, representing the StyleSheet rules for formatting data for a Web browser.

Box 7-7
XML with Reference to XSL and XSD

```
<?xml version="1.0" ?>
<!-- MyNoteToo.xml: A Database in XML. -->
<!-- Includes Document Type Definition (dtd) and html Style Sheet (xsl) -->
<?xml-stylesheet type="text/xsl" href="MyNote.xsl"?>
<!-- Here is the marked up Data: -->
<note
  xmlns:xsi="http://www.w3.org/2001/XMLSchema-instance"
  xsi:noNamespaceSchemaLocation="MyNoteToo.xsd">

    <to>Marie</to>
    <from>Kelman</from>
    <heading>Reminder</heading>
    <body> Don't forget to buy another 300 IBM!</body>
</note>
```

To	From	Heading
Marie	Stacy	Reminder

***The Message*: Don't forget to buy another 300 IBM!**

FIGURE 7-2   Browser display of XML message.

Box 7-8
DTD

```
<!-- MyNote.dtd: Rules for the Database (Meta-Data) in XML. -->

<!ELEMENT note (to,from,heading,body)>
<!-- A note has these 4 components -->

<!ELEMENT to (#PCDATA)>
<!ELEMENT from (#PCDATA)>
<!ELEMENT heading (#PCDATA)>
<!ELEMENT body (#PCDATA)>
```

Box 7-9
XSD

```
<!-- MyNoteToo.xsd: Rules for the Database (Meta-Data) in XML. -->
<xs:schema
 xmlns:xs="http://www.w3.org/2001/XMLSchema">
   <xs:element name="note">
    <xs:complexType>
     <xs:sequence>
        <xs:element name="to" type="xs:string"/>
      <xs:element name="from" type="xs:string"/>
      <xs:element name="heading" type="xs:string"/>
      <xs:element name="body" type="xs:string"/>
     </xs:sequence>
    </xs:complexType>
   </xs:element>
</xs:schema>
```

The tags <html>, <body>, <table>, <tr>, <th>, <td>, <h2> are markup tags for Web pages; the content is specified in terms of *HyperText Markup Language* HTML, international ISO standard 15445 (since 2000) that is maintained by W3C.

Note that to change the format of the display, all we need to do is change the XSL StyleSheet. This requires knowledge of HTML and XSL. Deep knowledge of the XML content is not that important. For example, we can create the browser display shown in Figure 7-3 without changing the XML document. All we need to do is to have the XML document link to MyNoteALT.xsl — a different StyleSheet file (in Box 7-11).

Box 7-12 shows text file MyNoteALT.xsl that contains the alternative StyleSheet.

Financial Markup Languages

Once we have defined XML schema for an application domain (specified with either DTD or XSD), we can launch an application XML standard protocol. For example, we can define *NotesML* as the XML standard for the processing of plain notes, defined by the corresponding DTD and XSD specifications. There are hundreds of such XML standards in many application domains (which adds a burden to many human acronym processors), specified by single companies, business consortia, and professional or trade associations.

The Message: Don't forget to buy another 300 IBM!		
Person From:	Person To:	Message Category:
Kelman	Marie	Reminder

FIGURE 7-3   Alternative display of XML message.

Box 7-10
XSL StyleSheet

```
<?xml version="1.0" ?>
<!-- MyNote.xsl: An XML Style Sheet to map MyNote.xml into html -->
<xsl:stylesheet xmlns:xsl="http://www.w3.org/TR/WD-xsl">
<xsl:template match="/">       <!-- match all of note -->
<html>                         <!-- insert html tags -->
<body>
<xsl:for-each select="note">
    <table border="2" bgcolor="grey">
        <tr>             <!-- insert table headings -->
          <th>To</th>
          <th>From</th>
          <th>Heading</th>
        </tr>
        <tr>               <!-- get values from note -->
          <td><xsl:value-of select="to"/></td>
          <td><xsl:value-of select="from"/></td>
          <td><xsl:value-of select="heading"/></td>
        </tr>
    </table>
    <h2> The Message: <xsl:value-of select="body"/></h2>
</xsl:for-each>                    <!-- close all wffs -->
</body>
</html>
</xsl:template>
</xsl:stylesheet>
```

Box 7-11
XML Link to Alternative XSL StyleSheet

```
<?xml version="1.0" ?>
<!-- MyNoteALT.xml: A Database in XML -->
<!-- ALT format. -->
<!-- Includes Document Type Definition (dtd) and html Style Sheet (xsl) -->
<!DOCTYPE Collection SYSTEM "MyNote.dtd">
<?xml-stylesheet type="text/xsl" href="MyNoteALT.xsl"?>
<!-- Here is the marked up Data: -->
<note>
<to>Marie</to>
<from>Kelman</from>
<heading>Reminder</heading>
<body> Don't forget to buy another 300 IBM!</body>
</note>
```

Box 7-12
XML Link to Alternative XSL StyleSheet

```
<?xml version="1.0" ?>
<!-- MyNoteALT.xsl: Another XML Style Sheet to map MyNote.xml into html -->
<xsl:stylesheet xmlns:xsl="http://www.w3.org/TR/WD-xsl">
<xsl:template match="/">     <!-- match all of note -->
<html>                        <!-- insert html tags -->
<body>
<xsl:for-each select="note">
<h2> <i>The Message</i>: <xsl:value-of select="body"/></h2>
<center>
      <table border="4" bgcolor="grey">
        <tr>            <!-- insert table headings -->
          <th>Person From:</th>
        <th>Person To:</th>
        <th>Message Category:</th>
        </tr>
        <tr>            <!-- get values from note -->
          <td><xsl:value-of select="from"/></td>
          <td><xsl:value-of select="to"/></td>
          <td><xsl:value-of select="heading"/></td>
        </tr>
      </table>
</center>
</xsl:for-each>              <!-- close all wffs -->
</body>
</html>
</xsl:template>
</xsl:stylesheet>
```

A standard protocol is useful only if it has a community of users. In addition to FIXML, here are a few XML standards related to financial technology that have stood the test of time:

- The mission of the *Financial products Markup Language* (FpML) is "to streamline the process supporting trading activities in the financial derivatives domain through the creation, maintenance, and promotion of an e-business language for describing these products and associated business interactions based on industry standards." The FpML consortium was formed by JP Morgan and PricewaterhouseCoopers in 1999; since November 2001, it has been under the aegis of the International Swaps and Derivatives Association (IDTA), the international trade association of the privately negotiated derivatives industry. Privately negotiated derivatives include OTC swaps, options, and other structured product contracts for interest rates, currencies, commodities, energy, credit, and equities. ISDA, chartered in 1985, is the organization that develops risk management and other standards for the industry. FpML models the structuring of deals, negotiating the terms of a transaction, executing and confirming the transaction, and communicating settlement details about the transaction (http://www.fpml.org/).

- *FinXML* was designed by the Integral Development Corporation in 1999 as a standard language for communicating data between systems involved with trade processing. It models deal capture, confirmation generation, risk management, payments, settlements, and accounting. It also models information about contra parties, settlement instructions, payment instructions, holidays, and master agreements formalized by the International Swaps and Derivatives Association. The patent for FinXML was approved in the United States in 2002: patent 6347307. (http://www.finxml.org/).
- In 2000, the American Institute of Certified Public Accountants (AICPA) developed a set of financial statements in XML. This evolved into the *eXtensible Business Reporting Language* (XBRL), a standard that models the "global business information supply chain to create, exchange, and analyze financial reporting information. The range of information that the organization covers includes regulatory filings, general ledger information, and audit schedules." The Securities Exchange Commission (SEC) accepts XBRL documents for regulatory reporting (http://www.xbrl.org/Home/).
- The International Press Telecommunications Council (IPTC), established in 1965 to safeguard the telecommunications interests of the World's Press, is also involved in developing industry standards for news. Their members (including *Reuters*, the *Wall Street Journal*, and other financial media firms) developed *NewsML* in 2000 (http://www.newsml.org/).
- *Really Simple Syndication* (RSS) is used to send XML files containing short descriptions of content, together with a Web link to the full version of the content. (The XML file called RSS feed, webfeed, RSS stream, or RSS channel.) In operation, a program called a feed reader or aggregator checks an RSS-enabled Web pages for a user; if any content was updated, then the Web-browsing user is notified. No software installation is required by the user: typically users link to an RSS feed by clicking on an orange rectangle with the letters XML or RSS. RSS feeds are now common on many news and financial Web sites. XML-based technology was developed by UserLand Software in 1997, and the first specification was published in 2000; since 2003 RSS has been maintained by an advisory board at the Berkman Center for Internet & Society at Harvard Law School.
- The *Open Financial Exchange*, a specification for the exchange of data between financial institutions, business, and consumers via the Internet, was created by CheckFree, Intuit, and Microsoft in 1997. *OFX* became XML compliant in 2000. The OFX online financial services standard helps over 2400 banks and brokerages, as well as major payroll processing companies connect to over three million individuals and small businesses (http://www.ofx.net/).
- The *Interactive Financial eXchange* (IFX) forum was also formed in 1997 to create a messaging standard based on OFX for financial services. IFX (developed in 2000) is a "mature, well-designed XML-based, financial messaging protocol, built by financial industry and technology leaders" that so far concentrates on "content rich conversations" in electronic bill presentment and payment; business-to-business payments; business-to-business banking (such as balance and transaction reporting and remittance information), automated teller machine communications; consumer-to-business payments; and consumer to business banking (http://www.ifxforum.org/).
- *FundsXML* is a model for the automated distribution and collection of organizational, structural, and historical information about investment funds. It was

developed by German and Swiss financial institutions in 2001
(http://www.funds-xml.org/).

- The Financial Information Services Division (FISD) of the Software &
  Information Industry Association (SIIA) developed the *Market Data Definition
  Language* (MDDL) in 2001. MDDL offers a common data interchange format and
  common data dictionary for the fields that describe financial instruments; corporate
  events affecting value and tradability; and market-related, economic and industrial
  indicators (http://www.mddl.org/).

- In 2001, a consortium of buy-side firms, sell-side firms, and vendors (such as
  Bloomberg, Reuters, Standard and Poor's, Thomson Financial) joined together to
  define an open standard for categorizing, tagging, and distributing global investment
  research. *Research Information eXchange Markup Language* (RIXML) standardizes
  the exchange of investment research between sell-side brokers and their asset
  manager buy-side clients. RIXML can tag "any piece of research content, in any form
  or media with enough detail for end users to be able to quickly search, sort and filter
  aggregated research" (http://www.rixml.org/).

- *Vendor Reporting Extensible Markup Language* (VRXML) is an XML-based
  interchange format and common data dictionary on the fields needed for market
  data billing, reporting, and inventory management. The initial draft was developed
  in 2002 by the New York Stock Exchange and Gemini Systems to improve the
  quality, timeliness, and efficiency of reporting information from vendors. The
  Software & Information Industry Association Financial Information Services
  Division (SIIA FISD) later assumed ownership and maintenance of the
  specification.

- *TWIST*, the United Kingdom-based *Transaction Workflow Innovation Standards
  Team* (before 2004: the *Treasury Workstation Integration Standards Team*) is a
  nonprofit industry group created in 2001 to develop standards for treasury,
  working capital management, and commercial payment systems. The organization
  was inspired by the treasury operations department of the Royal Dutch/Shell
  Group. TWIST nonproprietary XML-based standards "ensure interoperability
  between banks, their corporate and institutional clients, and electronic trading
  platforms, in order to achieve efficient and properly controlled industry-wide
  straight through processing of transactions." In October 2002, TWIST published a
  complete set of messages that cover the entire trade life cycle, covering the set up
  of trade relationships, trade origination, negotiation, execution, confirmation,
  settlement, reconciliation, and reporting across a variety of financial markets
  (http://www.twiststandards.org/).

- *RosettaNet* (a subsidiary of GS1 US, formerly the Uniform Code Council, Inc.) was
  founded in 1998 as a consortium of computer and consumer electronics, electronic
  components, semiconductor manufacturing, telecommunications, and logistics
  companies working to create and implement open business-to-business ("B2B")
  XML process standards for supply chain partners (http://rosettanet.org/).

- The *Open Applications Group, Inc.* (OAGi) is a not-for-profit open standards group
  formed in 1994 by enterprise resource planning vendors involved with building
  process-based XML standards for both business-to-business and application-to-
  application ("A2A") integration (http://www.openapplications.org/).

- *ACORD* (Association for Cooperative Operations Research and Development) is a
  global, nonprofit insurance association (organized in 1970) whose mission is to
  facilitate the development and use of standards for insurance, reinsurance, and
  related financial services industries. Their *ACORD XML* supports messages for

Life & Annuity, Property & Casualty/Surety, and Reinsurance sectors
(http://acord.org/).

- The *Object Management Group* (OMG) is a consortium (initially of computer hardware systems vendors) formed in 1989 to establish software component ("object") programming standards and standards for system modeling. The first standard, for Inter-Process Communication, was the 1991 Common Object Request Broker Architecture (CORBA). Their most popular standard is the *Unified Modeling Language* (UML), a language used to model the organization, behavior, architecture, business process, and data structure of an application system. Their *XML Metadata Interchange* (XMI) is an XML standard for communication (http://www.omg.org/).

Other financial XML standards were designed to harmonize other standards or to be a "standard of standards." Some of these superset standards include the following:

- The *Straight through Processing Modeling Language* (STPML) was intended to be a superset standard to support every industry standard data exchange format. It was initially developed in 1999 under the aegis of the Microsoft Distributed Internetworking Architecture for Financial Services (DNAfs) steering committee (including Microsoft, FIX, Merrill Lynch, NASD, Reuters, Bridge, ILX, Infinity, and the Financial Models Company). STPML was based on the trading cycle model of the Global Straight through Processing Association, a consortium formed in 1998 to "reduce the complexity, cost, and risk associated with cross-border trade processing and to promote the more efficient flow of information to all parties involved in cross-border trading." The GSTPA promoted paperless trading and quicker (i.e., $T+1$) settlement times. The GSTPA was dissolved in 2002 (http://www.stpml.org/).
- In 2001, XLM standard ISO 15022 XML was proposed (by SWIFT and FIX) to be a common message standard based on the 1999 ISO 15022 (Data Field Dictionary for Financial Messages). In 2003, an *International Standards Team Harmonisation* (ISTH) initiative, consisting of IFX, OAGi, SWIFT, and TWIST, was created to develop and promote a "single Core Payment XML Kernel" that can be used globally between any corporation and its servicing bank. In 2004, ISO 15022 XML evolved to ISO 20022: the UNIversal Financial Industry (*UNIFI*) message standard. Later that year, the ISTH recommendations for an XML-based financial messaging standard were also incorporated and registered into the UNIFI ISO 20022. (SWIFT is the registration authority for ISO 20022 as well as for the ISO 15022.) UNIFI was developed with the UML modeling methodology (to specify the financial business areas, business transactions, and message flows), together with a set of XML design rules that translate UML messages into XML schemas (http://www.iso20022.org/).

Many organizations take advantage of the availability of XML-based translators for messaging. For example, routing Fedwire transfers through SWIFTNet (instead of going through the native FEDNET network for Fedwire) requires that the Fedwire-formatted messages be wrapped in an XML "container" or "envelope." Senders and receivers must use translators or "adapters" for the XML wrapping and unwrapping process in the gateways between SWIFTNet and Fedwire systems.

Advantages and Disadvantages of Markup Languages

Messages containing markup are always larger than messages that do not contain markup. This can be seen by comparing the aforementioned FIX and the corresponding FIXML messages. Consequently, it takes longer to transmit messages containing markup than messages that do not contain markup.

This may be a problem with large messages or with messages where the XML envelope is much larger than the actual message. Many messages wrapped in their XML equivalents can be one or two orders of magnitude larger than the unwrapped version: XML is not a good choice for some high performance applications. (However, some applications may transmit compressed messages and expand the message at reception.) Moreover, some users get overwhelmed by the quantity of markup tags and the abundance of acronyms and of tag abbreviations; this combination of "too much" and "too little" can cause confusion for human readers.

However, the real advantage of markup languages is in the reduced costs of protocol modification, support, and maintenance. Adding a new data field in a proprietary message service requires programming changes to all user applications that use the service; with XML, changes would most likely be localized to an XML translator or adapter. Further cost savings result from the economies of scale resulting from relying on a user community for updates.

7.4. Representing Rules

Many messages and orders for trading and regulation depend on the representation and processing of rules. Rules are in order management systems (representing as trading alerts), algorithmic trading systems (representing trading strategies), and market regulatory systems (representing regulations that must be complied with at trading time). Rules are used to implement "best practice" policies and procedures for risk management. In general, rules are represented in most algorithms used for control.

A rule can be described in terms of "If a condition is true then perform an action." Conditions are expressions that can be evaluated in real time to be either true or false; actions involve any command to the processor. When a condition is observed to be true, and the action is performed, the rule is said to be *fired* or *triggered*. In many financial applications, *messages and orders correspond to the action part of rules.*

The syntax for rules differs for different language systems. In programming languages, "condition-action pairs" are represented by the language control structures. These include *if* statements, *case* statements, and *switch* statements seen in most programming languages. Condition–action rules are also represented when certain "exceptional" conditions are noticed by the program. In Ada or PL/I, these *exception handlers* are represented by *raise* and *on* statements: if a condition is observed during program execution, an exception is said to be *raised*. In other languages (C++, Java), exceptions and exception handling occur inside a *try* statement: an exception may be caught (using the *catch* statement) and thrown (by a *throw* statement) to be handled somewhere else in the program.

In many database management systems (especially relational systems), rules are called *stored procedures* or *database triggers*. Triggers (procedures usually written in a database system language that implement the "action part" of condition–action pairs) are fired when an event is detected. For example, trigger events can be defined every time a record in a particular table is inserted, deleted, or modified; trigger execution can also be ordered conditionally using *before*, *after*, or *instead* of conditions.

Here are a few rules, written in condition–action syntax, that mimic the dialog shown in Section 7.1.

IF (Stock.Price=UNKNOWN)
THEN send price request message to get more information.

IF (increasing(Stock.Price) AND Stock.NEWS>0 and TIME<Afternoon)
THEN issue a buy order to the broker.

IF (BUY.Symbol=SELL.Symbol AND BUY.Price=SELL.Price)
THEN execute the order by matching buyer with seller.

IF (FIXMSG.TAG54=TRUE AND FIXMSG.TAG54.VALUE=1)
THEN (set tickersym=FIXMSG.TAG55.VALUE;
      set size=FIXMSG.TAG57.VALUE;
      BUY(tickersym, size)
IF (BUY.Symbol=UNKNOWN)
THEN route order to someone who can execute the order.

We can also have "generic rules" involving variables that look like this:

IF (candidateBuy(ProductX) AND similar(ProductX, ProductY))
THEN assert (candidateBuy(ProductY))

This rule says "buy Y if you are buying X and X is similar to Y."

Processing Rules

Even though the syntax for rules differs for different authors and programming languages, the semantics of rules has been mostly unchanged for thousands of years. Aristotle (384 BCE–322 BCE) is credited for first discussing the "laws of logic." Centuries later, George Boole (1815–1864) showed how logic resembles algebra in the manipulation of true or false values. Claude Shannon (1916–2001) showed that Booles' notation (now called Boolean algebra) can represent switching circuits. (Boolean algebra is also called relational algebra in the world of relational database management systems.)

From a programming perspective, the rule IF X THEN Y can be viewed as a *declarative* as "IF X is True THEN assert Y is True" (where X and Y are either true or false) or it can be viewed as a *procedural command* as "If X is True Then perform Action Y" (where it assumed that by performing X, Y is also asserted to be true). Both interpretations are used in computer programs. We can also read IF X THEN Y in reverse, e.g., as "Perform Y IF X is True" or declaratively as "Y is True if X is True."

When do rules fire? We need a rule about rules (a "meta-rule") that specifies when a rule should fire. The one that is usually adopted is

IF X AND (there is a rule "IF X THEN Y") THEN Y. (Declarative)
IF X AND (there is a rule "IF X then do Y") THEN do Y. (Procedural)

This ancient meta-rule is sometimes called *modus ponens* (Latin: *modus* the way *ponens* that affirms, bridges, or supports). It is built into most programming languages.

Representing Conditions with Logic Operators

Rule conditions can be expressed in terms of comparisons denoting order. Numbers and text can be compared. For example, most programming languages support the comparisons (the syntax might be different):

$$123 < 456 \quad \text{``ABC''} < \text{``DEG''}$$

For example, typing in $=123 < 456$ in an Excel cell results in TRUE. Other languages (or matching libraries) support "wild card" matches: special symbols that match any single or arbitrary numbers, e.g.,

"A*B" matches "A123456B" and AB
"A$B" matches "A1B" and "AZB"
"ABB" does not match "ABC"

Notations for conditions are also expressed with the logical operator AND (also called conjunction, from Latin *conjunctus*, joined), the logical operator OR (also called disjunction, from Latin *disjunctus*, disjoint or separate), and the logical operator NOT (also called negation, from Latin *negatus*, denial). In Excel, these are represented as =AND, =OR, and =NOT. In C and Java they are represented by the symbols &&, ||, and !.

The full definitions of some logical operators are tabulated in the truth table shown in Table 7-1.

Note that according to the rules of logic specified in the truth table, IF X THEN Y can also be written as

Y OR NOT(X) or in Excel =OR(Y, NOT(X))

and as

NOT(X AND NOT(Y)) or in Excel =NOT(AND(X, NOT(Y)))

Note that conjunction AND and disjunction OR are both *associative*: which means they do not need to be grouped in order. This means (in Excel)

=AND(X,AND(Y,Z)) is the same as =AND(AND(X,Y),Z))
=OR(X,OR(Y,Z)) is the same as =OR(OR(X,Y),Z))

TABLE 7-1   Truth Table for Some Logical Operators

X	Y	NOT (X)	X AND Y	X OR Y	IF X THEN Y	X AND (Y IF X)
FALSE	FALSE	TRUE	FALSE	FALSE	TRUE	FALSE
FALSE	TRUE	TRUE	FALSE	TRUE	TRUE	FALSE
TRUE	FALSE	FALSE	FALSE	TRUE	FALSE	FALSE
TRUE	TRUE	FALSE	TRUE	TRUE	TRUE	TRUE

Inference and Decision Trees

Inference rules such as modus ponens allow rules to deduce other rules: condition–action pairs can be chained through a *decision tree*. For example, given the following three rules:

> A stock is undervalued if its price from an earnings model is greater than its current price.
>
> There is no news about the stock if there is no news about it for the last 5 hours.
>
> If a stock is undervalued and there is no news about it, then buy the stock.

In a programming language notation, the rules are

> IF   earningsModelPrice(Stock, P) AND currentPrice(Stock,CP) AND (P>CP)
> THEN undervalued(Stock)
>
> IF   currentnewsfeed(Stock, -5, empty)
> THEN noNews(Stock)
>
> IF   undervalued(Stock) AND noNews(Stock)
> THEN buy(Stock)

Structurally, the three rules can also be represented in terms of the following.

> IF   A, B, C
> THEN F
>
> IF   Z
> THEN E
>
> IF   F and E
> THEN D

This can be mapped into the "decision tree" as shown in Figure 7-4. So, for example, the three assertions

> earningsModelPrice(IBM, 90)
> currentPrice(IBM, 85)
> currentnewsfeed(IBM, -5, empty)

imply that we should buy IBM. Tracing the inferences from the top-down through the decision tree is sometimes called *goal driven*; tracing inference bottom-up is sometimes

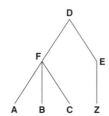

FIGURE 7-4   A decision tree.

called *event* (or *fact*) *driven*. These two ways of traversing the tree (and applying modus ponens) correspond to the procedural and declarative interpretations of rules.

The Need to Handle Uncertainty

In practice, assertions, rules, and conclusions are not necessarily known with total certainty. For example, predictions associated with an earnings model may involve statistical uncertainty given in terms of a standard deviation or other measure. Rules may also have uncertainty or a confidence metric attached to them. For example

> We observe that 85% of the time that if a stock is undervalued and there is no news about the stock then we should buy the stock.
> Latest reports indicate GE is undervalued with certainty 75%; IBM is undervalued with a 50% confidence.
> Media reports show 85% of the news is not about GE.
> The certainty that there is no news concerning is IBM 50%.

In a programming language notation:

```
IF   undervalued(Stock) AND noNews(Stock),
THEN buy(Stock)   CERTAINTY 0.85

undervalued(GE)     CERTAINTY 0.75
noNews(GE)          CERTAINTY 0.85

undervalued(IBM)    CERTAINTY 0.50
noNews(IBM)         CERTAINTY 0.50
```

The rule has a confidence or certainty of 0.85. Given the assertions about IBM and GE, we infer that we should buy both IBM and GE, but what is the confidence of this decision?

Note that without a method for handling uncertainty, logic tells us to buy both stocks. However, if we have a way of manipulating uncertainties, an *uncertainty calculus*, then we can have further decision criteria (e.g., buy the stock with the largest confidence factor; buy the top two subject to a threshold certainty value, etc.).

An uncertainty calculus is another rule about rules (meta-rule) that assigns a confidence, belief, or certainty to rules or assertions. Certainty measures are typically between 0 and 1 (1 denotes 100% truth or certainty and 0 denotes impossibility or something that is 100% false). Since all conditions can be built up by combinations of conjunction, disjunction, and negation, it is sufficient to define an uncertainty calculus for AND, OR, and NOT.

If beliefs are consistent with statistics and probability theory, then the resultant uncertainty calculus is a *probabilistic logic*; otherwise, the resultant structure is a *fuzzy logic*. Let us denote

$$p(X) = \text{the certainty of X}$$
$$p(Y) = \text{the certainty of Y}$$
$$p(X \text{ AND } Y) = \text{the certainty of X AND Y}$$
$$p(X \text{ OR } Y) = \text{the certainty of X OR Y}$$
$$p(\text{NOT}(X)) = \text{the certainty of NOT X}$$

In general, the certainty of X AND Y and the certainty of X OR Y both depend on the certainty of X and the certainty of Y. This can be written as

$$p(\text{X AND Y}) = ANDf\,[p(\text{X}), p(\text{Y})]$$
$$p(\text{X OR Y}) = ORf\,[p(\text{X}), p(\text{Y})]$$
$$p(\text{NOT(X)}) = 1 - p(\text{X})$$

If we have the certainty of a rule, then the certainty of the conclusion is the certainty of the modus ponens meta-rule IF X AND (RULE) THEN Y:

$$p(\text{X AND RULE}) = ANDf\,[p(\text{X}), p(\text{RULE})]$$

In any case, it turns that there is a fundamental bound to the certainties:

$$p(\text{X AND Y}) = ANDf\,[p(\text{X}), p(\text{Y})] \leq \min[p(\text{X}), p(\text{Y})]$$
$$p(\text{X OR Y}) = ORf\,[p(\text{X}), p(\text{Y})] \geq \max[p(\text{X}), p(\text{Y})]$$

Box 7-13

Popular Methods for Combining Uncertainty in Rule-Based Systems

Optimistic uncertainty calculus

$$p(\text{X AND Y}) = ANDf\,[p(\text{X}), p(\text{Y})] = \min[p(\text{X}), p(\text{Y})]$$

$$p(\text{X OR Y}) = ORf\,[p(\text{X}), p(\text{Y})] = \max[p(\text{X}), p(\text{Y})]$$

$$p(\text{Y IF X}) = \max[1 - p(\text{X}), p(\text{Y})]$$

Neutral uncertainty calculus

$$p(\text{X AND Y}) = ANDf\,[p(\text{X}), p(\text{Y})] = p(\text{X})^* p(\text{Y})$$

$$p(\text{X OR Y}) = ORf\,[p(\text{X}), p(\text{Y})] = p(\text{X}) + p(\text{Y}) - p(\text{X}) \cdot p(\text{Y})$$

$$p(\text{Y IF X}) = 1 - p(\text{X}) \cdot [1 - p(\text{Y})]$$

Pessimistic uncertainty calculus

$$p(\text{X AND Y}) = ANDf\,[p(\text{X}), p(\text{Y})] = \max[p(\text{X}) + p(\text{Y}) - 1, 0]$$

$$p(\text{X OR Y}) = ORf\,[p(\text{X}), p(\text{Y})] = \min[p(\text{X}) + p(\text{Y}), 1]$$

$$p(\text{Y IF X}) = \min[1 + p(\text{Y}) - p(\text{X}), 1]$$

Note: The minimum function $\min[a,b]$ returns the smaller value of a or b. The maximum function $\max[a,b]$ returns the larger value of a or b. Both functions are built into Excel and other programming systems.

Box 7-13 shows three uncertainty calculi that have been used in financial systems. Let us see how these three calculi compare on the firing of the following rule:

IF   undervalued(Stock) AND noNews(Stock),
THEN buy(Stock)   CERTAINTY 0.85

undervalued(GE)   CERTAINTY 0.75
noNews(GE)   CERTAINTY 0.85

undervalued(IBM)   CERTAINTY 0.50
noNews(IBM)   CERTAINTY 0.50

For GE, the conclusions for the three uncertainty calculi are summarized in Table 7-2. The conclusions to buy(GE) has confidence ranging from 45 to 75%.

For IBM, the conclusions for the three uncertainty calculi are summarized in Table 7-3. The conclusions to buy(IBM) has confidence ranging from 50 to 21.25%.

In many applications, certainties are used to prioritize decisions or initiate an action if a certain threshold is met: certainties are interpreted as scores. For example, in one application, a buy decision can only be made if the certainty is higher than 70%; in another application, this threshold could be 50%. In a third application, actions are performed only on the highest ranked object, regardless of the confidence. Other applications can combine different uncertainty calculi that depend on certain observables. This approach leads to a weighted average scoring method seen in case-based reasoning and other systems.

TABLE 7-2

RULE	85.00%	
X: undervalued(GE)	75.00%	
Y: noNews(GE)	85.00%	
	X and Y	RULE AND X AND Y
Optimistic	75.00%	75.00%
Neutral	63.75%	54.19%
Pessimistic	60.00%	45.00%

TABLE 7-3

RULE	85.00%	
X: undervalued(IBM)	50.00%	
Y: noNews(IBM)	50.00%	
	X and Y	RULE AND X AND Y
Optimistic	50.00%	50.00%
Neutral	25.00%	21.25%
Pessimistic	0.00%	0.00%

Box 7-14
Rules and Technical Analysis

The basic assumption of technical analysis and charting is to create a dictionary of patterns and pattern indicator rules that indicate buy signals, sell signals, signals indicating the start of a trend, or signals indicating the end of a trend. Many technical analysis rules are based on analyzing the patterns in bar charts, which display the three dimensions of high, low, and close of prices. Other rules are based on analyzing the patterns in Japanese candlestick charts — these charts have been used for centuries to display the four dimensions of high, low, close, and open prices in time.

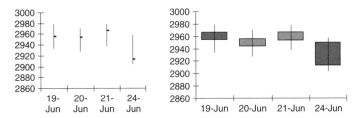

Both bar and candlestick methodologies provide colorful names for price patterns. For example, Western price patterns, such as a *Head and Shoulders* or *Moving Average Crossover*, or Eastern price patterns indicating a *Dragonfly Doji* are said to signal trend reversals or confirmations. Many market data vendors provide charting algorithms and can be instructed to fire pattern indicator rules. Many automated trading systems (especially in the commodities futures markets) claim that these techniques are very profitable.

7.5. Notes and References

The remarks by de la Vega can be found in
[0.1] Martin S. Fridon (ed.). *Extraordinary Popular Delusions and the Madness of Crowds and Confusión de Confusiones*. John Wiley & Sons, New York, 1996. ISBN 0 471 13312-4.

The observations by Norbert Wiener are in
[0.2] Norbert Wiener. *The Tempter*. Random House, New York, 1959.

The Anatomy of Orders

Different types of orders and order parameters are discussed from a technology perspective in
[1] The Order Audit Trail System (OATS) Reporting Technical Specifications. National Association of Securities Dealers (available at http://www.nasd.com/).

The Securities and Exchange Commission (SEC) has two rules for the public disclosure of order execution and routing. Markets that trade national market system securities must release monthly electronic reports and statistical measures of execution quality to the

public (Rule 11Ac1-5). Rule 11Ac1-6 requires broker–dealers that route equity and option orders to release quarterly reports that identify where the orders are routed to for execution to the public. The SEC wants these rules to inspire competition among market participants in order to provide the best prices for order execution. These rules are discussed at
[2] http://www.sec.gov/rules/final/34-43590.htm

Order Processing Technology: From Q-Codes to FIX

A good list of updated technology references on the Internet and other TCP/IP networks is maintained at Wikipedia:
[3] http://en.wikipedia.org/wiki/

The Internet Assigned Numbers Authority (IANA) is the central authority for Internet names and numbers.
[4] http://www.iana.org/

FIX is a public-domain specification owned and maintained by FIX Protocol, Ltd. at
[5] http://www.fixprotocol.org/

Some of the issues involved with creating a set of standard protocols for order routing, clearing, and back office messages are in
[6] Recommendations for Standardization of Protocol and Content of Order Flow Data. Technology Advisory Committee (Standardization Subcommittee), Commodity Futures Trading Commission, April, 2002 (available at
http://www.cftc.gov/files/ac/acrecommstandardreport.pdf).

Markup Languages

The World Wide Web Consortium (W3C) is a consortium that produces the software standards for the World Wide Web, including the standards and recommendations for XML. The latest standards are at
[7] http://www.w3.org/

Representing Rules

The technology of rules and uncertainty is described in
[8] Michael R. Genesereth and Nils J. Nislsson. *Logical Foundations of Artificial Intelligence*. Morgan Kaufmann Publishers, 1987. ISBN 0934613311.

[9] H. Guggenheimer. "Probabilistic Propositional Logic." *Polytechnic Notes on Artificial Intelligence*, Vol. 4, 1987.

[10] H. Guggenheimer and R. S. Freedman. "Foundations of Probabilistic Logic." *Proceedings of the Sixth International Conference on Artificial Intelligence*, IJCAI, 1987.

[11] H.W. Guggenheimer. "Limit Theorems for Dempster Composition in Probabilistic Logic." *Computers and Artificial Intelligence*, Vol. 9, No. 4, 1990.

[12] C. Alsina, M.J. Frank, and B. Schweizer. "Problems on Associative Functions." *Aequationes Mathematicae* 66, 2003.

Many patterns in technical analysis are described by
[13] Robert W. Colby and Thomas A. Meyers. *The Encyclopedia of Technical Market Indicators*. McGraw-Hill, New York 1988. ISBN 1-55-623049-4.

Candlestick chart techniques were invented by Munehisa Homma, a rice merchant who lived in the middle of the Japan's Edo Period of the Tokugawa Shogunate (1603–1868). Homma traded futures and options contracts for the physical delivery of rice at the Dojima Rice Exchange (Osaka). His techniques are described in many places, including
[14] Steve Nison. *Japanese Candlestick Charting Techniques* (revised edition). Prentice Hall, 2001. ISBN 0735201811.

Academics have traditionally dismissed technical analysis. An alternative view is by
[15] K.A. Kavajecz and E.R. Odders-White. "Technical Analysis and Liquidity Provision." Review of Financial Studies, Vol. 17, No. 4, 2004 (available at http://rfs.oxfordjournals.org/cgi/content/full/17/4/1043).

7.6. Discussion Questions

1. A standard TCP/IP utility that determines the route Internet messages (packets) take to reach a particular host is *traceroute*. Many servers provide access to traceroute as a free service; some vendors also provide a visual traceroute that shows the path on a map. The Microsoft Windows utility that performs a similar task is called *pathping*. Use either traceroute or pathping to see how messages are routed in the Internet.

2. How can a traceroute-type utility be used in connection with SEC Rules 11Ac1-5 and SEC Rule 11Ac1-6 (see [2]) that deal with order routing?

3. In its purest form, a peer-to-peer network does not have the concept of server and client. How can peer-to-peer messaging protocols be used in financial systems? Should they?

4. Can a program trade be a block trade? Can a block trade be a basket trade? How are these trades canceled?

5. The current buy price for 500 shares of a stock is $20. Suppose it is known that within a certain time, the price will fluctuate from $15 to $25. Associated with each $1 price increment is a transition probability. Create a set of buy limit orders with a size of 2000 shares and a VWAP of $20 that can protect against price fluctuations. If the current asset price increases, can this set of limit orders be adjusted (by cancel and new order) to reflect a moving price? Can you do this easily with FIX?

6. Is XML reliable?

7. Which financial XML standard(s) has the largest probability of success?

8. Explain how a financial messaging standard can be used for international transactions where both parties do not speak the same (human) language.

9. Database Management Systems (DBMS) can implement rules with "stored procedures" or triggers. Which vendors support these?

10. What are the alternatives of not using an uncertainty calculus in financial systems?

CHAPTER ♦ 8

Systems of Financial Systems

I was a technology person who was mystified by how much Instinet was charging for a basic transaction processing service.... I am more convinced than ever that our basic matching service is a commodity, it is a utility... our stock market is a transaction-processing engine.....
Last year at this gathering, I told this audience that they could not think of themselves as market makers. I stated that the sell side had to identify themselves as being in the customer execution business...... We have routing, we have the order types, we have the pricing, and we have the liquidity that the industry requires.

> —Remarks by Robert Greifeld, President and CEO of The NASDAQ Stock Market
> to the Securities Traders Association Conference, October 7, 2004

But I think the big problem is still sociology. People who understand the business don't understand the technology. And the people who understand the technology don't understand the business. That gap has not narrowed as far as I can see. There has to be an overlap between the customer and the technologist in order for a system to work. Both sides can have a sensible dialogue if there is a 50% overlap. But that is a process that, by and large, does not occur.

> — Remarks by Christopher Keith in Global Custodian (Spring 2000)

8.1. Describing Financial Systems

A system is a collection of integrated components that form a unified whole. Sometimes the components can be recursively decomposed into other components or *subsystems*. Consequently, these components induce a natural hierarchy: one component hierarchy can be considered a system with respect to *its* components.

Systems are, in some sense, "stand-alone" entities: the components work together by some means of communication and control. This is the basic difference between a system and an ordinary collection of components. A component must have an *observable* influence on the whole system if it is to be part of a system. Observability implies that there must be a model of component behavior, specified by some formal document.

Financial systems considered as a set of interacting and communicating entities are *Systems of Systems* (SoS); each component system may consist of large-scale, geographically separated systems that are managed and maintained by independent organizations.

Box 8-1
The Nature of Systems

The word system (from Latin *systema* or *sistema*: arrangement and Greek *syn*: together and *histonai*: cause to stand; related to *histos* mast) was first used in the title of a printed book in the 16th century. From the perspective of the 16th century, a system is a collection of components that has a life of its own.

One of the earliest best-selling books concerned with systems was *Systema Logica* (Logic Systems) by Bartholomew Keckermann (1571–1609). Keckermann was a merchant and Hebrew teacher; his book provided a new way to structure how subjects should be taught in the university. (The word *university*, dating from the 14th century, is from Latin *universitatem*: corporation or society, and is also related to *universus*: whole, or universe; it is also related to *unio* onion, reflecting the unity of an onion with its peels or layers.) The *Systema Logica* established an integrated curriculum surrounding a core set of topics. This approach differed from the component-based handbook model (like Pacioli's *Summa*) that taught a set of disjoint component subjects or computational methods such as commerce, abacus, algebra, and accounting. Keckermann's book went through more than 40 editions between 1599 and 1656.

The Keckermann approach influenced Johann Heinrich Alsted (1588–1638), a philosophy professor at the Herborn Academy, who wrote *Systema Mnemonicum Duplex* (Double Memory System), published in Frankfurt in 1610. In 1613, Alsted published the 3500-page *Systema Systematum* (System of Systems) and one of the first encyclopedias (1620).

Another best seller dealing with systems was the *Dialogo sopra i due Massimi Sistemi del Mondo* (Dialogue Concerning the Two Chief World Systems), published in 1632 by Galileo Galilei (1564–1642). The two systems in question were the heliocentric and geocentric models of the universe.

Diagrams of Financial Systems

Humans like to model systems by pictures and diagrams that show components, relationships, and behaviors. Generally, a diagram of a financial system consists of a network of nodes (also called boxes, circles, bubbles, or other labeled containers) together with lines or arrows connecting the nodes. These diagrams provide a map of the system structure. Nodes are mapped to system components; component relationships are shown by the way the nodes are arranged and by the number and direction of the lines between the nodes.

Sometimes nodes can be pictures or icons (e.g., of a bank or of a person working at a desk). Arrows can denote direction or just a "connection." Other conventions (involving shapes) depend on a particular systems engineering methodology.

For example, Figure 8-1 shows a typical "generic" description of a financial system of systems: two sets of 10 labeled boxes (labeled new client account system, purchase and sales system, etc.) with a few labeled bubbles (front-office order tickets, etc.). The labels indicate that each box is a component system.

By itself this diagram is ambiguous. What kind of relationships do the arrows denote? A control relationship is usually indicated by vertical placement: if a box is above another box and an arrow connects the upper box to the lower box, then system actions of the

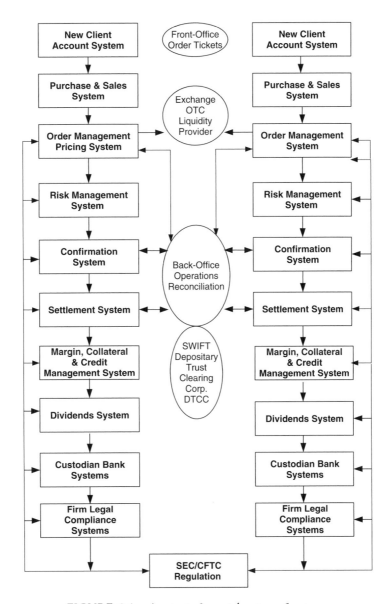

FIGURE 8-1   A generic financial system of systems.

upper box are performed before the actions in the lower box. Other relationships usually involve labeling the arrows.

There is also a problem with different component hierarchies. There seem to be five systems (of systems) displayed: one system is a collection of component boxes that represents a buyer; another collection of component boxes represents a seller; a bubble represents the market; another two bubbles represent clearing and settlement activities; and another box represents the regulatory systems that serve to oversee the other systems. The bidirectional arrows represent a kind of feedback.

Another source of ambiguity concerns whether the system shown is complete: are all components and relationships shown? For most systems (or systems of systems), these diagrams are usually *not complete* because of their complexity and quantity. Even though the diagrams may be shown on several pages, some component or relationship is probably left out. For example, where are the systems that acquire and process news? Which system computes and sends out tax forms? Where are the backup systems and recovery systems? There is also a problem with ellipses: aren't there more than one buy side, sell side, clearing house, exchange, or regulatory authority for different financial products?

It is best to consider system diagrams as one of many possible *views* of a system or system of systems. A particular view may be modeling a specific aspect of the system. Indeed, many popular systems engineering methodologies recommend the use of several *different types of diagrams* in order to provide a different view of how the system components work together. What is important is to keep the diagrams and rules consistent and unambiguous.

Hierarchy Models

Figure 8-2 shows a view of a clearing house and its members as a hierarchy. In general, arrows in a hierarchy are not directed and usually not labeled. The basic relationship is *has* (from top down) or *belongs* (from bottom up): components or systems in a lower level *belong* to (or are components of) a system or component in the next higher level. For example, a clearing house *has* house members; members clear and settle for clients as an *agency* for a fee (a client *belongs* to a non-member firm or a member firm). The client can also be an internal client of the member (a *principal*). Members maintain a net account for each financial product. The sum total of all the client or nonmember buys and sells for each

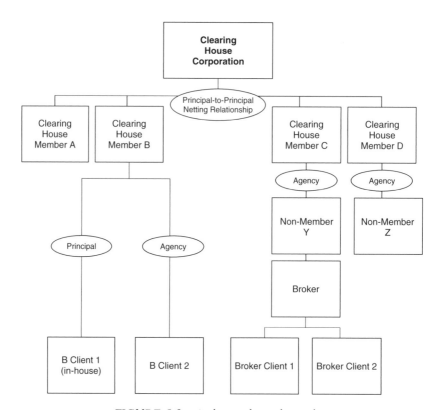

FIGURE 8-2   A clearing house hierarchy.

product are periodically cleared and settled between the members. The actual buyers and sellers of products are accounted for by record-keeping standards. Members perform relatively risk-free transactions between themselves through accounts maintained by the house (this is noted by the label principal-to-principal netting relationship). If a member defaults, then the other members cover the obligation. In some sense, this *multilateral clearing* arrangement is a generalization of the book entry database protocol that was used at the Amsterdam Stock Exchange in the 17th century (for stocks, options, and stock futures).

Models for Control Flow

Flow diagrams (or "flowcharts") model the behavior of a system or component by the behavior of a set number of subcomponents. The only relationship shown is an order that shows which system is active. The control flow specifies the name of the next component that will be executed. Typically, a control flow diagram does not specify the inputs or outputs of the components: usually only a single unidirectional arrow emerges from each container. (Special flowchart conventions provide *decision* or *switch* boxes that specify one of several paths that depend on an IF-THEN rule; other conventions may show bidirectional arrows or colored lines to indicate or highlight something different.)

Figure 8-3 encapsulates a financial system as three subsystems: trade booking, trade confirmation, and trade settlement. In trade booking, the control flow is: first initiate the client system, which invokes the sales system, the trader system, and the operations/back office system. Trade confirmation is initiated by purchase and sales; this system contacts trader, legal and credit, operations/back office. Feedback in the form of a confirmation is seen when control from operations/back office passes to purchase and sales and the

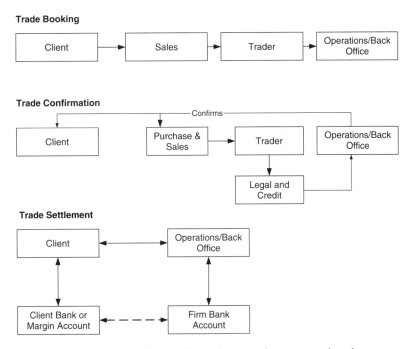

FIGURE 8-3   Control flows for booking, confirmation, and settlement.

client. Trade settlement shows a dialog of (bidirectional) control and a dashed arrow to indicate money flow.

Models for Layers and Interfaces

An "onion diagram" (or "layered diagram") is a diagram consisting of concentric circles. The innermost circle is the *core* or *kernel*: a component whose services are used by the next highest layer or peel. In general, outer layers are dependent on inner layers. Lines separating layers are sometimes called *interfaces*; lines separating different components on the same level are sometimes called *protocols*.

Figure 8-4 shows how financial system components are dependent on the core messaging systems consisting of FedWire, SWIFT, and SunGard. A *belongs* hierarchy is seen as well (e.g., a Funds system *belongs* to the buy side systems).

The onion model is probably what Keckermann had in mind when modeling courses for a university curriculum. It also resembles the structure of the universe (or what we now call the *solar system*) from a geocentric or heliocentric perspective: the aforementioned model shows the financial universe from a network-centric perspective. Note that the TCP/IP specification (Application Layer/Transport Layer/Network Layer/Physical Layer), usually represented as a rectangle, can also be represented as an onion (by topologically looping together the two vertical sides of the rectangle).

Onion diagrams became very popular in the 1970s to help explain the interoperability features of the standard Unix operating system: if the kernel is rewritten to run on another host computer, then all the outer layer utilities can be ported to that host computer.

FIGURE 8-4   Onion diagram of financial systems.

Modeling Arbitrary Relationships and Collaboration between Systems

An entity relationship diagram (ERD) defines systems or components as bubbles or boxes; relationships are specified by a directed arrow. A convention is that containers (systems or components) correspond to nouns and arrows correspond to verbs. In the object management group (OMG) unified modeling language (UML), an ERD is called a collaboration diagram. In the artificial intelligence literature, an ERD is known as a semantic network.

Figure 8-5 shows a financial system in terms of relationships that can actually be read directly via noun verb noun. For example, regulators correlate news and regulators surveil a market. A market participant complies with the regulators. Products are listed on a market.

To developers who build systems using languages that support object-oriented programming systems (OOPS), using languages such as C++ and Java, ERDs are interpreted as message specifications. For example, Products programming object receives an analyze message from the Market Participant programming object. In Java or C++ the message call can look like

```
Products.analyze();  or  MarketParticipant(Product).analyze();
```

The messages (relationships) can also be interpreted as socket calls between the entities that are represented as separate computer systems: the diagram provides no hint on the actual implementation.

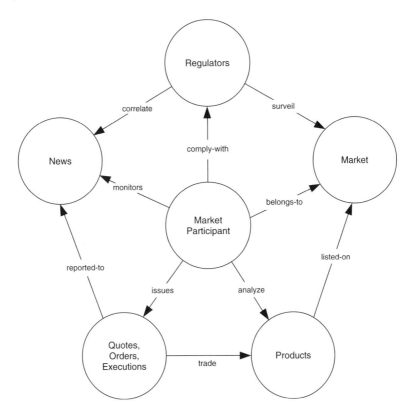

FIGURE 8-5   Entity-relationship diagram (ERD) of financial systems.

The six bubbles in the ERD of Figure 8-5 are too general to be useful in a practical implementation (outside of a simulation of an entire market); the view it provides is too abstract. Figure 8-6 shows an ERD view of the interactions among five other financial entities.

In order to understand this ERD without any instructions, one convention to follow is to start at the container in the upper left and follow the innermost arrows. This view says that an investment manager first routes an order for a block trade to a broker/dealer. (A block trade is a trade usually executed by institutional investors. For equities it corresponds to an order having a size of at least 10,000 shares; for bonds it corresponds to an order having a value of at least $200,000.) The broker/dealer routes the trade to an exchange specialist where it is presumably executed: the next (outward bound) arrow routes the execution back to the broker/dealer, who reports the average execution price back to the investment manager. Note that there could have been many executions over a period of time as no execution process or execution entity was specified.

The investment manager routes allocation instructions to the broker/dealer — presumably this large block trade pooled the orders of several clients together and now they must be accounted for separately so that each client owns the correct number of allocated shares.

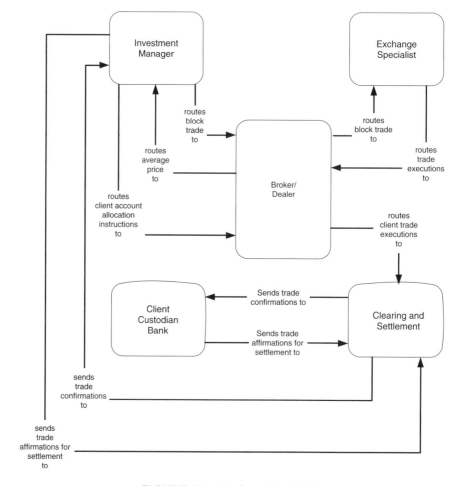

FIGURE 8-6   Broker–dealer ERD.

These instructions are assembled by the broker/dealer into execution allocations for the clearing and settlement entity, which in turn sends confirmations back to the investment manager. Confirmations are also sent to the investment manager's client's bank (custodian entered the English language in 1781 — it comes from Latin *custodia* guarding — and refers to one entrusted with keeping property or records). Finally, the investment manager sends settlement instructions back to the clearing and settlement entity. Any other details (showing more entities and relationships) would have to be specified "inside" the clearing and settlement container.

Note that this ERD does not show the contra side of the block trade and the details associated with clearing. There are also no specific legal or operating specifications or regulatory relationships.

What is the advantage of an ERD over a verbal description? From our financial technology perspective, the ERD shows structure and may provide common names for an implementation in terms of programming objects and messages. An ERD provides another map or view. However, formal verbal descriptions are usually mandated in specifications, contracts, and patents.

One of the drawbacks of an ERD is that the nature of data exchanged between entities — the information in the messages — is not shown clearly. This drawback is addressed by another system view called a data flow diagram.

Modeling Information Exchange

A data flow diagram (DFD) shows how information that is needed by one system component is created or transformed by another system component. A DFD does not explicitly specify control or timing. The DFD convention calls containers denoting system components (usually drawn as bubbles) *processes*; arrows coming into a process are the *inputs* and arrows going out of a process are *outputs*. All input and output arrows must be labeled. Processes can have multiple inputs and outputs. Figure 8-7 provides a different view of the aforementioned ERD.

This 12 bubble DFD is another representation of the "life cycle of a securities transaction" that shows some of the different systems involved with execution, clearing, and settlement.

Note that according to the DFD convention, nothing in this diagram suggests that one process must be finished before another process, regardless of the order that is implicit in the labels (i.e., 0.T, 2.T, 7.T+3, etc.). This is both a strength and a weakness. It indicates that processes can execute concurrently; however, sometimes it is necessary to indicate a sequence.

As in the other system diagrams, individual component containers can be considered systems in their own right and decomposed into subcomponents. This helps keep the diagrams simple and understandable. As the number of process bubbles and data flow arrows increases, the diagrams become less understandable (especially when lines start crossing).

The system specified in Figure 8-7 can be described as follows.

A. Trade Execution

1. Buying and selling customers place their orders with their respective brokers. (Customers may also provide payment or transfer instructions with their respective custodian banks.) Brokers confirm the receipt of the orders back to the customer.

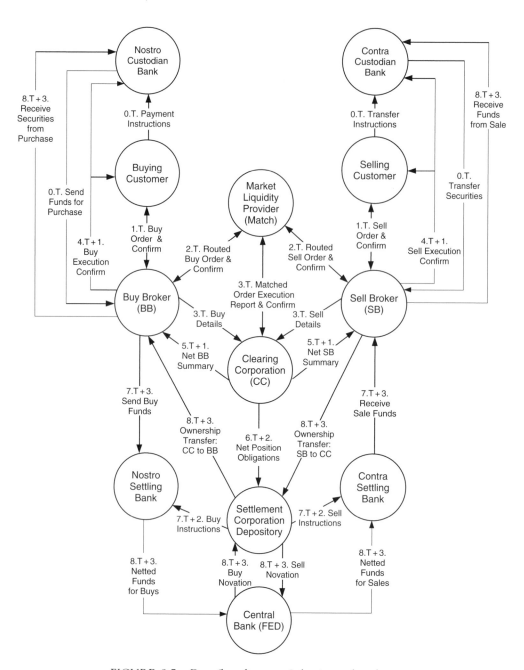

FIGURE 8-7   Data flow diagram of clearing and settlement.

2. The broker routes the customer orders to the market (such as an exchange, an electronic market such as Nasdaq or Instinet, or another broker via FIX). The Market confirms the receipt of the orders back to the broker. The market provides a utility that matches buyers with sellers.

3. Once matched, a trade is said to be executed. The market sends a Notice of Execution (NOE) to the clearing corporation and to the buying and selling broker.

In the diagram, these activities typically occur on the day of execution — denoted as T. Data flows correspond to the arrows with labels starting with 0.T, 1.T, 2.T. Essentially two parties agree to exchange an amount of securities for cash on a particular settlement date. As we have seen, transaction details could also be specified directly (e.g., using FIX) between the parties.

B. Trade Clearing
  1. Buying and Selling Brokers send trade details to the Clearing Corporation. Both brokers also deliver a confirmation to their respective customers containing the details of the executed order. Confirmations are also sent to the custodian banks.

  2. The Clearing Corporation compares each side of the trade and provides a report to each broker.

Clearing processes specify the who–what–where–when obligations of market participants and intermediaries for the delivery of securities and money. Data flows correspond to the arrows with labels starting with 3.T, 4.T. At this point it is known who owes what to whom. After execution, information relating to the trade needs to be recorded (this is sometimes called "trade capture") to assure that both sides agree to the terms of the transaction. Both sides must also review and confirm the details ("trade comparison, matching and confirmation"). In some cases the trades are matched by the market and are reported to the Clearing Corporation as *locked-in* transactions; trade matching is performed simultaneously with trade execution so that matching and confirmation details are sent with the market Notice of Execution. Ultimately, the securities are made available on settlement day through the broker's securities account in the Settlement Corporation Depository (as an entry in an account book). Brokers also have accounts at a Settlement Bank (with one side of the trade denoted by *Nostro* Our and the other side denoted by *Contra* Other). Funds are available before settlement time. In this DFD, the Clearing Corporation is the counterparty to all transactions; this substitution of one party for another (a technique first used in 1682) is called *novation* (Latin *novare*: to renew).

C. Trade Settlement
  1. The Clearing Corporation computes all settlement obligations and sends this information regarding net financial product and cash balances to the brokers. Note that before settlement time, funds from the buyer must be available to the buying broker, and financial securities from the seller must be available to the selling broker. (For short sales, arrangements must be made to borrow these securities; these arrangements are not shown in the DFD.)

  2. Securities are delivered to the buyer; funds are delivered to the seller. Actual financial products are delivered through book entry accounting systems via the Settlement Corporation Depository. Before the 1970s, many U.S. systems required the physical delivery of certificates and other documents from a depository to the customer. In this DFD, payments are arranged between settlement banks, which in turn maintain accounts at a central bank. Note that some financial products (such as futures contracts) settle in cash; securities are not transferred.

Settlement processes perform the who–what–where–when obligations that were specified by the clearing processes. The end result is the transfer of securities from seller to the buyer, and the transfer of money from buyer to seller. In most U.S. markets these processes take anywhere from T+1 to T+5 days; in developing countries, transfer may take T+30 days or more. Product is delivered only if there is payment and payment is sent only if a product is delivered. These deliveries are final unless there is some legal action such as a default. Typically, clearing members must make good on the obligations of a defaulted client; the Clearing Corporation makes good on the obligations of a defaulted clearing member.

Clearing, Settlement, and Payment

There are multiple implantations of clearing systems, settlement systems, and payment systems that form the core infrastructure of all financial systems. Depending on the scenario, these systems can be viewed as competitors of each other or of clients of each other. Some provide emergency backup for each other.

Payment and settlement systems for cash or funds transfer are not novation based (there is no house acting as the contra side to a transaction). FedWire Funds Service, probably the most important utility for all U.S. markets, provides a real-time continuous settlement system for organizations that are members of the Federal Reserve System. Each transaction is processed individually and cannot be reversed. Because there is no netting involved, it is called a gross settlement system. CHIPS, an acronym for Clearing House Interbank Payments System, is based on a patented algorithm for multilateral netting. The algorithm requires each CHIP participant to have a CHIPS account at the New York Federal Reserve Bank. Participants are told by CHIPS how to fund these accounts at the start of the day (using the FedWire Funds Service). During the day, participants settle payment funds transfer in CHIPS (not through FedWire); these transactions cannot be reversed. At the end of the day, CHIPS nets all unmatched payments and synchronizes its accounts with the CHIPS accounts held at the Federal Reserve. (Negative CHIPS closing positions are refunded to a positive position by the participant, synchronized with another FedWire transfer to their CHIPS Federal Reserve Account.)

Payment and settlement systems for bonds and other fixed income securities includes the FedWire Securities Service, which provides a book-entry system used by members of the Federal Reserve System for the settlement and transfer of U.S. treasuries, bonds for many federal agencies, and certain international agencies. (This system is different from the FedWire system used to transfer money.) It is not novation based; it requires the immediate and simultaneous transfer of securities against payment. FICC is an acronym for the Fixed Income Clearing Corporation, formed by the Depository Trust & Clearing Corporation (DTCC) in 2003 as a merger of the Government Securities Clearing Corporation (GSCC) and the Mortgage Backed Securities Clearing Corporation (MBSCC). FICC provides a netting system for the clearance and novation-based settlement of these products.

Payment and settlement systems for U.S. equities are provided by the National Securities Clearing Corporation (NSCC). NSCC provides novation-based clearing for most U.S. equity, corporate bond, and municipal bond transactions. It instructs its sister organization, the Depository Trust Company (DTC), a member of the Federal Reserve System, to process the settlement instructions and the transfer of products. Today both organizations are part of the Depository Trust & Clearing Corporation (DTCC).

The NSCC originated as the clearing house for the New York Stock Exchange in 1892. In 1920, the Clearing House became the Stock Clearing Corporation and began introducing new technologies to replace handwritten tickets for reporting clearing transactions, such as punched cards (1949), electronic computers (1959), and magnetic tape (1961). In 1968 the NYSE introduced a central certificate service to transfer securities electronically (eliminating physical delivery). As a result of the "paperwork crisis" (which forced the NYSE to close 1 day a week because of large trade volume), the Continuous Net Settlement (CNS) system was deployed in 1972. The Securities Industry Automated Corporation (SIAC) was organized to manage the clearing corporation, then called the National Clearing Corporation (NCC). In 1973, the NYSE Central Certificate Service was spun off to become the separate Depository Trust Company (DTC), and both CNS and DTC became linked in 1974 through automated book entry systems.

Payment and settlement systems for options, futures, and other derivative products are provided by the Options Clearing Corporation (OCC). The OCC is the sole issuer and novation-based settling agent for all stock options, equity index options, and single stock futures listed on U.S. exchanges. OCC also guarantees stock loan and borrow transactions. It is owned by the Chicago Board Options Exchange, American Stock Exchange, Philadelphia Stock Exchange, New York Stock Exchange, and the Pacific Stock Exchange. (Options on futures are cleared on futures clearing systems.) CCorp, an acronym for the Clearing Corporation, was established by the Chicago Board of Trade as the Board of Trade Clearing Corporation (BOTCC) in 1925 and was the first independent clearing house for futures markets in the United States. CCorp provides novation-based clearing systems for the futures and derivatives markets.

The clearing and settlement of international currency products (foreign exchange, abbreviated as FX) involves the transfer of a specified value of one currency for another. These transactions are typically settled bilaterally (between buyer and seller); there is no novation-based clearing corporation. These transactions involve transfers of funds through two separate national payment systems in their respective currencies (typically through central banks such as the Federal Reserve), using financial messaging systems such as SWIFT and utilities such as FedWire and CHIPS.

Different national payment systems and different central bank systems are not linked directly with each other. Because settlements in general occur over different time zones, settlement occurs over different time periods in the business day. These transactions can be especially risky when clearing depository receipts. (A *depository receipt* is a product traded on a domestic stock exchange, representing securities, usually stocks, issued by a foreign company. The depository receipt allows investors to own shares in a foreign company without opening foreign bank and foreign brokerage accounts; risk is transferred to brokerage intermediaries and settlement banks.) The risk to party A that makes the first payment transfer in currency Y is that receiving party B will fail to transfer to party A the payment of currency X due to problems with technology (or perhaps party B will default within the settlement time period).

Something like this happened. The Herstatt Bank in Germany was party B: Herstatt received payments in German marks and other parties were waiting to receive payments in New York in U.S. dollars. At the end of the (German) business day on June 26, 1974, German bank regulators shut down Herstatt Bank before Herstatt could pay the corresponding dollar amounts on their FX transactions. The other parties in New York were stuck waiting for their U.S. dollars. This caused disruptions of payments across CHIPS; some banks withheld payments and others experienced losses. It took 3 days to undo the damage in the New York foreign exchange markets. (Settlement risk in foreign exchange markets is sometimes called *Herstatt risk*.)

Box 8-2
How Many Bubbles to a Page? Seven (Plus or Minus Two) and Other Heuristics

During the 1950s, the Air Force Operational Applications Laboratory conducted various experiments on human memory, judgment, and communication. The results, published by George Miller in 1956, found that most people can distinguish between:

6 different audio tones;

6 different loudness levels;

6 different taste levels;

5 different sizes of squares;

8 to 15 different positions along a line.

After averaging the results, Miller showed that the mean number of distinguishable alternatives is 6.5; consequently, with 68% confidence, this means that most people can distinguish between 5 to 9 (7 ± 2) categories. Many system designers invoke Miller's observation and state the following heuristic rules:

1. A system diagram should not have more than 7 ± 2 containers per page.
2. A hierarchy should not have more than 7 ± 2 levels.
3. The number of menu items in a menu system should be less than 9.
4. Testing should be performed by 5–10 independent testers.

Miller noted that "this magical number seven applies to one-dimensional judgments" – the accuracy of distinguishing decreases for single dimensions. Different results apply for multidimensional problems. For example, a diagram with boxes of multiple sizes, colors, shapes, and line thickness might have a memorable arrangement. This implies that even though people can make crude judgments of complex patterns, "it was better to have a little information about a lot of things than to have a lot of information about a small segment of the environment."

There is another set of numbers that might relate to Miller's conclusions about human information processing. It is often stated that "research shows that people are likely to remember 10 percent of what they *read*; 20 percent of what they *hear*; 30 percent of what they *see*; 50 percent of what they *hear and see*; 70 percent of what they *say*; and 90 percent when they *say and do something at the same time*. (This may be a statistical paraphrase of a classic Chinese proverb: "When I see I forget; when I hear I remember; when I do I understand.") The percentages are from a study performed for the Socony-Vacuum Oil Company. (SOCONY – the Standard Oil Company of New York acquired Vacuum Oil in 1931 and became Socony-Vacuum; in 1955 it became Socony Mobil; it became Mobil Oil in 1966; today it is Exxon Mobil.) The study was done under Chaning R. Dooley (1878–1956), head of training at Socony. During World War II, Dooley, and Walter Dietz (of AT&T) ran the Training Within Industry program that helped technology-based industres rapidly train employees, emphasizing "on-the-job training" and training the trainers.

8.2. System Analogies

Diagrams are not the only way to represent system structure. Complex systems can frequently be represented in terms of simpler systems by *analogy*; an analogy maps system components to other system components and maps component relationships to other component relationships. For example, 19th century technologists described electricity and magnetism in terms of fluids: voltage corresponded to pressure and voltage relationships corresponded to fluid flow relationships. Complex financial systems are described frequently in terms of gambling systems and auction systems. Indeed, many terms from poker (such as action, add-on, blue chip, board, short, call, cap, cash in, check, close, deal, dealer, equity, expectation, fill, insurance, in the money, irregularity, limit, open, position, post, runner, and split) are used in analogous fashion in financial systems. Physical analogies are used as well (including terms from mechanics and physics such as liquidity, momentum, depth, continuity, pressure, resistance, and volume).

Analogies between systems were formalized mathematically by Samuel Eilenberg (1913–1998) and Saunders Mac Lane (1909–2005) in 1945. Essentially, analogies are made between *categories*. A category consists of two collections: a collection of *objects* and, for each pair of objects, a collection of relationships called *morphisms* from one object to another object.

In the Eilenberg–Mac Lane terminology, analogies (maps between categories) are called *functors*. A functor associates objects in one category to an object in the other category and morphisms in one category to morphisms in the other category.

Some examples of technology system analogies are shown in Table 8-1. The morphisms specify how objects interact with each other. For example, for electrical systems, morphisms are given by Maxwell's equations; for mechanical systems, the morphisms are given by Newton's laws; and for hydraulic systems, the morphisms are given by Navier–Stokes equations. Certain relationships are also true across all analogous systems. For example, power is always flow times potential (current times voltage; force times velocity; volume times pressure). In Eilenberg–Mac Lane terminology, there are functors between the categories of electrical systems, hydraulic systems, and mechanical systems.

Table 8-2 shows an analogy between communication systems and financial systems. Communication (i.e., telephone) exchanges match callers with receivers; financial exchanges match buyers with sellers. In this sense, the exchanges in both systems can be considered to be morphisms. Both systems use intermediaries as repeaters or routers. Modern communication systems multiplex (and demultiplex) messages to improve efficiency; multilateral clearing systems likewise use netting to multiplex (and demultiplex) transactions to improve efficiency (see Box 2-3). In communication systems, messages associated with "weak" (i.e., low voltage) signals are magnified by amplifiers to a higher

TABLE 8-1   Objects in Technology System Analogies

Object	Electrical	Mechanical	Hydraulic
Flow	Current	Force	Volume
Potential	Voltage	Velocity	Pressure
Integrating	Inductance	Elasticity	Inertance
Dissipating	Resistance	Friction	Resistance
Differentiating	Capacitance	Mass	Capacitance

TABLE 8-2   Communication and Financial System Analogy

Communication	Financial
Message	Transaction, order, quote
Caller	Buyer
Receiver	Seller
Repeater	Broker
Router	Routing broker
Amplifier	Margin; credit leverage
Multiplexer	Clearing agent
Demultiplexer	Settlement agent
Exchange	Exchange

voltage so that they can be processed at greater distances. In financial systems, "weak" (i.e., low volume or small size) orders or transactions can be magnified using margin or leverage so that the resultant gain or loss behaves as a high-volume gain or loss.

Categories are similar in spirit to classes in object-oriented programming systems. A class is a collection of programming data structures, together with a collection of relationships called methods, which are used to manipulate the data structures. Methods are similar to functions. An instance of a class (which assigns values and memory to the data structures and the methods) is called an object; this helps make the distinction between something that executes (the object) and something (the class serves as a template) that does not execute. Consequently, categories correspond to classes and morphisms correspond to methods. This can also be seen in analogies between the different system description diagrams and methodologies (Table 8-3).

Gambling System Analogies

Gambling houses (casinos) provide a place where professional players and the general public can bet on whether they can win at a probabilistic game. Players compete against each other, against a dealer, and against chance. (A race track does not have a dealer at each table or post but does have a market; in race track jargon, a market is the list

TABLE 8-3   Analogies between System Diagrams

System Description Categories	Objects	Morphisms
Network diagram	Nodes	Arrows, lines
Hierarchy chart	Elements; components	Belongs-to; has-a
Flowchart	Subroutines; modules; commands	Control sequence
ERD	Entities; objects	Relationships; messages
Onion	Layers	Interfaces; protocols
DFD	Processes	Inputs, outputs
OOPS	Classes	Messages, methods

of all horses in a race together with their odds in winning a race.) The casinos make money on the small "spread" between the true probabilities of winning and the casino's payoff probabilities. Gambling houses use technology to make games easier to play and to make games more accessible to professional players and the retail public. In gambling and financial systems, participants frequently agree that it is better to be lucky than to be smart.

There are several protocols for establishing an account at a casino. In one scenario, a new player goes to the cashier's cage and fills out forms to establish identification and credit (with checking accounts or credit cards). In the days of Casanova this would be accomplished with a letter of credit that is linked to a known social network of people who can guarantee payment. The casino establishes credit limits and gambling margins for the player (laws prohibit gambling with borrowed money). To reduce house clearing and settlement risks, funds may be withdrawn (from the player's checking account or via credit card cash advance) and placed in the player's account. Like the analogous financial system, all customer information is maintained in a customer master database so that returning players and good customers can be rewarded with soft dollar "comps" (complimentary) such as free meals, drinks, rooms, or transportation. Casinos are careful with authentication and guard against any misuse or stealing of identification ("ID theft") regarding players and casino employees who may play for their own accounts.

The player uses this credit line to obtain money surrogates — chips — that are specific to the casino. Each game has its own rules and protocols that are maintained in a game master database (analogous to the securities master file used in financial firms). Games are played at specific tables (such as the physical market maker positions or posts on physical trading floors, or analogous port numbers in TCP/IP connections). Unlike financial broker/dealers, casino dealers are usually employees of the casino; they earn salary and tips (unless they are casino partners).

Gambling activity is totally transparent and visible. Players are known and identified at every table. Every action is constantly monitored and archived in real time by surveillance systems (called the "eye in the sky") and compliance personnel. Archival material must be submitted on demand to regulatory organizations. Any suspicion of a rule violation by a player, dealer, or casino employee can result in disciplinary action such as expulsion from the casino, being barred from all casinos, or legal action such as jail time.

Casinos maintain social networks regarding criminals or suspicious players; associates of suspicious players are also suspect. These social networks act as a kind of "firewall" to keep suspicious players away from the tables; casino staff will prevent these players from entering the casino or may order them to leave if they are already playing. A staff of house detectives also monitors suspects; they may open formal investigations and may submit their findings or referrals to the police. Casinos are also on guard regarding casino closures or other kinds of denial of service attacks by criminal elements or competitors (these may be implemented as a "virus" attack on casino computer systems). Information about players may be shared between different casinos and regulators. Brokerages and exchanges comply with and enforce similar rules.

Periodically, casinos issue reports to regulators assuring that all practices are fair and orderly. The ultimate regulatory authority is the (state) government. The financial systems analog for this type of report is the Financial and Operational Combined Uniform Single Report, known as a FOCUS report. It provides the SEC and other regulators with a complete, detailed view of a firm's financial and operational conditions (in the form of answers to several hundred questions); summaries are submitted monthly and details are submitted quarterly.

Box 8-3
EDGAR

All SEC-registered entities (including foreign and domestic public companies, investment managers, and investment advisers) are required by law to file regulatory and compliance reports and forms with the U.S. Securities and Exchange Commission (SEC). These reports contain time-sensitive corporate information, such as registration statements, periodic reports (FOCUS), and other reports (such as Sarbanes-Oxley disclosures). This information must also be made available to regulators, investors, and others in the financial community in order to create fair and informed securities markets.

The SEC started developing an electronic disclosure system in 1983 in order to manage the submission (by companies), the receipt and acceptance (by the SEC), and the dissemination and analysis (by the financial community) of these reports and forms. The resultant system, the Electronic Data Gathering, Analysis, and Retrieval system (EDGAR), was deployed in 1993.

In 1993, electronic filing was by direct file transmission, diskette, or magnetic tape. Formats were text based. Today, EDGAR filing is Web based and also uses markup languages such as the eXtensible Business Reporting Language (XBRL).

Settlement occurs when a player goes to the cashier's cage and exchanges chips for cash or other fungibles. If a player owes money, then this amount is deducted from the credit line in real time. One of the technology innovations of the slot machine (invented in 1895) was its ability to settle in cash.

Unlike trading (betting on the value of financial products), casino betting games do not involve any events external to the table such as news or reports on what is happening at another table. In order to bet on external events, players can contact a *bookie* or *bookmaker*: an organization that is usually unregulated (or illegal) that takes bets, computes probabilities for the payoff, and either pays or collects.

Casino systems are closed systems (most casinos do not have windows or clocks). Players can only improve their profit performance by assessing event probabilities carefully; some of these activities (such as card counting) may also be banned by the casino. Players can also survey casinos in order to ascertain which casino offers the best terms, comps, and odds. Casinos know that if they offer better odds than their competitors, they stand to make less profit per player but more profit by volume (this was the strategy that Blanc used in Monte Carlo).

Auction House Analogies

An auction is a place where suppliers or producers meet to sell a product to a product to buyers or consumers. Auction systems have a mechanism of price discovery that is perceived to be fair by auction participants. There may be some amount of bargaining or negotiation. In exchange for coordinating the auction, the auction house receives a brokerage fee. The auction dealer (auctioneer) is an employee of the house.

Buyers and sellers need to be registered by the auction house. Depending on the house rules, buyers may need to establish credit in order to place bids; sellers need to establish ownership. Sellers may set a "reserve" price at the auction *open* that buyers must exceed if the auction is to proceed. Buyers compete against each other in order to win the product at a lowest price; in this sense, an auction is a (nonprobabilistic) game where the players are other bidders.

A normal auction is when players compete to buy: the winner buys the product at a price higher than the competition. When players compete to sell, the winner sells the product at a price lower than the competition (this is sometimes called a reversed or procurement auction). In this sense, the trading floors of most financial markets provide simultaneous normal and reversed auctions for the buying and selling of products. Some example auction systems include the following:

- **English auction**
  Players bid against one another, with each bid being higher than the previous bid. The auction ends when there are no more bids (or when a predetermined upper price is reached). The winning bidder pays the last bid price.

- **Dutch auction**
  The dealer starts at a high ask price (asking if players want to buy); the dealer lowers the price until a player offers a bid (or until a predetermined lower price is reached). The winning bidder pays the last announced price. The recent Google initial public offering was arranged as a kind of Dutch auction.

- **Sealed first-price auction**
  Bidders submit a single secret bid. The winner pays the submitted price.

- **Sealed second-price auction**
  Bidders submit a single secret bid. The winner pays the submitted price of the second highest bidder (not the winner's price), thus giving bidders an incentive to bid a true value. This auction is named after economics professor William Vickrey (1914–1996).

Most auction houses do not provide clearing and settlement services directly; they may provide settlement services through affiliated corporations. For example, eBay offers the payment services of the PayPal bank payment system. In general, a seller relies on the bono fides (good faith) of the buyer for payment, and a buyer relies on the bono fides of the seller for delivery. However, the auction house may maintain a reputation database in order for players to assess clearing and settlement risk.

Regulation and Surveillance of Fraudulent Activity

Auction houses and gambling houses, as well as trading firms and clearing corporations, keep their markets fair and orderly by continuous surveillance. Surveillance is difficult because of the large number of actions that must be examined. Here are some examples of the common jargon used in gambling systems, auction systems, and financial systems to indicate fraudulent or illegal activity.

Cornering the market is when a participant acquires large amounts of a product in order to control its price. Other participants are *cornered* ("trapped against a wall"). One purpose is to arrange a *short squeeze* of participants who need to sell at a low price after paying high prices. (*Short* is a term derived from poker meaning "unable to pay on time due to having insufficient chips; low on funds.") One way of performing a corner is with a *bear raid*; a participant acquires a product by price manipulation: first by selling (to lower the price) and then by buying back at the lower price.

Box 8-4

Gambling Games, Auctions, Game Theory and Beauty Contests

Game theory creates models of interacting decision makers called players. Players have actions; each player's action profile comes with a cost or benefit known as a payoff. These payoffs can be used to sort a player's action profile into a set of preferences. All actions and payoffs are known to all players. Moreover, the assumption is that players are rational and will always execute the optimal strategy.

A Nash equilibrium is an action profile for all players with the property that no player can do any better with any other action. In some sense, a Nash equilibrium is a stable solution to the problem of finding a player's optimal strategy in maximizing payoff in the game: if players can't do better then why would they change? The Nash equilibrium is named after John Nash (1928–).

Game theory in general and the search for Nash equilibrium in particular have been applied to price models in auctions, price competition strategies, and voting. However, many experiments performed with real people have revealed inconsistencies between game theoretical predictions and actual observed behavior.

For example, consider the following auction. Players pay \$10 to participate. They are all asked to estimate the value of a mystery prize, where the lowest value is 0 and the highest value is 100 (in other words, estimates must be in the interval [0, 100]). The dealer collects these estimates and computes the average value A from the players. The winner is the player whose estimated value is closest to 0.76 times this average estimate. We define "closest" as the value that minimizes the absolute difference between $0.76*A$ and the player's value. If there is a tie, then winners split the prize. For example, suppose there are 10 players and suppose each player's estimate of the value is as follows:

Player:	1	2	3	4	5	6	7	8	9	10
Value:	62	36	80	28	65	83	76	34	55	67

The average of all the guesses is $A = 58.6$ and $0.76*A = 44.536$. Player 2 is the winner because player 2's value of 36 is closest to 44.536.

In this game there is a unique Nash equilibrium. In order to derive it, note that all players assume that if the other players choose randomly then the average should be 50, so the best number to choose is then $0.76*50 = 38$. However, because all players are rational, they all know this too. So if everyone else picks 38, a winner should pick $0.76*38 = 28.88$. By the same reasoning, if everyone else picks 28.88 then a winner should pick 21.95, but then everyone else knows this too. By continuing in this style of iterative thinking, we should pick $0.50*0.76*0.76*0.76*. \ldots = 0.0$. The Nash equilibrium is 0 and if everyone picks 0 they all get to share the prize: they cannot do any better.

In experiments with people, the winning numbers depend on the sample population. Most people iterate one or two times (winning numbers cluster at 50 or 38); many business executives iterate two or three times (38 or 29); academics seem to iterate the most and choose the smallest numbers, which generally are too small so they do not win. This game shows that the real winner does not win with the theoretical optimum solution: the real winner only needs to be a single iteration ahead of everyone else.

Box 8-5

System Consequences of Investment Fraud

In the case of bankruptcy and default, clearing members make good on the obligations of a defaulted client, and the clearing corporation makes good on the obligations of a defaulted clearing corporation member. How is an investor protected? There is no insurance for investment fraud. To partially address this, the US Congress created a nonprofit corporation — the Securities Investor Protection Corporation (SIPC). SIPC, funded by its broker dealer members, works as a trustee in legal cases to recover investor assets: clients of a failed brokerage firm must be able to receive their registered securities. SIPC cash reserves cover other client claims (a maximum of $500,000, including $100,000 for cash claims).

Here are two examples where the SIPC was needed. Both involved the failure of NSCC member clearing corporations; both were victims of a short squeezer.

Adler, Coleman

Adler, Coleman Clearing Corporation cleared for 40 firms and had 65,000 customers before it failed in February 1995. Adler's default was caused by the failure of a client, Hanover Sterling & Company, a Nasdaq broker. One of Hanover's clients, Fiero Brothers, Inc., organized a bear raid on some stocks by created millions of illegal short positions. Hanover tried to stabilize the market and stop the shorts by encouraging Fiero to buy – by illegally selling Fiero stock below the market price. Hanover quickly ran out of capital; this led to it's shutdown by NASD. The next day Adler filed for bankruptcy. Almost $1.6 billion of Adler's buy and sell contracts was guaranteed by the NSCC before liquidation. During 1995, NSCC and SIPC agreed that NSCC would be liable for $17 million plus interest. To avoid similar problems in the future, NSCC created the Market Maker Domination System (MMD). Using executing broker identifiers, MMD compares trades across all NSCC member's client market makers in order to assess suspicious trading activity and to establish collateral limits for the clearing corporations.

MJK Clearing

MJK Clearing handled $12 billion in assets for 175,000 customers before it failed in September 2001. Like Adler, MJK was a victim of a short squeeze by one of its clients. In this case, it was in a thinly traded (low "liquidity") Nasdaq stock called GenesisIntermedia Inc. (GENI). The stock was cornered by the owners: they owned 77.5% of all shares. In 1999, the owners colluded with others to hype the $8 stock to $80. However, instead of short selling, the owners loaned the hyped stock (with cash collateral priced from the inflated stock as) to brokerages; the brokerages then loaned the stock to short sellers. At least 7.2 million shares of GENI stock short squeezed. As the price increased, the increased collateral flowed from borrowers (short sellers) to the owners. After the September 11 Attack, the price of GENI fell. MJK was able to refund $65 million of collateral to some clients; other clients owed MJK collateral that MJK itself used to borrow stock: one client owed MJK $40 million. When this client defaulted, MJK failed. After the SIPC coordinated liquidation, more than $10 billion was restored to investors. In this case, the NSCC was not liable for losses. It turns out that the MMD system helped the NSCC avoid liabilities by helping it maintain enough collateral to cover losses.

Capping is when a poker player illegally adds money to a bet by placing extra chips on a winning bet after receiving cards from a distracted dealer. *Pegging* is when a player marks cards in order to cheat. Cheating in cards corresponds to market manipulation of prices; for example, in financial systems, pegging manipulates the price of one product in order to influence the price of another product.

A *wash* gives the impression of high activity. It occurs when a participant sells (and buys back) a product at the same price at the same dealer or when a player wins and loses the same amount with the same dealer. *Overbidding* also gives the impression of high activity: a participant issues many unauthorized orders, many inflated orders, or many indications of interest.

Overtrading involves an arrangement with a dealer to buy a product not at a fair market price. Other *prearranged* actions may depend on prior arrangements of price, terms, and side. When a group manipulates prices, they are said to be *acting in concert*. A group may also set up a *daisy chain* that lulls a player into buying in a rising market: the bubble bursts after the unsuspecting player buys the product. Some arrangements hide ownership (to avoid fees or legal disclosures by) creating a set of fictitious activities (*parking*) or tax liabilities (*as of* activities). Group activities that are designed to manipulate prices, disguise ownership, or avoid legal requirements are examples of collusion.

A *front runner* is a horse that is in the leading position of a race. It also refers to someone with knowledge of an imminent event who profits by taking advantage of the information. For example, a broker receives a large buy order from a client; if the broker submits his own buy order in advance of the client buy order, then the broker is a front runner. (After the client buy order the price will increase, the broker can then profit by selling immediately.)

8.3. Characteristics of Systems of Systems

Functional views correspond to identifying what jobs and tasks a system needs to perform. Operational views correspond to measuring how these tasks perform in practice.

Functional vs. Operational Characteristics

From a functional view, some of the major functional attributes of financial systems of systems (SoS) include the following.

- **Completeness**
  There are models to identify and classify users and messages; subsystems can act on all messages and are able to understand their control instructions.

- **Time models**
  There are explicit models for time to indicate when the system is open for business, when actions can take place, and when actions are completed.

- **Finality**
  Some actions may be reversible and some may be irreversible.

- **Fees**
  There are models for compensation services for working and nonworking hours.

- **Fraud**
  There are models for actions that may be the result of criminal activities.

From an operational view, some of the major operational attributes of financial SoS include the following.

- **Operational independence**
  SoS components operate independently of the other components.

- **Managerial independence**
  SoS components are built or acquired independently, integrated independently, and maintained independently.

- **Evolution**
  An SoS evolves from a more technologically primitive and functionally simpler SoS. Major SoS changes can occur relatively quickly, with long periods of stability characterized by a minor change in between brief periods of major development. (This is sometimes called punctuated equilibrium: subsystems can die or mutate.)

- **Communications**
  Compliance to communication standards is usually more important than the operational capability of an individual component subsystem.

- **Backup**
  Systems must have compatible messaging formats so that in case of a disaster, competitors can be interoperable with each other. For example, even though FedWire, SWIFT, and CHIPS identify clients by different identification models, they have common message semantics to enable one system to be a backup for another system.

Sometimes it is easier to consider dysfunctional financial SoS — systems not having these functional or operational properties.

The principal technology driver for financial SoS has been the desire to eliminate physical processing or delivery for the simple economic reason that the resulting systems operate faster and cheaper. The side effect is that space and location become less important as communication technology improves.

From the view of a financial application system, the other core financial SoS network infrastructures (power, water, transportation) are utility systems. From this perspective, the independence and complexity of financial application systems demand an emphasis on protocol and interface design; ultimately, a financial SoS is defined by its communication standards.

Emergent Properties of Financial SoS: Analogies from Physics

The original definition of a system implies that a system has "a life of its own." In effect, one of the difficulties in describing a financial SoS is that it performs operations that cannot be localized to component systems. For example, purchasing 100 shares of stock involves many systems and depends on the particular systems at a broker, exchange, clearing house, compliance organizations, news organizations, power utilities, etc. This "self-emergent" property is one of the characteristics of a functional SoS.

Much of the terminology in SoS uses jargon from physics. For example, another SoS property is *criticality*: a point in time when the state or organization of an SoS changes suddenly. This can include communication breakdowns or restarts, e.g., when a connected (in physics: *percolating*) network decays to a non-connected (in physics: *non-percolating*) state (regarded as *a phase change*). *Self-organized criticality* is the ability of a SoS to maintain itself around a critical point. From an operational perspective, supposedly modest changes (such as a minor software update, a change in suppliers, a day having an unusual number of shares traded) can result in a period of undesirable chaotic behavior before the SoS is corrected and swings back to the equilibrium near the critical point; the SoS is said to be at "the edge of chaos."

In practice, such "bad events" are observed more often than under the traditional theoretical bell-shaped normal probability law. Bad events occurring with higher than normal frequency seem to follow a "fat tail" or "power" probability law. (This will be discussed in the next chapter.) In financial SoS jargon, such bad events are frequently called "glitches."

Measurement of percolation and connectivity can be visualized with the help of different types of system diagrams. For example, percolation is related to the question "What is the average number of steps needed for a message to pass from a source system to a target system?" In a network diagram, this parameter is called the *mean geodesic distance*. For TCP/IP-based SoS, the answer can be found by using the ping command. For networks of people (social networks), psychologists have discovered that two random U.S. citizens are connected by an average of six acquaintances. This is sometimes called the *small world effect* with six degrees of separation (the mean geodesic distance is 6). For power networks, the mean geodesic distance is much higher than that for social networks or for the Internet.

These considerations may be important when considering system *resilience*: the ability of a system to recover from a shock or disturbance. In a system network diagram resilience can be measured by seeing what happens when a node or subsystem is removed from a SoS; in general, removal increases the mean geodesic distance. Another parameter is the network degree: the average number of connections (arrows) per system node.

Many SoS are seen to form different community clusters (measured by network algorithms that compute a clustering coefficient). In some cases, one would expect that system node connectivity should be random; in reality, for many SoS (represented as a *scale-free* network), a few network system nodes (called "hubs") are far more connected than other system nodes. The Web is a scale-free network.

Electrical power networks have very low degree and low cluster coefficient; they have low resilience and are easy to break. Social networks have high degree and high cluster coefficient; they have high resilience and are harder to break. The Internet is somewhere in the middle. A scale-free SoS network with high-degree system hubs are easy to break — just break the hub systems (random system failures on ordinary system nodes have little effect on the SoS behavior). Usually, the more hubs (and redundant connections), the more resilient (the properties of a scale-free SoS become more like a small world SoS).

Box 8-6
Glitches

The word "glitch" refers to a malfunction or problem that causes a temporary setback. It entered the English language around 1962 (perhaps originating from the Yiddish *glitsch*: a slippery place). Media sources frequently use this word to identify problems originating in financial technology. (Indeed, a Google search executed in June 2005 on "NYSE glitch" and "Nasdaq glitch" yielded 21,900 and 26,600 hits, respectively.) The following events were headlined as glitches.

A trader at Morgan Stanley put in a routine order to buy a large portfolio of stocks: a "basket trade." The portfolio was valued in the millions of dollars; however, the trader mistakenly put in an order that valued the portfolio in the billions of dollars. The erroneous trade caused a 2.8% jump in the Russell 2000 index. (The trade was reversed by the buyer after NYSE specialists alerted the Morgan Stanley floor brokers that something was wrong. Nasdaq systems also alerted the buyer; the trade was electronically executed because there was no request to break the trade.) The event was similar to one that occurred at Lehman Brothers Holdings, when an order for a short sale was erroneously overstated by one billion dollars. Glitches similar to these are also termed fat finger syndrome, which blames bad orders on careless keyboard typing. (*Wall Street Journal*, February 16, 2005)

A "communication problem" halted trading at the NYSE and American Stock Exchange 4 minutes before the close on June 1, 2005. The problem occurred when a SIAC system and its backup were overwhelmed by an error message that duplicated itself millions of times. The problem was detected and corrected an hour later. (*Reuters*, June 2, 2005)

Shortly after the 9:30 open on January 20, 2005, "a network switch failed" at Nasdaq. The problems reached about 20 percent of Nasdaq's stocks as well as Nasdaq's trading of exchange-listed stocks (such as those listed on the NYSE). The problem was solved by 11 AM. (*Associated Press*, January 20, 2005)

On June 3, 2005 trading in the Japanese yen, Canadian dollar, Mexican peso, British pound, Swiss franc, and EuroFX futures was suspended at 8:15 AM CDT because some traders were unable to enter or cancel currency orders on the Globex system (the electronic dealing platform run by the Chicago Mercantile Exchange). The problem was resolved and trading was resumed at 9:45 AM CDT. (*Reuters*, June 3, 2005)

On April 8, 2005 "a systems glitch" shut down the electronic trading platform at the International Petroleum Exchange (London) for almost 2 hours on Thursday, just a day before the exchange switched to an all-electronic operation. Trading in Brent crude oil futures was suspended for 90 minutes due to an error relating to the input of reference prices. The systems failure was caused by "human error" and not by the technology in the electronic trading platform. (*Financial Times*, April 8, 2005)

On March 8, 2005, "sporadic connectivity issues" shut down e-cbot, the electronic trading system run by the Chicago Board of Trade electronic trading system at 9:20 AM. The outage affected other markets: the commodity exchanges at Winnipeg (Canada), Kansas City, and Minneapolis also stopped trading. Trading resumed at 12:30 PM. (*Finextra*, March 8, 2005)

Box 8-7
SNAFUs

A serious glitch is sometimes called a SNAFU, an acronym originating with the U.S. Army during World War II. Here are two examples:

Consequences of a broken network connection
In November 1985, a broken Fedwire connection prevented the Bank of New York (BONY) from delivering securities to buyers and settling payments with sellers. The network outage occurred at 10 AM on Thursday November 21, after installing a software update in a computer system, and the system was down all day. (At that time, Fed operations officially closed at 2:30 PM, and on November 21, Fed operations remained open, hoping that technologists could fix the system by the evening. The Fed remained open until 1:30 AM Friday morning.) The network problems were finally fixed by 1:30 PM Friday afternoon. Before then, BONY was unable to accept payments from clients all day Thursday and part of Friday, which left the clients with a surplus of $20 billion and diminished the need for their clients to borrow. This caused the interest rate for short-term borrowing (the federal funds rate) to fall from 8.375% to 5.5%. BONY was also unable to pay for and deliver billions of dollars worth of securities to client buyers on Thursday and part of Friday; consequently, BONY had to borrow a record $20 billion from the Federal Reserve Bank of New York so they could pay for securities already received. BONY repaid the $20 billion loan on Friday with a $4 million interest expense.
Source: "Computer Snafu Snarls the Handling of Treasury Issues" (*Wall Street Journal*, November 25, 1985).

Consequences of failing to process email
A Florida jury awarded a financier $604.3 million on his claims that his investment bank defrauded him. The amount could increase to almost $2.5 billion if punitive damages are awarded. Document search and retrieval, especially email, is crucial in legal proceedings: this judgment shows that having inadequate search systems can result in substantial legal fees. In this case, the investment bank kept uncovering new backup tapes; searches were unable to be processed "because of technology glitches" and many retrieved documents were incomplete or submitted late.
Source: "How Morgan Stanley Botched a Big Case by Fumbling Emails" (*Wall Street Journal*, May 16, 2005).

The New York Stock Exchange fined a member firm $2.1 million for failing to preserve electronic communications during a three-year period and for failing to supervise and maintain compliance, another example of the trend by regulators to penalize firms for failing to archive or retrieve emails.
Source: "NYSE Fines UBS, Claiming a Failure To Retain Emails" (*Wall Street Journal*, 14 July 2005).

Extra hubs and connections must also be balanced by cost considerations. Moreover, many SoS networks have the property that *improvements may make things worse for the average client*. For example, in transportation networks, it has been observed since the 1950s that the construction of a new highway connection (meant to improve traffic flow) results in a situation where the traffic congestion becomes worse, even when the quantity of traffic remains the same. This paradox was formalized by Dietrich Braess, a mathematics professor at Ruhr University (Bochuma) in 1968. This is another example where a Nash equilibrium is not necessarily a winning or desired solution.

8.4. Notes and References

The remarks by Robert Greifeld can be found at
[0.1] www.nasdaq.com/newsroom/presentations/documents/
STA_Greifeld_Speech_2004.pdf

The remarks by Christopher Keith can be found at
[0.2] http://home.globalcustodian.com/magazine.do?magid=7

Describing Financial Systems

Diagramming conventions used in the Universal Modeling Language (UML) are described at
[1] http://www.uml.org/.

Good discussions on the different types of payment, clearing, and settlement systems are available at international financial standards organizations and other places, including
[2] *Clearing arrangements for exchange-traded derivatives*. Bank for International Settlements, Basel Committee on Payment and Settlement Systems (CPSS), Publication No. 23, March 1997. ISBN 92-9131-501-X (available at http://www.bis.org/publ/cpss23.htm).

[3] Mario Guadamillas and Robert Keppler. *Securities Clearance and Settlement Systems: A Guide to Best Practices*, by The World Bank Policy Research Working Paper Series No. 2581, April 2001 (available at http://econ.worldbank.org/files/1690_wps2581.pdf).

[4] SEC 1997 Report to Congress: The Impact of Recent Technological Advances on the Securities Markets. September 1997 (available at http://www.sec.gov/news/studies.shtml).

[5] John C. Knight, Matthew C. Elder, James, Flinn, and Patrick Marx. *Analysis of Four Critical Infrastructure Applications*. Computer Science Department, University of Virginia Report No. CS-97-27, September 1998 (available at http://www.cs.virginia.edu/~techrep/)

[6] David M. Weiss. *After the Trade Is Made*. New York Institute of Finance, 1993. ISBN 0131776010.

[7] James Moser. Contracting innovations and the evolution of clearing and settlement methods at futures exchanges. Federal Reserve Bank of Chicago, Working Paper Series WP-98-26, 1998 (available at http://ideas.repec.org/e/pmo36.html).

During its 23-year history, the Congressional Office of Technology Assessment (the OTA closed in 1995) provided the U.S. Congress with objective and authoritative analysis of 20th century technology. These include

[8] Trading Around the Clock: Global Securities Markets and Information Technology. OTA-BP-CIT-66. U.S. Government Printing Office, July 1990. NTIS order #PB90-254087 (available at http://www.wws.princeton.edu/~ota/).

[9] Electronic Bulls and Bears: U.S. Securities Markets and Information Technology. OTA-CIT-469. U.S. Government Printing Office, September 1990. NTIS order #PB91-106153 (available at http://www.wws.princeton.edu/~ota/).

The classic paper that is a source of much of the psychological aspects of system design is by
[10] George A. Miller. "The Magical Number Seven, Plus or Minus Two: Some Limits on Our Capacity for Processing Information," by *The Psychological Review*, Vol. 63, 1956 (available at http://www.well.com/user/smalin/miller.html).

Another perspective on using complex system designs for presentation and analysis is by
[11] Edward Tufte. *The Visual Display of Quantitative Information*. Graphics Press (2nd edition), 2001. ISBN 0961392142 (papers available at http://www.edwardtufte.com/).

The classic Socony–Vacuum study is described by
[12] J.E. Stice. "Using Kolb's Learning Cycle to Improve Student Learning," *Engineering Education*, Vol. 77, No. 5, February 1987. Note that this paper reports that people remember "26 percent of what they hear," not 20%.

The Training Within Industry program is described by
[13] Channing R. Dooley. The Training Within Industry Report 1940–1945. Reprinted in *Advances in Developing Human Resources*, Vol. 3, No. 2, May 2000.

System Analogies

Category theory was first described by
[14] S. Eilenberg and S. Mac Lane, "General Theory of Natural Equivalences," *Transactions of the American Mathematical Society*, Vol. 58, 1945.

Various engineering analogies (from electrical, mechanical, translational, mechanical rotational, hydraulic, acoustic, and thermal engineering) are summarized by Keith E. Holbert at
[15] http://www.eas.asu.edu/~holbert/analogy.html

The SEC's EDGAR technology is described at
[16] http://www.sec.gov/info/edgar.shtml

A description of SEC forms and reports is available at
[17] http://www.sec.gov/about/forms/secforms.htm

Beauty-contest game experiments and iterative thinking are described by
[18] A. Bosch-Domènech, J.G. Montalvo, R. Nagel, and A. Satorra. "One, Two, (Three), Infinity, . . . : Newspaper and Lab Beauty-Contest Experiments." *The American Economic Review* 1, Vol. 92, No. 5, December 2002 (available on the Web).

[19] Rosemarie Nagel. "A Keynesian Beauty Contest in the Classroom." *Classroom Expernomics*, Vol. 8, Fall 1999 (available at http://www.marietta.edu/~delemeeg/expernom/f99.html).

[20] Jacob K. Goeree and Charles A. Holt. "Ten Little Treasures of Game Theory and Ten Intuitive Contradictions." *American Economic Review, American Economic Association*, Vol. 91, No. 5, 2001 (available on the Web).

[21] Colin F. Camerer. *Behavioral Game Theory: Experiments in Strategic Interaction.* Princeton University Press, 2003. ISBN 0-691-09039-4.

How do auctions start the price process? Different opening protocols are discussed in the context of financial technology by
[22] Ian Domowitz and Ananth Madhavan. "Open Sesame: Alternative Opening Algorithms in Securities Markets." To appear in *Building Better Stock Market: The Call Auction Alternative* (edited by Robert Schwartz), Chapter 24 (available at http://www.marshall.usc.edu/fbe/wp_pdf/99-16.pdf).

The Dutch auction system used in the Google IPO is described by
[23] Ruth Somon and Elizabeth Weinstein. "Investors Eagerly Anticipate Google's Public Offering: Dutch Auction-Type Process May Give Smaller Bidders a More Level Playing Field." *Wall Street Journal*, April 30, 2004.

The conflicts behind traditional floor-based auction systems and electronic-based auction systems are discussed in
[24] Kate Kelly. "Open Outcry: Big Board Chief's Tough Job: Selling Technology on the Floor: Mr. Thain Works to Convince Brokers, Specialists of Need for Electronic-Trading — Push Irked by a One-Minute Delay." *Wall Street Journal*, August 2, 2004.

Fraudulent practices that led to the Adler Coleman failure (Box 8-5) are described by
[25] New York State Attorney General Report on Micro-Cap Stock Fraud (Section 8: Clearing House Practices), Bureau of Investor Protection and Securities (December 1997) (available at http://www.oag.state.ny.us/investors/microcap97/report97d.html).

A list of failed financial services companies is maintained by
[26] http://www.weissratings.com/failed_brokers.asp

The MJK failure (Box 8-5) is described in
[27] Joseph Weber and Gary Weiss. "A Saudi Financier's Squeeze Play: How a Minnesota Brokerage Firm Fell Prey to a Complex Stock-Loan Deal," *Business Week*, May 12, 2003 (available at http://www.businessweek.com/magazine/content/03_19/b3832095_mz020.htm).

Characteristics of Systems of Systems

Systems of systems are discussed in
[28] M. Maier. "Architecting Principles for Systems-of-Systems," *Proceeding of the 6th Annual INCOSE Symposium*, pp. 567–574, 1996 (available at http://www.infoed.com/Open/PAPERS/systems.htm).

A good summary of some empirical studies of networked systems (including the small-world effect, degree distributions, and clustering) is by
[29] M.E.J. Newman. "The Structure and Function of Complex Networks." *SIAM Review*, Vol. 45, No. 2, June 2003.

Braess' paradox was first described in
[30] D. Braess. Über ein Paradoxon aus der Verkehrsplanung [On a paradox of traffic planning]. *Unternehmensforschung* 12, 258–268 (1968) (available at http://homepage.ruhr-uni-bochum.de/Dietrich.Braess/Index.html#paradox).

A financial system of system approach described by Chris Keith, former chief technology officer of the New York Stock Exchange, is in

[31] Chris Keith and Allan Grody. "Electronic Automation at the New York Stock Exchange." In *Managing Innovation: Cases from the Services Industries* (edited by Bruce Guile and James Quinn), National Academy of Engineering, Washington 1988. ISBN 030903891X (available at http://books.nap.edu/books/030903891X/html/82.html).

8.5. Discussion Questions

1. For what kinds of financial systems is it most appropriate to use control flow, data flow, entity relationship, or onion diagrams?

2. Use the UML sequence diagram to specify a sequence of financial messages in a financial system.

3. Can futures markets be used to bet on arbitrary events? Discuss how the Iowa futures market and companies such as TradeSports may be used to purchase futures contracts on political events. Also, describe how exchange-traded weather futures contracts can be used to bet on the weather. How do these systems differ from a bookie or a bucket shop?

4. Some economists and finance professionals believe that markets provide the most effective way of predicting (or at least, assessing) the future. With this in mind, DARPA put in place a futures market called PAM (an acronym for the policy analysis market) with the intent to predict political outcomes. Describe the goals of PAM. What happened to the futures market?

5. According to the SEC, insider trading is "buying or selling a security, in breach of a fiduciary duty or other relationship of trust and confidence, while in possession of material, non-public information about the security. Insider trading is illegal in U.S. markets. In the 1980s, insider trading scandals cost Wall Street firms hundreds of millions of dollars. Which firms were implicated? Are they still in existence? Can you give a total value to the scandal?

6. Comment on the demise of Drexel Burnham Lambert, Kidder Peabody, Barings, and Long Term Capital Management with respect to their SoS. Comment on their social networks and computer system networks.

7. Comment on the system of system issues described in [31].

8. Discuss how Braess' paradox could lead to a "glitch" in a financial system.

9. An expert system models human problem solving by automating the rules that people use to complete a task. In some financial applications, expert systems perform better than other systems that are based on finding a theoretical optimal solution. Use the beauty contest game to discuss when this might happen. Can you think of any financial applications where an expert systems approach would be more successful than an optimal theoretical approach? Can you think of any financial applications where an optimal theoretical approach would be more successful than an expert systems approach?

CHAPTER ♦ 9

Risk

The market unwittingly obeys a law which governs it, the law of probability.
— Louis Bachelier, *Théorie de la Spéculation*, 1900

Some years ago … the question of calculable risk came to my attention and the attention of Professor John von Neumann. I had been working on the mathematical theory of prediction, and I had devised methods which could be used on numerical series such as stock-market data…. For us to be able to use a statistical estimation method to cut down a calculable risk, it is necessary for the improvement produced by this method to be clearly calculable and even directly visible … every continuing undertaking must be regulated as to its performance by its results … something which is strictly analogous to what is called "feedback" in a control machine…. This feedback is the economic feedback of private enterprise.

Actuarial work can only be done when we have a sufficient number of instances, so that the degree of deviation can be assessed. This is never possible at the beginning of a radically new course of conduct. The result is that there is neither a calculated risk nor a calculable risk, and no amount of mathematical acuity can make up for statistical knowledge. "Calculated risk" has often become a cheap catch-phrase, and is very commonly meant to fool the public….
— Norbert Wiener, *Invention: The Care and Feeding of Ideas* (Chapter 9), 1954

Mathematics is, in fact, a crutch. When you feel unsafe with something, with concepts, you say, "Well now, let's derive it." Correct? Here is the equation, and if you manipulate with it, you finally get it interpreted, and you're there. But if you have to tell it to people who don't know the symbols, you have to think in terms of concepts…. It's not the partial derivative … it is really something you feel with your fingers so to speak.
— Mark Kac, from an interview published in *Los Alamos Science*, Fall 1982

9.1. Types of Risk in Financial Systems

Risk measures the statistical impact of a bad event appearing in a system. One key assumption is that the system is *observable*: *observability* is the ease of determining if specified system inputs affect system outputs. If a system is not observable, then an audit trail of events may not be meaningful. Observability is needed in order to distinguish between "good events" and "bad events." Observability is also needed to classify events into different risk categories in order to help identify significant risk factors, trends and meaningful event audit trails. Observability is also needed to assess whether a system (or organization) is following "best practices" in the industry, which can be measured by means of interviews, questionnaires, scorecards, and other data-gathering procedures.

Rational players seek to minimize risk by performing corrective actions — what Wiener meant by "feedback." Corrective actions are effective if the system is *controllable*: *controllability* is the ease of producing a specified output from a specified input. For example, in a trading system, one measure of controllability is *liquidity*: the ease of buying, selling, or liquidating a portfolio position in a given product at a specified price. A portfolio manager assumes controllability when she "forces" the system to a desired portfolio return: the system can be corrected (or regulated) if performance is not meeting specified objectives. Controllability is seen when a system (or organization) is forced to follow "best practices" or other standards. Note that one purpose of algorithmic trading is to increase the controllability of portfolios: without rule-based trading strategies, it might not be possible to buy and sell large volumes of securities without market impact — at the best executed price over time.

Systems that are both observable and controllable are called *testable*. From a financial technology perspective, one development goal is to improve the observability, controllability, and testability of financial systems.

Risk is an attribute of financial system components, financial systems, and financial system of systems. Its propagation across components and systems must be managed and controlled by organizations and regulatory authorities before the ultimate risk event — the failure of the entire system of systems — occurs. This ultimate type of risk is referred to as *systemic risk*.

The natural language for describing the frequency of bad events is the language of probability and statistics. Risk is frequently measured by an expected dollar cost of bad events subject to a degree of confidence (similar to that seen in rule-based uncertainty calculi).

In some sense, risk is a statistical description of danger and exposure (while reward is a statistical description of protection and profitability). In any case, most statistical approaches used to assess and manage risk are similar. First, historical data are collected and fitted to an assumed statistical model of bad events. If the statistical model is valid, then risk assessment is reduced to estimating the likelihood of bad events occurring over a given time horizon with respect to the model.

Nonstatistical approaches used to assess and manage risk identify systems or organizations (or people) that exhibit "best practices," which can be a firm with a good reputation over time, an "industry leader," or an acknowledged expert. In this approach, a model codifies observable features and characteristics of these systems (via questionnaires using weighted scoring methods) and identifies and ranks deviations from the ideal "best practices."

A simple example in life insurance contrasts these approaches. The statistical approach collects data across the population detailing accidents and causes of death in order to estimate risk factors. The "best practices" approach collects a set of 90 year olds and asks them what they eat and what they did to enable them to live so long. Both approaches require data and statistics. In any case, once an approach is in place, risk measures are calculated, timely risk reports are developed, and capital is set aside to provide an emergency fund for corrective measures (or insurance) and to assure regulators that the system complies with "best practices" rules.

Good models are understandable, easy to implement, and produce correct results. To avoid incorrect answers, many models have parameters that must be recalibrated according to a specific schedule or event. Some models ultimately must be rejected because of insufficient data, wrong data, or the wrong modeled functional relationship between data components. (The risk of using a wrong model is called *model risk*.)

Box 9-1
Risk Adjusted Capital Ratios

Risk-adjusted capital ratios are guidelines for banks and other institutions that are issued by governments and regulatory organizations in order to assure that these institutions have enough insurance money set aside to cover bad events. Most capital adequacy requirements are based on data recorded in standardized balance sheets and other accounting statements that specify assets and money flows (see Box 3-2). The amount of money to be set aside (insurance or regulatory capital — further classified in the United States as Tier 1, Tier 2, and Tier 3 capital) is specified as a fixed percentage of all "risk-weighted" assets.

Different regulatory organizations provide different ways of computing risk-weighted assets, ranging from fixed weights per given financial product (i.e., a 50% risk weight for mortgages) to a more general scheme involving market, credit, and operational risk.

For example, according to the Basel II Accord — the international standard specified by the Basel Committee on Banking Supervision of the Bank for International Settlements (BIS) — banks should hold total regulatory capital equivalent to at least 8% of their risk-weighted assets. Guidelines are based on a "best practices" approach. The actual regulatory capital depends on how the risk asset components are measured, which depends on the underlying statistical model used and the number of samples needed to come up with parameter estimates.

The technology implementation of Basel II (according to their 2005 Quantitative Impact Study) is essentially based on spreadsheet-based weighted sums. In that study's spreadsheet templates, over 2000 data points need to be provided.

Measuring Risk

Expected losses can be measured by averaging — over a number of days, months, years, or any other fixed time period — the frequency and cost of bad market movements; the frequency and cost of credit defaults (see Chapter 4); and the frequency and cost of other bad events (the cost of glitches, snafus, crashes, settlement failures, or system shutdowns). For financial systems, loss events are generally classified into market risk, credit risk, and operational risk. Some important risk values and probabilities that are common to these three risk categories are as follows.

- **Loss severity**
  This is the probability of a loss (usually given in units of money) per event over a set time period. For example, for one firm, historical data might show that in 5% of all the years, there was a recorded loss event that cost the firm at least $15 million. This corresponds to an event that happens, on average, once every 20 years.

- **Value at risk (VaR)**
  If we are given a table of loss severity probabilities, we can ask the opposite question: given a probability of a loss event over a year, month, day, or other set

time, what is the cash value of the loss? For example, for one firm, historical data might show that a loss event with a 0.1% probability over a year (an event happening, on average, once in 1000 years) corresponds to a loss (value at risk) of $100 million or more over the year.

- **Loss frequency**
  This is just the probability of the number of loss events per year. This can be used to estimate the average number of yearly defaults, glitches, snafus, crashes, settlement failures, or system shutdowns.

- **Reliability**
  Reliability is the probability that a loss event occurs after a specified time T (in other words, reliability is the likelihood that a bad event *does not occur before* T: the system works fine in $[0,T]$ and a failure or bad event happens after time T). A related concept is *maintainability*: the probability that the loss event can be corrected or restored within T time units. Another related concept is *availability*: the probability that a system is operating at time T.

Reliability and Risk Events

Different System of System (SoS) configurations can be used to assess reliability. For example, Figure 9-1 shows system components in a series configuration: outputs of one system are inputs to another system.

Given the reliabilities of the three component systems: what is the reliability of the system of systems? In general, the series SoS reliability is a function of the component reliabilities and satisfies the inequality

$$Rs(t) \leq \min[R1(t), R2(t), R3(t)]$$

The reliability is less than the least reliable component. If failures of component systems are independent, then the reliability of the SoS is the product of the individual reliabilities (this is always less than the least reliable component):

$$Rs(t) \leq R1(t)^*R2(t)^*R3(t) \leq \min[R1(t), R2(t), R3(t)]$$

For example,

$$\text{if} \quad R1(t) = R2(t) = R3(t) = 0.95, \quad \text{then} \quad Rs(t) = 0.857375.$$

System components that have a parallel configuration (Figure 9-2) are said to be *redundant*: the SoS reliability is greater than the individual subsystem reliabilities. In

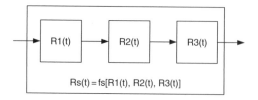

FIGURE 9-1   Systems components in series.

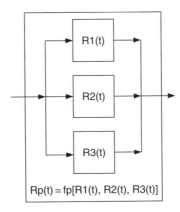

FIGURE 9-2   Systems in parallel.

general, the parallel SoS reliability is a function of the component reliabilities and satisfies the inequality

$$Rs(t) \geq \max[R1(t), R2(t), R3(t)]$$

The reliability is greater than the most reliable component. If failures of component subsystems are independent, the probability that the parallel SoS fails implies all subsystems must fail:

$$1 - Rp(t) = [1 - R1(t)] \cdot [1 - R2(t)] \cdot [1 - R3(t)]$$

or

$$Rp(t) = 1 - [1 - R1(t)] \cdot [1 - R2(t)] \cdot [1 - R3(t)] \geq \max[R1(t), R2(t), R3(t)]$$

For example,

$$\text{if} \quad R1(t) = R2(t) = R3(t) = 0.95, \quad \text{then} \quad R(t) = 0.999875.$$

Note that in general, the series reliability and the parallel reliability can be any function of the individual component reliabilities

$$Rs(t) = fs[R1(t), R2(t), R3(t)] \quad \text{and} \quad Rp(t) = fp[R1(t), R2(t), R3(t)]$$

as long as the functions result in a probability. The functions fs and fp are called copulas. They were initially seen with the uncertainty calculi used in rule-based systems (see Box 9-2).

Credit Failures and Defaults

A credit rating agency (see Box 4-5) rates companies with the following scale: AAA, AA, A, BBB, BB, B, CCC, and D, where D is the default state. What is the likelihood that a company rated AAA today will move to a BB-rated company next year? It is frequently

---

Box 9-2
Uncertainty Calculus and Copula

A copula (Latin *copula*: bond, connection related to *copulare*: to join) is a function that combines or joins two component probabilities to make a third probability. The *ANDf* and *ORf* functions in a probabilistic uncertainty calculus are copulas (Section 7.4 and Box 7-13). In the context of reliability models, the series connection corresponds to *ANDf* and the parallel connection corresponds to *ORf*.

A copula and an uncertainty calculus both model a dependence structure of events. Note that independence is specified by the *ANDf* "multiplication copula." Without copulas, dealing with the dependence structure of probabilities becomes very complicated. For example, the loss severity and loss frequency distributions are usually not independent. In other words, without copulas we need to estimate simultaneously, for example

$P = $ Probability[Number of Bad Events per Year $< b$, Cost of Bad Event per Year $< c$]

The copula allows the separate estimations of risk frequency and risk severity:

Prob(b) = Probability[Number of Bad Events per Year $< b$]
Prob(c) = Probability[Cost of Bad Event per Year $< c$]

and their combination via

$$P = ANDf\,[\text{Prob(b), Prob(c)}]$$

Copulas were investigated by A. Sklar, B. Schweizer, and M. Frank in the 1960's in their studies of multiple valued logics, fuzzy sets, and statistical dependence. The initial research goes back to Niels Abel (1802–1829). The earliest deployed applications of copulas were appeared in rule-based systems of the 1970s. Actuaries started using copulas in risk management applications in the 1980's; copulas started appearing in financial systems in the 1990's.

---

useful to distinguish between different failure and nonfailure events and consider the fact that ratings denote distinct system *states*. If the system is observable, we can estimate the transition probabilities.

System state transition probabilities are conveniently represented in a state transition table or a state transition matrix. Figure 9-3 shows an example of yearly transition credit rating probabilities in a spreadsheet table.

Credit rating agencies such as Moody's or Standard & Poor's compute tables of credit rating transition probabilities. There is much information in these tables. For example, the probability is 87.73% that a company rated AAA this year will be AAA rated next year; the probability that a company rated AAA this year will default (and be rated D) next year is 0.02% (fairly unlikely). Note that there is approximately an 11% chance that a AAA company will have a lower rating next year. A CCC-rated company has a 24.86% chance of improving to a B-rated company by next year. A defaulted company will stay in the default state.

Note that the probabilities of all the outbound arrows of a given node (on the diagram) corresponding to the probabilities across the columns of a given row in the table all sum to 1.

	A	B	C	D	E	F	G	H	I	J
1										
2		**AAA**	**AA**	**A**	**BBB**	**BB**	**B**	**CCC**	**D**	
3	**AAA**	87.73%	10.93%	0.45%	0.63%	0.12%	0.10%	0.02%	0.02%	
4	**AA**	0.84%	88.22%	7.47%	2.16%	1.11%	0.13%	0.05%	0.02%	
5	**A**	0.27%	1.59%	89.04%	7.40%	1.48%	0.13%	0.06%	0.03%	
6	**BBB**	1.84%	1.89%	5.00%	84.21%	6.51%	0.32%	0.16%	0.07%	
7	**BB**	0.08%	2.91%	3.29%	5.53%	74.68%	8.05%	4.14%	1.32%	
8	**B**	0.21%	0.36%	9.25%	8.29%	2.31%	63.87%	10.13%	5.58%	
9	**CCC**	0.06%	0.25%	1.85%	2.06%	12.34%	24.86%	39.97%	18.61%	
10	**D**	0.00%	0.00%	0.00%	0.00%	0.00%	0.00%	0.00%	100.00%	
11										

FIGURE 9-3   Yearly transition probabilities for credit ratings.

	A	B	C	D	E	F	G	H	I
12		**AAA**	**AA**	**A**	**BBB**	**BB**	**B**	**CCC**	**D**
13	**AAA**	77.07%	19.25%	1.66%	1.37%	0.37%	0.18%	0.05%	0.05%
14	**AA**	1.54%	78.11%	13.40%	4.36%	2.07%	0.32%	0.13%	0.07%
15	**A**	0.63%	3.03%	79.83%	12.95%	2.93%	0.36%	0.16%	0.10%
16	**BBB**	3.20%	3.73%	9.06%	71.73%	10.47%	1.05%	0.50%	0.26%
17	**BB**	0.28%	4.95%	6.70%	9.85%	56.91%	12.21%	5.57%	3.53%
18	**B**	0.51%	0.97%	14.85%	13.31%	5.13%	43.54%	10.63%	11.07%
19	**CCC**	0.18%	0.84%	5.21%	5.44%	14.89%	26.82%	19.01%	27.60%
20	**D**	0.00%	0.00%	0.00%	0.00%	0.00%	0.00%	0.00%	100.00%

FIGURE 9-4   Two-year transition probabilities for credit ratings.

Transition probabilities over several years correspond to matrix multiplication. In Excel this can be computed with the MMULT array function. To implement it, select another range of cells (i.e., B13:I20) and enter the following formula as an Excel array formula (using the Excel Control-Shift-Enter keys):

$$=MMULT(B3:I10,B3:I10)$$

Figure 9-4 shows the resultant 2-year transition probabilities. Here, the probability is 77.07% that a company rated AAA this year will be AAA rated in 2 years; the probability that a company rated AAA this year will default (and be rated D) in 2 years is 0.05% (fairly unlikely); note that there is a 23% chance that a AAA company will have a lower rating in 2 years.

Transition probabilities for 3 years can be computed by matrix multiplication of this 2-year matrix with the 1-year matrix. Note that as the number of years increase, all companies eventually default.

This approach in representing state transitions in a table originates with Andrei Markov (1856–1922), a professor of mathematics at Saint Petersburg University. The technology is now called a *discrete Markov chain*. Discrete Markov chains are used in many technology systems: one of the largest discrete Markov chains is used in the Google page rank algorithm.

9.2. Basic Properties of Probabilities

The first statistical model developed for market risk — the cost of potentially bad events due to market movements — was due to Louis Bachelier (1870–1946). Bachelier, a student of Henri Poincaré (1854–1912) at the Sorbonne in Paris, developed a model

---

Box 9-3

From Louis Bachelier's "Theory of Speculation" (Ph.D. dissertation, Paris 1900)

The determination of these [market price] fluctuations depends on an infinite number of factors; it is, therefore, impossible to aspire mathematical prediction of it…. The calculus of probabilities, doubtless, could never be applied to fluctuations in security quotations, and the dynamics of the Exchange will never be an exact science…. But it is possible …to establish the law of probability of price changes consistent with the market at [a given] instant. If the market…does not predict its fluctuations, it does assess them as being more or less likely, and this likelihood can be evaluated mathematically.

---

that showed how prices evolve with time. He used this model to derive probabilities of profitable trades for futures and options. Conversely, for potentially unsuccessful trades, Bachelier showed how to compute an expected loss over a given time period — a value at risk. In the model, the expected gains and losses for a given financial product depended on a key statistical parameter that he called "the coefficient of nervousness" (*nervosité*) or the "coefficient of instability." Bachelier showed that, in this model, the value at risk is proportional to the square root of time multiplied by the coefficient of nervousness. Risk increases with time, and larger values of the coefficient of nervousness lead to a "disturbed" market state, whereas smaller values lead to a "calm" market state.

Today, Bachelier's coefficient of nervousness is known by the rather dry phrase "standard deviation" or "volatility"; it is frequently abbreviated by the lowercase Greek letter sigma σ (Bachelier used the Latin letter k).

Figure 9-5 shows several potential price paths of a risky security. Each monthly security price was constructed by adding noise — generated by multiplying a coefficient of nervousness with Excel's random number generator RAND() — to a risk-free security having an annual simple return of 3%. The average price over all paths (the thick black line) is an annual return of 3% a year — the same price as the risk-free security. (Note that the slope of the line is 3% per year.) In some sense, Figure 9-5 shows how prices evolve in several (nonobservable) parallel universes. Only one of these price curves is the one we observe in our universe.

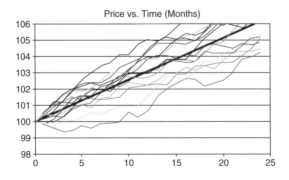

FIGURE 9-5   Possible price paths of a risky investment.

Financial Technology of Bell-Shaped Curves

An important technology used for analyzing a time series is the histogram: a chart that shows how often a value will appear in one of many intervals (called bins). The histogram is just a display of tabulated frequencies. (The ability to create histogram frequency tables and graphs is built into Microsoft Excel: it is called the Histogram Tool and is part of Excel's Data Analysis ToolPak.)

The word *histogram* (from the Greek *histos* mast, related to our root word for system, and *gram* write) was invented in 1891 by British statistician Karl Pearson (who apparently used histograms in his statistics lectures).

For example, suppose we have a set of daily prices of GE from October 2, 2003 to October 7, 2005. We are interested in the frequency of price transitions from the price on an arbitrary day to the price 10 days in the future. A histogram of this set of 498 price changes can characterize the fluctuations of GE. First, what should be the intervals of price ranges and how many bins should we create? The Excel default number of bins is the square root of the number of input values (rounded down): Excel creates this number (here 22) of evenly distributed bin intervals using the minimum and maximum values in the input range as start and end points. Figure 9-6 shows the Excel histogram of price changes showing the relative frequency (percentage) on the vertical axis.

The chart of frequencies looks like a bell-shaped curve, symmetric around its mean or average value (a daily price change of about $0.07). The histogram shows that it is very unlikely that the value of GE over the next 10 trading days will decrease less than $1.70 (about 5% of the time). About 90% of the time, the 10-day price changes fluctuate between −$1.50 and $1.50.

Suppose today's price of GE is $34.22. Can we use the histogram to infer facts about the future? If the probabilities of price movements follow the same underlying rule, as Bachelier observed, we can make inferences about the future likelihood of price movements. For example, the histogram shows that the value of GE will be less than $32.52 with a 5% chance in the next 10 days: i.e., there is a 5% chance that, in the next 10 days, we will lose more than $1.70 per share. This loss of $1.07 per share is the 10-day value at risk given a bad event having a 5% probability of occurring. In other words, on average we might lose $1.07 once in every twenty 10-day sequences.

The two main attributes of the bell-shaped histogram are where it is centered (this is called the mean) and the width of the histogram, showing where most of the probability is

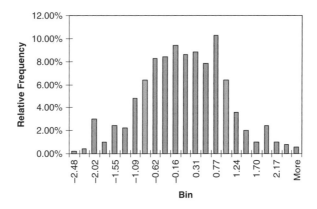

FIGURE 9-6   Ten-day price histogram of GE.

concentrated. The width is related to Bachelier's coefficient of nervousness: wider widths show greater price variability and greater price fluctuation.

Sometimes we also want to fit a curve to the frequencies at each bin, e.g., by using splines (Section 4.3) or any other curve-fitting technique. In this case, the resultant curve is called a *probability density*: given a price change interval, the area under this curve corresponds to the probability that the price change will occur in this given interval. The probability density can also be considered to model a histogram with an infinite number of bins.

Bachelier's model, still used today in financial engineering applications, showed that a representation of price changes (modeled as a set of random independent flips of a fair coin) also produces a bell-shaped histogram. Bachelier described the evolution of price changes x over time t by a special probability density function. Today we use the same density to describe the evolution of returns: recall (Box 2-9) that the simple return from time 0 to time T is just a kind of normalized relative price change. For simple single period compounding the return is

$$\text{return}(T) = \frac{\text{price}(T) - \text{price}(0)}{\text{price}(0)}$$

and for continuous compounding the return is

$$\text{return}(T) = \log \frac{\text{price}(T)}{\text{price}(0)}$$

In any case, for small returns, the price change is just

$$\text{price}(T) - \text{price}(0) = \text{price}(0)^*\text{return}(T)$$

Bachelier's probability density model for a return of value x at time t is, in today's notation,

$$p(x, t) = \frac{1}{\sigma \cdot \sqrt{2\pi \cdot t}} \cdot \exp\left(\frac{(x - \mu \cdot t)^2}{2 \cdot \sigma^2 \cdot t}\right)$$

There are two parameters that mimic the two main attributes of the bell-shaped histogram. The first parameter, denoted by the Greek letter mu (μ), helps specify the center of the curve. The second parameter, denoted by the Greek letter sigma (σ), is Bachelier's coefficient of nervousness and is related to the width of the curve — the bell where most of the area (probability) is concentrated.

Excel has a single built-in function for both normal densities and the areas (probabilities) under the curves (=NORMDIST). In MuPAD, the built-in functions are stats::normalPDF and stats::normalCDF. Figure 9-7 shows some examples of the evolution of returns (return values x are on the horizontal axis) for time t (measured in years) ranging from 1/12 (1 month) to 1 year, where $\mu = 20\%$ per year and $\sigma = 50\%$ per year.

Note that the center of the curve, corresponding to the mean in the histogram (at $x = \mu \cdot t$), drifts to the right at a speed that varies linearly with time. The parameter μ is sometimes called the mean return rate or the mean rate of return, or simply the drift. The width of this return density is proportional to $\sigma \cdot \sqrt{t}$ — the bell width increases with the square root of time. The parameter σ is sometimes called diffusion or volatility. The value of σ^2 (sigma squared) is sometimes called the variance. By looking at the graph, note that the return has less "nervousness" over the 1-month time frame (where the likelihood of returns varies about ±50% per year) and much more "nervousness" over the 1-year

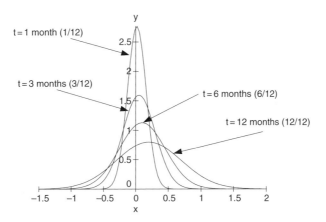

FIGURE 9-7   Frequency of annual returns in Bachelier's model: $t = 1$ month to 12 months.

period (where the likelihood of returns varies about $\pm 140\%$ per year). At very short time intervals, the likelihood that the annual return fluctuates very greatly is small.

Bachelier recognized that his probability density resembled the function studied by Gauss in 1821. This "Gaussian law" (derived when Gauss was analyzing error-prone astronomical measurements) also appeared as a special case in a model of voltage propagation in a telegraph wire (the complete solution to the telegraph problem was published by Bachelier's adviser, Poincaré in 1893). Consequently, this return probability density is called Gaussian density. Early 20th-century British academics preferred to call it the normal density; today normal and Gaussian are used interchangeably.

Bachelier's model assumes that the drift and volatility of the Gaussian returns are constant: this implies that these two parameters can be estimated with confidence from a historical time series (see Box 9-5).

Another Bell-Shaped Curve

Note that the markets and their observed histograms are under no obligation to follow a particular model for prices or returns. For example, another bell-shaped curve is the Cauchy density: Cauchy returns x follow this rule:

$$q(x, t) = \frac{h \cdot t}{\pi} \cdot \frac{1}{(x - a \cdot t)^2 + (h \cdot t)^2}$$

In MuPAD, the built-in functions for Cauchy densities and areas (probabilities) under the curves are stats::cauchyPDF and stats::cauchyCDF. Figure 9-8 compares, for $t = 1$, Cauchy density ($a = 0$ and $h = 1$) and Gaussian (normal) density ($\mu = 0$ and $\sigma = 1$).

The Cauchy density also has two parameters. Parameter a is like the mean — it helps specify the center of the curve. The second parameter h, called the half-width, is like σ. The reason why it is called the half-width is that 50% of the area (probability) under the Cauchy density is within the center $\pm h$.

Note that the center of the curve (at $x = a \cdot t$) drifts to the right at a speed that varies linearly with time (like the Gaussian return) and the bell width of this density also increases linearly with time (proportional to $h \cdot t$), not proportional to the square root

---

Box 9-4
Statistics and Parameters

In antiquity, authorities frequently collected data to register citizens and their property for taxation and other purposes. For example, to assess taxes it was necessary to ascertain the total and average numbers of persons living in a household, together with an estimate of average property income. (In ancient Rome this registration was called a *census*.) By the 17th century, the study of such state-collected data (called in Latin *statisticum*, from the word *status* a political entity or state) was a recognized activity. The word statistics, a shortened version of statisticum, was popularized in English by the Scottish financial economist John Sinclair (1754–1835) in his 21-volume *Statistical Account of Scotland* (1791–1799).

By the end of the 19th century, as shipping and insurance technologies developed, statistics referred to any collection of data to be analyzed, not only from government sources.

Sample values derived from data (values today called the sample average or mean, variance, and standard deviation) were initially called simply constants, coefficients, derivatives, or derivates. For example, the term "standard deviation" was first invented in 1893 by Karl Pearson (1857–1936), eugenics professor and then head of the Eugenics Record Office (later renamed the Department of Applied Statistics) at University College (London). In 1915, Ronald A. Fisher (1890–1962) called each of these quantities a *statistic*. (Fisher worked as an analyst at the Mercantile and General Investment Company before World War I; he succeeded Pearson as eugenics professor in 1933.) Since these statistical values fluctuated from data sample to data sample, Fischer denoted the "true value" of these statistics by the word *parameter*. Consequently, one goal of a statistical procedure is to estimate with confidence (i.e., with low probability of error) the value of a parameter from a given set of data and sample statistics derived from data. A major component of many financial systems for market analytics and risk assessment (and a major product of market data vendors) is concerned with statistical parameter estimation.

It turns out that data can be analyzed without estimating parameters. In 1942, Jacob Wolfowitz (1910–1981) introduced the idea of *nonparametric statistics*. [His son, Paul Wolfowitz (1943–), was the 10th president of the World Bank.]

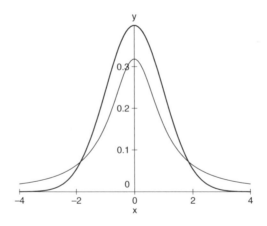

FIGURE 9-8   Gaussian density (thin tails) and Cauchy density (fat tails).

Box 9-5
Measuring Sample Statistics for Gaussian Returns

Suppose time is measured in days, and suppose we have closing prices for the previous 51 days: $V(0), \ldots V(50)$. At the end of each day, after the close, compute daily returns from successive price changes for the last 50 days:

$$R(k) = \frac{V(k) - V(k-1)}{V(k-1)}, k = 1..50 \text{ for returns under simple compounding or}$$

$$R(k) = \log \frac{V(k)}{V(k-1)}, k = 1..50 \text{ for returns under continuous compounding.}$$

For Gaussian returns with $t = 1$ (day), an estimate of μ is the sample mean return m, where

$$m = \frac{1}{50} \sum_{k=1}^{50} R(k)$$

For Gaussian returns with $t = 1$ (day), an estimate of σ is the sample standard deviation sig, the square root of the sample variance var, where

$$\text{var} = \frac{1}{50} \sum_{k=1}^{50} [R(k) - m]^2 \quad \text{and} \quad sig = \sqrt{\text{var}}$$

Sometimes the averaging factor for variance is the sample size minus 1 (i.e., 49). Excel and other systems have built-in functions for variance ($=VAR$) and standard deviation ($=STDEV$). Statistical procedures also provide confidence intervals for these estimates.

What would be the value of these estimates with tomorrow's data? In the *simple moving average* (SMA) method, only the most recent 50 days are included in the summation; on subsequent days, the statistics are computed with the same sample size but with a new value. The *exponentially weighted moving average* (EWMA) method replaces the fixed-sample average by a weighted sum. This requires a constant L (a "smoothing factor," frequently between 0.85 and 0.95). An EWMA estimate of today's sample mean and variance from the value of yesterday's mean and variance m and var and today's return R is

- m:=L*m + (1-L)*R:
- var:=L*var + (1-L)*(R-m)^2:

We can transform means and variances to other time units: under normal probabilities, the mean and variance scale linearly with time. (The standard deviation scales with the square root of time). For example, the normal probability statistics, for a year of 12 months, 52 weeks, 365 days are:

Mean (annualized) $= 1^*$AnnualMean $= 12^*$MonthlyMean
$\qquad\qquad = 52^*$WeeklyMean $= 365^*$DailyMean

Var(annualized) $= 1^*$AnnualVar $= 12^*$MonthlyVar $= 52^*$WeeklyVar $= 365^*$DailyVar

Sig(annualized) $= \sqrt{12^*}$MonthlySig $= \sqrt{52^*}$WeeklySig $= \sqrt{365^*}$DailySig

where $\sqrt{12} = 3.4641\ldots, \sqrt{52} = 7.2111\ldots, \sqrt{365} = 19.1049\ldots.$

Other time-scaling factors may also be used (e.g., instead of a 365-day year, use a 280-day year based on the number of holiday-free trading days).

of time as in the Gaussian density. Because of this, the Cauchy density has fat tails — returns that are relatively rare for the Gaussian density are much more common under the Cauchy density. It can be shown that an event having a 1% probability for a Gaussian density (i.e., it will occur once every 100 years) will occur once every 13 years if the underlying probability is Cauchy.

The Cauchy density has a strange property: the statistical estimation procedures specified in Box 9-5 are not valid for its mean and standard deviation.

Quantiles and Value at Risk

If we know the return histogram or probability density, we can answer questions like What is the asset return associated with a bad year that has a 5% chance of happening? If the asset is worth $1 million today, what is the VaR over the next year? The solution requires a function called the *quantile function* that is built into MuPAD, Excel (=NORMINV for normal density), and other systems.

For example, suppose time is measured in years and the volatility per year $\sigma = 0.25$ and drift per year $\mu = 0$ for one product with a Gaussian return, and $h = 0.25$ and drift per year $a = 0$ for another product with a Cauchy return. Suppose a very bad year occurs with a 5% probability. Then using the MuPAD Quantile functions the returns associated with the 5% event are

- `stats::normalQuantile(0, 0.25^2)(0.05)`, `stats::cauchyQuantile(0, 0.25)(0.05)`

  `-0.4112134067, -1.578437879`

For Gaussian returns, the bad year has an annual return worse than -41%; for Cauchy returns, the bad year has an annual return worse than -158%. The 1-year VaR for a $1 million asset is

$$\text{Price}(T) - \text{Price}(0) = \text{Price}(0)^*\text{Return}(T) = -\$411,213.41 \text{ for normal returns;}$$
$$= -\$1,578,437.88 \text{ for Cauchy returns.}$$

We can still assess VaR, even if we do not know the exact return probability densities. There are a few constraining inequalities for VaR, which depend on the general shape of the return distribution, that are named after Pafnuty Lvovich Chebyshev (1821–1894), chairman of the applied mathematics department at St. Petersburg University (and Markov's teacher). The inequalities are summarized in Box 9-6.

The 1-year VaR bounds for a bad event having a 1% probability of occurrence for assets with (with normal and Cauchy returns) having $\mu = a = 0$ and $\sigma = h = 0.25$ per year are summarized in the spreadsheet shown in Figure 9-9. The spreadsheet in Figure 9-10 displays the corresponding formulas.

The Bank of International Settlement recommends that a bank should have at least three times its total 10-dayVaR (assuming normal returns) for a cash reserve to protect itself against bad situations. A possible rationale for this multiplication factor of three might be because this amount would be sufficient to cover any return density that is symmetrical around its mean (compare cells T36 and T38 in Figure 9-9).

Box 9-6

Inequalities for VaR

The VaR is bounded by the following values that depend on the shape of the return probability density or histogram:

$$\text{VaR} < \text{Price}(0) \cdot \left(m - \frac{s \cdot \sqrt{P \cdot (1 - P)}}{P} \right) \quad \text{for general return densities}$$

$$\text{VaR} < \text{Price}(0) \cdot \left(m - \frac{s \cdot \sqrt{2 \cdot P}}{2 \cdot P} \right) \quad \text{for return densities symmetric around mean } m$$

$$\text{VaR} < \text{Price}(0) \cdot \left(m - \frac{s \cdot \sqrt{2 \cdot P}}{3 \cdot P} \right) \quad \text{for symmetric return densities with a single "hump"}$$

These Chebychev inequalities assume that statistical procedures specified in Box 9-5 are valid (m is the mean and s is the standard deviation of the returns over a given time period). This excludes Cauchy returns. Also note that these inequalities make no assumption on how the mean and standard deviation scale in time. In general, these VaR bounds are valid for the same time period as the return samples.

	R	S	T
31	Bad Event Probability	1%	Asset Value:
32	sigma s	0.25	$1,000,000
33	mean m	0	
34		1 Year Return	1 Year
35	**Density Shape**	**Quantile**	**VaR**
36	Normal	-0.581586969	-$581,586.97
37	Symmetric Single Hump	-1.178511302	-$1,178,511.30
38	Symmetric	-1.767766953	-$1,767,766.95
39	General	-2.487468593	-$2,487,468.59
40	Cauchy (half width=s)	-7.955128988	-$7,955,128.99

FIGURE 9-9   One-year VaR for an event occurring 1 in 100 years.

	R	S	T
31	Bad Event Probability	0.01	Asset Value:
32	sigma s	0.25	1000000
33	mean m	0	
34		1 Year Return	1 Year
35	**Density Shape**	**Quantile**	**aR**
36	Normal	=NORMINV(S31,S33,S32)	=1000000*S36
37	Symmetric Single Hump	=S33-S32*SQRT(2*S31)/(3*S31)	=1000000*S37
38	Symmetric	=S33-(S32*SQRT(2*S31)/(2*S31))	=1000000*S38
39	General	=S33-(S32*SQRT(S31*(1-S31))/S31)	=1000000*S39
40	Cauchy (half width=s)	=S33+S32*TAN(PI()*(S31-0.5))	=1000000*S40

FIGURE 9-10   One-year VaR for an event occurring 1 in 100 years: Formula display.

Box 9-7
Cheating, Fairness, Best Execution, and Compliance Risk

In a coin-flipping game, one way to cheat is by using a biased coin with one side heavier then the other. Another way is by using a trick coin, where for example, every sixth toss comes up exactly the same as the first. In a financial market system, using trick coins is equivalent to either fraud or the illegal practice of *price fixing*. Many of these tricks can be detected by computing the sample *covariance* and *correlation* relating two different time series. Given time series A and B, if mA and mB are the sample means and sA and sB are the sample standard deviations, then the sample *covariance* and *correlation* are:

$$\text{covariance}(A, B) = \frac{1}{samples} \sum_{k=1}^{samples} [A(k) - mA] \cdot [B(k) - mB]$$

$$\text{correlation}(A, B) = \frac{\text{covariance}(A, B)}{sA \cdot sB}$$

Covariance and correlation are built into Excel, MuPAD, and other systems. Using these statistics, market surveillance tests can detect the following "Worst Practice" activities:

- *Price fixing* occurs when market makers collude on unfair pricing arrangements.
- *Tape painting* occurs when a market maker creates fake trades to establish an artificial price. This tricks customers about the real price.
- *Quote painting* occurs when a market maker posts a deceiving quote in order to trick a customer about the real price.
- *Front running* occurs when market makers trade for their own account when holding a large buy (or sell) order from a customer. Trading before the customer's trade could causes the price to move and results in the customer paying a higher price (lower for a sell order); the market maker profits by later selling (or buying back) at the price established after the execution of the customer's order.
- *Backing away from quotes* occurs when market makers refuse to execute orders based on quotes seen by customers.
- *Late reporting of trades* could slow the market and reduce quick extreme price movements: this makes trading less risky and less costly for market makers.

These activities violate the SEC principal of *best execution*: a market maker's duty to execute an order in the best available manner. For example, in 1994, William Christie and Paul Schultz published a statistical analysis of market maker quotes; they concluded that Nasdaq market makers quoted prices primarily on even eighths (avoiding odd eighths). In a fair market, even and odd eighth quotes should be equally likely. This led to a $1.03 billion settlement of a class-action lawsuit against 37 Nasdaq brokerages involving possible collusion (in addition to a 1996 settlement, where NASD agreed to spend $100 million to improve market surveillance).

Circuit Breakers

A *circuit breaker* is an electrical component that is designed to protect an electrical system from damage caused by an unusual surge of voltage or current (due to a sudden overload or short circuit). Circuit breakers are designed to be reset (either manually or automatically) so that the underlying system can resume normal operations. (A fuse protects only once; it must be replaced after every surge event.) In financial power networks, circuit breakers protect financial components against rare events such as lightening strikes or power network overloads.

From the perspective of emergent SoS properties, sometimes at a time of criticality, the best recourse is to shut down system components and restart. (This can be formally shown in the context of a Markov chain analysis.)

In practice, it has been noticed that periodically restarting a system to a previous state decreases the consequences of "unscheduled" serious system failures. From the reliability perspective (assuming that bad events will occur), system faults may lie dormant for a long time before an unlucky combination of circumstances causes them to be observable. In that case, unpredictable failures can have costly consequences. In computer operations, failures include database corruption, extreme memory leakage (from memory allocation and deallocation), improper message processing, and eventual application paralysis.

This behavior has also been observed in the financial markets. For example, the New York Stock Exchange uses several types of *circuit breakers* (Rule 80A and Rule 80B) to shut down and restart the market in order to "reduce market volatility and promote investor confidence." The market crashes in October 1987 and October 1989 led to the adoption of these rules. Market data vendors frequently indicate when NYSE Rule 80B is triggered with an indicator that says CURBS IN (in red for a decreasing market or green for an increasing market).

Sometimes there is a dramatic reduction in costs when circuit breakers are involved to shut down a system periodically. One reason for this is that the cost per hour for unscheduled down time is usually substantially greater than the cost per hour for scheduled down time.

9.3. Portfolios and Risk

A portfolio is a set of two or more financial products that is treated and analyzed like a separate product. In some sense, a portfolio is similar to a system of systems. Box 5-9 discusses how each product can be assigned a portfolio component weight given its price and the total value of the portfolio. (Recall that the sum of all weights is 100%.)

How is the portfolio return related to the component product returns? Note that if the shares held in the component products are fixed, the portfolio weights can vary; conversely, if the component weights are fixed, the number of component shares can vary. This can be seen in the simple two product portfolio seen in the spreadsheet of Figure 9-11.

Initially the portfolio has 100 shares of XYZ ($50 per share) and 150 shares of ABC ($100 per share). The starting value of the portfolio (the "net asset value," usually abbreviated as NAV) is $20,000 with 25% of the value in XYZ and 75% in ABC. In 1 year, the values of XYZ and ABC are $75 and $120, respectively; the new portfolio NAV is $25,500 and the new weights are 29.412 and 70.58824%, respectively. The portfolio return based on the portfolio NAV change is 21.57%. It turns out the portfolio return can also be represented in terms of the returns of the portfolio components and the most recent weights (see the formula display shown in Figure 9-12).

Box 9-8
Financial Circuit Breakers

Circuit breakers are set thresholds, based on values of the Dow Jones Industrial Average (DJIA), at which trading is halted. NYSE circuit breaker levels are set every 3 months and correspond to 10%, 20%, and 30% drops of the DJIA closing values of the previous month (rounded to the nearest 50 points). For second quarter 2008, the NYSE Rule 80B circuit breakers were as follows.

- **10% circuit breaker**
  If a 1200 point DJIA decline occurs before 2 PM then trading halts for 1 hour and resumes. If the decline occurs between 2-2:30 PM then trading halts for 1/2 hour and resumes. There is no halt if the decline occurs after 2:30.

- **20% circuit breaker**
  If a 2450 point DJIA decline occurs before 1 PM then trading halts for 2 hours and resumes. If the decline occurs between 1-2:00 PM then trading halts for 1 hour and resumes. If the decline occurs after 2:00 then trading halts for the rest of the day.

- **30% circuit breaker**
  If a 3650 point DJIA decline occurs at any time then trading halts for the rest of the day.

Other circuit breakers are called collars: these breakers restrict a certain type of program trading. The NYSE defines a program trade as either (i) the simultaneous trade of a basket (portfolio) of 15 or more stocks from the Standard & Poor's 500 Index or (ii) any basket of stocks from the Standard & Poor's 500 Index valued at $1 million or more. Note that futures contracts based on the Standard & Poor's 500 Index are traded at the Chicago Mercantile Exchange: these contracts give rise to short-term arbitrage opportunities when the cash price of the NYSE-traded S&P 500 stocks are unsynchronized with the price of a CME-traded S&P 500 futures contract. Collars are designed to restrict program trading resulting from *index arbitrage strategies:* strategies that involve the simultaneous program trading of S&P 500 stocks at the NYSE and the trading of S&P 500 futures contracts at the CME. For example, in July 2005, the NYSE Rule 80A collar rule (which was eliminated in late 2007) was

- If the DJIA drops 200 points or more, then all index-arbitrage sell orders of the S&P 500 stocks must be stabilizing for the remainder of the day, unless on the same trading day, the DJIA advances 100 points or less below its previous day's close. This only affects S&P 500 stocks; this "uptick downtick rule" restricts sells to upticks (increasing prices) and buys to downticks (decreasing prices). When the last price was down, a sell cannot be executed at a lower price; when the last price was up, a buy order cannot be executed at a higher price.

Futures exchanges sometimes call circuit breakers "price limits." For example, trading is halted between 2 and 10 minutes on the CME S&P 500 futures contract if the contract price is below the previous day settlement by 5%, 10%, 15%, and 20%. There are circuit breakers at the CBOT on their DJIA futures contracts with levels and actions similar to the NYSE halts. The CBOE synchronizes its circuit breaker trading halts in equity options with the NYSE.

	J	K	L	N	P	Q
17		XYZ	ABC			
18	Starting Shares	100	150			
19	Starting Weights	0.25	0.75		Weights	
20		XYZ	ABC	Portfolio	XYZ	ABC
21	Year1 Values	$50	$100	$20,000	0.25	0.75
22	Year2 Values	$75	$120	$25,500	0.29412	0.7058824
23						
24	Return	33.33%	16.67%	21.57%	Return	21.57%
25	Year2 Shares	85	159.375			

FIGURE 9-11   Returns, portfolio weights, and number of product shares.

	J	K	L	N	P	Q
17		XYZ	ABC			
18	Starting Shares	100	150			
19	Starting Weights	0.25	0.75		Weights	
20		XYZ	ABC	Portfolio	XYZ	ABC
21	Year1 Values	50	100	=K21*K$18+L21*L$18	=K21*K$18/N21	=L21*L$18/N21
22	Year2 Values	75	120	=K22*K$18+L22*L$18	=K22*K$18/N22	=L22*L$18/N22
23						
24	Return	=(K22-K21)/K22	=(L22-L21)/L22	=(N22-N21)/N22	Return	=P22*K24+Q22*L24
25	Year2 Shares	=P21*N22/K22	=Q21*N22/L22			

FIGURE 9-12   Returns, portfolio weights, and number of product shares (formulas).

Monte Carlo Simulation of Portfolio Returns

One of the problems with assessing the risk in a portfolio is in choosing the correct return probability density. If the portfolio components are all stocks, where returns are assumed to follow Bachelier's Gaussian density, then the portfolio return will also follow a Gaussian density. However, if the portfolio has a mix of different products — stocks, bonds, options, and other contracts — then it is not clear what the portfolio return density is. The assumption of a Gaussian density would probably underestimate the VaR.

Because of this, technologies were developed to simulate portfolio returns. If the underlying probability densities (with their parameters) of the portfolio components are known, then random price paths can be generated for each component using a built-in random number generator (as in Figure 9-5). These price paths can be used to generate, over a given time period, a histogram of an observed value (such as Figure 9-6). We can use the histogram to make inferences with confidence. This method was developed and implemented on the first computers used at the Manhattan Project during World War II.

Generating such "Monte Carlo" (i.e., simulated random) samples for a portfolio of different products involves the creation of random number algorithms that can generate different samples from different probability densities (today this is not a problem). The implementation must also provide utilities to tabulate and analyze the resultant statistics and their associated confidence intervals (see Box 9-9).

Bootstrapping

A similar technology involves random resampling (with replacement) from an original set of data observations. This method, called *bootstrapping*, was developed in the early 1980s by Stanford University statistics professor Bradley Efron. It is nonparametric (see Box 9-4), as we do not have to assume anything about the density of the portfolio components.

Box 9-9
Simulation Technology and Monte Carlo

The Monte Carlo method was developed during World War II at the Los Alamos Research Labs by Mark Kac (1914–1984) and Stan Ulam (1909–1984). Kac (Kac is the Polish spelling for Katz) and Ulam were close friends; both got their Ph.D. from the University of Lvov. Ulam is credited with coining the phrase "Monte Carlo method."

In 1945, the U.S. Army Air Forces created the RAND Corporation (an acronym for Research and Development) to capitalize and develop World War II technologies. One of those technologies involved using Monte Carlo methods to simulate complex systems: synthetic random events would be input to the system and histograms of the outputs would be created in order to assess system behavior.

In the late 1950s, it was recognized that building special purpose system simulations was tedious and expensive using the existing Fortran-based technology. To address this, RAND started developing a programming language and system called SIMSCRIPT (Simulation Script) that enabled Monte Carlo model builders, not Fortran programmers, to quickly build system simulations. According to Harry Markowitz (1927–), RAND's principal designer of SIMSCRIPT, the new language "reduced programming time by allowing the programmer to describe (in a certain stylized manner) the system to be simulated rather than describing the actions which the computer must take to accomplish this simulation." In July 1962, RAND put SIMSCRIPT in the public domain. Markowitz and associate Herb Karr (author of the SIMSCRIPT user manual) left RAND and formed a company called CACI, an acronym for California Analysis Center, Inc. (later an acronym for Consolidated Analysis Centers, Inc.), to offer new versions of SIMSCRIPT, as well as training and consulting on system simulation. SIMSCRIPT was based on viewing a system as a collection of entities, attributes, sets, and events — a view consistent with an entity–relationship diagram approach.

One legacy of SIMSCRIPT was its influence on the development of other programming systems that represented entities, attributes, and sets for compute-intensive systems. SIMSCRIPT influenced Simula (in 1965 an acronym for Simulation Language, and in 1967 an acronym for Simple Universal Language), the language that many believe started the current trend of object-oriented programming systems.

In the early 1980s, the World Bank began work on a system that would take as input a problem description used by financial and economic model builders; the output was a computer representation that could be executed on different computer processors or architectures. The World Bank system was later called the Generalized Algebraic Modeling System (GAMS). GAMS consists of a language compiler and a system of component computational solver engines. GAMS has been maintained by the GAMS Development Corporation since 1987.

A few years later, a similar system called A Mathematical Programming Language (AMPL) was developed at Bell Laboratories (by some of the same people that developed C and Unix). Like GAMS, AMPL is integrated with component solver systems. In 2003, development and support of the AMPL system were transferred from Lucent Technologies, Inc., to AMPL Optimization LLC, a company formed by the inventors of AMPL.

Here is an example how it works. Suppose we have 10 sample observations, shown in Figure 9-13, where X1 and X2 denote some observable value associated with two portfolio components and Y denotes a value associated with the entire portfolio. To get the first bootstrap sample we need to "shuffle" the data randomly. Because the records are numbered between 1 and 10, we need to pick 10 numbers randomly in the range 1 to 10 that correspond to the records in the original sample. For example, Figure 9-14 shows a first bootstrap sample. A second bootstrap sample is shown in Figure 9-15.

With bootstrap sampling, essentially a resampling with replacement from the empirical probability distribution, we can specify percentiles and confidence intervals, without resorting to probability density assumptions, statistical procedures, or algorithms. All we need is the ability to create a histogram. In practice, the original sample can be duplicated many times to create an expanded artificial sample. Note, however, that the resultant confidence intervals are conditional (and biased) on the original sample.

In some sense, this bootstrap generation of random samples destroys any sequence dependencies between data records. For example, if the original sample is a day-to-day

Sample	Y	X1	X2
1	6	5.9	0.2
2	5	0.8	6.1
3	3.5	6	7
4	8.7	5.5	6
5	3.2	6.3	6.2
6	9.6	9.5	8.5
7	5.9	2.1	1.3
8	9.3	8.6	4.9
9	1.1	1.8	0.6
10	8	9.9	0.1

FIGURE 9-13   Original sample for bootstrap.

Bootstrap Sample1	Y	X1	X2
4	8.7	5.5	6
6	9.6	9.5	8.5
9	1.1	1.8	0.6
7	5.9	2.1	1.3
10	8	9.9	0.1
9	1.1	1.8	0.6
3	3.5	6	7
3	3.5	6	7
7	5.9	2.1	1.3
2	5	0.8	6.1

FIGURE 9-14

Bootstrap Sample 2	Y	X1	X2
6	9.6	9.5	8.5
4	8.7	5.5	6
6	9.6	9.5	8.5
2	5	0.8	6.1
5	3.2	6.3	6.2
2	5	0.8	6.1
5	3.2	6.3	6.2
9	1.1	1.8	0.6
3	3.5	6	7
1	6	5.9	0.2

FIGURE 9-15

time series, then any correlations between Monday and Tuesday are lost. In order to prevent this loss of serial correlation information, we can generate samples of moving blocks. For example, suppose the block size is 2 and the random record selected is record number 8. Instead of selecting record 8 for the new artificial sample, we select record 8 and record 9. This block selection preserves next day correlations. A block size of length 3 preserves Monday–Tuesday–Wednesday correlations. Note that special rules need to be made if the selected record is one of the last records in the original sample (such as a wrap-around rule).

Mean Variance Technology

Suppose a portfolio contains two products A and B with $w(A)$ the proportion of A and $w(B)$ the proportion of B. The average portfolio return is the weighted sum of the component returns (see Figure 9-11):

$$\text{Return} = w(A) \cdot \text{return}(A) + w(B) \cdot \text{return}(B)$$

If we use the formulas in Box 9-7, we can compute the portfolio variance as

$$\text{Variance} = [w(A)]^2 \cdot \text{var}(A) + [w(B)]^2 \cdot \text{var}(B) + 2 \cdot w(A) \cdot w(B) \cdot \text{covariance}(A, B)$$

There are similar formulas for an arbitrary number of products. Note that the covariance can be negative, positive, or zero (Box 9-7). One consequence is that the portfolio risk, if defined as an alias for the variance of the portfolio return, can be reduced if the portfolio has a mix of products that have zero or opposite covariances (or correlations).

The formulation of portfolio risk in terms of the covariance of portfolio components is associated with Harry Markowitz (1927–) and his 1952 paper on "Portfolio Selection." The paper discussed the problem of *portfolio optimization*, namely given the individual component statistics, find the portfolio weights that maximize return and minimize risk subject to a set of constraints (such as the maximum amount of each asset to purchase or sell short should be less than 50% of the portfolio value). Markowitz showed that the solution to the problem can be stated in terms of the mathematical language of *quadratic programming*. (In this context, the word programming refers to an older meaning as scheduling, as in radio or television programming. It is now used as a synonym for optimization.)

The Markowitz "means-variance" approach influenced a generation of asset allocation professionals. More formally, the portfolio optimization problem is

Find the weights w(1), w(2), . . . that maximizes the
objective: Return – Risk*RiskAdversionParameter;
subject to the constraints: sum{i in Products} w(i) = 1;

The "risk aversion parameter" can vary from 0 (which gives the portfolio with the maximum return) to any very large number (which gives the portfolio with the minimum risk). A chart that graphs the pair of (risk, return) for each risk aversion value traces a curve called the "efficient frontier." In 1956, Markowitz successfully analyzed a portfolio of 25 products on an IBM 602A system (a punched card system with 192K memory). Each run took several hours.

Using today's technology, it is very easy to solve the portfolio optimization problem with a specification language such as AMPL. Quadratic programming solvers exist on many different hosts and architectures. For example, Box 9-10 shows an AMPL program that computes an efficient frontier. It was submitted to the Network-Enabled Optimization System Server (NEOS), a project of the Optimization Technology Center (OTC) of Northwestern University and Argonne National Laboratory. Sample output is shown in Box 9-11.

Other objective functions to maximize (or minimize), and other constraints can be formulated. For example, one another popular objective function is to maximize

$$\frac{\text{portfolio return} - \text{spot interest rate}}{\text{portfolio standard deviation}}$$

This is also known as the Sharpe ratio, in honor of William Sharpe (1934–), a younger colleague of Markowitz at RAND. Sharpe showed that using a simple *regression model* (Box 9-12) for portfolio returns, the solution to the portfolio optimization problem can be stated in terms of the mathematical language of *linear programming*.

9.4. Risk and Hedging

A portfolio manager controls the performance of a portfolio by buying or selling component products based on the movements of portfolio components. From another perspective, the value of some portfolio products can depend on the value of other underlying products, indices, or parameters. What is the new price of a security given a change in some underlying factor?

Suppose the price of a security depends on some underlying factor, such as the interest rate. Suppose we also know how the price of the security changes when the interest rate changes. This ratio of price change to rate change is actually the slope of a line as Figure 9-16 shows.

Given two points (yesterday's and today's rate and price) we can draw a line that approximates (or predicts) a future price based on any given interest rate movement. Note that this extrapolation is only a linear approximation of what may be the actual price: the error in the approximation increases in time and increases for large changes in the underlying interest rate. The slope of the line is a measure of price sensitivity. Depending on the underlying factor, these price sensitivities have special names. Moreover, explicit formulas for these sensitivities have been derived under the Bachelier assumption of normal returns.

Price Sensitivities: "The Greeks"

Many traders, portfolio managers, and risk managers give special names to slopes and sensitivity relationships. Collectively, they are known as "Greeks" because most of them are named after Greek letters. They can also be described with the difference notation discussed in Box 2-9. The Greeks are also known as *partial derivatives*.

Box 9-10

Portfolio Optimization in AMPL on NEOS (Specification)

Commands to the coordinating NEOS server are written in uppercase; the AMPL model specification is written in lowercase.

```
TYPE NCO
SOLVER MINOS-AMPL
BEGIN.COMMENT
  Email this entire program to neos@mcs.anl.gov
END.COMMENT
BEGIN.MOD

    set Products;
    param X{Products};                 # Product Returns
    param COV{Products, Products};     # Product Covariance Matrix
    param aversion default 10;         # risk aversion parameter
    var Return;                        # unknown portfolio Return
    var Risk;                          # unknown portfolio Risk
    var w{Products}>=0;            # unknown portfolio weights (constrained)

    maximize obj: Return - aversion * Risk;
    subject to
        con1: Return = sum{j in Products} w[j]*X[j];
        con2: Risk =
            sqrt(sum{i in Products} w[i]*(sum{j in Products} COV[i,j]*w[j]));
        total: sum{i in Products} w[i] = 1;
END.MOD
BEGIN.DAT
    data;
    set Products:= STOCKS BONDS FUTURES;
    param X:=
    STOCKS 0.09
    BONDS 0.03
    FUTURES 0.15;
    param COV:
        STOCKS BONDS FUTURES:=
        STOCKS 0.36 0.09    0.18
        BONDS 0.09 0.09     0.18
        FUTURES 0.18 0.18   2.25;
END.DAT
BEGIN.COM
    option solver_msg 0; # hide most solver messages
    let {i in Products} w[i]:= 1/card(Products);      # initialize
    let Risk :=0.1;                                   # initialize
    for {s in 1...10} { # Run 10 optimizations for efficient friontier
        let aversion := 0.05 * s; # from 0.05 to 0.5
        solve;
        printf "Return: %f; Risk: %f; obj: %f; ",Return, Risk, obj;
        display aversion;
        display w;
    }
END.COM
END-SERVER-INPUT
```

Box 9-11

Portfolio Optimization in AMPL on NEOS (Output Excerpts)

```
%% YOUR COMMENTS
   Email this entire program to neos@mcs.anl.gov

%%%%%%%%%%%%

%% MINOS OUTPUT %%%%

5 variables:
    3 nonlinear variables
    2 linear variables
3 constraints; 11 linear nonzeros
    1 nonlinear constraint
    2 linear constraints
1 linear objective; 2 nonzeros.

MINOS 5.5: outlev=1
timing=1
MINOS times:
read:  0.00
solve: 0.01
write: 0.00
total: 0.01

Return: 0.126153; Risk: 0.979796; obj: 0.077164; aversion = 0.05

w [*]:=
BONDS 0
FUTURES 0.602558
STOCKS 0.397442
;
Return: 0.105063; Risk: 0.641427; obj: 0.040920; aversion = 0.1

w [*]:=
BONDS 0
FUTURES 0.251047
STOCKS 0.748953
;
..........
Return: 0.038222; Risk: 0.308335; obj: -0.115945; aversion = 0.5

w [*]:=
BONDS 0.862962
FUTURES 0
STOCKS 0.137038
;
```

Box 9-12
Regression and the Method of Least Squares

The regression algorithm, implemented by built-in functions in Excel and other systems, computes the slope and intercept of the line from a set of data points. The algorithm was invented by Carl Friedrich Gauss (1777–1855) and was used to predict the position of the recently (1802) discovered asteroid *Pallas* (now called the planetoid or minor planet 2 *Pallas*). Gauss formalized the "method of least squares" in his 1821 *Theoria combinationis observationum erroribus minimis obnoxiae* (theory of the combination of observations least subject to error). In two dimensions, a regression line showing the relationship between the price of IBM stock and DJIA looks like

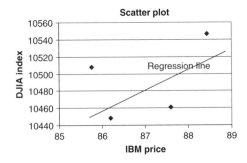

Gauss was a contemporary of Paul Julius Reuter (see Section 1.5) when they both lived in Göttingen. (Before traveling to London, Reuter visited Gauss when Gauss was experimenting with electricity and telegraphy.) In the early 20th century, British statisticians started calling the least-squares method the *formula for regression*.

In many financial and economic models, slopes of regression lines are denoted by beta and the value when the line crosses the y axis is called alpha.

For example, if V is a price, ∂V is the change in price with respect to some quantity. The following Greeks are computed and distributed by market vendors:

- $\dfrac{\partial V}{\partial S}$ is called *delta*.

  Delta measures the sensitivity of the price V to the price of another product S, with all other factors held constant.

- $\dfrac{1}{V} \cdot \dfrac{\partial V}{\partial S}$ is (sometimes) called *lambda*.

  Lambda measures the relative sensitivity of the price with respect to an underlying product S with all other factors held constant. It is a "normalized" delta.

- $\dfrac{\partial V}{\partial t}$ or $\dfrac{\partial V}{\partial T}$ is called *theta*.

  Theta measures the sensitivity of the price to a time t or a time T with all other factors held constant.

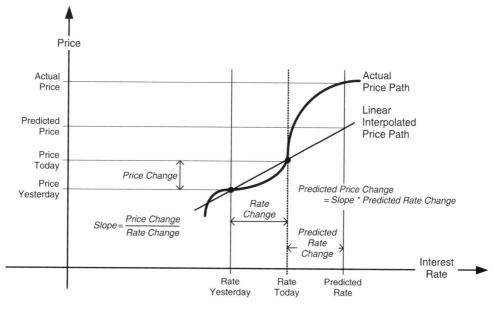

FIGURE 9-16

- $\dfrac{\partial V}{\partial r}$ is called *rho*.

  Rho measures the price sensitivity to an interest rate, usually the shortest spot interest rate, with all other factors held constant.

- $\dfrac{1}{V} \cdot \dfrac{\partial V}{\partial t}$ is the *return* per unit time — the *rate of return*.

  Note that the time unit is explicit in the rate of return: it has the same units as a yield (units are per month, per year, per week . . .).

- $-\dfrac{1}{V} \cdot \dfrac{\partial V}{\partial r}$ is called *duration*.

  Duration is used in bonds and other fixed income products. Duration measures a normalized sensitivity of the price V with respect to an interest rate or yield r with all other factors held constant. If duration is one of the supplied market analytics, then price change due to a yield is

  $$\partial V = V \cdot \partial r \cdot \text{duration}$$

  The units of duration are time units.

Years ago, specialized calculators, such as the Monroe Model 360 Bond Trader (released in 1979 at a cost of $1200), were designed to compute durations and bond yields (see Section 4.2). It typically took about 15 seconds per bond to compute these values. The first spreadsheets increased the speed of this computation by orders of magnitude; customized software executing on today's PCs can compute at least a million yields or durations per second. The only limitation is due to the latency in integrating prices and market data with the analytic system. This was solved in some sense by services such as Bloomberg that explicitly integrate data, computation, and analytics.

- $\dfrac{\partial C}{\partial \sigma}$ is usually called *vega* (and sometimes called *kappa* or *K*).

Because most of the Greeks depend on an underlying Gaussian return probability, we can also measure the sensitivity to the model parameters. Consequently, we can compute the sensitivity of the price C to the coefficient of nervousness (volatility) σ. Vega is not a Greek letter; its probability is a mnemonic for volatility.

We can also look at the sensitivities of sensitivities: the rate of change of the rate of change. Such "second-order Greeks" include

- $\dfrac{\partial^2 V}{\partial S^2} = \dfrac{\partial delta}{\partial S} = \dfrac{\partial}{\partial S}\left(\dfrac{\partial V}{\partial S}\right)$ is called *gamma*.

   Gamma measures the sensitivity of the delta to the price of the underlying product S with all other factors held constant.

- $-\dfrac{1}{V} \cdot \dfrac{\partial^2 V}{\partial r^2} = -\dfrac{1}{V} \cdot \dfrac{\partial duration}{\partial r} = -\dfrac{1}{V} \cdot \dfrac{\partial}{\partial r}\left(\dfrac{\partial V}{\partial r}\right)$ is called *convexity*.

   Convexity measures a normalized sensitivity of the duration with all other factors held constant.

Hedging Technology

One application of computing market analytics such as the Greeks is to create hedges: a hedged product has reduced risk. A product is hedged perfectly if another product can be found that mimics it perfectly; if a trader is long the product and short the perfect hedge (or vice versa), all risk is eliminated, but so is the potential profit. Consequently, we can approximate the change in value of the portfolio if we know all portfolio deltas, gammas, and other hedge ratios (the partial derivatives of V with respect to the portfolio components).

Hedging with Two Products: Delta Hedging

Suppose we want to mimic the performance of V by a linear combination of two products, $P(1)$, and $P(2)$. The pricing relationship is that the price of the portfolio should equal the price of the hedged product:

$$w(1)^* P(1) + w(2)^* P(2) = V$$

Suppose all three products depend on another factor, like a stock price or interest rate. Then, another desirable relationship is that the delta (with respect to the factor) of the portfolio should equal the delta of the hedged product:

$$w(1)^* \text{Delta}(1) + w(2)^* \text{Delta}(2) = \text{Delta}(V)$$

Assuming we know and can look up the deltas and the prices for all products, we see that we have two equations in two unknowns: $w(1)$ and $w(2)$.

Using computer algebra, the symbolic solution is found by

- `solve({w(1)*P(1)+w(2)*P(2)=V,`
  `    w(1)*Delta(1)+w(2)*Delta(2)=Delta(V)},[w(1),w(2)])`

The solution, in C notation, is just

```
w(1)=(V*Delta(2) - Delta(V)*P(2))/(P(1)*Delta(2) - P(2)*Delta(1));

w(2)=(V*Delta(1) - Delta(V)*P(1))/(P(2)*Delta(1) - P(1)*Delta(2));
```

Such a hedge is sometimes called *delta neutral*.

Example: Hedging with Duration

Suppose we want to hedge the 3-year zero coupon bond V with 2- and 5-year zero coupon bonds using duration. Figure 9-17 shows the market analytics. We can use the same weight formula that was derived for delta hedging. The weights are

```
w(1)=(86*5-3*77)/(90*5-77*2) = 0.6722...
w(2)=(86*2-3*90)/(77*2-90*5) = 0.3310...
```

Thus one unit of V can be hedged with 0.67 units of P(1) (at a cost of $60.51) and 0.33 units of P(2) (at a cost of $25.49), adding up to one unit of V (costing $86). If we hedge with convexity, the convexities of the bonds imply that the weights are approximately 0.75 and 0.24, respectively.

Note that as long as we have the hedging formulas, the portfolio weights can be recomputed whenever new prices and Greeks become available.

Hedging with Three Products: Delta Gamma Hedging

If we want to hedge V with three products, we need another relationship. This can involve the Greek derived from first-order (rho, theta) or higher partial derivatives (i.e., gamma). So, for example, hedging a product based on gamma and delta implies the following:

- `solve({w(1)*P(1)+w(2)*P(2)+w(3)*P(3)=V,`
  `    w(1)*Delta(1)+w(2)*Delta(2)+w(3)*Delta(3)=Delta(V),`
  `    w(1)*Gamma(1)+w(2)*Gamma(2)+w(3)*Gamma(3)=Gamma(V)},`
  `    [w(1),w(2),w(3)])`

A special simple case is when V is an option, P(1) is cash, P(2) is the underlying product, and P(3) is another option on the underlying product. The delta and gamma are computed with respect to the underlying stock: for cash, (delta=gamma=0), and for the underlying stock, delta=1 and gamma=0.

	P(1)	P(2)	V
Price	90	77	86
Duration	2	5	3
Convexity	4	25	9

FIGURE 9-17

Let us call the underlying product S and the other option P. The hedging equations are solved via

- ```
solve({w(S)*S+w(P)*P+Cash=V,
    w(S)+w(P)*Delta(P)=Delta(V),
    w(P)*Gamma(P)=Gamma(V)},
    [w(S),w(P),Cash])
```

In C notation, the solution is

```
w(S)=(Gamma(P)*Delta(V)-Gamma(V)*Delta(P))/Gamma(P);
w(P)=Gamma(V)/Gamma(P);
Cash=V-(S*w(S)+P*w(P))
```

Such a hedge is sometimes called *delta gamma neutral.*

Suppose we want to hedge 1000 options (i.e., 10 contracts) on a stock with a portfolio of the underlying stock, with borrowed cash, and with another option on the stock. The portfolio must mimic the delta and gamma of the underlying. How much cash, how many shares, and how many options do we need? Figure 9-18 shows the market analytics.

The weights are

```
w(S)=(0.05*550-80*0.35)/0.05=-10.0
w(P)=80/0.05=1600
Cash=2450-(50*(-10)+1.15*(1600))=-1110
```

We need short 10 shares of stock (yielding $500 income), purchase 1600 options (160 contracts) of P (at a cost of $1840), and hold $1100 in cash: the total portfolio value is $2450 (the value of the hedged option).

Hedging with Four or More Products

We can hedge a product V with any number of products subject to any strategy involving the hedge ratios, as long as we end up with "N equations in N unknowns" — a standard problem in linear algebra whose solution is implemented in most programming systems.

For example, market analytics and portfolio weights for a four-product hedge are shown in Figure 9-19. The unknown weights are computed by the Excel's built-in linear algebra functions for matrix multiplication (=MMULT) and matrix inverse

	S	P	Cash	V
Price	50	1.15	−1	2450
Delta	1	0.35	0	550
Gamma	0	0.05	0	80

FIGURE 9-18

	A	B	C	D	E	F	G	H	I	J
4		W1	W2	W3	W4		V		weights	
5	Price	38.3425	39.7873	1.44481	1.208566		100		0.2307	w1
6	Delta	-112.5707	-26.71621	-139.2869	-113.1054		-50		2.3008	w2
7	Gamma	330.4993	17.93931	-312.5599	-182.8852		200		-0.2513	w3
8	Theta	3.578765	1.117112	-2.461653	0.678042		4		-0.0215	w4

FIGURE 9-19
```

Box 9-13

The Greeks and Partial Differential Equations

Quantitative models are rules that explain how certain quantities change with respect to other quantities. Good models mimic the way real objects behave, whether we are talking about voltage fluctuations or price changes. It should not be too surprising at this point to realize that most of the rules that govern these models are based on formulas that relate small rates of changes among different quantities. For example, suppose we look at the Greeks of a product V with respect to another product S and the short-term spot interest rate r. It turns out that the price of V and the price of S are related through the following formula:

$$\text{theta} + (r \cdot S) \cdot \text{delta} + \frac{k^2 \cdot S^2}{2} \cdot \text{gamma} = r \cdot V$$

This is the Black–Scholes equation, derived by Fisher Black (1938–1995), Meyron Scholes (1941–), and Robert Merton (1944–). Here, k is Bachelier's constant "coefficient of nervousness" for the returns of product S. Using the definition of the "greeks," the Black–Scholes equation can also be written as

$$\frac{\partial V}{\partial t} + r \cdot S \cdot \frac{\partial V}{\partial S} + \frac{k^2 \cdot S^2}{2} \cdot \frac{\partial^2 V}{\partial S^2} = r \cdot V$$

This formula, relating small rates of changes, is also called a "partial differential equation," a phrase originating with William Rowan Hamilton (1805–1865) in the 1830s. The solution to many technology problems can be rephrased to finding the solution to one or more partial differential equations.

For example, Bachelier found that the *probability density p* for returns x satisfies the following equation:

$$\frac{\partial p}{\partial t} + \mu \cdot \frac{\partial p}{\partial x} = \frac{\sigma^2}{2} \cdot \frac{\partial^2 p}{\partial x^2}$$

The solution to this equation is the Gaussian density. In fact, both the Black–Scholes equation and the Bachelier equation are both examples of the Diffusion Equation — the equation that was used to model the diffusion of voltages in the Atlantic cable (see Section 6.2). There are many connections between probability densities and partial differential equations. For example, the more general Telegrapher's Equation

$$\frac{\partial^2 p}{\partial t^2} + 2a \cdot \frac{\partial p}{\partial t} = c \cdot \frac{\partial^2 p}{\partial x^2}$$

solved by Bachelier's teacher Poincaré is connected with a probability density for price changes (or returns) that exhibit sudden jumps from a trend: here, price changes and returns are not independent. The probability densities used in reliability likewise are connected with partial differential equations. This connection of probability with small rates of change shows that many partial differential equations can be solved by Monte Carlo methods.

	I	J
4	**weights**	
5	=MMULT(MINVERSE(B5:E8),G5:G8)	w1
6	=MMULT(MINVERSE(B5:E8),G5:G8)	w2
7	=MMULT(MINVERSE(B5:E8),G5:G8)	w3
8	=MMULT(MINVERSE(B5:E8),G5:G8)	w4

FIGURE 9-20

(=MINVERSE). The matrix inverse function is implemented via an algorithm called Gaussian elimination (Gauss used it to solve the regression problem resulting from his asteroid computations). The Excel formulas are shown in Figure 9-20.

9.5. Notes and References

Bachelier's dissertation is available at Project NUMDAM, devoted to the digitization of ancient mathematics documents, at
[0.1] http://www.numdam.org/item?id=ASENS_1900_3_17__21_0

An English translation of a Bachelor's dissertation by A. James Boness is reprinted in Chapter 2 of
[0.2] Paul H. Cootner (editor). *The Random Character of Stock Market Prices*. MIT Press, Cambridge, 1964.

The observations by Norbert Wiener are in
[0.3] Norbert Wiener. *Invention: The Care and Feeding of Ideas* (Chapter 9), unpublished manuscript, 1954. Published posthumously by The MIT Press, Cambridge, 1993. ISBN 0262231670.

The remarks by Mark Kac are from
[0.4] M. Feigenbaum. "Reflections of the Polish masters: An interview with Stanislaw Ulam and Mark Kac." *Los Alamos Science* Fall, 1982. Reprinted in other places, including the *Journal of Statistical Physics*, Vol. 39, No. 5-6, 1985 (available on the Web).

Types of Risk in Financial Systems

The concepts of observability, controllability, and testability were developed in the 1960s by control system engineer Rudolph E. Kalman (1930–). They were used successfully in the NASA Apollo program. See
[1] R.E. Kalman, P.L. Falb, and M.A. Arbib. *Topics in Mathematical System Theory*. McGraw-Hill, New York, 1969. ISBN 007033255X.

Obervability, controllability, and testability applied to software systems are discussed by
[2] R.S. Freedman. "Testability of Software Components," *IEEE Transactions on Software Engineering,* Vol. 17, No. 6, June 1991.

The Basel II Accord — the international standard specified by the Basel Committee on Banking Supervision of the Bank for International Settlements—is described at
[3] http://www.bis.org/publ/bcbsca.htm

A good survey paper discussing copulas and uncertainty calculi is
[4] C. Alsina, M.J. Frank, and B. Schweizer. "Problems on Associative Functions." *Aequationes Mathematicae* 66, 2003.

The application of discrete Markov chains to credit risk is described by
[5] R.A. Jarrow, D. Lando, and S.M. Turnbull, "A Markov Model for the Term Structure of Credit Risk Spreads." *Review of Financial Studies*, Vol. 10, No. 2, Summer 1997.

The Google application of discrete Markov chains to Web page ranking is described by
[6] L. Page, S. Brin, R. Motwani, and T. Winograd. The Pagerank Citation Ranking: Bringing order to the Web. Technical Report, Stanford University Database Group, 1998 (available at http://dbpubs.stanford.edu:8090/pub/1999-66).

Basic Properties of Probabilities

The research leading up to the NASD lawsuit concerning best execution is described by
[7] William Christie and Paul Schultz. "Why Do Nasdaq Market Makers Avoid Odd-Eighth Quotes." *Journal of Finance*, Vol. 49, No. 5, December 1994.

[8] William Christie, Jeffrey Harris, and Paul Schultz. "Why Did Nasdaq Market Makers Stop Avoiding Odd Eighths?" *Journal of Finance*, Vol. 49, No. 5, December 1994.

[9] Susan E. Woodward, Price Fixing at Nasdaq? A Reconsideration of the Evidence. Paper prepared for the Congressional Budget Office, Contract No. 96-0228, 1997.

Financial circuit breakers are described by
[10] http://www.nyse.com/press/circuit_breakers.html

[11] http://www.cboe.com/TradTool/circuitbreaker.pdf

Portfolios and Risk

Markowitz's autobiographical remarks about SIMSCRIPT and other technologies are from
[12] Harry M. Markowitz. *Portfolio Selection: Efficient Diversification of Investments* (2nd edition). Basil Blackwell, Inc., Cambridge 1991. ISBN 1-55786-108-0.

SIMSCRIPT is maintained by CACI at
[13] http://www.caci.com/

AMPL was first described publicly by
[14] Robert Fourer, David M. Gay, and Brian W. Kernighan. "A Modeling Language for Mathematical Programming." *Management Science*, Vol. 36, 1990.

GAMS was first described by
[15] Jan Bisschop and Alexander Meeraus. "On the Development of a General Algebraic Modeling System in a Strategic Planning Environment," *Mathematical Programming Study*, Vol. 20, 1982.

Bootstrap sampling is described by
[16] B. Efron. The jackknife, the bootstrap, and other resampling plans. Society of Industrial and Applied Mathematics (SIAM), CBMS-NSF Monograph 38, 1982.

The original model for portfolio risk appeared in
[17] Harry M. Markowitz. "Portfolio Selection." *Journal of Finance*, 7(1), 1952 (available at http://cowles.econ.yale.edu/P/cp/p00b/p0060.pdf).

Commands to the NEOS server also use XML (see this book's website showing Box 9-10 with NEOS XML tags). NEOS is available at
[18] http://www-neos.mcs.anl.gov/

Risk and Hedging

The traditional "Greeks" are described in many places. Another source is
[19] John Hull. *Options, Futures, and Other Derivative Securities*. Prentice Hall, Englewood Cliffs, NJ, 1989. ISBN 0-13-639014-5.

Hedging algorithms are described by
[20] Robert Jarrow and Stuart Turnbull. *Derivative Securities*. South-Western College Publishing. Cincinnati, 1996. ISBN 0-538-84255-5.

Connections between the Diffusion Equation and the Black–Scholes equation are described in
[21] Paul Wilmott, Sam Howison, and Jeff DeWynne. *The Mathematics of Financial Derivatives: A Student Introduction*. Cambridge University Press, Cambridge 1997. ISBN 0-521-49789-2.

9.6.   Discussion Questions

1. Given the 1-year credit transition probabilities in Figure 9-11, what are the 10- and 20-year credit transition probabilities?

2. Circuit breakers are involved to shut down a system periodically. Show two examples, i.e., when there is a reduction in costs and when there is no reduction in costs.

3. There are several sample portfolio optimization problems specified on the Web in AMPL or GAMS. Find one and use NEOS to solve it.

4. Explain how to build a statistically based alerting system for unusual stock price movements.

5. Can you compute the delta of a product without a formal price model? Explain.

6. Explain how circuit breakers increase the reliability of a financial system.

7. Can circuit breakers affect the statistical measurements of volatility? Can winsorizing (Box 5-8) solve this problem?

Index